AF737866

FRENCH ADMINISTRATIVE LAW AND THE COMMON-LAW WORLD

BERNARD SCHWARTZ

PROFESSOR OF LAW AND DIRECTOR OF THE INSTITUTE OF COMPARATIVE LAW,
NEW YORK UNIVERSITY

PROFESSEUR À LA FACULTÉ DE DROIT ET DES SCIENCES POLITIQUES
DE L'ÉCOLE LIBRE DES HAUTES ÉTUDES

INTRODUCTION BY

ARTHUR T. VANDERBILT

CHIEF JUSTICE, SUPREME COURT OF NEW JERSEY

THE LAWBOOK EXCHANGE, LTD.
Clark, New Jersey

ISBN-13: 978-1-58477-704-5
ISBN-10: 1-58477-704-4

Lawbook Exchange edition 2011

The quality of this reprint is equivalent to the quality of the original work.

THE LAWBOOK EXCHANGE, LTD.
33 Terminal Avenue
Clark, New Jersey 07066-1321

Please see our website for a selection of our other publications and fine facsimile reprints of classic works of legal history:
www.lawbookexchange.com

Library of Congress Cataloging-in-Publication Data

Schwartz, Bernard, 1923-
French administrative law and the common-law world / Bernard Schwartz.
p. cm.
Originally published: New York : New York University, c1954.
Includes bibliographical references and index.
ISBN-13: 978-1-58477-704-5 (alk. paper)
ISBN-10: 1-58477-704-4 (alk. paper)
1. Administrative law--France. 2. Administrative courts--France. 3. Administrative procedure--France. 4. Judicial review of administrative acts--France. 5. Administrative law--United States. 6. Administrative courts--United States. 7. Administrative procedure--United States. 8. Judicial review of administrative acts--United States. I. Title.
K3400.S39 2005
342.44'06--dc22 2006004394

Printed in the United States of America on acid-free paper

FRENCH ADMINISTRATIVE LAW AND THE COMMON-LAW WORLD

BERNARD SCHWARTZ
PROFESSOR OF LAW AND DIRECTOR OF THE INSTITUTE OF COMPARATIVE LAW, NEW YORK UNIVERSITY
PROFESSEUR À LA FACULTÉ DE DROIT ET DES SCIENCES POLITIQUES DE L'ÉCOLE LIBRE DES HAUTES ÉTUDES

INTRODUCTION BY
ARTHUR T. VANDERBILT
CHIEF JUSTICE, SUPREME COURT OF NEW JERSEY

NEW YORK UNIVERSITY PRESS
WASHINGTON SQUARE • NEW YORK
LONDON: GEOFFREY CUMBERLEGE • OXFORD UNIVERSITY PRESS

Copyright 1954 by New York University

Library of Congress catalogue card number: 54-5276

Printed in the United States of America

CARISSIMAE UXORI SUAE

PREFACE

The establishment of the Institute of Comparative Law at the New York University School of Law is symptomatic of the interest in comparative law that prevails in the legal profession in the United States. Such interest appears at present, indeed, to be at an all-time high among American lawyers. In a sense, this is but a part of the general acceptance by the United States of a significant role in world affairs. If that role is to be performed adequately, Americans must give up their parochial attitude toward foreign institutions. In the field of law, specifically, American lawyers must abandon their reluctance to study other systems, and American law schools must provide facilities for foreign lawyers to study the Anglo-American system. The continuance of legal isolation in the United States has become an anomaly at a time when political isolation is recognized as no longer practically feasible. It may be that the common law and the civil law are too far apart in fundamental approaches and techniques to justify hope of an early unification of the two great systems, but, if there must be one law in Europe and another in America, it is at least feasible for the modern lawyer to have some familiarity with both systems, for contemporary legal problems may transcend national boundaries.

To help build the necessary bridge between American and non-American law is the primary purpose of the new Institute of Comparative Law. To achieve it, the Institute offers a rich program of study and research for American lawyers in the field of foreign law and for non-American jurists in the law of the United States. In addition, the Institute is engaged in what will develop into an extensive publication program. It is inaugurating a new series of volumes on comparative law. The first of these is the present work on French administrative law.

It is appropriate that the comparative law series should be initiated with this study by Dr. Bernard Schwartz, the director of the Institute. Dr. Schwartz is internationally known as a specialist in comparative administrative law and as a writer of legal texts and contributor to American and foreign legal periodicals. He spent fifteen months in France obtaining the materials upon which this book is based. The work itself seeks to explain the fundamentals of the *droit administratif* to an

English-speaking audience. The author does so by use of the comparative method, rather than by the more usual type of straight exposition. Approach through the comparative method takes as its point of departure knowledge already possessed by the reader in the American system of law and proceeds thence to point out similarities and differences. In so far as possible, the American lawyer is thus enabled to learn French administrative law in terms of his own law and not as a distinct but unrelated system.

Russell D. Niles, Dean
New York University School of Law

ACKNOWLEDGMENTS

It would be an act of uncommon ingratitude for the author not to record his obligation to those on both sides of the Atlantic who have made this work possible. For the kindness of his reception in France, special thanks are due to M. L. Julliot de la Morandière, dean of the Law Faculty of Paris, and M. Marc Ancel, president of the First Chamber of the Court of Appeal of Paris and secretary-general of the Institute of Comparative Law of Paris; and, in so far as the Council of State, whose facilities were made available upon the fullest possible basis, is concerned, to M. Henry Puget, councilor of state and director of section of the Institute of Comparative Law of Paris, M. Maxim Letourneur, *maître des requêtes* and senior government commissioner, and M. Alain Plantey, first-class auditor. The latter two are entitled to particular gratitude for their willingness to read over portions of the manuscript, especially those dealing with the organization and procedure of the Council of State. Their comments and criticisms have, it is hoped, enabled the author to avoid many of the pitfalls that might otherwise beset the common lawyer in a study of this type. Access to the working of the Prefecture Councils has been facilitated by M. F. Fagnot, councilor of the Interdepartmental Prefecture Council at Versailles.

In this country, Chief Justice Vanderbilt, who has kindly consented to write an Introduction, which is a far cry from the usual platitudinous preface written by one in the Chief Justice's position, and Dean Russell D. Niles must be paid public thanks for their encouragement and assistance in ensuring adequate publication. The Guggenheim Foundation and the State Department, through a fellowship and an advanced research grant under the Fulbright Act, rendered financial assistance without which this book would have been impossible. I also wish to acknowledge the aid I have received from New York University Press in producing this volume, especially Wilson Follett for his editorial work on the manuscript and Anne Koreny who handled the technical details of production. Thanks are also due to the *Canadian Bar Review* for permission to use material that originally appeared in its pages.

And, finally, mere words can never adequately express my debt to her to whom this study is dedicated.

BERNARD SCHWARTZ

INTRODUCTION

This book is a significant contribution to the slowly growing literature on comparative law. Habitually we resort to comparisons in deciding cases in the courts, not only utilizing the authorities in our own state but also borrowing freely from the experience of other common-law jurisdictions in our search for sound principles of law adapted to the needs of the time. Legal scholars, however, with rare exceptions have shied away from employing the comparative method of studying law on a grand scale, even though the comparative method comes nearer to the scientific methods of modern research than any other method open to the law, planned experiments in the law being generally unavailable. Our legal scholars have been preoccupied, first with the analytical, and then with the historical, and more recently with the sociological approach to the law, or with a combination of two or more of these methods.

The reasons for the failure to pursue the comparative method of studying law more assiduously are not hard to find. To the very real difficulties arising from differences in nomenclature in different systems of law and to the necessity of comprehending two or more systems of law in their entirety before undertaking to write about any one phase of them comparatively (for there is no gainsaying the truth that law, like history in Maitland's aphorism, is a "seamless web") must be added the heavy task of understanding the economic, political, and social background of each system of law studied comparatively (for the significance of a system of law cannot be grasped apart from the environment in which it functions) and—most important and to the legal scholar most burdensome of all—the need of finding out how the particular subject under consideration actually *works* in each of the legal systems under review as distinguished from what has been written about it in the books. The researcher in comparative law cannot hope to do all of his work in the library or in his study. He must venture forth into the field where the law is in daily operation and he must not only observe what is going on there but he must make searching inquiry from all manner of men who are expert in actively dealing with the law in action. For thus and thus only may one hope to avoid the pitfall of finding superficial resemblances or differences in the systems of law under review, when in fact no such resemblances or differences exist. Indeed, we have a striking example in this very book of how the difference between the French administrative system in operation and what had been written about it drove Professor Schwartz to change his views on a fundamental question of French administrative law. The question was whether French administrative law is consistent with the reign of law,[1] a principle to which most English-speaking lawyers are devoted. Suffice it to say, however, that, had Professor Schwartz been obliged to answer the question in the negative, French administrative law would have lost most of its significance for us, but, with his carefully reasoned and documented answer in the affirmative, French administrative law immediately acquires a new significance for all of us who had been misled by the superficial views of Professor Dicey and his school.

The greatest deterrent to the comparative study of law from the standpoint of the legal scholar has yet to be mentioned. It is the provincial, one might almost say the parochial, attitude of our bench and bar toward "foreign law," meaning the law of any country other than our own. What a change from the post-Revolutionary attitude of a century and a half ago, when we find the pages of Kent and Story illuminated by numerous references to the great writers on the civil law and when our reports were being enriched by the deliberate use of French authorities! Says Kent, speaking of his work on the Supreme Court of New York before he became Chancellor: "The Judges were republicans & very kindly disposed to everything that was French, & this enabled me without exciting any alarm or jealousy to make free use of such [French and civil] authorities & thereby enrich our commercial law."[2]

This change from our post-Revolutionary days in the intellectual attitude of the profession toward the law is not to our credit. It has inevitably had its baleful effect on the comparative study of the law, for no man likes to gather precious seed from afar and at great expense and sow it on barren ground, however much the ground may need it. In this very field I may cite two conspicuous instances of the untoward effects of our modern American aversion to "foreign law." Forty years ago I studied administrative law under Frank J. Goodnow, a great scholar and a great teacher, whose *Comparative Administrative Law*[3]

[1] See chap. 10, *Droit Administratif* and the Rule of Law, *infra* p. 306.
[2] I Select Essays in Anglo-American Legal History 827, 843 (Boston, 1907).
[3] New York, 2 vols., 1893.

and *Principles of the Administrative Law of the United States*[4] were the pioneer works on the subject. *Comparative Administrative Law* dealt with the subject, then much simpler than now, as it had developed in England, France, Germany, and the United States. But American lawyers in so far as they were interested at all in administrative law were concerned only with American administrative law and completely allergic to foreign experience. Long before I arrived in his class Goodnow had learned that he must concentrate on American administrative law, and his epoch-making volumes on comparative administrative law were never referred to except as an item in the bibliography announced at the first lecture. Ernst Freund, who carried on in this field where Goodnow left off, likewise confined his teaching and writing to the American scene, although he was admirably equipped by reason of his foreign training to have dealt with the subject comparatively.

The limitations thus imposed on the scope of Goodnow's and Freund's teaching were not the only ones that restricted their work. Half a century ago administrative law was a new subject in the law. In fact, it has only been recently that administrative law found its way into the digests and the encyclopedias under its own name. It was quite neglected by "practical" students intent on pursuing the "bread and butter" subjects in private law. To them administrative law, along with international law, taxation, and municipal corporations, was but a legal phase of political science. A mere handful of students pursued Professor Goodnow's inspiring courses while across the corridor hundreds of "practical" students took a dull course in corporations. These "practical" students could not foresee that administrative law would become the outstanding legal development of the twentieth century, reflecting in the law the hegemony of the executive arm of the government, any more than they could anticipate that taxation would become as important a factor in any business transaction as the consideration itself.

So vast has been the development of administrative law here, especially in the Federal Government, that our *substantive* administrative law is quite unknown to any one individual, and what we call administrative law is in fact nothing more than administrative procedure and its constitutional background. This procedure, moreover, despite the benign intentions of the Federal Administrative Procedure Act of 1946, threatens to become as involved a labyrinth as the cumbersome and technical systems of common-law and equity procedure before the

[4] New York, 1905.

Judicature Acts and the ensuing rules of court in England and similar reforms here.

The prime difficulties that confront us in administrative law today, however, deal with even more fundamental matters than mere procedure. The members of the Attorney General's Committee on Administrative Procedure split not merely on the important problems of the scope and practice of judicial review and on the necessity for legislative standards of fair procedure but also on the vital issue of separating the prosecuting and judicial functions in administrative law.[5] The President's Committee on Administrative Management had previously enunciated the views of the minority of the Attorney General's Committee with respect to administrative organization. In its report to the President it epitomized its views of the organization of the executive branch of the Federal Government in these clear terms:

> The Executive Branch of the Government of the United States has . . . grown up without plan or design. . . . Commissions have been the result of legislative groping rather than the pursuit of a consistent policy. . . . They are in reality miniature independent governments set up to deal with the railroad problem, the banking problem, or the radio problem. They constitute a headless 'fourth branch' of the Government, a haphazard deposit of irresponsible agencies and uncoordinated powers. . . . There is a conflict of principle involved in their make-up and functions. . . . They are vested with duties of administration . . . and at the same time they are given important judicial work. . . . The evils resulting from this confusion of principles are insidious and far-reaching. . . . Pressures and influences properly enough directed toward officers responsible for formulating and administering policy constitute an unwholesome atmosphere in which to adjudicate private rights. But the mixed duties of the commissions render escape from these subversive influences impossible. Furthermore, the same men are obliged to serve both as prosecutors and as judges. This not only undermines judicial fairness; it weakens public confidence in that fairness. Commission decisions affecting private rights and conduct lie under the suspicion of being rationalizations of the preliminary findings which the Commission, in the role of prosecutor, presented to itself.[6]

The Committee recommended to the President that the administrative agencies should "be divided into an administrative section and a judicial section. . . . The judicial section . . . would be wholly independent. . . . Its members would be appointed by the President with the

[5] Final Report of the Attorney General's Committee on Administrative Procedure 202-50 (Washington, 1941).

[6] Report with Special Studies 32-33, 39-40 (Washington, 1937).

approval of the Senate for long, staggered terms and would be removable only for causes stated in the statute. . . . The administrative section . . . would formulate rules, initiate action, investigate complaints. . . . It would of course do all the purely administrative or sub-legislative work now done by the commissions—in short all the work which is not essentially judicial in nature. The judicial section would sit as an impartial, independent body to make decisions affecting the public interest and private rights. . . . This proposed plan . . . guarantees the complete independence and neutrality for that part of the work which must be performed after the manner of a court."[7]

President Roosevelt, who certainly was not a novice in politics or administration, transmitted the report to Congress with the following message: "I have examined this report carefully and thoughtfully, and am convinced that it is a great document of permanent importance. . . . The practice of creating independent regulatory commissions, who perform administrative work in addition to judicial work, threatens to develop a 'fourth branch' of the Government for which there is no sanction in the Constitution."[8]

Other impartial authorities have reached similar conclusions. Thus Professor Robert E. Cushman in his *The Independent Regulatory Commissions* concludes that "nothing short of complete separation goes to the root of the evil of the prosecutor-judge combination."[9]

Meanwhile the already vastly complex problems of the executive branch of government have been still further complicated by the Second World War, the cold war that ensued it, the undeclared war in Korea, and rapid inflation. The number of administrative agencies, permanent or emergency, is constantly increasing; the number of federal employees is growing by leaps and bounds from day to day; and national expenditures as well as the national debt have reached astronomical proportions. While no one these days would dream of attempting to abolish administrative law or the administrative agencies, it is inescapable that, with the conditions confronting us, sooner or later the entire administrative establishment will be resurveyed in the light of sound principles. In this process we shall need all the light we can get from every possible source. Professor Schwartz's earlier works have demonstrated his familiarity from the comparative point of view with

[7] *Id.* at 41-42.
[8] *Id.* at iii-vi.
[9] P. 726 (New York, 1941).

English and American administrative law.[10] Now he has shown us clearly how much we can learn from the French. We are the beneficiaries of Professor Schwartz's intensive study over the years of American administrative law and of his pursuit of the subject first in England and then in France, not only in the universities but in the field, an experience that has enabled him to overcome the difficulties I have mentioned as inherent in the comparative study of law.

A comparative study of French administrative law with English and American administrative law (the latter two themselves differ widely in constitutional premises and in actual practice) might have become as involved as our federal administrative law of today—and as discouraging. Fortunately for us, Professor Schwartz's study has an almost delusive simplicity which, while revealing the breadth of his learning and the depth of his insight, quite conceals from anyone who has not previously worked in this field the immense labor that must have been put into his analysis of the French administrative system in comparison with the Anglo-American systems and the pruning away of nonessential details so that the essentials of each system may stand out in bold relief. In setting before us the fundamental problems of these three diverse yet not altogether dissimilar systems of administrative law, Professor Schwartz paints his picture with a broad brush, making it possible for us to see the woods and not merely the trees. At the same time his scholarship is such that every stroke of his brush is marked by painstaking accuracy. There is no evasion of difficult problems, no fuzziness of thinking, no vagueness in language as he probes the vital problems of administrative law in our complicated modern industrial era in three different administrative establishments. In so doing he again makes it clear to us that administrative law involves much more than administrative procedure and that at the heart of administrative law lie some of the most vexing issues of modern government, having to do on the one side with the relations of each of the three great branches of government—legislative, executive, and judicial—to each other and on the other side the relations of local government to state government and of state government to Federal Government—and the effect of the sum total of all of these relations on the freedom of the individual on the one hand and on the other hand their effect on the strength and stability of the State.

There is nothing academic about these issues; they continue to per-

[10] Law and the Executive in Britain: A Comparative Study (New York and Cambridge, 1949); American Administrative Law (London, 1950).

plex our executives, our legislatures, and our highest courts and to play their part in our national relations and our international relationships. Particularly have I been impressed as I have read and reread the manuscript how time and again a short statement of a problem, a brief quotation from an outstanding authority, and a word of comment from the author will illuminate the problem through a comparative approach where a study of the same problem by itself in a single system of administrative law would prove ineffectual.

The temptation is strong to comment on the many helpful suggestions contained in this study, but it would be unfair to both the author and the reader for me to do so.

Arthur T. Vanderbilt

CONTENTS

French Administrative Law and the Common-Law World

Chapter One

A COMMON LAWYER LOOKS AT THE *DROIT ADMINISTRATIF*

The common lawyer seeking to pursue research in a civil-law system such as that of France soon finds that he must work in directions to which he is wholly unaccustomed. The concepts and techniques that have served him so well in his own law are all too often handicaps to accurate understanding. He is now in a system in which the case law is of secondary significance—in which the legislative *ought* is, at least in theory, of more importance than the *is* of the decided case. For he is in a realm where the Code reigns supreme. "Franco-German doctrine rests upon the absolute sovereignty of the written law."[1] Legal principles are deduced from the law laid down by the legislator. The role of the judge is limited to interpretation and to filling in the lacunae in the Code. The inductive method, second nature to the common lawyer, leads only to misconceptions.

The French Code was, however, promulgated at a time when legal thought was concerned primarily with the field of private law. Public law in the modern sense had only begun to evolve. Codification was hence largely a codification of the rules of private law. When with the diffusion of the democratic ideal there came the need for a system of legal principles to govern the relations of the State with the citizen, such a system had to be shaped without the aid of a detailed set of authoritative principles laid down in a Code. If such a system were to be developed at all in the absence of legislative intervention, it had to be developed by the judge by practices thoroughly familiar to the Anglo-American lawyer. In this field the judicial role was not limited to filling

[1] Alibert, Le Contrôle juridictionnel de l'administration 15 (1926). (Translations from French sources are by the author of this book except as otherwise noted.)

in the gaps in the Code. The judge was confronted, much as were the creators of the common law, with a *tabula rasa.*

The normal reluctance of the judge in a civil-law system to make law, in the Anglo-American sense, had to give way in the face of the need for defined rules in the field of public law. The need for such rules has been at least as pressing in countries governed by the civil law as in the common-law world. "How to fit ancient liberties, which have gained a new preciousness, into solution of those exigent and intricate economic problems that have been too long avoided rather than faced, is the special task of Administrative Law," wrote Mr. Justice Frankfurter in 1941.[2] An adequate system of administrative law fulfills this task by ensuring that governmental functions shall be exercised "on proper legal principles"[3]—"according to the rules of reason and justice,"[4] and not at the mere caprice of the magistrate. It affords a remedy to the citizen adversely affected by improper governmental action.

It is in the modern State that the need for an adequately developed system of administrative law has become especially evident. When the French Code was promulgated, the role of the State was, after all, not nearly so important as today. Government was then but one of many competing power structures. In the contemporary State, on the other hand, "there is not a moment of his existence where . . . man does not find himself in contact with government and its agents."[5] Government today tends more and more, by taking over or controlling the functions heretofore performed by private institutions, to become the all-dominant factor in society. As it does so it comes into ever-increasing contact with the individual life. "It is in this ceaseless contact of the individual with the State that the danger of arbitrariness has especially arisen."[6]

As has been indicated, the development of a system of administrative law to help minimize this danger has been, in France as in the common-law world, largely the handiwork of the judge. In this respect the *droit administratif*, unlike most other branches of French law, bears a close resemblance to the kind of law prevalent in the Anglo-American system. The French administrative lawyer, like his confrere in the com-

[2] Foreword, 41 Col. L. Rev. 585, 586 (1941).

[3] Pioneer Laundry and Dry Cleaners, Ltd., v. Minister of National Revenue, [1940] A.C. 127, 136.

[4] Sharp v. Wakefield, [1891] A.C. 173, 179.

[5] Duguit, Manuel de droit constitutionnel 39 (1923).

[6] *Id.* at 40.

mon-law world, is accustomed to derive the basic principles of his system inductively from the decided cases. Since these principles have not been clearly expressed by the legislature, they have had to be worked out by "the gradual process of judicial inclusion and exclusion,"[7] much as in Anglo-American law. The judge, having to seek a correct solution in the infinite variety of cases presented to him, and finding no clear guide in a Code enunciating the fundamentals of administrative law, has had to establish these fundamentals himself.[8] It is this necessity that gives to the common lawyer seeking a comparative understanding of the *droit administratif* a facility of comprehension that he achieves in almost no other area of a civil-law system. French administrative law, like that of the system in which he has been grounded, is judge-made law.

There is, however, an essential difference between the judge who has made the *droit administratif* and the judge who has made Anglo-American administrative law. In the common-law world the basic principles of administrative law have been worked out by the ordinary courts by analogy from the principles of private law. In France, on the other hand, the law courts concerned with the dispensation of justice between individuals have played only a minor part in this field. French administrative law has been the work of a series of administrative courts —a group of tribunals created outside the ordinary judicial system. Under the Anglo-American system the State is subject to the same law and the same judges as the individual. The citizen adversely affected by administrative action has his remedy before the ordinary courts. The *droit administratif* is based on the existence of a special law for cases involving the administration and of special courts to decide them.[9]

The common lawyer normally feels that one of the great virtues of his system has been that control over administrative action is maintained through the same institutions that administer the ordinary law of the land and on the same fundamental principles of justice. This relationship has been the basis of the rule of law in the common-law world, and its absence in the French system led to the well-known criticism of the *droit administratif* by A. V. Dicey. With us, Dicey insisted, it must be the law courts that determine questions of administrative law, and the applicable principles are those worked out from the ordinary private law by judicial empiricism. This sequence, indeed, is implicit in his

[7] Davidson v. City of New Orleans, 96 U.S. 97, 104 (1877).
[8] Waline, Traité élémentaire de droit administratif 21 (6th ed., 1951).
[9] Laubadère, Traité élémentaire de droit administratif 25 (1953).

third meaning of the rule of law in his classic definition of that concept. The "law of the constitution, the rules which in foreign countries naturally form part of a constitutional code, are not the source but the consequences of the rights of individuals, as defined and enforced by the courts; . . . in short, the principles of private law have with us by the action of the courts and Parliament been so extended as to determine the position of the Crown and of its servants."[10] This is the cardinal principle under which administrative power is controlled in our polity. "Any official who exceeds the authority given him by the law incurs the common law responsibility for his wrongful act; he is amenable to the authority of the ordinary courts, and the ordinary courts have themselves jurisdiction to determine what is the extent of his legal power, and whether the orders under which he has acted were legal and valid."[11]

The French lawyer, on the other hand, has been no less attached to what he sees as the virtues of a system in which the control of administrative authority is vested in special administrative tribunals rather than in the ordinary courts. "In reality," states a leading contemporary treatise on the *droit administratif*, "for France the system is, on the whole, satisfactory. It is wise not to submit cases involving the knowledge of administrative law and of the necessities of administrative life to the law courts. The law courts do not possess this knowledge. They would be inclined either to exaggerate the prerogatives of the administration or to neglect them through ignorance or partisanship. The administrative judge knows administrative law. By reason of the manner of his recruitment, he can understand the facts and grasp their reality and complexity. From this understanding his decision acquires the authority needed to make an administration naturally disposed to abuse its prerogatives defer to it."[12]

The difference between the Anglo-American and the French system of administrative law, so far as it concerns the organs in which the control of administrative action is vested, can be attributed to differing interpretations of the doctrine of the separation of powers. That doctrine has been of basic importance in the constitutional theory of both systems. Though Montesquieu may have erred in assuming that free government, like all Gaul, is divided into three parts, there clearly must be some separation of governmental authority in the democratic State.

[10] Law of the Constitution 203 (9th ed., 1939).
[11] *Id.* at 389.
[12] Rolland, Précis de droit administratif 277 (10th ed., 1951).

Of late there has been a tendency to overlook this necessity—to consider the separation of powers as an outmoded idea of the eighteenth century, "said to belong to the age of etiquette, the age of overrefinement, when every practical activity was embarrassed by ceremonial and checks."[13] Yet, as the British Committee on Ministers' Powers pointed out, this extreme view loses sight of the need for some distinction between the branches of government. "One of the main problems of a modern democratic state is how to preserve the distinction, whilst avoiding too rigid an insistence on it, in the wide borderland where it is convenient to entrust minor legislative and judicial functions to executive authorities."[14]

The common lawyer has been accustomed to think of the separation of powers as one of the leading characteristics of his constitutional system. "It is believed to be one of the chief merits of the American system of constitutional law," the United States Supreme Court has asserted, "that all the powers entrusted to government, whether state or national, are divided into the three grand departments, the executive, the legislative, and the judicial. That the functions appropriate to each of these branches of government shall be vested in a separate body of public servants, and that the perfection of the system requires that the lines which separate and divide these departments shall be broadly and clearly defined."[15]

In the Anglo-American system the doctrine of the separation of powers has become in effect a doctrine of the *specialization* of powers. Each branch of government is to exercise the type of power conferred upon it—legislative, executive, or judicial—free of interference from the other branches. As for the courts, the delegation to them of *the* judicial power has meant that to them is confided the resolution of all justiciable controversies; and this control has meant that they are competent to decide cases involving exercise of authority by the executive branch. Thus, in the common-law world, the courts have come to control the legality of administrative action. With us, as was stated by Farwell, L.J., an administrative "tribunal is not an autocrat free to act as it pleases, but is an inferior tribunal subject to the jurisdiction which the Court of King's Bench for centuries, and the High Court since the

13 Pound, Administrative Law 45 (1942).

14 Report 4 (Cmd. 4060, 1932).

15 Kilbourn v. Thompson, 103 U.S. 168, 190 (1880). See Vanderbilt, The Doctrine of the Separation of Powers and Its Present-Day Significance (1953).

Judicature Acts, has exercised over such tribunals."[16] Nor, in the Anglo-American view, does this judicial control compromise the independence of the executive branch required by the separation-of-powers doctrine. The judicial function is seen as solely to determine the law applicable to controversies. The simple fact that the administration happens to be one of the parties in a particular case does not mean that a court, in deciding that case, is exercising other than purely judicial power.

In France, as in the common-law world, the separation of powers forms a cornerstone of constitutionalism.[17] The doctrine there has, however, received an interpretation wholly unlike that to which the common lawyer is accustomed. Anglo-American constitutional history is a record of attempts by legislature and courts to restrain excesses by the executive branch. French constitutional theory, on the other hand, has been influenced by the memory of constant obstruction of the executive branch by the *Parlements*—the common-law courts of appeal under the *Ancien Régime*. Rightly or wrongly, it was felt that they had unduly opposed efforts toward necessary administrative reforms in order to conserve their own privileges and prerogatives. "It is . . . the memory of these struggles [*i.e.*, between the *Parlements* and the executive] and of the detrimental effect on the country's administration which explains the deep distrust with which subsequent French Constitution-makers viewed all judicial activities, and which resulted at the time of the First Revolution in a complete separation not only of the judicial and administrative functions, but also of the judicial and administrative jurisdictions."[18] In the Anglo-American world the struggle of the common-law courts with the executive led to the supremacy of the courts over the executive. In France a like conflict has led to the opposite result.

The necessity of destroying the *Parlements* was one of the dominant ideas of the Constituent Assembly of 1789, and it did away with them as early as November 3 of that year.[19] But the members of the Assembly sought also to prevent a return of the *Parlementary* abuses by forbidding the courts created in place of the pre-Revolutionary tribunals to interfere with the working of administrative agencies. The consequence was the enactment of the basic law of August 16-24, 1790, that proclaimed the separation of administrative and judicial functions: "Judi-

[16] Rex v. Board of Education, [1910] 2 K.B. 165, 178.
[17] Sieghart, Government by Decree 157 (1950).
[18] *Id.* at 153.
[19] Waline, *op. cit. supra* note 8, at 45.

cial functions are and will always remain distinct from administrative functions. Judges may not, under penalty of forfeiture of office, interfere in any manner with the workings of administrative bodies, nor summon administrators before them in connection with the exercise of their functions." It was the enactment of this principle that restrained the French law courts from asserting a control over administrative action similar to that exercised by Anglo-American courts. In the common-law world much of constitutional history has been concerned with securing the independence of the judiciary from the executive. In France there has been in addition an even stronger movement aimed at securing the independence of the executive from the judiciary.[20]

With the enactment of the principle of the separation of administrative and judicial authorities the principal anxiety of the men of the Revolution over judicial competence was eliminated. But where did this enactment leave the individual citizen adversely affected by administrative action? In actual fact he was left with only whatever remedy was available to him in the administration itself. "Actually, though the reform was proclaimed in 1790, it was only half realized: the judges were indeed prevented from administering, but the administrators were not prevented from judging. On the contrary, they were given every incentive to judge. To be specific, let us imagine a citizen who has a complaint against the administration. The law courts cannot receive his complaint; to whom, then, can he bring it? He has no remedy but to file a petition, a humble request, either with the author of the act complained of or with his superior. . . . Thus the administration was appointed its own judge."[21]

Such a system, under which one organ was at the same time judge and interested party, would appear today to be the very negation of justice.[22] "Of course," said Cotton, L.J., in an important case, "the rule is very plain that no man can be plaintiff, or prosecutor, in any action, and at the same time sit in judgment to decide in that case."[23] A concentration of functions in administrative agencies much less invidious than that involved in the French system in the post-Revolutionary period has been the object of constant criticism in the common-law world. Indeed, as the United States Supreme Court has recently explained, one of the fundamental purposes of the Federal Administrative Procedure Act of

20 Compare Report of the Committee on Ministers' Powers, 110.
21 Waline, *loc. cit. supra* note 19.
22 Labaudère, Manuel élémentaire de droit administratif 41 (3d ed., 1951).
23 Leeson v. General Council of Medical Education (1889), 43 Ch. D. 366, 379.

1946 was to curtail and change the practice of embodying in one person or agency the duties of prosecutor and judge. That "Act did not go so far as to require a complete separation of investigating and prosecuting functions from adjudicating functions. But that the safeguards it did set up were intended to ameliorate the evils from the commingling of functions . . . is beyond doubt."[24]

The French system of the post-Revolutionary period, under which there was no judge of the validity of administrative action except the active administration itself, was subject to even greater dangers than those involved in the concentration of the functions of prosecutor and judge in Anglo-American administrative law. It is not surprising, therefore, that efforts were soon made to eliminate these dangers—efforts to prevent the active administration from being the final judge of its own action. At the same time, however, there was the need to have *some* judge of the legality of administrative action. Such a judge has been found through the development of a series of administrative courts wholly distinct from the active administration. "To prevent the law courts from judging cases affecting the administration, to preclude the administration from being the judge in its own cause, and nevertheless to find a judge—these requirements seemed to amount to the squaring of the circle. French law has, however, resolved the problem very neatly by the creation of two orders of jurisdiction; to wit, two systems of courts subject to two different supreme courts: the judicial and the administrative jurisdiction. The latter is distinct both from the judicial order and from the active administration."[25] The application of the separation-of-powers doctrine in France has thus had two stages. The first consisted in removing cases involving questions of administrative law from the cognizance of the law courts. The second consisted in removing such cases from the cognizance of the active administration and vesting them in a series of separate administrative courts.

To the common lawyer the term "administrative court" appears self-contradictory. A *court*, to his way of thinking, is an organ "discharging judicial power with all the implications of the judicial function in our constitutional scheme."[26] An organ characterized as *administrative* stands on a wholly different footing. As was aptly pointed out by Lord Greene, a court in the common-law world is ill fitted for the

[24] Wong Yang Sung v. McGrath, 339 U.S. 33, 46 (1950).
[25] Waline, *op. cit. supra* note 8, at 47 (italics omitted).
[26] Frankfurter, J., dissenting, in Penfield Co. v. Securities and Exchange Commission, 330 U.S. 585, 604 (1947).

determination of the type of dispute normally referred to an administrative body. "Certain types of questions are not so suitable for decision by courts of law as by a different type of tribunal. A court of law must necessarily be guided by precedent. Its functions are first to ascertain the facts and then to apply the law to the facts as ascertained. In applying the law it must be guided by previous decisions. If it does not do this the law becomes chaotic. The whole tradition and practice of legal administration makes it extremely difficult for the judges to administer a law by which the tribunal is to grant or withhold rights according as they think it just or reasonable to do so."[27] The advantages of decision by administrative organs—directness, expedition, freedom from the bonds of purely technical rules, and the consequent ability to give effect to the legislatively expressed policy[28]—can only be bought at the cost of many of the traditional checks on courts. Certainty and predictability, the technique of decision according to authoritative principles, and the bridling of the magistrate's individual will by formalized rules of procedure—these must inevitably be lessened as freer play is given to administrative discretion.

The basic dissimilarity between courts and administrative organs in the common-law world was underlined by the well-known attempt by the Committee on Ministers' Powers to distinguish between "judicial" and "administrative" decisions. A judicial decision was said by the Committee to presuppose an existing dispute between two or more parties and to involve four requirements: (1) the presentation of their case by the parties to the dispute; (2) the ascertainment of questions of fact by means of evidence adduced by the parties; (3) the submission of legal argument on questions of law; and (4) a decision disposing of the whole matter by a finding upon the facts in dispute and an application of the law of the land to the facts so found.[29] An administrative decision is something entirely different. Indeed, asserted the Committee, the very word "decision" has a different meaning in the two spheres. "In the case of the administrative decision, there is no legal obligation upon the person charged with the duty of reaching the decision to consider and weigh submissions and arguments, or to collate any evidence, or to solve any issue. The grounds upon which he acts, and the means which he takes to inform himself before acting, are left entirely to his discretion."[30]

[27] Law and Progress 20 (Haldane Memorial Lecture, 1944).
[28] See Pound, "Justice According to Law" 14 Col. L. Rev. 1, 24 (1914).
[29] Report, 73.
[30] *Id.* at 81.

One grounded in the Anglo-American emphasis upon the sharp distinction between administrative and judicial functions cannot but feel that an "administrative court" is a singular kind of hybrid. An organ is either an administrative agency or a court: it cannot, at one and the same time, be both. When, investigating the *droit administratif*, the common lawyer is confronted with a series of organs termed "administrative courts," said to be the sole supervisors of the legality of administrative action in France, he will seek to probe more deeply into their true nature to determine whether the administrative or the judicial element in them preponderates—*i.e.*, whether they are actually administrative agencies or, in the common-law sense of the term, courts.

In post-Revolutionary France, then, the only remedy available to citizens adversely affected by improper administrative action was within the administration itself. As time went on there was a natural tendency to defer the complaints of such citizens to an organ of the administration specialized in the handling of such complaints. It was felt that the earlier system of having such complaints decided only by the agency whose action had caused the grief complained of gave the individual citizen no serious guarantee of justice.[31] The obvious step toward obviating this difficulty, in view of the impotence of the law courts under the French interpretation of the separation-of-powers doctrine, was to carry such complaints to the head of the executive branch, supposed to be less subject to partisanship than a subordinate official.

A chief executive, however, even a Bonaparte, is not omnicompetent. He cannot himself personally perform all the functions exercised in his name. The actual accomplishment of many such functions must be delegated. In our suppositious case the examination of complaints brought by citizens adversely affected by improper administrative action was vested in a newly created organ—the Council of State. It is this body that was to evolve into the supreme administrative court in the French system.

There is little doubt that the Council of State was, at the time of its creation, more an administrative agency than a court. "No member of the Council specialized as a judge. If many of its members were jurists, many were also from a military or naval background."[32] The resolution of individual grievances was but a small part of the work of the Council. It had in addition important legislative and administrative functions;

[31] Rolland, *op. cit. supra* note 12, at 273.

[32] Sauvel, "Les Origines des commissaires du gouvernement auprès du Conseil d'État statuant au contentieux" Revue du Droit Public 5, 9 (1949).

it was in effect part of the hierarchical head of the administration, acting as the consultative organ of the chief executive. In dealing with the complaints of individuals adversely affected by administrative action, it was not bound to dispose of them in accordance with purely legal concepts. Its decisions were swayed just as much by policy as by law. Thus its decisions were patently not those of a court. To adopt once more the terminology of the Committee on Ministers' Powers, they were at most "quasi-judicial." Any Council of State decision, at the time of its creation, was " 'quasi-judicial,' and not judicial, because it [was] governed, not by a statutory direction to [it] to apply the law of the land to the facts and act accordingly, but by a statutory permission to use [its] discretion after [it] ha[d] ascertained the facts and to be guided by considerations of public policy. This option would not be open to [it] if [it] were exercising a purely judicial function."[33]

"The natural tendency of administration is to treat each case by itself, to give more weight to facts than to principles, and to prefer an easy solution of policy to a difficult solution of law. The natural tendency of a court, on the other hand, is to relate each case to a general rule, to look for the question involved rather than for the interests at stake, and to subordinate the expediency of administration to the exactitude of juridical theory."[34] The history of the post-Napoleonic Council of State has been one of uniform evolution from the former to the latter tendency. It was entrusted at the outset with legislative, administrative, and quasi-judicial functions. It prepared and edited the text of statutes;[35] it performed the role of a superior council of administration; and it dealt with the grievances of individuals who professed to have been adversely affected by improper administrative action. The concentration of the functions of legislator, administrator, and judge in the one organ militated against the exercise of the judicial function in a truly judicial manner. Pressures and influences properly enough directed toward officers responsible for formulating and administering public policy constituted an unwholesome atmosphere in which to adjudicate private rights.[36] "Could the Council of State be impartial when it would have to judge the legality of an act upon which it may have

[33] Report, 74.

[34] Waline, *op. cit. supra* note 8, at 71.

[35] It was, indeed, the Council of State that was called upon to draw up the great Codes of the Napoleonic era.

[36] Report of the President's Committee on Administrative Management 36 (1937).

been consulted beforehand and given its approval?"[37] The obvious means of meeting this defect was by specialization and division of labor within the Council of State. "The danger would be eliminated if organs and functions were differentiated internally within the Council, with certain of its members judging, the others giving administrative advice."[38]

The development within the Council of State in this respect has been very similar to that urged by the President's Committee on Administrative Management in 1937 to deal with the problems arising from the concentration of the functions of prosecutor and judge in American administrative agencies. The Committee recommended a redistribution of functions within the federal regulatory agencies. They "would be divided into an administrative section and a judicial section." The former "would formulate rules, initiate action, investigate complaints . . ." and the latter "would sit as an impartial, independent body to make decisions affecting the public interest and private rights."[39]

Within the French Council of State there has been a complete separation of functions not unlike that advocated by the President's Committee. As early as 1806 there was created a separate section to deal with cases touching the validity of administrative action. "It was the Emperor himself who decided to put an end to the unsatisfactory existing situation. He recognized . . . that among the cases which he decided every day in accordance with the advice of the Council of State were many which affected the reputation and property of citizens . . . and thought that such decisions were veritable judgments, for which it was necessary to organize within the Council a *true tribunal* which would follow established procedures, and which would, above all, give the parties an opportunity to be heard. This led to the decree of July 22, 1806, which set up, within the Council, the judicial section, whose function it was to examine these cases, and laid down a procedure to be followed by it whose main features still subsist today."[40]

Subsequent stages saw the enlargement of this judicial section's competence and the development of a duty to exercise its functions in a truly judicial fashion. Of no less importance was the insulation of the administrative judiciary thus established from the active administration. If the separation of functions within the Council of State were to be

[37] Waline, *loc. cit. supra* note 34.
[38] *Ibid.*
[39] Report, 41-42.
[40] Sauvel, *supra note* 32, at 10.

more than a merely formal one, it was not enough to divide the Council into administrative and judicial sections. Steps had to be taken to ensure that those exercising administrative functions could not participate in the work of those deciding cases. As was provided for in the American Administrative Procedure Act, no one engaged in nonjudicial functions could be permitted to share in the work of the judicial section.[41] This insulation of the judging process in the French Council of State dates from two ordinances of 1831 and 1839 that eliminated from the deliberations of the Council in its judicial capacity those of its members connected with the work of the active administration. "But the precautions have been carried even further; as a rule no Councillor can act as a judge with regard to any administrative operation on which he has previously given advice. If, for instance, a decree has been prepared by the Council of State and the same decree forms the subject-matter of litigation, all Councillors who have taken part in the deliberations on the draft are debarred from acting as judges in the law-suit."[42]

With the separation of administrative from judicial functions the essential step was taken to enable the Council of State to perform in a truly judicial manner its role of deciding cases involving the administration. Of even more importance, perhaps, is the fact that, once this step was taken, the judicial section of the Council of State could evolve into a veritable court. Though there is little doubt that the Council of State began as an administrative agency exercising at most some quasi-judicial functions, it seems clear that the judicial section of that body is today a court exercising judicial power in the Anglo-American sense of the term.

The basic difference to the common lawyer between a court and an administrative organ has already been mentioned. It is not one of mere terminology or even of form. "In endowing this Court with 'judicial power,' " as Mr. Justice Frankfurter has said, "the Constitution presupposed an historic content for that phrase and relied on assumption by the judiciary of authority only over issues which are appropriate for disposition by judges."[43] A court entrusted with the review of administrative action is not in the position of a hierarchical superior of the administration. Such an organ may be as much concerned with policy and administrative efficiency as with legality, and it may act on its own

41 Compare the problem involved in cases like Errington v. Minister of Health, [1935] 1 K.B. 179.

42 Sieghart, *op. cit. supra* note 17, at 226.

43 Coleman v. Miller, 307 U.S. 433, 460 (1939).

initiative to ensure effective carrying out of the policy of the administration. The judicial function is a more limited one. Judicial power, however large, has an orbit more or less strictly defined.[44] It "could come into play only in matters that were the traditional concern of the courts at Westminster and only if they arose in ways that to the expert feel of lawyers constituted 'Cases' or 'Controversies.' . . . Even as to the kinds of questions which were the staple of judicial business, it was not for courts to pass upon them as abstract, intellectual problems but only if a concrete, living contest between adversaries called for the arbitrament of law."[45]

If we look once more at the requirements defined by the Committee on Ministers' Powers for judicial decisions and apply them to the work of the judicial section of the French Council of State, it will become evident that that body today renders true judicial decisions. According to the Committee, the key factor distinguishing judicial decisions from those normally rendered by administrative agencies is their disposition of an existing dispute between two or more parties "by a finding upon the facts in dispute and an application of the law of the land to the facts so found, including where required a ruling upon any disputed question of law."[46] The dispute must, in other words, be decided by the application of appropriate legal precepts; or where none are directly applicable the judge must reason from them by analogy in accordance with the trained technique of the judicial process.

Now, this is precisely what the judicial section of the Council of State does in deciding cases. It acts upon the initiative of private parties professing to be adversely affected by illegal administrative action, after argument submitted on behalf of such parties and of the administration. Unlike a superior in the administrative hierarchy, it has nothing to do with the wisdom or expediency of challenged action. It is concerned only with the legality of such action, and it determines the question of legality in accordance with applicable legal principles. Nor does the fact that most of these principles have been formulated by the Council of State itself mean that that body has been exercising other than judicial power. The common lawyer, living under the empire of judge-made law, cannot characterize the French tribunal as other than a

[44] Frankfurter and Fisher, "The Business of the Supreme Court at the October Terms, 1935 and 1936" 51 Harv. L. Rev. 577, 621 (1938).

[45] *Loc. cit. supra* note 43.

[46] Report, 73.

court merely because the legal principles it applies are derived primarily from its own case law.[47]

It can, of course, be argued that a tribunal is not necessarily a court simply because it renders judicial decisions. The authority to render such decisions can, in fact, be vested in an administrative agency. "The fact that [such decision] is not reached by a court so-called, but by a Minister acting under statutory powers and under specialised procedure, will not make the decision any less judicial."[48] When such authority is conferred upon an administrative agency, however, it constitutes but a part of the work of that agency. If a body has been vested, as the judicial section of the French Council of State has been, with only the power to render judicial decisions, it has come very close to attaining the status of a court. If its decisions are rendered in accordance with judicial technique and procedure by judges secure in their tenure and insulated from political pressures and prejudices, then it has in fact attained that status.

That the Council of State has evolved from a purely executive tribunal to a court should not be a source of surprise to the common lawyer. Anglo-American legal history is rich in analogous developments. Indeed, the early evolution of the courts at Westminster—the very matrix of law in the common-law world—from the *Curia Regis* of the Norman kings was roughly similar to that of the French body. Both histories show the submission of petitions to the advisory council of the chief executive; specialization within the council to dispose of such petitions; and a judicialization of the specialists, accompanied by their separation from the other, purely executive, parts of the council. If the judicial section of the Council of State has not yet in form wholly split off from the administrative sections of that body, as the common-law courts split off from the *Curia Regis*, it is nevertheless for all practical purposes a separate judicial organ.

For the common lawyer seeking to understand the essentials of the *droit administratif* a realization that the so-called administrative courts in France, of which the most significant is the Council of State, are today courts and not administrative agencies is the beginning of knowledge. If the Council of State and the tribunals subordinate to it are considered as courts, then the French system loses much of the strangeness that it may at first exhibit to one grounded in the common

47 Compare Garner, "La Conception anglo-américaine du droit administratif" in Mélanges Maurice Hauriou 360 (1929).

48 Report of the Committee on Ministers' Powers, 74.

law. Likewise, the criticisms leveled at the French system by Anglo-Americans lose much of their force. For example, the famous denunciation of the *droit administratif* by A. V. Dicey was largely based on the assertion that administrative action in France is not subject to any judicial control. "The slightly increasing likeness between the official law of England and the *droit administratif* of France must not conceal the fact that *droit administratif* still contains ideas foreign to English convictions with regard to the rule of law and especially with regard to the supremacy of the ordinary Law Courts."[49]

But even if we admit with Dicey that freedom of administrative action from all judicial control is inconsistent with the rule of law, that admission does not mean that the French system must necessarily involve the negation of the constitutional principle. In France as in the common-law world, review of administrative action is available before courts. That they are termed administrative courts instead of law courts does not make them any less judicial than the courts set up to render justice in cases involving individual citizens. "It is very true that at the outset the Council of State was in large measure a servile instrument of the Emperor, and there was thus some basis for Dicey's criticism. . . . But after 1872, when the Council became an independent court, his criticism no longer had any basis. Since that time the Council, as every Frenchman knows, has shown its independence with respect to the government and has continually extended its control over the conduct of administrative authorities until today almost any act of an administrative authority . . . can be annulled if it is *ultra vires*."[50]

In the modern French legal system there are in reality two distinct sets of courts: one to dispose of disputes between individual citizens, the other to deal with cases in which the administration is involved. The former courts, which are the older, are concerned with controversies of the kind that have always been adjudicated by judicial tribunals. The development of the latter is more recent. The justice that they dispense has become a necessary complement to that rendered by the law courts only by virtue of the modern expansions of the role of the State. With the growth of State power has come the realization that such power must be subjected to judicial control; that the earlier solution, control only within the executive branch, was insufficient to protect private parties affected by administrative action.

[49] Dicey, Law of the Constitution xlvii (8th ed., 1915).
[50] Garner, *supra* note 47, at 358.

If the common lawyer considers the French legal system in this manner, as containing two orders of courts disposing of two different types of cases—the one concerned with private and the other with public-law disputes—he should not find its workings difficult to comprehend. Such a system should not seem singular to one who is familiar with the history of courts of law and courts of equity in the Anglo-American system. In the common-law world exactly as in the French system today, there were two different sets of courts to administer justice until the Judicature Acts and their American equivalents. Each had its distinct structure, personnel, and procedure; each applied the legal principles appropriate to its own system of law. The Court of Chancery, like the common-law courts before it, was in its origins an offshoot of the council of the chief executive, and the Chancellor acted more as an administrative agency than as a court. His decisions were rendered more in accordance with magisterial discretion than with legal principles. Early equity was thus in effect a system of justice without law, for the element of will or discretion was largely operative as the determinative factor. It was this aspect of equity that called forth the vigorous criticisms of such common lawyers as John Selden, who complained that the justice dispensed by Chancery was so uncontrolled by authoritative principles that it might just as well have depended on the size of the particular Chancellor's foot. But the executive tribunal came in time to be wholly judicialized and fitted into its place in the pre-existing legal order. The result was the co-existence in the common-law world of two distinct sets of courts, each with its separate jurisdiction and its autonomous system of law.

Such is more or less the situation in the French legal system today. The relation of the so-called administrative courts to the law courts can be compared to that which existed between courts of equity and courts of law in the common-law world. It thus becomes possible for the Anglo-American to determine the real nature of the French administrative courts. Courts of equity developed into true courts after starting out as executive tribunals; the French administrative courts like the Council of State have followed a similar pattern.

But what about the self-contradiction in the use of a term such as "administrative court"? The contradiction exists only for the outsider not familiar with the actuality of the French tribunals. Here once more the courts of equity can furnish a useful analogy to the common lawyer; for there is the same apparent self-contradiction in a court characterized solely as one of equity. One who understands the Anglo-American system realizes that the courts of equity were those organs in our legal system that administered the legal principles characterized under the rubric "the law of equity." Similarly, the French administrative courts are those organs in the French legal system that administer the principles of the *droit administratif*. The courts of equity were courts created to complement the common-law courts; they were true courts, and not mere organs of executive equity. Likewise, the work of the French administrative courts complements that of the courts rendering justice between individuals. They, too, are true courts today, and not mere organs of the administration.

Chapter Two

THE ADMINISTRATIVE COURTS

Disparagement of French governmental institutions has become fashionable of late in the Anglo-American world. So far as the law is concerned, censure of institutions that are not of common-law origin finds a ready response in the Anglo-American legal profession, for the common lawyer has always been notoriously insular in his outlook. Ever since the abortive attempt of the civilians to import the Roman law into his system, he has tended to look with distrust upon foreign systems of law. This distrust has been particularly evident in the field of public law. Here especially the common lawyer has felt that he has little to learn from foreign legal theories. Has not the public law of the common-law world proved itself in the centuries of Anglo-American constitutional development? With Dean Pound, the common lawyer has invoked the pragmatist criterion. "Our theory has worked—to adapt the answer of Diogenes, *solvitur gubernando*. Continental European theories have produced no such results."[1]

The common lawyer's misgivings were strongly reinforced by the conclusions of A. V. Dicey about the workings of the *droit administratif*. As Dr. Allen has pointed out: "Chiefly through the misrepresentations (later recanted) of . . . Dicey, French administrative law has been grievously misunderstood in this country."[2] But misrepresentation though Dicey's account may have been, no one can doubt the widespread effect of his teaching. "Despite frequent counterblasts to Dicey, there is still something in the very term 'administrative law' which stirs the English lawyer's deepest suspicions."[3] Nor need one seek far for the reason for Dicey's influence. The common lawyer would be more than human if he did not look with complacency upon an account emphasizing the superiority of his own system.

1 Pound, Administrative Law 56 (1942).
2 Foreword to Sieghart, Government by Decree x (1950).
3 *Ibid.*

Such complacency about his system of public law is, however, much less justified today than it was when Dicey wrote. Many in the common-law world are, in fact, coming to realize this. ". . . jurists and lawyers of divergent political views have become deeply disturbed at the trend of constitutional development in Britain during recent decades. Their anxiety is caused partly by the immense administrative powers of a discretionary character acquired by the central government; partly by the vast increase in the legislative powers delegated to ministers; partly by the decline in local government and the tendency towards centralization; but chiefly by the decline or elimination of judicial control as an effective barrier against arbitrary or irresponsible public administration."[4]

The supposed inadequacy of the law courts effectively to control administration has led many in the common-law world to propose that control be vested in specially created administrative courts. A bill introduced in the American Congress would set up a five-judge court to be known as the Administrative Court of the United States. Upon it would be conferred jurisdiction (1) in cases involving judicial review of administrative action, otherwise cognizable in any federal court other than the Supreme Court, and (2) in cases involving the civil enforcement of the rules, orders, or investigative demands of administrative agencies.[5] It should be noted that the jurisdiction of this proposed Administrative Court would be permissive and not mandatory. Persons adversely affected by administrative action would still have a choice of bringing their review action before the ordinary courts of law.

Similar proposals have been made with regard to the British system, although they have not yet reached the stage of proposed legislation. Perhaps the earliest suggestion was that of Professor Robson in his evidence before the Committee on Ministers' Powers.[6] He advocated the creation of an administrative Appeal Court, "grafted on to the Privy Council," a proposal that involved the abolition of both the supervisory and the appellate jurisdiction of the English High Court in matters pertaining to administration and the vesting of such jurisdiction in the proposed tribunal.

Although the Committee on Ministers' Powers saw fit to advise

[4] Robson, Book Review, 21 Pol. Q. 411 (1950).

[5] Caldwell, "The Proposed Federal Administrative Court: The Arguments for Its Adoption" 36 A.B.A.J. 13 (1950).

[6] Committee on Ministers' Powers, Minutes of Evidence 58 (1932).

"without hesitation"[7] against the adoption of Dr. Robson's proposals, his views have recently been reaffirmed both by himself[8] and by other writers. Thus, R. C. Fitzgerald, writing for a Canadian audience in 1950, after posing the problem presented by the present position in the common-law world, goes on to assert: "Surely what is wanted is a Supreme Court of Administration with power (a) to inquire in disputed cases into the motives for exercising an administrative act affecting private interests; (b) to annul an executory administrative decision; and (c) to award damages for loss suffered as the result of a wrongful act committed by an agent of a public service in the exercise of his administrative function."[9]

The advocates of this type of appellate administrative tribunal have found an unexpected supporter in Dr. C. K. Allen, heretofore one of the most doughty exponents of the virtues of the existing common-law system of control of administration by the ordinary courts. "For many years," says Dr. Allen (speaking of himself in the third person), he "has believed, or hoped, that administrative law, as a separate and distinct branch, could continue to be fitted into the existing framework of our judicature, without any special machinery. He is now inclined to believe that the time has come, in view of the great and increasing pressure of administrative problems, to assign this type of jurisdiction to special courts. . . . There is no reason why an appellate administrative tribunal should not combine the purely judicial with the expert administrative elements."[10]

The student of administrative law who examines these proposals of Anglo-American jurists for the creation of specialized administrative courts cannot but conclude that they represent a significant step in the direction of the *droit administratif*. "The main difference between the English and the French method of judicial control lies in the fact that in England the general jurisdiction over litigation to which the administration is a party belongs to the ordinary Law Courts, whereas in France it belongs to administrative Tribunals and foremost to the Council of State."[11] The setting up in the Anglo-American world of separate administrative courts to perform the function of controlling

[7] Report of the Committee on Ministers' Powers 110 (Cmd. 4060, 1932).

[8] Robson, Justice and Administrative Law 618 (3d ed., 1951).

[9] Fitzgerald, "Safeguards in the Exercise of Functions by Administrative Bodies" 28 Can. B. Rev. 538, 556 (1950). See also Sieghart, Government by Decree 317 (1950).

[10] *Supra* note 2, at xiii.

[11] Sieghart, *op. cit. supra* note 9, at 72.

administration, heretofore vested in the common-law courts, would go far toward eliminating this basic difference between the French and the Anglo-American systems.

The common lawyer, influenced by the distrust that Anglo-Americans feel for French governmental institutions in general and by his own antipathy to foreign legal institutions in particular, tends cavalierly to reject any proposal tending to a *rapprochement* between his system and the *droit administratif*. With Lord Hewart, he feels that *droit administratif* is "completely opposed to the first principles of our Constitution,"[12] and that is enough, in his view, to condemn suggestions that may involve any implantation of the French system in the common-law world.

One wonders, however, whether the time has not come for the common lawyer to abandon his insular prejudice and to appraise the working of the *droit administratif* on its merits. Such objective appraisal of the French system would do more than anything else to give the Anglo-American the foundation for a proper judgment of proposals to create administrative courts in the common-law world. What better basis can there be for assessment of the merits of such proposed tribunals than an equitable examination of the functioning of an actual system of administrative courts such as that in France?

The Anglo-American lawyer, if he wishes properly to conduct such an examination, will have to forgo the legal isolationism that has characterized the common lawyer. It is not enough today to declaim with Dicey that the principles of the *droit administratif* are foreign to the spirit and traditions of common-law institutions.[13] Though the common-law world is not necessarily obliged to imitate the French system, it should at least take the trouble to understand it before thanking God for having been preserved from it.[14]

An understanding of the *droit administratif* is largely to be derived from an understanding of the working of the administrative courts that have created French law in this field. It is only after the Anglo-American comprehends the functioning of these law-creating organs that he can hope to grasp the details of the substantive law laid down by them. A survey that seeks to unfold the *droit administratif* to the common lawyer must therefore concentrate first of all upon the French adminis-

[12] The New Despotism 41 (1929).

[13] Dicey, Law of the Constitution 326 (8th ed., 1915).

[14] Compare Morgan, Introduction to Robinson, Public Authorities and Legal Liability lxxii (1925).

trative courts. Their organization, jurisdiction, and procedure must be explained before any attempt can be made at analyzing the substantive details of the *droit administratif*.

Council of State

"Of all French governmental institutions, the Conseil d'Etat is to an English observer perhaps the most interesting. Stable and continuous but responding empirically to its changing environment, it has evolved a system of case-law as elaborate almost as the Common Law itself; and by that system it has achieved for the French nation a solution of the critical political problem of to-day—the reconciliation of the powers of the executive with the rights of the subject and the rule of law."[15]

The Council of State is the most important of the French administrative courts. It has been both the apex and the base of the French system, for, as we shall see, to it has been confided the most important original and appellate jurisdiction in the *droit administratif*. Its key position was recently underlined by its vice-president. "In its action, either preventive or *a posteriori*, against arbitrariness, the Council of State may be only a cogwheel of our public-law machinery, but it is a vital wheel whose influence extends far beyond the individual cases of which it has cognizance. Its very presence holds the prospect of potential control over the administration and maintains the confidence of the public in law and liberty."[16]

Although the modern Council of State was not set up until December 25, 1799—its one hundred and fiftieth anniversary was commemorated by impressive ceremonies held in Paris on June 9, 1950—French students generally see in the Council in its present form but a renaissance of the King's Council that existed under the *Ancien Régime*. So regarded, the Council of State dates back to the earliest years of the French monarchy; it has been characterized as, "with the French language and our cathedrals, one of the oldest living institutions of our country."[17]

An outside observer seeking to comprehend the organization of the Council of State need not, however, tarry long over its historical de-

[15] Hamson, "Rule of Law in France: I. The Conseil d'État and the Executive" The Times (London), February 20, 1951, p. 5.

[16] Conseil d'État, Études et documents 19 (1949).

[17] Conseil d'État, Études et documents 180 (1950), by M. Cassin, vice-president of the Council of State.

velopment. For his purposes the basic materials are the Ordinance and Decree of July 31, 1945,[18] the organic instruments under which the Council was reconstituted after the Liberation. It should be noted that the Constitution of the Fourth Republic, like that of its predecessor of 1875, makes no mention of the Council of State as an institution, limiting itself to an almost casual reference to the appointment of its senior members.[19] Nor, in the French view, is this lack of specific constitutional provision to be regretted. "Overdetailed legal texts can be a source of inconvenience—the rules of judicial jurisdiction should retain a flexibility not always consistent with the rigidity of constitutional provisions."[20]

The actual composition of the Council of State is as follows:

1. 1 vice-president, who is today its actual head
2. 5 presidents of sections
3. 46 councilors of state in ordinary service
4. 12 councilors of state in extraordinary service
5. 49 *maîtres des requêtes*
6. 38 first-class auditors
7. 10 second-class auditors

If one adds up the list, one will see that the Council of State contains 161 members. The first reaction of the common lawyer to this figure will undoubtedly be surprise. One nurtured in Anglo-American judicial traditions can picture a legislative body or a consultative assembly of over 150 members, but only with the greatest difficulty can he visualize a court of such dimensions. The entire federal judiciary in the United States (district courts, courts of appeal, and Supreme Court), he will say, is composed of some 281 judges. Is it then to be wondered at if he looks with astonishment on one French court of 161 judges?

A closer examination of the distribution of members in the French tribunal and of the manner in which it performs its functions will, we believe, show that its size is not actually disproportionate. In the first place, it should be realized that even the law courts in the French system tend to be much larger than their Anglo-American equivalents. Thus, the Court of Cassation, the supreme law court in France, is composed of 65 judges. And, even more important, the Council of State has been not only the ultimate appellate body in the French

[18] As amended by a law of February 11, 1950.
[19] Constitution of 1946, Article 30.
[20] *Loc. cit. supra* note 17.

system of administrative law but also the most important jurisdiction of first instance. Historically, thus, the proper analogy has been not between the Council of State and a body like the United States Supreme Court, but rather between it and a combination of the Federal Supreme Court and the district courts into one large tribunal endowed with both original and appellate jurisdiction.

Moreover, in considering the size of the French body one should constantly bear in mind that the Council of State is not exclusively, or even mainly, a court. The common lawyer who examines the Council will naturally be interested primarily in its role as a judicial tribunal. When he looks at it as a whole, however, he sees that its judicial functions constitute but a part of its work. In addition to its job as a court the Council is also the chief advisory body of the administration. "The main business of the Conseil as a whole is to tender advice to the Government and to the Executive."[21] As a consultative council it can quite properly have a larger membership than might be considered necessary for a purely judicial organ.

The common lawyer will doubtless be skeptical of the judicial efficacy of a court set up to control the legality of administrative action when it is also the consultative collaborator of the administration. Such skepticism would have been wholly justified at the time of creation of the Council of State. Since, as we have seen,[22] there has been a separation of administrative and judicial functions within the Council, so that its work as a court is carried on independently of its work as a consultative council. The actual mechanics of such separation will be discussed more fully in our analysis of the internal organization of the Council.

Appointment—The composition of the Council of State as given above shows that it consists of three types of members: the councilors of state, the *maîtres des requêtes*, and the auditors. These positions correspond to three echelons within the Council, the councilors being at the top of the scale and the auditors at the bottom.

It should perhaps be pointed out that the name of those at the bottom of the hierarchy, the auditors, is today wholly a misnomer. Originally, it is true, they were mere "listeners" as far as the work of the Council was concerned. The auditors were then younger members of the administration assigned to aid the members of the Council in

21 Hamson, *supra* note 15.
22 *Supra* pp. 12-13.

their duties, and without an effective voice in the work of the Council. Today the auditors are full members of the Council of State, with an equal vote in the deliberations in which they take part, though the name of "listener" has persisted.

Since the great majority of members start their career as second-class auditors, *i.e.*, at the lowest level of the hierarchy within the Council, the manner by which they are appointed is of cardinal significance. Until 1946 the second-class auditors were chosen directly by competitive examination emphasizing legal knowledge, open to those between twenty-one and twenty-six years of age. Since that time such direct recruitment by open examination has been done away with. Instead, the auditors are chosen from among the graduates of the National School of Administration. This institution was set up by the French Government in October 1945 as an administrative laboratory, as it were, to prepare those destined for careers at the upper level of the French administration. Admission to the School is by annual competitive examination. There are two types of examinations. The first is open to university graduates of less than twenty-six years; the second is intended for those who have already had at least four years of service in the administration and are between twenty-four and thirty years of age. There is thus a conscious effort to ensure that a substantial proportion of those admitted to the School shall have had previous administrative experience. The examinations are both written and oral. The outsider is struck by their general make-up: they are intended to test the general culture of candidates and their ability to analyze and synthesize, rather than their detailed technical competence in specific fields of administration. The course of study, of three years' duration, includes practical training in various administrative agencies as well as the more normal type of academic study. While at the School, students are in effect in the position of civil servants, and they receive a fixed salary from the State.

Once each year the French Government fixes the number of positions open to graduating students in the careers for which the National School of Administration prepares. These include careers in the various branches of the domestic and foreign civil service as well as that of second-class auditor in the Council of State. The career to which a specific graduating student is assigned depends on his own choice if a sufficient number of positions are available. If more choose a particular career than there are situations available, the positions are assigned on the basis of the students' graduating rank. The status and prestige of the Council of State ensure its obtaining the best graduates for the positions of second-class auditor that may happen to be open in a particular year.

Appointment to the lowest echelon within the Council of State is thus the end result of (1) open competitive examination and (2) closed competitive selection over a three-year period of study. Neither the examination nor the selection is part of a process intended only, or even primarily, to secure members for the Council of State: their main function is to obtain qualified young persons destined for the upper levels of the active administration. Only a portion of those so obtained are allotted to the Council instead of to the administration.

To one trained in common-law traditions the method of appointment just outlined—which, it should be emphasized, is now the method by which the great majority of members originally come to the Council of State—seems a singular way of choosing the members of a tribunal entrusted with the task of controlling the legality of administrative action. The way in which the second-class auditors are chosen smacks more of the manner in which, not judges, but civil servants are appointed in the Anglo-American world. Indeed, to the common lawyer the very notion of choice by competitive examination, followed by a period of schooling at governmental expense, seems wholly out of place for recruitment of members of a judicial tribunal, especially when examination and schooling are part and parcel of an over-all scheme for securing competent candidates for careers in the active administration.

Once more it must be emphasized that, even today, the whole Council of State is not a court. As we shall see, it contains important administrative sections that serve as a consultative organ of the administration, as well as the judicial section that controls the legality of administrative action. Clearly the method of appointment outlined is a proper way of selecting those who are to participate in the administrative sections of the Council. But, even for the tasks entrusted to the judicial section, the manner of appointment is not, by French usages, extraordinary.

In France the entire judiciary is considered as more or less a branch of the civil service.[23] The very judges of the law courts are recruited at an early age by means of open competitive examinations. Those ap-

[23] Thus, according to Brethe de la Gressaye and Laborde-Lacoste, Introduction général a l'étude du droit 428 (1947), "Les magistrats . . . sont des fonctionnaires de l'État."

pointed start at the lowest echelon of the magistrature, and in recent years there has even been advocated the idea of a further period of schooling for the fledgling judge before he actually begins his judicial career—something not unlike the schooling received in the National School of Administration by future auditors of the Council of State.

The way in which the lowest level of administrative judges in the Council of State is appointed, then, corresponds roughly with the way the French judiciary in general is recruited. Indeed, whatever difference there is seems to the French administrative lawyer, at least, to be in favor of the system used for the Council of State. He thinks it not undesirable that those destined for careers as administrative judges should acquire some knowledge of administration first. Appointment solely by competitive examination on legal matters, the practice before 1946, he sees as greatly deficient in that the chosen auditors came to the Council of State with merely legal training and inclination and no practical experience of administration. Today, he says, with appointments being made from among graduates of the National School of Administration, that defect is corrected.[24]

The French administrative lawyer's solution of the problem of appointments to his principal administrative court has found an echo in the writings of Anglo-Americans who have urged the creation of administrative courts in the common-law world. What, in their view, is needed in the personnel of these proposed tribunals is "a combination of legal training with special experience or training in the particular field in which the jurisdiction is to be exercised. . . . The administrative judiciary of the future should consist of youngish men who have had a training in law . . . and who have also a knowledge of the social sciences such as economics, government, public health, business administration, or educational science."[25]

The French method of appointment to the administrative judiciary carries this concept of an administrative judge who is both an expert lawyer and an expert administrator even farther than these Anglo-American jurists have advocated. That there are advantages in securing review of administrative action by judges who are specialists in administration as well as in law cannot be denied. What simpler way is there of solving the problem of control of the expert administrator than by having such control exercised by an equally expert judge?

24 Waline, Traité élémentaire de droit administratif 73 (6th ed., 1951).

25 Robson, *op. cit. supra* note 8, at 600-1. See also Sieghart, *op. cit. supra* note 9, at 317.

It is one thing, however, to understand the French method of appointment in its own setting and another to advocate it in connection with administrative courts that might be set up in the common-law world. The French method of appointment to the administrative judiciary is not unreasonable if one bears in mind the normal manner of judicial appointment in France. Even so, one may have some doubts about the merits of a system in which a man destined to perform the role of a controller of administration receives the same administrative schooling as the prospective administrator. There is always the danger of some unconscious bias in favor of administration in the future member of the Council of State. The expertness of the administrative judge may thus be bought at too high a price. It is, of course, still too early to say whether this danger is a purely theoretical one, for the system of appointment of second-class auditors in the Council of State through the National School of Administration has been in effect only since the latter part of 1947, when the first graduating class left the School.

Promotion—Once appointed to the Council of State, the second-class auditor can look forward to a lifetime career within that body after he has successfully weathered a two-year probationary period. Within that time he may be transferred to some other public function if his "abilities do not appear to meet the demands of his duties with the Council." After the two-year period the auditor can confidently expect promotion in due course to the higher ranks of the Council—to first-class auditor, then to *maître des requêtes,* and ultimately to councilor of state.[26]

To avoid the jockeying for promotion that mars many French institutions, the Council of State has adopted an absolute rule of promotion by seniority alone.[27] To the common lawyer, accustomed to Anglo-American concepts of competitive stimulus, such a rigid rule, with no attention at all to individual merit, seems the least calculated to ensure the advancement of those best suited for higher positions. Moreover, it would seem wholly to lose sight of the need for incentive to ensure the proper performance of duties by junior members. If, however, the method of promotion that prevails in the Council of State is judged solely in comparison with that in other French governmental institutions, its advantages appear to outweigh these defects. The danger of purely political promotion is one that hangs heavy over the

26 The councilors of state must be at least forty years of age when appointed.

27 Hamson, "Rule of Law in France: II. Form and Function of the Conseil d'État" The Times (London), February 21, 1951, p. 5.

public servant in France, and he has to perform his duties with an eye to the wishes of those in the government responsible for advancement. This necessity has even applied to the French judiciary, for, though French judges hold office for life, their advancement has been wholly in the hands of the Minister of Justice, a political official.[28] The importance of this dependence can be realized if one does not look at the French judiciary with common-law conceptions of judicial office. Judicial office in France is a lifetime career. The French judge starts at an early age at the bottom of the judicial ladder, and his constant hope is of promotion to a more desirable position. It is not surprising, therefore, that efforts to obtain promotion have been as characteristic of the French judiciary as of other branches of French public life.

The rule of promotion by seniority alone was adopted by the Council of State to avoid this sort of thing. The choice before the Council was less between promotion by merit and promotion by seniority than between a rule leaving promotion to the discretion of the government, with political considerations often proving the determinative factor, and an inflexible rule of advancement that would eliminate the danger of political promotions. So viewed, the rule adopted by the Council of State seems not so unreasonable as it at first appears. The newly appointed second-class auditor can at least devote all of his efforts to his duties without having to curry favor with those responsible for his promotion.

"Outside" Members—In addition to the members of the Council of State who begin as second-class auditors and progress up the hierarchy by the rule of promotion according to seniority, there are within the two upper echelons of the Council a certain number of members appointed from the outside. For example, only three quarters of the *maîtres des requêtes* must be chosen from among the first-class auditors. The other quarter may be chosen from employees of the active administrations who are over thirty years and have had at least ten years of public service. And the proportion of the councilors of state that may be chosen from outside the Council is even greater. Only two thirds of them need be appointed from among the *maîtres des requêtes*: the other third are chosen at the discretion of the government. In practice

[28] An attempt to remedy this situation was made by the provisions of Articles 83 and 84 of the Constitution of 1946. Under it, promotions within the judiciary are made on the recommendation of the Superior Council of the Judiciary, a body composed of members chosen from the legislative, executive, and judicial branches of the government and the legal profession. See *infra* p. 58.

the choice of these councilors from the "outside" is from among distinguished civil servants. These outside members, once appointed, become ordinary members of the Council and participate in its work on terms of full equality.

In addition to the outside members there are also attached to the Council twelve councilors of state in extraordinary service. These are chosen from among "qualified persons in different domains of national activity." They too are normally selected from the upper levels of the civil service, though others, such as distinguished law professors, may also be appointed. These councilors in extraordinary services are not in the position of ordinary members. They are appointed for terms of only one year (though their terms are renewable), and they may participate only in the work of the administrative sections of the Council, not in that of its judicial section.

To the French administrative lawyer the fact that not all of the appointments to the two higher echelons are made from within the Council gives it a great advantage over the French law courts. Like most common lawyers who have looked at the French judicial system, he feels that one of its great defects is the failure to provide for the infusion of outside blood into the upper ranks of the judiciary. Vacancies in the superior courts are filled solely out of the lower levels of the judiciary, from among men who have made the judicial career a lifetime one. French students have often pointed to the superiority of the common-law system of judicial appointment, under which it is common for high judicial office to be bestowed upon those who have distinguished themselves otherwise than by service at the lower levels of the judiciary. The appointment of some outsiders to the higher ranks of the Council of State constitutes a step in the direction of the Anglo-American system of recruiting judges—probably as long a step as is possible in France. The common lawyer may regret that in practice the choice of such outside members is limited to those in the active administration itself. Still, it is difficult to see how it could be otherwise in France. French tradition knows nothing like the elevation to the bench of the leading members of the bar, the chief source of supply for the common-law judiciary.

Tenure—The common lawyer rightly looks upon security of tenure as one of the cardinal safeguards of the proper performance of judicial functions. "It is quite evident," the United States Supreme Court has asserted, "that one who holds his office only during the pleasure of another cannot be depended upon to maintain an attitude of independence against the latter's will."[29] It was only when tenure during good behavior became the accepted practice that independence of the judiciary in the common-law world was effectively secured.

The rule of irremovability from office is expressly stated to be the principle that governs the tenure of judges of the French law courts. Such security in office, though provided for only in the statute law of the Third Republic, has attained the status of a constitutional principle with the inclusion of an express provision for irremovability in the Constitution of 1946.[30] One will, however, look in vain in both the French statute book and the organic instrument for a similar provision about the tenure of members of the Council of State. All that he will find is a statement in the ordinance governing the Council's organization that councilors of state can be removed from office only by a decree of the French Cabinet, rendered on the initiative of the Minister of Justice. As for the other members of the Council, *i.e.*, the *maîtres des requêtes* and auditors, a power of removal is given to the vice-president of the Council, acting on consultation with its section presidents.[31]

Security of tenure is not, then, provided for in the French legal texts for members of the Council of State. This omission appears at first glance to be a most unfortunate one, especially in a country in which the *lex scripta* is of such significance. But, as in so many other aspects of the *droit administratif*, the legal texts do not tell the whole story. Though "it is annoying in principle that the members of the Council of State are not irremovable, because of their exercise of judicial functions, in practice this fact has never presented any disadvantages."[32] The right to remove members of the Council has not been exercised for nearly a century, and its exercise today would be almost unthinkable. Even "if, according to the letter of the law, members of the Council may be removed from office by the government, in actual practice their situation is as secure as that of the French or English judiciary. . . . French public opinion today would not tolerate either the removal of a councilor of state for political reasons or the exertion of pressure upon him to obtain a decision favorable to the administration."[33] Secu-

[29] Humphrey's Executor v. United States, 295 U.S. 602, 629 (1935).
[30] Article 84.
[31] Ordinance of July 31, 1945, article 17.
[32] Waline, *op. cit. supra* note 24, at 74.
[33] Garner, "La Conception anglo-américaine du droit administratif" in Mélanges Maurice Hauriou 355 (1929). Writing in 1929, Professor Garner was able to assert, *ibid.*, that he had received "the assurance from distinguished members of

rity of tenure for members of the Council of State has thus attained the standing of a constitutional convention in France—a standing that the common lawyer can readily appreciate by reference to the constitutional experience of his own system. Constitutional practice, if not the letter of the law, ensures to members of the Council their tenure during good behavior until the retiring age of seventy, free from any subservience to the executive.[34]

Presidency—The vice-president is today the actual head of the Council of State. True, according to the ordinance of 1945 prescribing its composition, the presidency is legally vested in the French Prime Minister (*Président du Conseil*) and, in his absence, in the Minister of Justice. In practice, however, this right has never been exercised by the Prime Minister; and, as for the Minister of Justice, it has become a custom for each newly appointed Minister to pay a visit to the Council and preside over a purely formal session. Aside from such state occasions the Council is in practice headed by its vice-president, although in a body of such size it is only natural that much of the detailed leadership should come from the presidents of the sections, whose work will shortly be discussed. Both the vice-president and the section presidents are chosen from the senior members of the Council. To them rigid promotion by seniority does not apply. They are appointed at the discretion of the government, though normally on the advice of the senior members of the Council.

Administrative Sections—The Council of State, in addition to its functions as an administrative court, has important legislative and administrative functions. With regard to them its role is primarily that of a consultative organ. For example, the government asks its advice on drafts of bills that it intends to submit to the legislature. It must also be consulted before certain important administrative regulations are promulgated.[35] In addition, statutes often provide that the Council must be consulted by the administration before certain decisions can

---

the Council of State that there is no basis for the Anglo-American opinion that the councilors of state are not entirely independent in the exercise of their judicial functions"—an assurance recently repeated to the present writer by equally distinguished members of the Council.

34 Hamson, *supra* note 15.

35 Another advisory role, potentially of great significance, is that conferred upon the Council by the ordinance of 1945 authorizing it to call the attention of the government to those reforms, legislative or administrative, that appear to the Council, acting on its own initiative, to be desirable—a role first exercised during 1949.

be made. Such consultations often occur, indeed, even when there is no statutory requirement that the advice of the Council be sought.[36]

Within the Council there is a separation of functions to ensure the insulation of those engaged in the work of the judicial section from those engaged in consultative tasks. The consultative work is actually entrusted to the four administrative sections into which the administrative portion of the Council is divided. These are known as the sections of the interior, finances, public works, and social problems. Each is concerned with a certain number of related government departments and deals with matters involving them. They are composed of a president and six councilors of state, and they contain in addition a certain number of *maîtres des requêtes* and auditors. In connection with legislative texts and important administrative regulations that must be submitted for the advice of the Council, the administrative sections do only preparatory work. The actual advice on such matters is given by the general assembly of the Council as a whole, which meets every week.

In the Council of State, conceived as the consultative organ of the administration, the French have very neatly solved a problem that has sorely troubled the common-law world. The common lawyer, too, has often sought a means by which competent disinterested advice could be made available to the administration before it undertook particular action. Where delegated legislation is involved, Anglo-American efforts have run to setting up *ad hoc* or permanent advisory bodies attached to particular administrative agencies. But the composition of such advisory bodies has always been problematic. The general tendency has been to try to make them representative of the interests to be affected by the administrative regulations—a tendency that results, of course, in anything but impartial advice.[37] A body such as the French Council of State, composed of specialists in administration and administrative law, wholly independent of the active administration, seems ideally suited to this type of consultative task.

The existence of the Council of State as a central advisory organ has also prevented French jurists from feeling the need for executive consultation of the judiciary of the type that has at times been advocated in the common-law world. That the need for expert judicial advice has often been felt by Anglo-American administrators is shown by

[36] During 1946-47, for a recent example, the Council was consulted on 2,691 occasions by the administration.

[37] See Schwartz, American Administrative Law 40 (1950).

their attempts to introduce advisory-opinion procedures whereby the validity of administrative action could be tested in advance. The best known such attempt is the English Rating and Valuation Bill, 1928.[38] Efforts to use the advisory-opinion technique in the field of administrative law have been consistently resisted by the common lawyer, who has felt that for the courts to give advice to the executive is inconsistent with common-law notions of the judicial function. Yet the problem with which the proponents of administrative consultation of the judiciary seek to deal—namely, to enable the administration to act without undue fear of later judicial invalidation—still remains. The administrative sections of the Council of State help the French administrator avoid a similar difficulty.

Judicial Section—The administrative lawyer who examines the organization and functioning of the Council of State will perforce devote most of his attention to its judicial section. To it is entrusted the task of dealing with litigation that arises between the public and the administration, and it is the judicial section alone, rather than the Council as a whole, that can properly be designated as an administrative court.

Although there is only the one judicial section in the Council, as compared with four administrative sections, to this one is assigned over half of the Council's ordinary personnel. With so many members the judicial section is too unwieldy a body to function as one judicial tribunal. It is, in fact, divided into a number of smaller units, each of which constitutes a separate court with full powers of decision in the cases that come before it. These units within the judicial section are known as subsections. There are nine of them, each composed of a president, two other councilors of state, and a certain number of the twenty-eight auditors and thirty *maîtres des requêtes* assigned to the judicial section. These subsections are designated according to number. The first four are preparatory organs: they study and prepare the records until particular cases are ready for judgment. Such cases are then decided by two of these subsections combined, under the direction of the president of the judicial section. The other five subsections have the power to decide cases by themselves, and they are given jurisdiction in numerous less important types of cases.

The normal organ of judgment in the judicial section is thus one of the last five subsections or else two of the first four combined. It deals with the more or less ordinary cases that arise. When a case of greater

38 See Schwartz, Law and the Executive in Britain 202-4 (1949).

difficulty comes up—if, for example, the question to be decided is a novel one or the amount involved in the litigation is very great—it is reserved for the judicial section as an entity, which, for such purposes, includes its president, the nine presidents of the subsections, and the two councilors of the subsection in which the case first came up. Finally, if a case is considered of even greater importance and difficulty, it is decided by what is known as the plenary assembly of the judicial section. This consists of the vice-president of the Council of State, the president of the judicial section, the presidents of its subsections, and four councilors elected from the administrative sections by their colleagues. The decisions of all these organs of judgment, it should be pointed out, have the same juridical authority; all are considered equally as judgments of the Council of State.

Within the judicial section the work of deciding cases is carried on in accordance with a defined division of labor among the various levels of the hierarchy within the Council. The task of the auditors and *maîtres des requêtes* is essentially to prepare the record for decision; that of the councilors of state is wholly to decide. This division does not mean that the lower ranks of the judicial section do not play a part in the crucial stages of the decision process. They have the same voice as the councilors in the final decision, and indeed the rule of an equal vote for each member, regardless of his age or position in the hierarchy, governs all the work of the Council. "All are equals within the house and the interchange between the most senior and the most junior is truly remarkable."[39]

The need for a division of labor in the judicial section arises from the procedure followed. The procedure of a French administrative court such as the Council of State is totally unlike that to which the common lawyer is accustomed. To him, judicial procedure is synonymous with adversary procedure. The mind of the judge is informed at an adversary hearing largely directed by the advocates of the parties, and it is only within the narrowest limits that he can direct his mind to materials other than those presented by the parties.

But common-law procedural concepts are wholly out of place in connection with the French administrative courts. Largely for historical reasons, their procedure has always been inquisitorial rather than adversary, much like that of the criminal courts in civil-law countries. The inquisitorial type of procedure is directed by the judge, not by

[39] Hamson, *supra* note 27.

the parties. His role is not solely that of an umpire: he has a duty actively to inquire into facts and legal issues on his own motion and is not limited to materials presented by the parties. This duty necessitates in each case an investigatory stage in which the facts and the law are inquired into by the court. In the judicial section of the Council of State this investigatory work is entrusted to the auditors and the *maîtres des requêtes.* A complaint received by the judicial section is allocated to an auditor or a *maître des requêtes,* whose job it becomes to examine the record as developed by the parties and to work up a tentative opinion. If he is not sure on any matter, he may and, indeed, should seek to clarify that matter by independent investigation. It is only after this preparatory stage that the affair is actually submitted for decision to the relevant organ of the judicial section, one of whose members has actively investigated it.

The need for a division of labor within the judicial section, which arises from the use of the inquisitorial type of procedure, has been most neatly met by the partition of work among the hierarchy that has existed in the Council of State from its origin. The existence of such a hierarchy is perhaps the most notable difference of organization between the French tribunal and the courts in the common-law world. It enables the judicial section to carry on its work through a co-operation between very different age groups that to an outside observer is most striking. The judicial section is "the only Supreme Court which comprises persons varying in age between 25 and 70: the balance in fact achieved is admirable."[40] This constant contact and collaboration between youth and age helps account for the success of the Council in molding its case law to meet changing conditions in a manner that would do credit to the best common-law courts, and that in a country in which changes in the law are more normally the work of the legislature than of the courts.

Extent of Separation of Functions—To the common lawyer a body such as the Council of State, which is both the consultative organ of the administration and the supreme tribunal that decides cases arising between the administration and private individuals, can seem to function properly, if at all, only if there is a sharp differentiation between its administrative and its judicial functions. The essentials of such separation do, in fact, exist within the Council of State in its internal division into administrative and judicial sections. As has been shown, the

[40] *Ibid.*

administrative sections discharge the duties of the Council as a consultative organ; it is only the judicial section that performs the role of an administrative court.

It is, however, a mistake to think of the Council of State as divided into wholly watertight administrative and judicial compartments. In the first place, it should not be forgotten that both the administrative and the judicial sections still form a part of the one corporate entity. "The Conseil calls itself *la maison* and has a strong corporate spirit."[41] All of its sections are housed in the same building, and there is inevitably much personal contact among the personnel of the various sections. It is, indeed, not unusual for members of the judicial section to discuss cases pending before them with colleagues in the administrative sections. To a common lawyer, it is true, such ex parte discussions by an administrative judge with those engaged in advising the administration would seem greatly to compromise the possibility of a fair trial. But in a system in which the inquisitorial procedure prevails such contacts by the judge are not looked upon with disfavor. Ex parte investigation by the judge is an essential element of inquisitorial procedure.

Another matter that might cause some uneasiness in an Anglo-American is the possible interchange of personnel between the administrative and judicial sections of the Council of State. A member of the Council need not remain permanently in one or the other section. In recent years a tendency has developed for members to specialize in administrative or judicial tasks. But a change of functions is still possible, and it is normally granted when requested by a member. When a transfer occurs from an administrative to the judicial section, efforts are made to minimize the inconveniences involved. For example, if particular administrative action upon which a member has helped to give advice while on an administrative section is challenged as to its legality after that member has been transferred to the judicial section, the case will, if possible, be assigned to another subsection.

Among the councilors of state themselves there is a direct interchange between the administrative and judicial sections when an issue is being dealt with by the plenary assembly of the judicial section and the general assembly of the Council. The plenary assembly of the judicial section, we have seen, is that organ of judgment which disposes of the most delicate cases that arise. The councilors elected from the four administrative sections participate in the work of the plenary

[41] *Ibid.*

assembly, even though the particular case may involve the legality of administrative action upon which the administrative sections have been consulted. The general assembly of the whole Council gives the advice of that body on proposed bills and on certain important administrative regulations. It is composed of all the councilors of state, and the councilors of the judicial section can and do participate in its work. No difficulty arises from this body's consideration of proposed statutes, for such legislative texts cannot be challenged before the Council of State. The administrative regulations on which the advice of the general assembly is given are quite another matter. Their legality can be questioned before the judicial section. There is, however, no provision for the recusation of councilors who have participated in the work of the general assembly when it considered particular challenged regulations.

The common lawyer may find it difficult to see how one who has previously given advice with regard to the subject matter of litigation can later approach such litigation with that "cold neutrality of an impartial judge" of which Burke speaks. True, even in the Anglo-American world mere prejudgment of a case is generally not enough to disqualify a judge.[42] But to admit that is far from saying that the judicial function can be properly performed by a judge who has previously acted in a consultative capacity for one of the parties.

The fact that the separation between the administrative and the judicial sections of the Council of State is not so complete as the common lawyer might desire does not, however, mean that the judicial section is not acting as a court in controlling the legality of administrative action. The important consideration is the insulation of the administrative judiciary from the active administration, and that insulation has unquestionably been achieved in the Council of State. It must be remembered that full judicial guarantees of security of tenure and independence of the administration are as fully provided for members of the administrative sections as for those of the judicial section. French students of the Council insist that its members are in no way bound by their vote in a matter before the general assembly or the administrative sections if the matter later comes up while they are participating in the work of the judicial section.[43] In essence, what is involved here

[42] See Schwartz, "Disqualification for Bias in the Federal District Courts" 11 U. of Pitts. L. Rev. 415 (1950).

[43] For a similar view with regard to the members of Anglo-American administrative agencies, see Franklin v. Minister of Town and Country Planning, [1947] 1 All E.R. 396, 398; Federal Trade Commission v. Cement Institute, 333 U.S. 683 (1948).

is a prejudgment by the administrative judge. One who has given advice with regard to particular administrative action is bound to be predisposed in favor of the validity of such action, even though he be wholly independent of the administration. The possibility of such prejudgment is much greater in the Council of State, because of the relations between its administrative and judicial sections, than would be possible in the Anglo-American judicial process. Yet this fact alone does not destroy the judicial character of the French tribunal, however much the common lawyer might prefer a complete dichotomy between the consultative and judicial organs within the Council.

To the French administrative lawyer, indeed, the fact that there is some participation by members of the administrative and the judicial sections in each other's work constitutes one of the great virtues of the Council of State. In his view this interchange between the sections helps account for the expertness that has enabled the Council so successfully to perform its functions. As perhaps the greatest of modern French administrative lawyers has stated, the Council of State is "at the same time a court and a consultative body; if it were only a court, its members would acquire only the legal competence of the judge, but since it is also a consultative body its members, constantly involved (by the framing of advice) in the preparation of the business of the active administration, acquire and retain an adequate assortment of the competences of the expert."[44] In the French view much more would be lost than gained by wholly depriving the administrative and judicial sections of the advantages of each other's *expertise*.

Jurisdiction—The key position of the Council of State in the development of the *droit administratif* becomes evident when one examines the matters over which it has had jurisdiction. In this respect as in many others, the French tribunal is different from any to which the common lawyer is accustomed. In the Anglo-American world the courts are generally divided into tribunals of first instance and those of appeal. Although there may be some blending of the two types of jurisdiction in one common-law tribunal—for example, the United States Supreme Court can exercise original jurisdiction in a limited number of cases, in addition to its appellate functions—even in such cases the court involved is still predominantly either an original or an appellate tribunal. The French Council of State, on the other hand, has been neither exclusively, nor even primarily, a court of first instance or a court of appeal. It has been entrusted with both original and appellate jurisdic-

[44] Hauriou, Précis de droit administratif 7 (12th ed., 1933).

tion, and in both areas its jurisdiction has been by far the most important in the French system of administrative law.

The original jurisdiction of the Council of State was established in an important decision of 1889[45] in which the Council laid down the principle that it was henceforth the tribunal of general jurisdiction (*juge de droit commun*) in the field of administrative law. This decision meant that the Council was competent in every administrative-law case except where jurisdiction was expressly conferred upon some other administrative tribunal. The Council has thus been the court of first instance in the *droit administratif* in every case unless a statute prescribed submission to some other tribunal. In such cases, it should be noted, the decision of the Council of State has been final, for there has never been an appellate tribunal above it in the French system.

The original jurisdiction assumed by the Council of State, much as the Courts at Westminster once assumed it in the common-law world, has been of basic importance in the French system. As a jurisdiction limited only by the boundaries of the *droit administratif* it could comprehend every dispute arising between the citizen and the administration. The French tribunal has made widespread use of its original jurisdiction. Proceeding on the assumption that for every administrative act that unduly injured a citizen there had to be a remedy, it has in effect made the *droit administratif* coterminous with the activities of the administration. The result has been a review of administrative action in the French system on a wider scale of availability than exists in the Anglo-American world. Whether or not the citizen was provided with a statutory remedy in his controversy with the administration, the Council of State has stepped in. And statutory attempts to provide for administrative finality have been treated as incompetent to override the basic principle that the Council of State might decide any dispute in the field of administrative law.

Only where an express statutory provision has given the citizen an adequate remedy in some other tribunal—and the Council has insisted that the remedy be an effective one—has the original jurisdiction of the Council of State been barred. And even in such cases the Council has been vested with appellate jurisdiction. Such appellate authority still maintains the pre-eminent position of the Council in the *droit adminis-*

[45] Cadot, December 13, 1889. The decisions of the Council of State are customarily cited by the name of the plaintiff and their date. They are reported in chronological order in the Recueil des arrêts du Conseil d'État statuant au contentieux, often called the Recueil Lebon, after its founder.

tratif, even though, as we shall see, most of its original jurisdiction is now to be devolved upon other tribunals. The decision of every other French administrative tribunal is subject to appeal to the Council of State—either full appeal on the law and the facts (*appel*) or appeal more or less limited to points of law (*cassation*). This principle obtains even where there is a statutory provision that the decision of the other tribunal shall be final.

This summary statement of jurisdiction should serve to show the pre-eminent position of the Council of State in the *droit administratif*. In the French system "every administrative decision is subject to challenge before a judge. That judge is either the Council of State, acting as a court of first and last instance, or, if a statute has so provided, another administrative tribunal subject to the appellate jurisdiction of the Council of State. Directly or indirectly, then, either on first instance or appeal, the Council of State has cognizance of every action brought against the administration, of which it is thus the supreme controller."[46]

Prefecture Councils—"Administrative Courts"

Organization—The type of judicial system familiar to the common lawyer is one with a number of tribunals of first instance at its base, with their jurisdiction normally defined on a territorial basis, and a supreme appellate tribunal at its summit. Our analysis of the Council of State has shown that the apex of the French administrative judicial system has been unlike that to which the common lawyer is accustomed. The Council of State, in addition to its role as a supreme court, has been vested with the general jurisdiction of first instance in the French system. Important original jurisdiction has, however, also been conferred on a territorial basis upon the interdepartmental Prefecture Councils.

Ever since the Revolution the unit of territorial administration in France has been the department. A law of 1800 set up within each department a Prefecture Council with a limited jurisdiction in administrative-law cases. At the beginning these bodies were closely connected with the prefects, the heads of the active administration in the departments. But, like the Council of State, they were to evolve in the course of the nineteenth century into veritable judicial tribunals. The most important step in this direction was a decree of 1862 imposing upon the Prefecture Councils rules of judicial procedure, including one that required the holding of an oral public hearing before

[46] Odent, Cours de contentieux administratif 165 (1949-50).

decision. The detailed rules of procedure for these Councils were laid down in a law of 1889. The procedure thus prescribed, which has not since been changed in essentials, is basically similar to that followed by the Council of State. In 1926 the Prefecture Councils, with the exception of that for the department of the Seine, were abolished and replaced by twenty-two interdepartmental Prefecture Councils with each having jurisdiction over several contiguous departments. And, by a decree of September 30, 1953, as we shall see, the Prefecture Councils are to be given the title of the "Administrative Courts" (*Tribunaux administratifs*) and vested with most of the general original jurisdiction formerly exercised by the Council of State.[47]

These twenty-two tribunals are each composed of a president and four councilors.[48] Before 1926 the presidency of the Prefecture Councils was vested in the prefects, and members of the prefects' staffs also participated in their work. Since that time such participation by members of the active administration has been done away with. There are two classes of councilors in these courts.[49] Those of the second class are chosen from among the graduates of the National School of Administration, much as the second-class auditors are appointed to the Council of State. First-class councilors are chosen from among the members of the class just below them, although, as in the Council of State, a certain number of "outside" members (here, one quarter) may be appointed from the civil service. The presidents are appointed from among the first-class councilors, although here, too, a choice may be made among designated civil servants. Within these tribunals there is a division of labor not unlike that among the echelons within the Council of State. The need for such division is caused by the use of an inquisitorial procedure similar to that of the Council of State.

Jurisdiction—The Prefecture Councils, unlike the Council of State, have been competent solely in cases in which express jurisdiction was given them by statute. They have been wholly tribunals of first instance. Their decisions have never been final; an appeal might be taken from them to the Council of State in every case, however small the

47 Under the 1953 decree, it should be noted, the "Administrative Courts" are to take the name of the city in which they sit, rather than that of the departments over which they have jurisdiction, as has been the case with the Prefecture Councils.

48 That of Paris (or for the department of the Seine, as it has been called) consists of twelve councilors and a president.

49 Such is the provision of the September 30, 1953, decree referred to above. In the Prefecture Councils, there have been three classes of councilors.

amount involved. Furthermore, the jurisdiction of the Prefecture Councils has been essentially territorial. They have been competent only in cases within their departments. It should be noted that the territorial jurisdiction of these tribunals does not primarily depend on domicile, as it normally does in an Anglo-American court. It is not "determined by either the domicile of the plaintiff or the seat of the defending administrative agency, but by the place where the administrative operation which gave rise to the actual litigation was carried out. Thus any litigation in connection with public works has to be brought before that [Prefecture] Council in whose territory the actual work has been done."[50]

The jurisdiction of the Prefecture Councils, which, it should be recalled, has been a competence specifically conferred by statute, has extended over a number of administrative-law matters. It has included the cognizance of all cases connected with public works; with direct taxes; with the sale of public property; with elections to local assemblies; and with the enforcement of health legislation applicable to business premises. In 1934 the competence of the Prefecture Councils was extended to include cases involving most of the acts—other than those growing out of rule-making activities—of local administrative agencies, as distinguished from agencies connected with the central government. And, on September 30, 1953, there was promulgated, as has been mentioned, a decree by which the Prefecture Councils (under their new title of "Administrative Courts") are to be vested with general original jurisdiction in administrative-law cases. Henceforth, it is they who are to be the first-instance controllers of the legality of administrative action in France, subject, of course, to the full appellate supervision of the Council of State.

Other Administrative Tribunals

The outside observer who seeks to analyze the *droit administratif* will be concerned primarily with the Council of State and the first-instance "Administrative Courts" (*Tribunaux administratifs*), as the Prefecture Councils are now to be termed. He should, however, realize that there is also a large number of other tribunals that the French administrative lawyer considers a part of his administrative judicial system, all subject to the appellate jurisdiction of the Council of State. Among these are the Colonial Councils, which have a jurisdiction

[50] Sieghart, *op. cit. supra* note 9, at 232.

similar to that of a Prefecture Council in the overseas territories of the French Union; the Court of Accounts, which oversees the expenditure of public funds by a control analogous to that exercised by the Court of Exchequer in the early common-law system; the Superior Council of National Education, which decides appeals from decisions in the field of education; the Review Councils, set up under the compulsory military service laws; and the Assistance Commissions, which hear appeals in the field of national assistance.

The foregoing is intended merely as an illustrative list, by no means complete. In recent years the French legislature has set up an ever-increasing number of administrative tribunals to deal with cases arising out of specified administrative activities. There has been a growing tendency to remove the decision of cases arising between the administration and the public from the competence of the active administration and to vest decision in independent tribunals. A similar tendency has existed in the common-law world, especially in Britain, where since the Second World War there has been a veritable mushrooming of such administrative tribunals. To the common lawyer they do not come within the concept of courts. The French bodies, on the other hand, are treated as courts by administrative lawyers in France, although they are similar in many ways to the British administrative tribunals. Such treatment is explained by the desire of the Council of State to hold these newly created bodies to stricter procedural rules than those imposed in the French system on the active administration. These tribunals, if found to come within the concept of administrative courts, can be required to follow the usual rules of judicial procedure.

Administrative Justice in Slow Motion

Anglo-American jurists who have advocated the setting up of administrative courts in the common-law world have often pointed to the great delays involved in litigation before the ordinary courts as one of the main reasons for their proposals. Judicial justice, they say, is dispensed ever so slowly, though it may be dispensed exceedingly well. The vesting of administrative-law jurisdiction in specialized administrative courts would both relieve the work load of the law courts and enable the administrative-law cases themselves to be disposed of more speedily.

The experience of the French Council of State indicates, however, that the mere establishment of separate administrative courts will not of itself solve the problem of delay in the dispensation of justice. The administrative court may take as long in deciding cases as the law court, whether because of the inadequacies of the administrative tribunal itself or, as in the Council of State, because of the number of cases brought before it.

One who looks through the decisions of the Council of State rendered during 1948 may chance upon the *Jacquin* case, decided on appeal from the Prefecture Council on May 14 of that year. The decision appealed from was handed down May 6, 1938, a mere ten years earlier; but that decision dealt with the consequences of an accident that occurred on July 14, 1914, thirty-four years before the decision of the Council of State. Nor did the Council in 1948 decide the case on the merits. It held only that the case did not involve an administrative-law question and hence came within the competence of the French law courts rather than of the administrative courts. We are not told what is the ultimate outcome of this French version of *Jarndyce v. Jarndyce* —which is undoubtedly now winding its weary way through the French law courts—but clearly, in the words of a commentator, "no example is better calculated to show the slowness of the administrative courts."[51]

The *Jacquin* case is the horrible example; but the normal delay involved in decisions of the Council of State, though not nearly so extreme, has still been considerable. According to one student who analyzed a large number of cases, the average time for decision has been three years after the filing of the complaint or petition of appeal.[52] This is a considerable delay, especially if one realizes that the granting of intermediate relief against the administration is the exceptional thing in the *droit administratif*. In the absence of a power of temporary injunction or *supersedeas* such as is exercised by Anglo-American courts, a three-year lag in the granting of relief against the administration may in fact destroy the effectiveness of such relief when it is obtained. As one observer comments, "justice that takes so long is no longer justice, but a parody on it."[53]

Since 1947 the Council of State has published a yearbook entitled *Studies and Documents* containing articles and other materials on vari-

[51] Waline, Note, Revue du Droit Public 600, 601 (1949).

[52] Liet-Veaux, "La Justice administrative au ralenti" (1948) Dalloz, Chronique 133. The present writer was assured by members of the Council of State that two years would be a more accurate figure.

[53] Gassie, La Réforme des Conseils de Préfecture 7 (thesis, 1947).

ous aspects of the Council's work. Included in these volumes are detailed statistics on the work of the judicial section that enable the outside observer to obtain an over-all picture of its case load for the past few years. It is this case load, ever-increasing since the Liberation, that has been primarily responsible for the delay noted. The following table, taken from the statistics published in the yearly *Studies and Documents*, should serve to prove the point:

	Cases Filed	*Cases Decided*
1944-45	2,581	2,307
1945-46	6,893	2,782
1946-47	6,772	4,308
1947-48	7,201	4,219
1948-49	5,699	4,777
1949-50	6,665	4,874
1950-51	5,857	4,022

These figures clearly show the reason for the lag between the filing of a complaint or appeal and the decision by the Council of State. And they show that the cause of delay has not been the inefficiency of the Council as a deciding organ. Quite the contrary! To consider the volume of cases decided by the judicial section is to be impressed by the amount of work performed. The decision of well over four thousand cases a year has been made possible only by the thoroughgoing division of labor within the Council, already discussed, and by the extreme devotion of its members to their work. Indeed, as the table indicates, the Council has made an increasingly successful effort to catch up with its judicial business. But the ever-growing number of cases filed has made the Council feel as if it were working on a treadmill. As the vice-president has stated, "however great may be the devotion of my colleagues and the constant improvement in our methods of work, the number of cases decided remains very perceptibly below that of the new cases filed. The backlog has, it is true, increased less during 1949 than in previous years. But still it did increase, and it is continuing to increase."[54]

It is impossible for any one tribunal, even one as well organized for the purpose as the Council of State, properly to dispose of the number of cases that have been filed with the Council. That number, which

[54] Conseil d'État, Études et documents 17 (1950). On August 1, 1949, the Council of State had a backlog of 18,933 undecided cases. By August 1, 1951, this had grown to 22,599, and by the beginning of 1953 to some 24,000.

has increased tenfold in the past seventy years, has been due primarily to the success of the Council as an administrative court. Its effectiveness in controlling the action of the administration and its willingness to intervene at the request of those adversely affected by administrative action have made the French citizen turn to it with far more frequency than the Anglo-American does to his courts in analogous cases. The very effectiveness of the Council as the controller of administration has led, paradoxically, to its impaired efficiency, for it produced the ever-increasing resort to the Council by the public and a resultant case load too heavy for any one tribunal. The Council is thus "in danger of being overwhelmed by its own success."[55]

The answer to the problem is the devolution of the Council of State's jurisdiction of first instance to other tribunals. In 1889, when in the *Cadot* case[56] the Council laid down the principle that it was the general jurisdiction of first instance in the *droit administratif*, the number of administrative-law cases was only one tenth of what it is today. A system with only one court of general first-instance jurisdiction could then be workable. As a contemporary defender of the *Cadot* decision observes, "there was only one urban praetor in Rome for the whole empire."[57] Today, however, such a view overlooks the practical reality of congestion in the Council of State. With the tremendous increase in administrative-law cases, "the maintenance of only one administrative court of general jurisdiction for all of France becomes an indefensible anomaly."[58]

Administrative-Court Reform

A bill introduced in the French Parliament during 1950 by the government, with the approval of the Council of State, sought to transfer most of the original jurisdiction of the Council to the Prefecture Councils. According to its terms, these were to become, with some exceptions, the tribunals of general first-instance jurisdiction (*juges de droit commun*) in the field of administrative law, though their decisions were still to be subject to appeal to the Council of State. After having tried unsuccessfully for three years to have this bill come to a vote in the National Assembly, the government did succeed in July 1953 in having the legislature authorize it to promulgate a so-called "decree law" in the

[55] Hamson, *supra* note 27.
[56] *Supra* note 45.
[57] 2 Hauriou, La Jurisprudence administrative de 1892 à 1929, 440 (1929).
[58] Waline, *op. cit. supra* note 24, at 80.

field of administrative-court reform. As we shall see,[59] the French executive has been given what amounts to plenary legislative power to govern by decree, and its "decree laws" issued in pursuance of such authority have the full effect of statutes.

On September 30, 1953, the French Government promulgated a "decree law" putting most of the provisions of the 1950 administrative-court reform bill into operation and, when operative, this will have exactly the same legal effect as if the bill itself had actually been passed. Under this decree, the rules of jurisdiction that had governed the working of the *droit administratif* since the *Cadot* case[60] are to be completely altered. Henceforth, it is the Prefecture Councils that are to have general original jurisdiction in administrative-law cases. They are to be competent in all such cases unless jurisdiction has been expressly conferred by statute upon some other tribunal. With some important exceptions,[61] the Council of State is now to be solely an appellate court, whose chief function will be to hear appeals from the Prefecture Councils. The appellate power of the Council of State is to be a full one on both the law and the facts, and appeals to it can be taken as a matter of right in every case.

It is recognized by the draftsmen of the 1953 decree that its successful implementation will depend upon the effectiveness with which the Prefecture Councils carry out the important functions conferred upon them. They have, therefore, sought to ensure that the Councils will have a status and dignity adequate to their newly conferred responsibility. As has already been mentioned, the decree changes the name of the Prefecture Councils to the "Administrative Courts" (*Tribunaux administratifs*). The intent here is clearly to complete the process of judicialization of these tribunals and to make them, in the field of administrative law, as nearly as possible the equivalent of the ordinary first-instance law courts.

As the September 30, 1953, decree asserts, the merits of the reform worked by it cannot be contested. Our analysis of the congestion in the Council of State calendar has shown that that tribunal has been unable,

[59] *Infra* pp. 95-101.

[60] *Supra* note 45.

[61] These exceptions include: (1) actions to secure review of decrees of the national executive; (2) cases involving civil servants appointed by decree; and (3) cases involving administrative acts which are effective in more than the jurisdiction of any one "Administrative Court" (as the Prefecture Councils are to be termed).

despite its constant efforts to keep abreast of its work, to function effectively as the court of original jurisdiction in the *droit administratif*. Now that its first-instance competence is to be devolved upon a score of courts located throughout the country, it is to be hoped that administrative justice in slow motion will become a thing of the past in France.

The 1953 decree working this reorganization of the administrative-court system must, under the law giving the government the authority to promulgate it, be submitted to Parliament for ratification. Unless the legislature expressly refuses to ratify, however, its provisions are to go into effect one month after a regulation is promulgated by the government putting it into operation. At the time of present writing, there has been neither legislative ratification nor issuance of the regulation referred to. Nevertheless, as both ratification and the regulation appear reasonably certain,[62] the reform worked by the decree has been treated in this book as virtually in effect. Even if, French politics being what they are, a government crisis should cause the decree to remain inoperative, since the reform effected by it is urgently desired by all French administrative lawyers, it appears definite that a similar measure will be adopted in the near future. When the September 30, 1953, decree, or a measure like it, does finally go into effect, the structure of the French administrative judicial system will, as has been indicated, be radically altered. Original jurisdiction in most cases will then be conferred upon a number of tribunals of territorial competence located throughout the country, with appeals lying from their decisions to a central court. With such a symmetrical pyramidlike structure the organization of the judicial system in the *droit administratif* will be of a type more familiar to the common lawyer than the French system that has prevailed until now.

[62] According to one commentary, the requirement of ratification in the 1953 law conferring the "decree law" power is a mere formality. Fauvet in *Le Monde*, October 1, 1953, p. 1, col. 4. Indeed, there is a strong possibility that the Parliament may never act on the administrative-court reform decree. In that event, there will be, in effect, a de facto ratification, for, as has been pointed out, the decree's provisions will be operative until the Parliament expressly refuses to ratify.

Chapter Three

THE LAW COURTS

"Two systems of courts seem so natural to the average Englishman that he cannot conceive of any other condition."[1] A similar comment can well be made on the average Frenchman today. The outstanding characteristic of the French legal system, as we have seen, is the coexistence of two distinct sets of courts, one to administer the law applicable to cases arising between private citizens, the other to dispose of controversies to which the administration is a party.

To the French lawyer the need for two systems of courts seems as manifest as it appeared to the common lawyer before the merger of law and equity in the Anglo-American world. It is wholly natural, in his view, that different types of cases should be decided by specialized judges with special guarantees of *expertise*. As the leading contemporary treatise on the *droit administratif* states, "the division of the courts into two systems appears to be a simple application of the principle of the division of labor. Since the application of two clearly distinct systems of law is involved, it is preferable to divide the work among different courts: each will know better how to do its own job."[2]

The common lawyer who seeks to understand the workings of the French legal system has a ready analogy at hand in the system that prevailed in the Anglo-American world before the merger of law and equity. As in the French system today, there were two distinct sets of courts to administer justice before the Judicature Acts and their American equivalents. Each functioned independently, had its own distinct personnel and procedure, and applied the legal principles appropriate to its own system.

The relationship between courts of law and courts of equity was not always a harmonious one. The very existence of two sets of courts of

1 Smith, in Vanderbilt, Studying Law 334 (1945).
2 Waline, Traité élémentaire de droit administratif 48 (6th ed., 1951).

theoretically equal competence, with the demarcation between them never drawn with mathematical precision, soon made conflicts between Chancery and the law courts well-nigh inevitable. At first sporadic, such conflicts grew in intensity with increasing extensions of the jurisdiction of the Court of Chancery. A settlement became essential if the legal system itself were not to break down under internecine strife. A settlement was in fact achieved with the resolution by James I of the famous controversy between Lord Chief Justice Coke and Lord Chancellor Ellesmere.

The royal decision upholding the power of the Chancellor could not, however, completely resolve the problems inherent in a legal system in which justice was administered by two distinct sets of jurisdictions. The needless duplication in an artificially dichotomized administration of justice was scarcely affected by the settlement of the Coke-Ellesmere controversy. As time went on, the reasons for maintaining two separate systems became more and more difficult to comprehend. The inconveniences of such dualism, especially those flowing from the uncertainties that persisted in the rules marking out the respective jurisdictions of law and equity, were as burdensome to the litigant as they were unnecessary. "The division of remedial justice into two systems, with two courts entirely distinct from each other, intensified the defects inherent in each system. A litigant not unfrequently would have to be sent out of court to bring his action in another tribunal simply because he had chosen the wrong one. Since the rules governing the choice of tribunal were not always clear and easy of application, the harm to innocent seekers for justice was great."[3]

The common lawyer who looks at the workings of the French legal system will naturally do so through the lenses gained from centuries of experience with a dichotomized administration of justice in his own legal system. He will seek to find out whether the division of remedial justice in France between the administrative courts and the law courts has resulted in inconveniences similar to those that flowed from the division between law and equity in the Anglo-American world. Cognizant of the incessant conflicts between Chancery and the law courts in his own system, he will endeavor to see whether there have been analogous conflicts between the administrative courts and the law courts in France and, if so, what efforts have been made to resolve them. He will concentrate especially on the rules of jurisdiction developed to

[3] Clark, Handbook of the Law of Code Pleading 17 (2d ed., 1947).

parcel out the field between the two sets of tribunals; for he knows from his own experience that a dualized system of justice can be intolerable for the average litigant unless the rules of jurisdiction are clear and easy to apply. Nor will the Anglo-American be misled by the widespread belief of the French legal profession that two systems of courts are a necessary and wholly natural device for dealing with two basically distinct types of case. He will recall how a similar belief that the distinction between law and equity inhered in the very nature of things delayed for centuries in the common-law world the fusion that had become necessary.

Organization of the Law Courts

Our analysis of the French administrative courts has shown us that until now the structure of the administrative judicial system in France has been most unlike that to which the common lawyer is accustomed. In the Anglo-American world it is customary for the courts to be divided into tribunals of first instance and courts of appeal. And the jurisdiction of our courts is normally conferred upon a territorial basis. The French system of administrative courts, on the other hand, has been characterized by the pre-eminent position of the Council of State as both a court of first instance and an appellate tribunal. That body, as we have seen, has been both the supreme administrative court in the French system and the general jurisdiction of first instance. Nor has its competence been limited on a territorial basis. Its jurisdiction, like that of the King's Courts at Westminster (and like that of the English High Court today), has extended throughout the country.

The structure of the French judicial system has always been more like that with which the common lawyer is familiar. The law courts in France are organized in the pyramidlike manner so commonplace to the Anglo-American. Original jurisdiction is conferred upon a large number of tribunals of territorial competence located throughout the country. From them there is an appeal to a smaller number of intermediate appellate courts whose jurisdiction is also territorially defined. At the apex is a central court with ultimate appellate jurisdiction in certain cases. The situation here is basically similar to that which prevails, for example, in the federal judicial system in the United States, and the structure of the French judicial system should consequently present few difficulties for the Anglo-American lawyer.

General original jurisdiction in the French judicial system is vested in what are known as the Courts of First Instance. There is in principle one such court in every *arrondissement,* one of the basic units of territorial administration, of which there are some 350 in France. It has come to be recognized, however, that in many of the smaller *arrondissements* there is not sufficient judicial business to justify the maintenance of a full court. This recognition led in 1926 to the attempted abolition of the *arrondissement* courts and the substitution of a first-instance court for each department, the next larger unit of territorial administration. This reform was not to be long-lived, for it conflicted with local traditions that had grown up since the Revolution, and, more important, it met the determined opposition of that part of the legal profession that had monopolized the work before the smaller local courts. The result was the re-establishment of the *arrondissement* courts in 1929 and 1930.

An effort was made to deal with the problem of the smaller *arrondissement* having insufficient business to occupy a full court by classifying the courts themselves in three categories. Which class a particular court comes within depends on the size of its territorial unit. Only courts of the first and second classes must consist of three or more judges. Courts of the third class may contain only one member. The actual composition of a given court depends on its individual importance; *i.e.*, the population of its territorial unit.[4] A court of the third class sitting in a small *arrondissement* may consist of one judge, whereas the Court of First Instance for Paris is composed of over 160 judges. The work of the latter is, indeed, so complicated that it has had to divide itself into nineteen chambers (eleven civil, seven criminal, and one juvenile) that specialize in certain types of cases.

Above the Courts of First Instance in the judicial hierarchy are the Courts of Appeal. There are twenty-seven such tribunals in the French system, and each has territorial jurisdiction over one or more specified departments. Their size depends, like that of the Courts of First Instance, on the importance of their particular territorial units. The smallest consists of some six members. The Court of Appeals for Paris is composed of over ninety judges and is divided into fourteen chambers.

Barring an express statutory provision to the contrary, all decisions of the Courts of First Instance may be appealed from to the appropriate Court of Appeal. Nor, it should be noted, is the review power of the appellate tribunal of the limited type familiar in the Anglo-Amer-

[4] There are, at present, 35 Courts of First Instance of the first class, 94 of the second class, and 226 of the third class.

ican world. The Court of Appeal may reconsider any issue of law or fact involved in the case. It "proceeds, in other words, to a new examination of the case just as though it were itself the judge of first instance."[5] If the judges of appeal are in doubt on any matter, they may order the taking of new evidence. They must themselves render the judgment that they think proper; they may not merely reverse or remand the case to the Court of First Instance.

The concept of full review by the appellate court on both the law and the facts has been of the greatest consequence in the French legal system. It has meant that the administrative courts, in working out the scope of their review of administrative action, have not had their only guidance in the analogy of limited review by an appellate court of the decisions of subordinate judicial tribunals, such as has influenced the courts in the common-law world in this field. Anglo-American courts have quickly come to the view that the findings of the administration are entitled to at least as much deference as those of a trial judge or the verdict of a jury. The French Council of State, without the example of only limited review by appellate courts to sway it, has, as we shall see, fashioned a theory of broader review over administrative action.

At the apex of the French judicial system is the Court of Cassation. This is a central court, composed of sixty-five judges, that sits in Paris. The concept of full appeal discussed above is wholly inapplicable to its work. The reviewing power of the Court of Cassation is essentially limited to questions of law. It is erroneous, as French jurists point out, to "think of it as merely a third step in the appellate ladder, a sort of higher Court of Appeal. It is nothing of that sort, for it does not decide the case *de novo;* it rather judges the decisions that are certified to it, 'quashing' them if they are contrary to law. In consequence the Court of Cassation is not concerned with the *facts* of the case: they are not within its competence; it takes them as they have been found in the decision of the lower court and looks to see whether these facts have been judged in accordance with law."[6] The Court of Cassation is, then, that body in the French judicial system which is vested with the function of ensuring that there shall be a uniform application of the law by the courts of the land. As such a body, it has a role analogous to that played by the United States Supreme Court in the federal judicial system or by the House of Lords in Britain.

[5] Morel, Traité élémentaire de procédure civile 489 (2d ed., 1949).

[6] Brethe de la Gressaye and Laborde-Lacoste, Introduction générale a l'étude du droit 257 (1947).

Personnel

The common lawyer tends to think of judicial office as a reward for service at the bar. He looks upon promotion to the bench as the culmination of a distinguished professional career. "In England judges—both of inferior and superior courts—are appointed from practising members of the Bar. They have thus a tradition of independence and their affinities are with the Bar rather than the Executive or its servants. They are, too, less concerned with promotion."[7] The French conception of judicial office is an entirely different one. "In continental countries judgeship is a career. The young judge starts his career in one of the lowest courts and hopes to advance through judicial office and other posts under the Ministry of Justice to the highest courts."[8]

The method of appointment to the administrative courts in France is, as we have seen, one that the common lawyer would consider more appropriate for the recruitment of civil servants than for the selection of judges. The same is true of appointment of judges of the law courts. "Judges are civil servants (*fonctionnaires*) of the State," states a recent French treatise, "recruited by means of a competitive examination."[9] Such examinations are open to every French citizen over the age of twenty-five who has a law degree and has been either a member of the bar for two years or an employee of the Ministry of Justice for one year. The young law-school graduate in France normally chooses at the very outset whether his career shall be at the bar or on the bench. If his choice is for judicial office, he will seek to pass the examination given to would-be judges. In the normal course only those who qualify at the examination are appointed to judicial positions.

It will be immediately realized that the road to judicial office in the French system is basically similar to that for appointments to the administrative judiciary. Would-be councilors of state, it will be recalled, start their careers at the lowest echelon of that administrative court after having been recruited by competitive examination and schooled at the National School of Administration. In like manner the successful applicant for judicial office begins as a member of one of the lowest courts. In recent years it has been recognized that this system allows entry into the magistrature of young persons who have only academic

[7] Wade and Phillips, Constitutional Law 232 (4th ed., 1950).
[8] *Ibid.*
[9] Brethe de la Gressaye and Laborde-Lacoste, *op. cit. supra* note 6, at 428.

legal training with little or no practical experience. It has been urged that those who pass the competitive examination for the judiciary be given further training at government expense to prepare them adequately. A like argument as to the administrative courts has led, we have noted, to the provision for further schooling in the National School of Administration for would-be councilors of state and prefecture councilors. In 1945 an ordinance did actually provide for such schooling for fledgling judges by means of a three-year probationary period during which they would assist in the work of the courts, much as, in the American system, a young law-school graduate may serve as the law secretary of a judge. The provisions of this ordinance, however, were suspended by a law of 1946; and candidates successful at the competitive examination for judges are still appointed directly to posts at the bottom of the judicial hierarchy.

Promotion

The fledgling judge in the French system starts his career, then, at the foot of the judicial ladder. Few competent young lawyers would be willing to spend their lives as junior members of an unimportant court in a minor provincial town. The constant hope of the newly appointed French judge is to improve his position by promotion within the judicial hierarchy. In opting for judicial office he hardly limits his ambition to membership in some insignificant Court of First Instance; rather, his goal is membership in one of the more prominent Courts of Appeal or even in the Court of Cassation.

It is this consideration that makes the system of promotion in the French judicial system of such cardinal significance. True, French judges do enjoy the guarantee of secure tenure. The principle of irremovability is, indeed, now expressly provided for judges of the law courts in the Constitution of 1946.[10] But that provision disposes of only part of the problem. "If irremovability is a safeguard necessary to preserve the independence of judges, its benefits are perceptibly diminished whenever the promotion of judges is at the discretion of the government. The ideal would be for judges not to advance; so it is in the English system, in which the judge is named at the outset to the post that he will hold for his entire career. In France, on the contrary, the bench is a career begun young, in which one advances in office."[11]

10 Article 84.
11 Morel, *op. cit. supra* note 5, at 135.

Until a comparatively recent time the promotion of judges was wholly at the discretion of the French Government. Some improvement was made by the setting up in 1906 of a promotion list prepared by a commission composed mainly of members of the Court of Cassation and representatives of the Ministry of Justice. No judge can be promoted to a position carrying with it an increase in salary unless his name has been put on the promotion list. The problem of political promotion is, however, not resolved by this system. In the first place, the highest judicial offices are not subject to the requirement of inclusion in the promotion list. Even more important, inclusion does not of itself give a judge the assurance that he will receive an available promotion. Although only those on the list can be appointed to higher judicial office, promotion can be given, at the discretion of the government, to anyone whose name is on the list. Many judges have, in fact, had their names on the list for years without receiving promotions. Advancement has thus continued to be largely in the hands of the Minister of Justice, a political official. "The present system still leaves a large share open to favoritism and influence," observes a leading recent treatise on the subject.[12] One should not be too surprised, therefore, to find that the struggle for promotion is as persistent among the judiciary as among others in French public life.

An attempt has been made in the French Constitution of 1946 to remedy this situation. Under its provisions[13] promotions within the judiciary are now made by the President of the Republic on the recommendation of the Superior Council of the Judiciary. This is a newly created body composed of members chosen from among the legislative, executive, and judicial branches of the government and the legal profession. It is not, however, clear whether its creation will do away with the problem of political promotions. In the first place, those chosen by the political branches of the government constitute the majority of the Superior Council. And, perhaps of even greater significance, the Council has, according to the letter of the constitutional provision, merely the power of recommendation. Its suggestions need not be followed by the appointing authority. The recommendations of the Superior Council may ultimately be followed almost as a matter of course; but unless and until such a tradition develops, it is difficult to see how the constitutional provisions of 1946 have effected any real improvement.

12 *Id.* at 136.
13 Articles 83 and 84.

The Law Courts

Erroneous Comparison with Common-Law Courts

Anglo-American scholars who have criticized the workings of the *droit administratif* have proceeded, as we saw, upon a misconception of the actual character of the French administrative courts. But they have also been led to their views by an erroneous tendency to compare the law courts in France with those with which they have been familiar in the common-law world. They have proceeded on the basic assumption that control of the administration by the ordinary courts of law has constituted the foundation stone of the rule of law under which Anglo-Americans have lived since the victory of the common-law courts over the executive. Looking at the French system, they have found that its law courts have been barred from exercising a control over the administration analogous to that asserted by Anglo-American courts. Not unnaturally they have concluded that *droit administratif* is wholly inconsistent with the rule of law.

That conclusion overlooks the possibility of two sets of "law courts" in one legal system. One should hardly expect it to be overlooked by Anglo-Americans who have had long experience with a system of that type. After the judicialization of the Court of Chancery it was as much a "law court" as any court of common law. Nor could it be maintained that it was contrary to the rule of law for control over administrative action to be exercised by a separate court of equity through injunctive authority, rather than by an ordinary law court through the prerogative writs. Either way, control over the administration was being asserted by true judicial tribunals, within the doctrine of the rule of law.

To assume that only the law courts in France are true judicial tribunals in the common-law sense is to start with an erroneous conception of their nature as compared with that of the French administrative courts. Our analysis thus far should have shown how wrong it is to dichotomize the French system on the basis of Anglo-American conceptions of courts of law as opposed to administrative agencies exercising judicial powers. It is not fair to judge an administrative court in France, such as the Council of State, by comparing it with the law courts in the Anglo-American world, or to assert that the *droit administratif* is defective because it is administered by tribunals not fully up to common-law judicial standards. Such an approach assumes that the deficiencies of the French system would be remedied if administrative-law jurisdiction were vested in the law courts instead of in a system of separate administrative tribunals. The criticism loses all meaning if, in reality, the French law courts are more like the French administrative courts than like the courts in the common-law world, and if they therefore suffer themselves from the very shortcomings that Anglo-Americans criticize in the French administrative courts.

The account of the French law courts given above should indicate sufficiently the fallaciousness of the assumption that they are precisely like the law courts familiar to the common lawyer. In fact, the very conception of judicial office in France differs radically, as we have seen, from that held in the Anglo-American world. The French judge is recruited in a manner that the common lawyer would think more fitting for civil servants than for those destined to hold judicial office. He looks upon the judiciary as a career to be begun at the bottom of the judicial ladder at an early age, with the hope of ultimate advance to judgeships in the more important courts. Whether the would-be judge hopes for a career in the Council of State or in the French law courts, his point of view is the same.

In certain respects, indeed, the councilor of state is more like the judge in the common-law world than his confrere in the French law courts. To the common lawyer the great lack of the French judicial system is its comparative failure to provide for the infusion into the judiciary of "outside blood." The Anglo-American judge normally attains judicial office after many years of service at the bar or with the government. He brings to his judicial tasks a broader outlook than could be acquired merely through labor at the lower levels of the judiciary. But in the French administrative courts, too, we saw there is provision for the appointment of "outside" members. Up to one third of the councilors of state may be chosen from among those who have had no previous connection with the Council. True, a power also exists to appoint outside members to the French law courts. It has, however, been exercised very rarely, for the normal judge in the higher courts is still one who has progressed through the various levels of the judicial hierarchy. In the matter of "outside" blood the administrative courts consequently resemble the courts of the Anglo-American world more than the French law courts do.

That the administrative courts are closer than the law courts to the courts of the common-law world is true also respecting a point of crucial significance: namely, the independence of the judge vis-à-vis the administration. It is on this point that Anglo-American critics of the *droit administratif* have made their greatest error. Quite rightly, they have insisted on the need for the control of administrative action to be vested in judges wholly free of any subservience to the executive. They have, however, gone too far in assuming that in the French system, as in their own, such judges must necessarily be members of the law courts. An administrative tribunal like the Council of State, A. V. Dicey insisted, "was to a considerable extent an official or governmental body, the members of which, when acting in the discharge of quasi-judicial functions, were likely to be swayed by ministerial or official sentiment. . . . the *Conseil's* idea of justice was not likely to be exactly the same as that entertained by judicial or common law courts."[14] But, in actual fact, the administrative courts display toward the administration more independence than the law courts. "Whoever is familiar with the case-law of the Council of State and the Court of Conflicts,[15] especially during the past twenty-five years, knows well that their decisions have been more liberal, more generally founded on equitable considerations, than those of the Court of Cassation, . . . particularly in the development of remedies for the protection of ordinary citizens against illegal and arbitrary administrative action."[16] That the French law courts have displayed greater timidity[17] than the Council of State toward the administration is not to be wondered at. The assurance of independence is "so much stronger, when the action is brought before the *Conseil d'Etat*, because the rules of promotion for the members are somewhat more definite and less arbitrary than the corresponding rules for the promotion of judges."[18] The young member of the Council of State can look forward with assurance to promotion within the Council. He knows that political considerations are all but eliminated by the Council's rigid rule of promotion by seniority. The newly appointed judge of the French law courts has no such assurance. Political factors, as has been noted, may and often do enter into judicial promotions in France.

It is not surprising, therefore, that French citizens have come to look to the Council of State rather than to the law courts as their principal protector against administrative arbitrariness. "The Council of

[14] Law of the Constitution 353 (9th ed., 1939).

[15] See *infra* pp. 62-64.

[16] Garner, "La Conception anglo-américaine du droit administratif" in Mélanges Maurice Hauriou 357 (1929).

[17] The term used recently by a French observer. Pinto, in Conseil d'État, Études et documents 22 (1949).

[18] David, in Dicey, *op. cit. supra* note 14, at 499.

State has thus come to be considered by Frenchmen as the principal guardian and defender of the rights and liberties of the people against a more or less bureaucratic and strongly centralized administration. And it is well known that whenever an individual in his controversies with the State has a choice of jurisdictions, he will bring his action before the Council of State rather than before a law court, particularly if his petition is based on principles of equity and natural law."[19] To look at the French system in terms of the common-law conception of the law courts as the natural safeguard against administrative arbitrariness is, then, to get a wholly false picture. As a prominent French administrative lawyer has stated, "one must take into account that in France the ordinary courts have little prestige and are afraid of displeasing the administration."[20]

Court of Conflicts

The mere existence of two systems of courts, each with jurisdiction limited to certain types of cases, makes conflicts between the two almost inevitable. Even if both orders of tribunals are wholly unmotivated by a desire to extend their own competence, the impossibility of an accurate jurisdictional demarcation leads perforce to a large penumbra of borderline cases in which each set of courts may differ about jurisdiction.

Unless some means is provided for settling such conflicts of jurisdiction, the two-court system itself may break down. The common lawyer can well appreciate this risk by reference to the history of his own system. Until the settlement of the Coke-Ellesmere controversy by James I, conflicts between Chancery and the law courts could not be finally resolved. The result in the common-law world was anything but a properly functioning legal system.

In the French system, too, a means for the resolution of conflicts of jurisdiction has had to be provided. The first efforts to deal with such conflicts vested final authority in cases involving them in the Council of State itself—a solution not unlike that adopted by James I, for his decision, as is well known, established the supremacy of the Court of Chancery in cases in which its decision conflicted with that of a law court. French jurists have felt, however, that a settlement of conflicts

[19] Garner, *supra* note 16, at 358.
[20] Jèze, quoted in Uhler, Review of Administrative Acts 49 (1942).

of jurisdiction by establishing the superiority of one or the other of the two orders of courts in a given case was an insufficient solution. "In effect, since what is involved is the maintenance of the rule that attributes two distinct domains to different orders of tribunals, the judgment of the question of competence, the resolution of conflicts of jurisdiction, cannot be confided to a court of one of the two orders, however high it may be, for it would inevitably be led to extend the jurisdiction of the order to which it belongs; and accordingly its impartiality will be doubted."[21]

If neither of the two orders is to be able itself to resolve conflicts of jurisdiction, resolution must be sought in the creation of a superior tribunal whose decisions will be final in such cases. "The solution of the problem can be found in the establishment of a special court that will belong to neither the law-court nor the administrative-court system, but will be composed of judges borrowed from the highest courts of the two systems and, under the presidency of a member of the government, will decide conflicts of jurisdiction and so enforce the rule of separation of the two orders of tribunals."[22]

This, in practice, is the solution finally adopted by the French system. With the establishment of republican government on a firm basis the earlier arrangement, under which conflicts of jurisdiction were decided by the Council of State, gave way to one in which such matters were to be dealt with by a newly created body, the Court of Conflicts. This tribunal, set up under a law of 1872, is composed of nine members. Three of them are councilors of state, elected from among that body; three are members of the Court of Cassation, elected by their colleagues on that tribunal; two are elected by the other members of the Court of Conflicts (the practice is for one to be a councilor of state, the other a judge of the Court of Cassation); and the president of the Court is the Minister of Justice. The judges of the Court are elected for a term of three years, and there is no limit to re-election.

The Court of Conflicts is not intended to be wholly independent of the administrative-court and law-court systems. Its members, with the exception of the president, are chosen in equal numbers from the highest courts of the two orders of jurisdiction. This equal division is not, however, fully carried out, for its president, the Minister of Justice, is a political official and hence, it might be argued, will tend

21 3 Duguit, Traité de droit constitutionnel 58 (3d ed.).
22 *Id.* at 59.

to be predisposed in favor of the administration and the administrative courts.

This danger has proved in practice more theoretical than real. In the first place, the Minister of Justice does not take an actual part in the work of the Court of Conflicts except when its other members are evenly divided. It is only to break such a tie that he casts his vote, that the Court may be able to hand down a decision. Even division has actually been extremely rare. Only four times has it been necessary for the Minister of Justice to take part in the proceedings since the Court was established in 1872. At other times, the Court is presided over by its vice-president; elected from its membership, he is by tradition alternately a councilor of state and a judge of the Court of Cassation.

Conflict Procedure

Positive Conflicts—The most important type of case over which the Court of Conflicts has jurisdiction is that involving what is known as a "positive conflict." Such a conflict occurs when a case is brought before a law court which, under the French application of the doctrine of separation of powers, comes within the exclusive jurisdiction of the administrative courts. In such a case a request is addressed to the law court to decline jurisdiction. This request is made by the appropriate prefect, the administrative head of the department, the basic unit of territorial administration in France. If the court rejects the prefect's request, he promulgates a decree of conflict, and this has the effect of transferring the case to the Court of Conflicts for decision on the jurisdictional question.

The Court of Conflicts must decide the question within two months, a time limit the brevity of which is justified by the need to prevent the conflict procedure from being used as a dilatory device. If the Court of Conflicts does not render a decision within the two-month period, the law court is revested with jurisdiction. The decision of the Court of Conflicts will either confirm or set aside the prefect's decree of conflict. If the decree is confirmed, the law court is completely divested of jurisdiction; the plaintiff must begin all over again before the competent administrative court. If the decree of conflict is set aside, the case goes back to the law court, which proceeds as though the question of conflicting jurisdiction had never been raised.

Negative Conflicts—A two-court legal system such as the French tends to make the life of the litigant a most difficult one. Unless he brings his case before the right set of courts, all he will get for his pains is a judgment dismissing his action for lack of jurisdiction, and he must begin his weary round of litigation all over again in the other set of courts. If he commences in the law courts an action that should have been brought in the administrative courts, his complaint will ultimately be dismissed, either by the law courts themselves or by the Court of Conflicts, and he will have to bring another action before the administrative courts.

If he brings his case in the first instance before the administrative courts and it is one that falls within the jurisdiction of the law courts, his lot may be even harder. For the procedure of conflicts is applicable only to cases improperly brought before the law courts. If the case is in the administrative courts, it is the Council of State that must ultimately dismiss for lack of jurisdiction—a process that may take quite a while, the congestion of that tribunal's calendar being what it is. The Council of State may decide many years after the cause of action arose that it was improperly brought before the administrative courts, and the plaintiff must then recommence his sad search for justice before the law courts. Truly, to paraphrase Mr. Justice Frankfurter, this danger, or even likelihood, of marching the king's men up the hill and then marching them down again seems a mode of judicial administration to which one cannot yield concurrence.[23]

And the position of the plaintiff in the French system may be even more difficult. He may bring his action before the administrative courts, which decide ultimately (and there may well be a lag of several years before the final decision of the Council of State) that the cause of action is one over which only the law courts have jurisdiction. The plaintiff, slightly the worse for wear after his rounds in the administrative courts, now tries again in the law courts. But they, not being in any way bound by the decision of the Council of State, finally decide (and here, too, the process may take years, for the case can start in a Court of First Instance, then go to a Court of Appeal, and ultimately get to the Court of Cassation for final resolution of the jurisdictional issue) that the case really is one falling within the jurisdiction of the administrative courts. The plaintiff in such a case is in the unenviable position of having a cause of action but no court to accept jurisdiction over it.

The solution has been adopted of having such "negative conflicts"—*i.e.*, those in which both the administrative courts and the law courts

[23] Dissenting, in City of Yonkers v. United States, 320 U.S. 685, 694 (1944).

have declined jurisdiction, each on the ground that only the other was competent—resolved by the Court of Conflicts on the petition of the plaintiff. But it is important to note that, from his point of view, this development merely gives him another hill over which to march the king's men. The Court of Conflicts does not deal with the complaint on the merits. It decides only whether the administrative courts or the law courts are vested with jurisdiction. And the plaintiff, probably by now much older and wiser in the ways of a two-court legal system, must start his action all over again in the set of courts held competent by the Court of Conflicts, hopeful, if he has survived thus long, of at last obtaining a judgment on the merits.

"*Denial of Justice on Merits*"—There is another type of case that, though very rare, tends to make the situation of the French litigant even harder at times. It can perhaps best be described by example. An accident has occurred between a private automobile and a government vehicle driven by a civil servant in the course of his employment. The plaintiff is a third person injured by the accident. He brings an action before the appropriate French law court against the driver of the private automobile on the ground that his negligence caused the accident. The court finds that the accident was caused by the driver of the government vehicle and dismisses the complaint. Under the French system, as we shall see, actions based on the negligence of government employees acting in the course of their employment can be brought against the State, but only in the administrative courts. The plaintiff therefore brings his action against the State in the appropriate tribunal for such suits, but it holds that the private driver and not the government employee was negligent, and it, too, dismisses the complaint.

In this type of case, plaintiff was left before 1932 without a real remedy. In 1932 the French Parliament enacted a law that vests jurisdiction in the Court of Conflicts in cases in which the decisions of the administrative courts and the law courts on the same cause of action clash on the merits in a way to produce a denial of justice. In this type of case, it should be noted, the Court of Conflicts decides upon the merits. But the plaintiff has still had to bring his action in three sets of courts before being able to obtain judgment on the merits.

Rules of Jurisdiction

Before going farther into the vagaries of a two-court legal system, it may be worth while briefly to analyze the rules of jurisdiction developed in France to determine whether a particular case falls within the competence of the administrative courts or of the law courts. If these rules are clear and easy to apply, the litigant's difficulties just described are largely theoretical. In practice, the litigant will normally know where to bring his action in the first instance. But if the rules of jurisdiction have not been worked out with sufficient clarity, then the difficulties are very real ones that may make the working of a dualized system of justice intolerable to a large number of litigants.

Ever since the Revolution the basic principle of French public law has been the one that forbids the law courts to exercise jurisdiction in administrative-law cases. "Judicial functions are and will always remain distinct from administrative functions," reads the basic law of August 16-24, 1790. "Judges may not, under penalty of forfeiture of office, interfere in any manner with the workings of administrative bodies, nor summon administrators before them in connection with the exercise of their functions." And a later law expressly precludes the law courts from "taking cognizance of acts of the administration, of whatever kind they may be."[24]

The mere legislative statement barring the French law courts from exercising a control over administrative acts similar to that exercised by the courts in the common-law world could not, however, of itself completely solve the problem of jurisdiction in administrative-law cases. For it did not answer the basic question of when a case involved an issue of administrative law within the meaning of the statutory prohibition. This question has had to be answered by the courts themselves—both administrative courts and law courts—in the post-1790 case law.

If a given case involves only two or more private citizens, then it is clearly one within the jurisdiction of the French law courts. But the converse—*i.e.*, that all cases in which the administration is a party fall within the competence of the administrative courts—is not necessarily true. If it were, the French rules of jurisdiction would be much simpler to apply than they actually are.

The starting point for a discussion of the rules of jurisdiction is the *Blanco* case, decided by the Court of Conflicts in 1873[25] and probably still the most famous case in the *droit administratif*. In that case the

[24] Law of 16 Fructidor, year III of the Revolutionary era.

[25] February 8, 1873. The decisions of the Court of Conflicts, like those of the Council of State, are usually cited by the name of the plaintiff and the date. They are reported in chronological order in the Recueil Lebon, together with the decisions of the Council of State.

court laid down the proposition that the jurisdiction of the French administrative courts was coextensive with the field of the "public services" administered by the State. As one of the greatest of modern French administrative lawyers explained in a later case: "Everything that concerns the organization and operation of public services, national or local—whether the administration act by means of contract or by a unilateral act—constitutes an administrative act which is, by its very nature, within the domain of the administrative courts. . . . All actions between administrative agencies and third persons, or between administrative agencies themselves, based upon the performance, the nonperformance, or the faulty performance of a public service, come within the jurisdiction of the administrative courts."[26]

The rule of jurisdiction thus laid down is, however, complicated by the indefiniteness of the concept of "public service" on which it rests. "The general rule of jurisdiction thus established in relation with the notion of public service would offer a clear enough basis for the determination of jurisdiction except for the difficulty which there is in certain cases of knowing whether or not a particular administrative enterprise is a public service."[27]

In the French view public service includes the services performed by the administration that are conceived of as necessary to promote the well-being of the community. "A public service is thus a means provided by the public authorities to satisfy general social needs."[28] And there is a tendency to hold that this definition applies whether or not the service concerned is operated strictly speaking by the administration itself or by private enterprise under administrative authorization. Consequently, services affected with a public interest, to use the familiar American terminology, tend to come within the jurisdiction of the administrative courts, whether the services are operated by the administration or by private enterprise.

But the converse is also true. If an activity does not come within the concept of public service, then cases concerning it are within the competence of the French law courts, even if the particular activity happens to be one carried on by an administrative agency.

All this would not be too difficult if the concept of public service were defined with sufficient precision. Unfortunately it is not so de-

[26] Conclusions of M. Romieu, government comissioner, in Terrier, Council of State, February 6, 1903.

[27] Bonnard, Précis de droit administratif 209 (3d ed., 1940).

[28] Appleton, Traité élémentaire du contentieux administratif 114 (1927).

fined, and that deficiency makes a difficult situation for the litigant seeking to determine whether to bring his borderline case before the administrative courts or the law courts. "A precise definition of public service is vitally necessary. It would be a great exaggeration to say that it has ever been furnished, even almost eighty years after the *Blanco* decision. Doctrine and case law both manifest with regard to this doctrine an uncertainty, the strangeness of which it has often been necessary to emphasize."[29]

And the confusion here tends to be worse confounded by the apparent departure of recent cases from the public-service concept as the sole test of jurisdiction. It has been held, for example, that the French law courts are competent with regard to contracts entered into with the administration if such contracts contain only the usual provisions found in ordinary private contracts, even if they relate to the functioning of a public service.[30] And, more recently, the Court of Conflicts has held that, if a particular public service is industrial or commercial, cases concerning it are for the law courts rather than the administrative courts.[31] But it is not clear from the case law exactly when a contract contains only the "usual" contractual provisions or when a public service is "industrial or commercial." As one scholar has stated, the recent law on this point "leaves to the unfettered discretion of the judge in each case the task of determining the commercial or noncommercial character of the service, and hence the jurisdiction that is competent."[32] Clearly, this uncertainty tends to make matters even more difficult for a plaintiff trying to decide whether to bring his action in the administrative courts or the law courts. "It must be stated in the plainest fashion that the case law has begun to develop in a direction that is most distressing and injurious to litigants."[33]

Prejudicial Questions

One familiar with the working of law and equity in the common-law world will realize that the difficulties arising from a two-court

[29] Morange, "Le Déclin de la notion juridique de service public" (1947) Dalloz, Chronique 45.

[30] Bonnard, *op. cit. supra* note 27, at 211.

[31] Waline, *op. cit. supra* note 2, at 63.

[32] *Id.* at 310.

[33] Bonnard, *op. cit. supra* note 27, at 209. For a strong recent criticism, see Laubadère, "Réflexions sur la crise du droit administratif français" (1952) Dalloz, Chronique 5.

system of justice are due not merely to uncertainties in the rules of jurisdiction. A case may clearly come within the jurisdiction of one order of tribunals, but the decision of it may involve the resolution of an issue that falls within the competence of the other order. The classic example in the common-law world was the action in equity to enjoin the commission of a trespass to land where the defendant disputed the plaintiff's title. In such a case the court of equity had to wait until the suitor's title to the land was first made out at law.[34] The grant of a permanent injunction was conditioned on the plaintiff's successful pursuit of an action in ejectment in the law courts.

This type of case is of common occurrence in the French legal system. And the way in which it is disposed of by the French courts tends to make the lot of the litigant in France an even harder one than has thus far been shown.

The general rule developed in the French system requires the court before which an action is brought to stay its decision where a question within the competence of the other order of tribunals must be resolved before the decision can be rendered. "Such a question is called 'prejudicial' where it does not come within the jurisdiction of the judge on the merits, and he must then stay his decision until the prejudicial question has been answered by the competent judge."[35] A common example of a prejudicial question is the case of an alien against whom a deportation order has been issued and who seeks to have the order annulled by the appropriate administrative court on the ground that he is a French citizen. The administrative court, which alone is competent to decide the legality of the deportation order, is not able, under the French theory, to deal with questions of citizenship. It must therefore postpone its decision until that question has been decided by the French law courts, just as, in the days when law and equity were separate systems in the Anglo-American world, courts of equity had to postpone granting an injunction against injuries to land where the title was disputed, until the question of title was resolved by the common-law courts.

In cases of this type the prejudicial question is not automatically sent to the competent jurisdiction for decision. It is up to the plaintiff to bring an action in the appropriate court to have the question determined. Until he does so he cannot obtain a favorable decision in his

[34] Paraphrasing Cardozo, J., dissenting, in City of Syracuse v. Hogan, 234 N.Y. 457, 464 (1923).

[35] Odent, Cours de contentieux administratif 33 (1949-50).

original action; and it has been held that, if he delays too long in doing so, his original complaint may be dismissed.[36]

That this method of dealing with cases is a most unsatisfactory one from the point of view of litigants has been recognized even by French students. According to perhaps the most eminent of them, the separation of the administrative courts and the law courts in France "appears to litigants and businessmen only as a complication, a cause of uncertainty and difficulty in litigation."[37] The individual seeking justice on what is essentially one cause of action is not likely to see the need for bringing what is in effect two actions, with the consequent loss of time and money, every time a prejudicial question is encountered by the judge from whom justice is sought. This recognition has produced a tendency to limit the prejudicial-question doctrine to cases in which the resolution of the question at issue is doubtful. If the answer that the competent judge would give to the question is clear, the question is not considered prejudicial, and it may be decided by the judge before whom the action is brought. It is, of course, not always easy to determine whether a question asserted to be prejudicial is doubtful or clear. But that uncertainty is merely one more of the risks that the French litigant must run in his two-court system.

A variant of the prejudicial-question problem arises in criminal cases in which a defendant prosecuted for violation of an administrative regulation interposes the defense that the regulation is illegal. The applicable section of the French Penal Code[38] provides that those "who have violated regulations legally made by the administration" are subject to criminal penalties. The French courts, both administrative and judicial, have uniformly held as follows: The provision that only the violation of regulations *legally made* is punishable by law confers upon the criminal courts by implication the power and the duty of examining the validity of regulations with the violation of which defendants are charged. Only if the regulation violated is a legal one has a crime been committed.

The posture of the French courts here is basically similar to that of the Anglo-American judiciary. With us, too, a defendant in a criminal case charged with violating an administrative regulation may raise the defense that the regulation is illegal. "There is something basically wrong and unjust," Mr. Justice Murphy has asserted, "about a judicial

[36] Société Convert et Cie., Council of State, June 26, 1946.
[37] 1 Hauriou, La Jurisprudence administrative de 1892 à 1929, 49 (1929).
[38] Article 471 (15).

system that sanctions the imprisonment of a man without ever according him the opportunity to claim that the charge made against him is illegal. . . . To sustain the convictions of the two petitioners in these cases would require adherence to the proposition that a person may be criminally punished without ever being accorded the opportunity to prove that the prosecution is based upon an invalid administrative order. That is a proposition to which I cannot subscribe."[39]

Voie de Fait

A word should be said about a development in the case law that has tended further to complicate the rules of jurisdiction in the field of administrative law in France. French legal theory, like that in the common-law world, has proceeded on the assumption that every administrative officer has marked out for him a certain area of competence. If he oversteps that area, his act is illegal and will be annulled by a competent court. In the French system such a case falls within the jurisdiction of the administrative courts, which alone can annul *ultra vires* administrative action.

Anglo-American theory treats similarly all cases involving illegal administrative acts. The only question for our courts is whether a challenged administrative act is *ultra vires;* if so, it will be set aside. French legal theory, on the other hand, has assumed that individual administrative acts are susceptible of varying *degrees* of illegality. And in the French view illegality can attain such flagrant proportions that it destroys the very administrative quality of the affected act.[40] There is then no longer mere illegality, but a veritable usurpation of power by the official concerned, who is acting no longer as an agent of the administration, but as an ordinary private citizen committing a wrongful act. When that is the fact it follows that the French law courts, not the administrative courts, have jurisdiction over cases brought by those adversely affected by the act, for it is no longer an act administrative in character.

The French theory on this point is well stated by Laferrière, the founder of modern French administrative law. "There is a situation," says he, "in which the act of an administrator pretending to exercise public power ceases to be an administrative act beyond the jurisdiction of the law courts. That is the fact where the administrator not only

[39] Concurring, in Estep v. United States, 327 U.S. 114, 131, 125 (1946).
[40] See Uhler, *op. cit. supra* note 20, at 139.

acts beyond his own jurisdiction, but exceeds the very sphere of administrative authority as such. If, for example, an administrator confiscates property, deprives a citizen of his liberty, suppresses a newspaper, forbids a legal trade or industry, the principle of the separation of powers does not prevent the aggrieved party from seeking the aid of the law courts; on the contrary, it requires that their jurisdiction be exercised as freely as if an administrative decision were not involved. Such decision, in fact, is not only subject to being set aside: it is nonexistent in law as an administrative act, since it is foreign in its purpose to the exercise of the administrative function."[41]

An administrative act that attains the requisite degree of flagrant illegality is characterized as a *voie de fait,* a term that has been translated as an administrative trespass,[42] but that actually means something stronger, for it includes the concept of taking the law into one's own hands. It is not, however, clear just what constitutes an illegality so flagrant as to make an administrative act a *voie de fait.* "If a *voie de fait* always presupposes an illegal action, the converse is not true: not every illegal action constitutes a *voie de fait.* The difficulty, which has not been resolved in a satisfactory manner, is to determine with precision what degree of illegality is necessary to create a *voie de fait.*"[43] The notion of *voie de fait* is, indeed, as a member of the Council of State has recently concluded, one of the vaguest and most confused in French law.[44] Yet it is essential for the litigant in France to be able to determine whether a *voie de fait* does exist in his case, for if it is a mere illegal administrative act that he is challenging, he must bring his action in the administrative courts, whereas if the illegality is so flagrant that a *voie de fait* exists, only the French law courts are competent. It can be imagined how many hills the king's men may have to be marched up and then down again before the French litigant can secure a judgment on the merits if his action happens to involve a borderline *voie de fait* type of case.

Rejection of Two-Court System

Those who urge the creation in the common-law world of a set of administrative courts modeled on those in the French system would do

[41] Laferrière, Traité de la juridiction administrative et des recours contentieux 479 (2d ed., 1896).

[42] Uhler, *op. cit. supra* note 20, at 138.

[43] Fréjaville (1946) Dalloz, Jurisprudence 173.

[44] Delvolvé, in Conseil d'État, Études et documents 32 (1950).

well to ponder the painful plight of Messieurs Jacquin and Peyrusse and the City of Narbonne. The City of Narbonne and M. Jacquin had entered into a contract under which Jacquin was to provide on the evening of July 14, 1914, a display of fireworks for the inhabitants of the city. M. Peyrusse, who, like all good Frenchmen, was among those enjoying the display provided every year on the national holiday, happened to be injured by a rocket, apparently set off negligently. An action was brought by Peyrusse in the appropriate Prefecture Council against the city, which impleaded Jacquin as a party to the action on the ground that he was liable to it as a guarantor under the contract between them.

On May 6, 1938, the Prefecture Council reached its decision. It held the city liable to Peyrusse for 20,000 francs; but it also held Jacquin responsible to the city in the same amount. Both Jacquin and the city appealed to the Council of State. That tribunal rendered its decision on May 14, 1948. It affirmed the judgment below against the city. M. Peyrusse has thus finally got his damages, a mere thirty-four years after the accident. But let not those who would rejoice at this final vindication of justice do so prematurely. For the case is not yet settled as between the city and M. Jacquin. The Council of State reversed the judgment of the city against Jacquin. Nor did it do so on the merits. It found only that the case involved a contract containing only the usual provisions found in private contracts, and that hence the law courts and not the administrative courts were competent. Thus the city, thirty-four years after the facts upon which its cause of action is based, knows only that it must start again in the law courts. And what if they, after the case has wound its weary way up to the Court of Cassation, should decide after all not to defer to the view of the Council of State and should hold that the case really falls within the jurisdiction of the administrative courts? The city and Jacquin will then have to march the king's men over to the Court of Conflicts to have the issue of jurisdiction resolved. Only then can the case be brought before a competent tribunal for a final decision on the merits.

It was precisely to avoid this sort of thing that the common-law world abandoned its earlier division of remedial justice into two systems. Ever since the first attempts at the merger of law and equity the trend in the Anglo-American world has been toward the unification of justice. To import into our system a set of administrative courts similar to those in France would be to reverse this trend. It would risk the revival within our legal system of all the defects inherent in a dualized system of justice.

Whatever advantages there may be in having administrative-law cases resolved by specialized administrative courts, the account here given of the French system shows that these are outweighed by the deficiencies inherent in a two-court legal system. That the common-law system of control of the administration by the ordinary courts is far from perfect, few will deny. But the answer is not to divide our system of remedial justice in two, unless we wish to return to all the jurisdictional difficulties that confronted Anglo-American litigants when law and equity were separate and competing systems of justice.

Chapter Four

THE ADMINISTRATION

The common lawyer who examines the administration of a Continental country such as France perceives before long that it is vested with broader powers than those possessed by administration in the Anglo-American world. "In almost every continental community the executive exercises far wider discretionary authority in the matter of arrest, of temporary imprisonment, and the like, than is either legally claimed or in fact exerted by the government in England; and a study of European politics now and again reminds English readers that wherever there is discretion there is room for arbitrariness, and that in a republic no less than under a monarchy discretionary authority on the part of the government must mean insecurity for legal freedom on the part of its subjects."[1]

The difference in degree of administrative authority between the civil-law and the common-law worlds in large part is due to dissimilar historical backgrounds. Anglo-Americans have lived for almost three centuries under governments with limited powers. Not so the citizens of Continental countries. Just a few years before Blackstone delivered his famous eulogy of English law, Voltaire—as typical as any man of his time of enlightened Continental opinion—was given reason to know how exceptional was the limited government that then prevailed in England. In 1717 he was sent to the Bastille for a poem that he had not written, whose author he did not know, and with whose views he did not agree. When Voltaire visited England "his predominant sentiment clearly was that he had passed out of the realm of despotism to a land where the laws might be harsh, but where men were ruled by law and not by caprice."[2]

French administrative law took as its starting point an absolute

[1] Dicey, Law of the Constitution 188 (9th ed., 1939).
[2] *Id.* at 189.

administration with virtually unlimited powers. Nor was its authority dependent on delegations by the legislature. The head of the State, as chief of the administration, possessed all the necessary powers as being inherent in his person. The point of departure in the common-law world in this respect was a wholly different one. Ever since the defeat of Stuart attempts at autocracy the common lawyer has denied the existence of autonomous administrative authority. In his view the administration possesses only those powers that are delegated to it by the elected representatives of the people, and, historically, such delegations have in fact been limited ones.

But these were only starting points, and the situation has changed substantially in both systems since the eighteenth century. In France the powers of an absolute State had been used to build up an equally absolute centralized administration, and it was only after the introduction of representative government that administrative authority came to be limited and, in time, subordinated to laws passed by a representative assembly. While administrative power in France was thus subjected to restrictive tendencies in the nineteenth century, an opposite tendency prevailed in the common-law world. With us the authority of the administration has had to be drastically increased if it were to perform the role assigned to it by modern public opinion. "Central administration, if it was to function at all, had to be invested with the necessary powers; it stood in even greater need of these powers as the units of local government were not subordinate to the central Government to the same extent as in many continental countries, where the hierarchy of a bureaucratic administration provided a wider range of means for ensuring obedience to its command."[3]

There is clearly a tendency for the scope of administrative authority in the common-law world to approach that of a Continental country such as France. The point of departure, limited administrative power, is more and more giving way with us as greater grants of authority are deemed essential. In France, on the other hand, the powers of a previously absolute administration have come progressively to be limited as legal theory has become permeated with the republican ideal. So much is not to say, however, that even today the details of administrative authority are the same in both systems. The difference in starting points leads to differences in results, and the authority of the administration

[3] Sieghart, Government by Decree 107 (1950).

in France is still, as we shall see, greater than that to which the common lawyer is accustomed.

One wonders, indeed, whether the difference in starting points does not still mean something more significant than mere matters of detail. "Whoever travels in the United States," reads a famous passage from Alexis de Tocqueville, "is involuntarily and instinctively so impressed with the fact that the spirit of liberty and the taste for it have so pervaded the habits of the American people, that he cannot conceive of them under any but a Republican government. In the same way it is impossible to think of the English as living under any but a free government."[4] The same is not true, in Tocqueville's view, of Continental countries, even of those with a republican form of government. And he chooses as his example the Swiss Republic, for, at the time he wrote, France was governed by the monarchy of Louis Philippe. "But if violence were to destroy the Republican institutions in most of the Swiss Cantons, it would be by no means certain that after a short state of transition the people would not grow accustomed to the loss of liberty. In the United States and England there seems to be more liberty in the customs than in the laws of the people. In Switzerland there seems to be more liberty in the laws than in the customs of the country."[5]

It would not be wholly fair to assert that what Tocqueville found true of the Switzerland of 1836 is true of France today. But there are undeniable elements of similarity. It was the absence of a theory of limited administrative power and of limitations on authority that could be delegated to the executive that made the transition to a totalitarian regime in France in 1940 a more easily accomplished one. The administration that had served the Third Republic was able to transfer its allegiance to the new chief of State without any need for drastic revisions in constitutional theory. "It is important to note that the introduction of a totalitarian regime in France was achieved in the form of a delegation of the constituent power from the national assembly to the head of the Executive and not by the misuse of any alleged emergency power."[6] In 1940 French administrative law returned to its point of departure of an absolute administration in whose head were concen-

[4] Quoted in Dicey, *op. cit. supra* note 1, at 186.

[5] *Ibid.* Tocqueville's remarks are clearly not applicable to the Switzerland of today, as any visitor to that country soon realizes. They were made before the Swiss Federal Constitution of 1848, when liberty in the Anglo-American sense was still almost unknown in Continental countries.

[6] Sieghart, *op. cit.* note 3, at 302.

trated both the legislative and the executive power. That the return to absolutism was acquiesced in by millions of Frenchmen who looked upon Marshal Pétain as the sole legitimate repository of authority shows that the French system has not departed so far as one would have hoped before 1940 from its starting point of unlimited administrative authority.

Organization of the Administration

To the Anglo-American, French politics appears as an exciting but more or less mysterious game. The fantastically large number of parties, the lack of a workable majority in the legislature, and the resultant constant changes in government, all make him wonder how effective government can be carried on at all.

The outside observer tends, however, to overlook a factor vital in the French system: continuity of administration. This tendency is especially characteristic of the American student, who thinks, even today, of a change in government as being necessarily accompanied by a veritable upheaval of personnel in the top levels of the administration. The constitutional implication must be, Mr. Chief Justice Taft stated in *Myers v. United States*, "in the absence of any express limitation respecting removals, that as [the President's] selection of administrative officers is essential to the execution of the laws by him, so must be his power of removing those for whom he cannot continue to be responsible."[7] And American Presidents, on their accession to office, have not hesitated to use their removal authority.

The situation in France is entirely different. A change in government there means a change only at the very apex of the administrative hierarchy. The administration as such continues, and it is its continuity that enables France to be effectively governed, even during protracted periods of cabinet crisis. This continuity makes the French administration an even more important factor in the life of the nation than the government that is its titular head. It is the higher permanent civil servants, rather than the political heads of the government, who wield much of the substance of governmental authority. It is they who "possess the substance of administrative power, with the ministers exercising only a political control."[8] The political life expectancy of a

[7] 272 U.S. 52, 117 (1926).
[8] Hauriou, Précis de droit administratif 159 (12th ed., 1933).

French minister being as short as it is, it is not to be wondered at if his influence on administration tends to be more or less ephemeral.

In this respect France is more like Britain than it is like the United States. The British, however, are able to avoid the worst aspects of the French system by having only two major political parties, one of which is usually able to rely on a stable parliamentary majority. The British administration is thus subject to much stronger control than the French from the political officials who head the various departments of the government.

In organization, too, the French administration bears a closer resemblance to the British than to that with which American students are familiar. It is, in the first place, much more centralized than is possible in a country with a federal system of government. Control from Paris is much more extensive than from Washington, even in an age that has witnessed a heretofore unprecedented expansion of federal activity. Moreover, the French administration, like the British and unlike the American, is based on a system of parliamentary government. Its titular heads are members of the legislature, dependent on legislative approval for their continuance in office.

At the apex of the administration in France is the Prime Minister (*Président du Conseil*) of the French Republic, the head of the Cabinet, which is vested with the direction of the executive branch. The Cabinet is composed of the ministers who head the various government departments. They are chosen by the Prime Minister and, like him, are political officials, subject to the direct control of the legislature, of which they are members.

The number of ministers in the French government has constantly grown. In 1791 a law fixed their number at six, and Napoleon was able to govern with only ten. Before the First World War there were twelve. Since that time, however, the Cabinet has grown apace, so that at times there have been almost as many ministers as there were political parties. In 1917 there were forty ministers in the French Cabinet, in 1936 thirty-eight, and in 1939 thirty-five. Since the Liberation their number has declined, and there were, for example, in 1949, only fifteen major ministries in the French Government.[9]

[9] These were the Ministries of Finance and Economic Affairs; Justice; the Interior; National Defense; National Education; Public Works, Transportation, and Tourism; Industry and Commerce; Agriculture; Overseas Territories; Labor and Social Security; Reconstruction and Urbanism; Veterans' Affairs; Public Health and Population; Merchant Marine; and the Office of the Prime Minister, consid-

The fluctuation in the number of ministries is to be explained in part by the fact that their number is fixed by executive regulation rather than by statute law, as has normally been the case in the American system. It is really up to the head of the French Cabinet to fix the number of ministerial posts that he deems necessary to his program. All too often the number has been determined by the need of offering ministerial positions to the leaders of the large number of parties whose support is necessary to ensure the formation of a government in a country in which no one party has anything even approaching a workable majority.

The central government departments in France are organized in a manner that should not seem unduly strange to the Anglo-American. The ministries themselves are set up to perform certain connected governmental functions, and each has as its sphere one of the important aspects of modern governmental activity. Thus, the Ministry of Public Health and Population is charged with ensuring the health and social welfare of the country and, so charged, administers the health laws and various schemes of social aid and insurance, which are as common in France as they have become in Britain since the Second World War. Each ministry in France is departmentalized into divisions that specialize in particular tasks. The Health Ministry, for example, is composed of a division of public hygiene and hospitals, a division of social hygiene, a division of pharmacy, and an assistance division. The divisions are headed by permanent civil servants, and it is they who are the effective heads of the French administration. Added specialization is attained within each division by its further partition into sections, which are in turn subdivided into bureaus on a pattern that should be familiar to any Anglo-American student of public administration.

Each ministry has its central offices in Paris, which formulate its general policies, and its agents throughout the country to execute these policies. The details of field organization vary from ministry to ministry, but in general it is customary for each of the ministry's bureaus to be divided into a number of regional offices, one in each important center of population. These offices in the field are, as a leading study points out, the "combatants" in the actual tasks of administration, but, like all local agencies, they are dependent on the "noncombatants" in the ministry; *i.e.*, those in the central offices in Paris.[10]

---

ered as virtually a ministry by French students. 3 Dalloz, Nouveau répertoire de droit 155 (1949). Since 1949, the number of ministers has again increased, though not to the extremes noted before the war.

[10] Hauriou, *op. cit. supra* note 8, at 160.

Decentralization

Ever since the Revolution France has been looked upon by Anglo-Americans as an outstanding example of a State with a fully centralized administration. It is, however, erroneous to think of French administration as dominated solely by a centralizing tendency. "The organization of every administrative machinery is influenced by two opposing tendencies: centralization and decentralization. Usually, no organization expresses either of these tendencies to the exclusion of the other but combines both."[11] The administration in France is no exception to this general rule, even though the centralizing tendency is of greater influence in it than in administration in the common-law world.

In this respect France should be sharply distinguished from a country with a federal system of government, such as the United States. Decentralization in France can never be so thoroughgoing as in the American system. If it were, French political organization would be wholly changed in form. A unitary State like France that is "completely decentralized is logically inconceivable, for that would be a State in which all administrative authority would be retained by the local units, so that the central power would no longer have any authority; and that amounts to saying that the wholly decentralized units would no longer be integrated in a State: rather, they would be the States. Decentralization can thus never logically be total: if it were, it would destroy itself and give way to another form of political organization."[12]

Decentralization in France, then, compared with that of a system such as the American one, is characterized by its incompleteness. Local administration, though it exists and is in fact fully developed, is closely controlled by the central administration and dependent on it. The most important local official in the French administration is the prefect, who is wholly an agent of the central government. There is one prefect for each of the ninety departments, the basic units of territorial administration in France. They are appointed at the discretion of the government, though in practice they tend to be chosen from among the lower echelons of what is known as the prefectoral corps, which consists of the prefects themselves, the subprefects, and civil servants of the administrative class who work directly under the prefects.

[11] Sieghart, *op. cit. supra* note 3, at 206.
[12] Waline, Traité élémentaire de droit administratif 199 (5th ed., 1951).

The Administration

The administration of the departments by the prefects is a Napoleonic conception: the minister issues his commands to the prefects, who in turn issue them to the citizens. There is still a large trace of the Napoleonic idea in the French system. As Napoleon had wished, the prefects are still both very dependent on the central government and very powerful in their departments.[13]

According to the Constitution of 1946 the prefects are charged with ensuring "co-ordination in the activities of State civil servants, the representation of national interests, and the administrative control of local territorial units."[14] Since all the French ministers rely on the prefects for local execution of their policies, he is in a sense their subordinate. In matters of promotion and discipline he is directly under the Minister of the Interior—a circumstance that helps to explain the key position of that official in the French governmental structure. The functions of the prefect are so numerous today that it would be vain to attempt a complete list. We are told that the prefect actually exercises some 1,300 functions involving quasi-judicial powers of decision.[15]

In addition to being an important link in the hierarchical chain of administration that starts from Paris, the prefect is also the head of the local administration in each department. As such, he is charged with executing the decisions of the General Council, a body elected in each department by universal suffrage. The General Council is vested with control over matters of purely local administration; for each department has its own administrative machinery, distinct from that of the central government, though, as has been indicated, this machinery is headed by the prefect, the direct representative of the central government.

The departments themselves are divided into communes, the lowest level of administration in France. Local government in each commune is administered by a mayor, who is the head of the communal administration, and a Municipal Council elected by the citizens of the commune. The mayor, elected by the Municipal Council, executes any decisions that it may make pertaining to communal administration. But he is also looked upon as to some extent the agent of the central government, responsible to, though not appointed by, it. Thus, he may in certain circumstances be suspended from office by the prefect or re-

13 *Id.* at 227.

14 Article 88. The powers of the prefects were strengthened by an important decree of September 26, 1953.

15 Waline, *op. cit. supra* note 12, at 230.

moved by the Minister of the Interior. And the prefect is able to intervene in specific situations in which he considers a mayor to be performing his functions improperly. The prefect is also vested with a general supervisory power over the Municipal Council, many of whose actions must be approved by him, including that most important of them, the vote of the communal budget.

It can be seen, then, that the French administration is of an essentially centralized character. True, it also has, like every other administrative organization, some decentralizing tendencies. These have found expression in the departments and communes, each with its own local officials and administrative machine. But even over local administration the essential control is still retained by Paris. The key figure in French local government is the prefect, an official appointed and closely controlled by the central government. It is his superintendence of the local administrative machinery that maintains the predominantly centralized cast of French administration.

Personnel

The Anglo-American administrative lawyer has generally not been concerned with what he terms the law of public administration. Matters touching upon it he sees as primarily the concern of the political scientist rather than of the lawyer. "Administrative law, as the term is here used," states a leading American text, "is limited to law concerning powers and procedures; . . . a large portion of the law of public administration is thus excluded."[16]

To the French student the approach of the Anglo-American administrative lawyer leaves out much that is essential to a branch of the law which has for its aim the canalization of administrative authority by law. His point of view can be seen in the Preface recently prepared by a distinguished member of the French Council of State for a book seeking to explain American administrative law to the French lawyer. That book written by an American administrative lawyer "furnishes us," he says, "with a summary of administrative law in the narrow sense in which that term is understood in the author's country; the reader should not expect a picture of the American administration's machinery, services, jurisdiction, and means of action. The book . . .

[16] Davis, Administrative Law 2 (1951).

covers a field much less vast than that of an even summary manual of French administrative law."[17]

It must be admitted that French criticisms of the Anglo-American administrative lawyer's approach to his subject contain a great deal of force. As is stated by an English writer, one of the few to have expressed this view in the common-law world: "Administrative law should be regarded as the law relating to public administration, in the same way as commercial law consists of the law relating to commerce or land law the law relating to land."[18] For the administrative lawyer to abdicate the law of public administration, leaving its development almost entirely to the political scientist, is to risk leaving a great part of the law governing administration in an unsystematized state.

An example of the difference in approach between the French and the Anglo-American administrative lawyer is their attitude toward the law of the civil service. To the Anglo-American this is something that does not concern the administrative lawyer, and, in fact, treatises on administrative law in the common-law world make little if any reference to it. To the French administrative lawyer, on the contrary, the law of the civil service constitutes a vital aspect of his subject. "The administration is worth only as much as the civil servants who represent it and act for it," asserts the foremost contemporary treatise on the *droit administratif*.[19] And, in accord with this view, French writers on administrative law generally devote a substantial portion of their work —often almost one tenth—to a detailed analysis of the law of the civil service.

The difference in emphasis here between French and Anglo-American administrative lawyers is to be explained in part by a basic difference in the conception of public employment. The Anglo-American tends to regard employment by the State as analogous to employment by a private employer. The relationship between employer and employee is a contractual one, and the employee has only the rights and obligations contained in his employment contract. Civil servants, in the common-law conception, are thus solely "employees" of the government, and, as such, have merely the status that the law generally accords to employees. "The situation of the Government employee is

17 Puget, Preface to Schwartz, Le Droit administratif américain: notions générales vi (1952).

18 Robson, "Administrative Law in England" in British Government since 1918, 88 (1950).

19 Waline, *op. cit. supra* note 12, at 322.

not different in this respect from that of private employees."[20] In the absence of provisions to the contrary in statutes or regulations, the State has the same discretion with regard to the appointment and dismissal of its employees that any private employer has.

The result of this assimilation of the position of the Anglo-American civil servant to that of the ordinary private employee is that the civil servant is not protected, *qua* employee, by the principles of administrative law developed by the common-law courts. Anglo-American administrative law is a system governing the relations between the administration and private individuals. Its principles are not applicable where the administration acts only with reference to its employees in matters relating to their employment. In the common-law world the government employee is not treated as one vested with "rights" that the courts will enforce. "The petitioner may have a constitutional right to talk politics," reads a famous statement of Mr. Justice Holmes, "but he has no constitutional right to be a policeman."[21]

The Continental conception of public employment is a different one. The civil servant adversely affected by administrative action that bears on his employment has the same remedies available as the ordinary citizen injured in his personal or property rights. The French civil servant who is damaged in his career by an administrative decision may obtain review of that decision by the administrative courts, just as a private individual can whose property rights are adversely affected by a decision of the administration. Under the French conception the government employee is thus not merely one who has the same status as a private employee. He is afforded the same protection by the *droit administratif* as a private citizen whose property or person is adversely affected by administrative action.

This assimilation of the civil servant in French law, not to the private employee, but to the ordinary citizen vested with personal or property rights, stems in part from the fact that his relationship to the government is not conceived as a contractual one. "The situation of the civil servant vis-à-vis the administration is wholly governed by statutes and regulations," reads the law of October 19, 1946, now the basic law governing the legal status of the French civil servant. If he is adversely affected by administrative action, he is affected not in his contract rights, but in the rights given him by statutes and regulations.

[20] Bailey v. Richardson, 182 F. 2d 46, 60 (App. D.C. 1950).
[21] McAuliffe v. Mayor of New Bedford, 155 Mass. 216, 220 (1892).

And, in the French view, he may resort to the administrative courts if those rights are violated, just as any Frenchman can whose personal or property rights are infringed by the administration.

All but the very highest posts in the French administration are filled, as we have seen, by members of the permanent civil service. Appointment to the civil service in France, as in most countries, is by means of open competitive examinations. It has been urged that these examinations have placed too much emphasis on specialized technical knowledge and not enough on the general cultural background of candidates, especially those destined for supervisory posts in the administration, where a broad background is at least as important as specialized knowledge. Similar complaints have been made of civil-service examinations in the United States, and both French and American students have tended to consider the British method of appointment of those destined for positions in the administrative grade of the civil service as a model. In France efforts have been made in this direction by the establishment since the Liberation of the National School of Administration, whose graduates alone are to fill the more important administrative posts in the civil service. The work of this School has already been discussed in connection with the appointment of second-class auditors in the Council of State.[22] Although it includes a certain amount of technical instruction, its emphasis is on the general administrative culture of the future civil servant.

The civil servant in France has one right conceded only after some hesitation to his counterpart in the common-law world: the right to organize collectively. The right of government employees to join unions is, indeed, now expressly recognized in the basic law of October 19, 1946. The French civil service is in fact almost fully unionized today, and from its unionization spring many of the practical obstacles to effective administration in postwar France. For the right of collective organization leads inevitably to an assertion of the right of collective action. Yet how can a right to strike be recognized in civil servants, in view of the public interest in the continuance of vital administrative services?

The French Constitution of 1946 expressly preserves the right to strike in its preamble, but states that it is subject to whatever laws may regulate it. Thus far no such laws have been passed that affect the civil service, but the government has often sought to take disciplinary action

22 *Supra* p. 26.

against striking government employees. Such attempts have been sustained by the Council of State, which has held that the right to strike is subject to government regulation in view of the primordial need of continuity in the operation of administrative services.[23] The answer given by the French court is thus basically similar to that arrived at in the Anglo-American world. But its answer has not prevented the civil service in France from going on strike many times since the Liberation. The existence of powerful collective organizations, provoked by the inadequacy of wages in the face of an ever-rising cost of living as well as by political factors, has thus far defeated the efficacy of the legal principle that demands continuous operation of administrative services.

Powers of the Administration

Anyone contemplating the powers of modern administration cannot fail to note that they fall into two general categories in their effect on private individuals. On the one hand the administration is vested with authority to promulgate rules of general applicability. On the other it has the power to render decisions adversely affecting the person or property of particular citizens.

In this respect the powers exercised by the administration can be compared to those normally possessed by the legislature and the courts. The legislature usually acts by determinations of *general* applicability addressed to indicated but unnamed and unspecified persons and situations. A court, on the contrary, acts by decisions that are *specific* in applicability and addressed to particular individuals or situations.[24] Legislation is thus distinguished from adjudication in that "the former affects the rights of individuals in the abstract and must be applied in a further proceeding before the legal position of any particular individual will be definitely touched by it; while adjudication operates concretely upon individuals in their individual capacity."[25]

The possession of legislative and judicial powers is perhaps the most striking characteristic of modern administration on both sides of the Atlantic. As the Attorney General's Committee on Administrative Procedure has stated, the distinguishing feature of an administrative

[23] Dehaene, July 7, 1950.

[24] See Fuchs, "Procedure in Administrative Rule-Making" 52 Harv. L. Rev. 259, 265 (1938).

[25] Dickinson, Administrative Justice and the Supremacy of Law 21 (1927).

agency is its possession of the authority to determine, either by rule or by decision, private rights and obligations.[26] The grant to the administration of legislative and judicial powers is essential if it is effectively to perform the regulatory tasks entrusted to it by the legislature. "If in private life we were to organize a unit for the operation of an industry, it would scarcely follow Montesquieu's lines."[27] Nor can the regulation of industry be adequately carried out under a rigid separation of powers. The administration has consequently been made the repository of all three types of governmental power. In the administrative process the various stages of making and applying law, traditionally separate, "have been telescoped into a single agency."[28] Rule making and adjudication have become the chief weapons in the administrative armory.

Rule Making: Inherent or Delegated Power?

The common lawyer who examines the administrative rule-making power in France is immediately struck by the fact that the administration is invested with an inherent authority to promulgate rules with the force of law. This authority is something foreign to Anglo-American conceptions of executive power, for with us the administration possesses only the rule-making authority delegated to it by the legislature.[29]

True, even in the common-law world administrative rule-making authority has been vastly extended in the last fifty years. If, as the Attorney General's Committee pointed out, "the promulgation of general regulations by the Executive, acting under statutory authority, has been a normal feature of federal administration ever since the Government was established,"[30] the area of administrative authority has certainly increased by leaps and bounds since the founding of the Republic. In mere volume, indeed, the amount of administrative rule making completely dwarfs the statutes enacted by the Federal Congress. And what is true of volume is true also of degree of authority. Anglo-American legislatures are tending more and more to enact legislation of the "skeleton" type, which sets up only the broadest standards

[26] Report 8 (1941).
[27] Landis, The Administrative Process 10 (1938).
[28] Report of the Attorney General's Committee, 204.
[29] This principle received striking reaffirmation in Youngstown Sheet & Tube Co. v. Sawyer, 343 U.S. 579 (1952), the famous steel-seizure case.
[30] Report, 97.

to limit the administrative rule-making power. The flesh and the blood —not to mention the soul—of the schemes of legislative regulation have to be provided by the rules promulgated by the administration.[31]

Yet, even though the administrative rule-making power is an enormous one today in the common-law world, it is still one that has its source in delegations by the legislature. In Anglo-American theory it is only the elected representatives of the people who have been vested with the inherent power to legislate. Other governmental organs may exercise legislative authority only by virtue of an express grant from the legislature. It is in this sense that the common lawyer has become accustomed to the term "delegated legislation," meaning the exercise by the administration of rule-making authority delegated to it.

It is the possession of only delegated rule-making authority that distinguishes the Anglo-American administration from its French counterpart. In the French system the administration is vested, in addition to the authority conferred upon it by the legislature, with inherent rule-making powers that exist even in the absence of legislative delegation.

The French Constitution, like the American, contains a general direction to the head of the executive branch to ensure the execution of the laws. It has been argued by some that the grant in Article II of the American Constitution to the President to "take care that the laws be faithfully executed" implies a vast residue of authority in the Executive—fully as sweeping as that inferred from the "necessary and proper" clause of Article I. "It would seem to include the power to take all steps 'which shall be necessary and proper for carrying into execution' the laws of the United States, except those which conflict with Constitution or statute. The Executive power is thus not limited to specific constitutional or statutory grants, but includes the power to take measures and exercise authority not specifically conferred."[32]

Although this view of inherent executive power finds support in the opinion of Mr. Justice Miller in an important case,[33] it has not been generally approved, for it is inconsistent with the basic principle that requires the rule-making authority of the American administration to have its source in a legislative delegation. In the French system, on the contrary, the theory of an inherent administrative rule-making power

[31] Compare Allen, Law and Orders 122 (1945).
[32] Schwartz, "The War Power in Britain and America" 20 N.Y.U. L. Q. Rev. 465, 486 (1945).
[33] In re Neagle, 135 U.S. 1, 63-4 (1890).

derived from a grant of authority to ensure the execution of the laws is the one generally adopted.

Under the Constitution of 1946 the French Prime Minister (*Président du Conseil*) is the head of the executive branch, and it is he who is charged with the execution of the laws. For his rule-making authority he has no need of an express legislative delegation. A general rule-making authority is to be found in his "inherent powers." This is the term used by the Council of State in a famous case in which the executive power was expressly stated to be based on the constitutional charge to ensure the execution of the laws.[34]

Under the French theory the inherent rule-making authority of the executive is a very broad one. It includes the power to promulgate any rule deemed necessary to promote public order, safety, health, and tranquillity—which, in effect, means any rule that the executive deems to be in the public interest. Nor, it should be noted, is the inherent power to issue such rules limited to the head of the French executive. To be sure, only the Prime Minister has the general authority to promulgate rules regulating any aspect of the national life; but ministers too may, without statutory authorization, issue rules necessary for "the proper operation of the administration placed under their control."[35] And the various local authorities possess similar powers; for example, prefects and mayors possess inherent authority to promulgate rules regulating public order, safety, and health in the departments and communes.

It should not be imagined, however, that the inherent rule-making power possessed by the administration is unlimited. In the French as in the Anglo-American system the administrative rule-making authority is considered as an essentially subordinate one. In Anglo-American theory the subordinate status of the rule-making power flows naturally from its source in a delegation by the legislature. "The power to legislate, when delegated by Parliament, differs from Parliament's own power to legislate. Parliament is supreme and its power to legislate is therefore unlimited. . . . But any power delegated by Parliament is necessarily a subordinate power, because it is limited by the terms of the enactment whereby it is delegated."[36]

[34] Labonne, August 8, 1919. This case arose under the Constitution of the Third Republic, which vested the power to ensure the execution of the laws in the President of the French Republic. Under the Constitution of 1946, as has been pointed out, this authority is now conferred upon the Prime Minister.

[35] Jamart, Council of State, February 7, 1936.

[36] Report of the Committee on Ministers' Powers 20 (Cmd. 4060, 1932).

In the French system, too, the rule-making power of the administration is inferior to the law-making authority of the legislature. "The hierarchy of legislators continues down to the administrative legislator, and just as an ordinary law is subordinate to the Constitution, so an administrative rule is in turn subordinate to the ordinary law. Thus an administrative rule may not be contrary to a statute or modify its terms."[37] The rule-making authority of the French administration, though not derived from Parliament, is thus "subordinate to the legislative power to the extent that it cannot suspend, alter, or repeal existing laws; that it is not allowed to act *contra legem*."[38]

The subordination of the rule-making power to the authority of the legislature has important consequences in limiting the inherent rule-making power of the French administration. In the first place, as has already been stated, an administrative rule cannot be contrary to existing statute law. And just as significant is the fact that, in the French system, only a statute can bring about certain legal results. For example, it is only the French legislature that can impose a new tax or increase an existing one.[39] And, similarly, the administration cannot itself promulgate rules that impose upon private individuals penalties not provided for by the legislature.[40] Nor can an administrative rule be issued that is retroactive in effect.[41] The legislature alone, according to the French theory, can produce such an effect.

Restrictions on Delegation

In the inherent rule-making power of the administration there is a great difference between the French and the Anglo-American systems. Even with the limitations noted, the administration in France still possesses an inherent authority to promulgate rules far broader than that vested in administration in the common-law world.

In the matter of delegations of authority to the executive the common lawyer who examines the French system will tend to find more resemblance to that with which he is familiar. In this respect a

37 Bonnard, Précis de droit administratif 300 (3d ed., 1940).

38 Sieghart, *op. cit. supra* note 3, at 259.

39 Syndicat Français des Directeurs de Cinémas, Council of State, February 28, 1947.

40 Guilloux et Ramatis, Council of State, March 10, 1950; Beauzet, Council of State, February 28, 1947.

41 Société Civile de l'École Gerson, Council of State, March 2, 1949; Société L'Aurore, Council of State, June 25, 1948; Devouge, Council of State, May 2, 1947.

sharp differentiation must first be made, however, between the situation in Britain and that in the United States. British constitutional law rests on the doctrine of the supremacy of Parliament—a doctrine utterly inconsistent with the notion of restrictions on the power that can be delegated to the executive. There are no limitations in Britain to restrain Parliament from assigning authority where and how it will. In the American system, on the contrary, grants of power by the legislature are subject to scrutiny by the courts to see that they are not inordinate. "In Great Britain, excessive delegations of Parliamentary powers are political concerns; in the United States, they are primarily judicial."[42]

Paradoxical though it may sound, either the American or the British administrative lawyer will find points of similarity to his own system in the French law on the subject of delegations of power to the administration. The American will immediately feel at home on finding that the French system, like his own, is based on the doctrine against the delegation of legislative power to the executive. "In effect," states a contemporary treatise on the *droit administratif*, "Parliament does not possess the legislative function as an inherent and original power: that power has been delegated to it by the Constitution. Parliament thus possesses, not a right that it can delegate at will, but a competence that the Constitution obliges it to exercise itself. It cannot legally delegate its legislative functions to the government. Such a delegation would be unconstitutional."[43]

It is well known that in the American system the doctrine against delegation has not prevented the legislature from conferring essentially legislative powers upon the executive. Indeed, it has come to be seen that a literal application of the doctrine against delegation could well make effective modern government impossible. The need for delegations under present-day conditions is perhaps nowhere better put than in the British Report of the Committee on Ministers' Powers. "The truth is," reads the Committee's conclusion on the subject, "that if Parliament were not willing to delegate law-making power, Parliament would not be able to pass the kind and quantity of legislation which modern public opinion requires"[44]—a conclusion that applies with equal force to the American Congress.

42 Weeks, "Legislative Power Versus Delegated Legislative Power" 25 Geo. L. J. 314, 330 (1937).

43 Bonnard, *op. cit. supra* note 37, at 295.

44 Report, 23.

That the doctrine against delegation does not prevent the grant to the American administration of powers legislative in essence does not, however, mean that there are no restrictions on delegations to the executive. The approach to the delegation problem in this country has shifted from formal application of an inflexible principle against delegation to a practice of determining whether legislative grants of power are in fact inordinate. "Congress cannot delegate any part of its legislative power except under the limitation of a prescribed standard," the Supreme Court has declared.[45] Thus, only where there are no adequate standards defined in the enabling legislation will delegations of legislative power to the executive be held invalid today in this country. At the same time the validity of particular delegations is still, with us, primarily a judicial question. It is our courts that have the last word on whether the standards defined in a given enabling act are adequate.

It is with regard to the question of judicial control that the French practice on delegations of authority to the administration differs from the American. And in this respect France resembles Britain more closely than it does the United States. French jurists, it should be noted, tend to deny that there is any such resemblance between their system and that in Britain. The question of delegation, asserts a recent French text on constitutional law, involves a special legal problem in countries which, like France, have a written Constitution. "In effect, in systems such as the English one, the absolute supremacy of Parliament, unlimited by any formal Constitution, allows Parliament to delegate to the government all the powers it deems necessary. In countries with a written and rigid Constitution, on the contrary, Parliament possesses legislative authority only from the Constitution and cannot, without violating it, charge the Executive with legislating in its place."[46]

From a practical point of view, however, the situation in France with regard to limitations on the authority that may be delegated to the executive is basically like that in Britain because of the lack of any judicial control of the validity of the laws enacted by the legislature. "The restrictions placed on the action of the legislature under the French constitution are not in reality laws, since they are not rules which in the last resort will be enforced by the courts. Their true character is that of maxims of political morality, which derive whatever strength they

[45] United States v. Chicago, M., St. P. & P. R. Co., 282 U.S. 311, 324 (1931).
[46] Vedel, Manuel élémentaire de droit constitutionnel 498 (1949).

possess from being formally inscribed in the constitution and from the resulting support of public opinion."[47]

The situation in France in this respect is of particular significance for Americans prone to criticize the system of judicial review of the constitutionality of statutes that prevails in this country. The French experience shows that a Constitution that cannot be judicially enforced contains but empty words. It is judicial review that ensures the inviolableness of the American Constitution and gives that instrument its practical meaning. It is the failure of the French courts to assert a review power over the constitutionality of acts of the legislature that has made the various Constitutions in France mere paper instruments and has in effect placed the French legislature in a position of practical supremacy not unlike that enjoyed by the British Parliament.

The doctrine against the delegation of legislative power to the executive, which French students have stated to be a basic principle of their constitutional law, has thus, like other constitutional doctrines in France, been of no more effect than a mere maxim of political morality. It has not in practice served to limit the grants of authority conferred upon the administration by the French Parliament. Nor has the situation been changed by the insertion in the French Constitution of 1946 of an express prohibition against the delegation of legislative power by the Parliament.[48] The failure of the French courts to assert a review power over the constitutionality of statutes has left the legislature as the final judge of the validity of its delegations—a position that means, of course, that there are in practice no restrictions on the authority that may be delegated by the French legislature to the administration.

Decree Laws

The truth of the foregoing assertion can best be tested in connection with the most extreme type of delegation made by the French Parliament: that of the authority to promulgate so-called decree laws.

It has already been shown that the rule-making power of the French administration is subordinate to the legislative authority of the French Parliament. This subordination means that an administrative rule in the French, as in the Anglo-American, system is invalid if contrary to statute law. But what if the legislature expressly delegates to the ad-

[47] Dicey, *op. cit. supra* note 1, at 135.
[48] See *infra* p. 100.

ministration the authority by its rules to modify or amend existing statutes?

In the United States such an attempt by the legislature to confer authority upon the administration to amend statutes would probably be held to exceed the permissible bounds of legislative delegations. As Mr. Justice Sutherland has stated: "The only authority conferred, or which could be conferred, by the statute is to make regulations to carry out the purposes of the act—not to amend it."[49]

In Britain, on the other hand, there are no limitations to restrain Parliament from delegating the power to amend statutes. In fact, the type of delegation about which there has been the most controversy in the British system—the so-called "Henry VIII clause"—involves essentially the grant of authority to amend acts of Parliament. These clauses, in effect, have conferred power upon the executive to modify the provisions of the relevant enabling act so far as may appear to it to be necessary for the purposes of bringing the act into full operation. Because of the supreme position of Parliament the validity of such delegations has, of course, been beyond question in the British courts. This does not, however, mean that the Henry VIII clause has not been strongly criticized by British students, who have constantly urged that its use should be abandoned in enabling statutes. Such, indeed, was the recommendation of the Committee on Ministers' Powers[50] appointed by the Lord Chancellor in 1929 to investigate the subject of administrative law; and its suggestion has, in practice, led to the virtual disappearance of the Henry VIII clause from recent British legislation.[51]

In France as in Britain there have not been any practical restrictions on the delegation by the Parliament of the authority to amend statutes. Such delegations have, in fact, been made a number of times in the period between the First and the Second World Wars in connection with the authority to promulgate so-called decree laws. These decree laws, like the regulations promulgated under the British Henry VIII clause, have as their primary characteristic that they are not subject to the normally basic subordination of administrative rules to statute law. The French decree laws, like the regulations issued under

[49] Miller v. United States, 294 U.S. 435, 440 (1935).

[50] Report, 65.

[51] For a more detailed account of the Henry VIII clause see Schwartz, Law and the Executive in Britain 57 *et seq.* (1949).

the Henry VIII clause, are valid even though their terms conflict with those of existing statutes.

The British type of delegation is, however, not nearly so broad as its French counterpart. The Henry VIII clause is intended to enable the administration to bring a defined legislative scheme into practical operation by allowing it to alter legislative provisions that prove unworkable in practice. The power to promulgate decree laws is not one delegated with reference to any defined statutory program. Rather, the administration is empowered to take whatever measures it deems necessary to deal with the nation's economic problems.

The extent of administrative authority can be seen with reference to the law of February 28, 1934, an illustrative statute of this type providing that "the Government is authorized, until June 30, 1934, notwithstanding any laws to the contrary, to take, by decrees . . . , the economic measures that the balancing of the budget demands." The decrees promulgated under this law were to be submitted to the Parliament for ratification by October 31, 1934, but were to be valid until the legislature refused to ratify.

If ever a statute provided for wholesale delegation, it was this one. The French Government was in effect given authority to promulgate any decrees that it deemed necessary to the balancing of the budget, and such decrees were to have the full force and effect of law, even though they conflicted with existing statutes—whence the term "decree laws." These decree laws, in the words of French students, involved an extreme concentration of legislative and executive power,[52] but such concentration was deemed justified by the pressing exigencies of the economic crisis. The various French Governments in the interwar period, faced with the need to reduce administrative expenses, balance the budget, and stabilize the franc, felt that the only way these problems could be coped with was by extended use of the administrative rule-making power. "In this situation of grave crisis requiring urgent measures that could not be adopted with the delays inherent in legislative procedures, the Parliament assumed the right to extend the administrative rule-making authority without excepting from it the matters normally reserved for the legislature alone."[53]

The extent of the power given to the French Government by the law of February 28, 1934, can be measured by a case in which the exer-

[52] Waline, *op. cit. supra* note 12, at 25.
[53] *Id.* at 28.

cise of the power was questioned. The administration had promulgated under that law a decree that regulated the dimensions, weight, and loads of vehicles using the public highways. Against the contention that such a decree had no relation to the statutory standard of "economic measures that the balancing of the budget demands," the Council of State held the decree to be valid. "The legislature intended to enable the government to realize all reforms that might lead to a reduction in the expenses of the State . . . [and] it is established that the limitation of the dimensions, weight, and loads of vehicles allowed on the public roads will lead to a reduction in the costs of upkeep of such roads."[54] That a law authorizing the promulgation of decrees necessary to aid in the balancing of the budget is construed as authorizing a traffic regulation of the type here upheld shows that the executive is in effect given plenary powers to take the measures it deems necessary to deal with the economic situation of the country. Such, at any rate, was the view of the various French Governments with regard to the authority conferred by the law of February 28, 1934, and by subsequent similar laws. "It is by the hundreds, as is well known, that the decree-laws have appeared, notably in 1935, 1936, and 1938, the government having dealt out in massive doses the remedy placed at its disposal"[55] by the legislature.

Nor could it be validly contended that a statute like the law of February 28, 1934, provided for an unconstitutional delegation of legislative power to the executive. Such a contention was, in fact, made in a case decided by the Council of State in 1936, but that tribunal held that it was not competent to deal with the constitutional question. "In the present state of French public law this contention is not one that can be raised before the judicial section of the Council of State."[56]

The American administrative lawyer who seeks to understand the scope and effect of the French statutes authorizing the promulgation of decree laws has a ready analogy in the act held invalid in *Schechter Poultry Corp. v. United States.*[57] As interpreted by the Supreme Court, the National Industrial Recovery Act, like the French laws we have been considering, empowered the executive, in the exercise of its rule-making authority, to take any measures that it deemed necessary to aid in the economic recovery of the nation. Under the Recovery Act "the

[54] Union des Véhicules Industriels, June 25, 1937.
[55] Josserand, "Les Déformations récentes de la technique législative" (1939) Dalloz, Chronique 9, 10.
[56] Arrighi, November 6, 1936.
[57] 295 U.S. 495 (1935).

discretion of the President in approving or prescribing codes, and thus enacting laws for the government of trade and industry throughout the country, is virtually unfettered."[58] As Mr. Justice Cardozo stated: "This is delegation running riot. No such plenitude of power is capable of transfer."[59]

In the French system such "delegation running riot" had become, by the time of the Second World War, the normal means of dealing with economic and other emergencies. Laws like that of February 28, 1934, vesting plenary powers in the government to deal by decree with the nation's economic situation, were enacted in 1935, 1937, 1938, and 1939. On the eve of the war the French system had thus become accustomed to the existence of a legislative power in the executive coextensive with that possessed by the Parliament in the economic field. It is no wonder, then, that the transition to the government of Vichy in 1940 was not so difficult as it might otherwise have been. "The developments already discussed show us that the serious alterations made in the Constitution in July 1940 were not without their precursors."[60] The vesting of complete legislative power in the chief of state in 1940 was not such an innovation for a country already accustomed to confer plenary powers upon the executive to promulgate decree laws. "After having again and again delegated its legislative powers, Parliament could, without the risk of shocking public opinion, attempt to delegate its constituent power and by this process destroy the Constitution by quasi-constitutional means."[61]

True, the vesting of plenary powers in the men of Vichy was not the same thing as conferring them upon the men of the Third Republic, whose mandate in office depended on the confidence of the nation's elected representatives. But personal confidence in the delegate is itself no answer to the question of restrictions upon delegations. "It is not your dictatorship of which I am afraid, Mr. Prime Minister," stated a legislative opponent of one of the laws conferring upon the French government the authority to promulgate decree laws. "Other men may replace you."[62]

[58] *Id.* at 542, per Hughes, C. J.

[59] *Id.* at 553. It should be noted that, under the National Industrial Recovery Act, no attempt was made to give the executive the authority to amend existing laws.

[60] Waline, *op. cit. supra* note 12, at 29.

[61] Sieghart, *op. cit. supra* note 3, at 303.

[62] Quoted *id.* at 308.

Decree Laws of 1948

The French themselves have not been slow to realize that the widespread use by the executive of the authority to promulgate decree laws was among the factors that facilitated the transition to a totalitarian regime in 1940. And the desire to prevent a return to such delegations running riot in the France that was to be constituted after the Liberation led to the inclusion in the Constitution of 1946 of a formal prohibition against the delegation of legislative power. "The Parliament alone may vote laws," reads Article 13 of that instrument. "It may not delegate that right." Although there is no express condemnation of the decree-law practice in this article, "such must be the meaning of its two short sentences, if weight is given, as is necessary, to the preparatory work and the discussion of the article before the Constituent Assembly. It follows from them that the members of the Assembly very clearly intended, though in a way unfortunately somewhat ambiguous, to condemn the decree-law practice, which was considered as one of the gravest faults of the Third Republic."[63]

The French Constitution of 1946, however, like its predecessors, provides for no mechanism by which its provisions can be enforced. The French courts today, like those under the Third Republic, uniformly refuse to assert the authority to declare acts of the legislature invalid, even though they conflict with the provisions of the organic instrument.[64] Article 13 of the present French Constitution is thus, in practice, a maxim of political morality violable at will by the legislature.

That the practical situation in France has not in fact been changed by the express constitutional prohibition against the delegation of legislative power is shown by the enactment by the very first Parliament under the Constitution of 1946 of an enabling act as broad as those authorizing the promulgation of decree laws. The law of August 17, 1948, in effect authorized the executive to take by decree any measures deemed necessary to deal with the economic situation; and, as in con-

[63] Morange, "La Réalisation de la réforme fiscale par la voie réglementaire" (1948) Dalloz, Chronique 177, 178.

[64] Chambre Syndicale des Agents Généraux, Council of State, February 4, 1949; Thomas, Council of State, June 2, 1948.

nection with the decree laws, it was expressly stated that the decrees promulgated might modify or replace existing legislative texts.[65]

The law of August 17, 1948, seems clearly to mark what has been termed an offensive return of the decree-law practice.[66] As was stated during the parliamentary debates, "The term 'decree law' is not in the text, but even without the term, it contains the reality of the decree laws."[67] Both during the legislative debates and since the enactment of the 1948 law grave doubts have been expressed with regard to its constitutionality. "It is impossible to admit that Parliament could have thus delegated wholesale its legislative power without violating Article 13 of the Constitution," asserts the pre-eminent contemporary work on the *droit administratif*.[68] But there is little doubt that the return of the decree-law practice is now an accomplished fact, despite Article 13. "Constitutional or not, the law of August 17 [1948] seems destined to be applied in a country in which there is no judicial control of the constitutionality of laws and in which such political control as has been provided for appears to be entirely illusory."[69]

Administrative Powers of Decision

Modern administration, in addition to its authority to promulgate rules of general applicability, is vested with significant powers of decision in cases affecting particular persons. This statement is as true of administration in France as of that on this side of the Atlantic. "Unlike rule making which tends to few general patterns with readily under-

[65] It should be noted that the 1948 law contains no time limit upon the exercise of the powers conferred by it. In fact, some of the most important decrees issued under the 1948 statute were promulgated in the latter part of 1953.

[66] Waline, *op. cit. supra* note 12, at 36. Unlike their prewar counterparts, decrees issued under the 1948 law do not have to be ratified by the Parliament. They consequently take effect immediately and remain in operation until the legislature acts positively to annul them.

[67] Quoted in Donnedieu de Vabres, "Décrets-lois et pouvoirs réglementaires d'après la loi du 17 août 1948" (1949) Dalloz, Chronique 5, 8.

[68] Waline, *op. cit. supra* note 12, at 37.

[69] Morange, *loc. cit. supra* note 63. For a more recent discussion, see Laubadère, "Des 'pleins pouvoirs' aux 'demis décrets-lois'" (1952) Dalloz, Chronique 36.

Since 1948, the decree-law practice has become, as it was before 1939, an established part of the French system. Especially significant in this respect have been the extensive powers of decree law exercised under both the law of August 17, 1948, and a law of July 11, 1953, by the government of Premier Laniel. The reform of the administrative-court system, discussed *supra* pp. 48-50, was initiated by decree of the executive, after the Parliament had failed for three years to pass a bill to accomplish that end.

standable variations in detail, administrative adjudication is more complex."[70] It would serve no useful purpose to attempt here to catalogue the many different types of decisions that the French administration is empowered to make. It has been calculated that one official, the prefect, actually exercises some 1,300 functions that involve powers of decision over individual rights and obligations.[71]

It should, however, be noted that in one important respect the authority of the French administration differs from that of its American counterpart. In this country the most significant powers of decision exercised by the administration have been conferred in connection with administrative regulation of various aspects of the economic scene. Such regulation is generally of two kinds. It is recognized that in certain fields the normal rules of free competition are inapplicable. In those fields the State tolerates the existence of virtual monopolies, but by a scheme of stringent administrative regulation it ensures that the monopolistic power shall not be abused. This sort of arrangement is the usual thing in the field of public utilities in this country. In other areas of economic activity the rules of free competition govern, but the State has intervened to prevent certain abusive practices that are conceived to be deleterious to the working of a free competitive system. An agency such as the Federal Trade Commission, to take the outstanding example, is set up to take action against unfair methods of competition in commerce.

In France the type of administrative adjudicatory regulation of the economic system that is so familiar to the American student has not been of great importance. In the field of public utilities the dominant theme in the French system has been, not regulation, but operation. Since the State itself operates most public utilities, there is no place for the Interstate Commerce Commission kind of regulation, which is of such significance in the American system. And as for the Federal Trade Commission type of regulation of abusive economic practices, the French system has tended to adopt a hands-off policy. It is this tendency that has made the growth of large cartels a matter of such consequence in a country like France, where their abusive practices have been almost wholly free from administrative regulation.

[70] McFarland and Vanderbilt, Cases and Materials on Administrative Law 214 (2d ed., 1952).

[71] Waline, *op. cit. supra* note 12, at 230.

Sanctions

The decision of an administrative agency, like that of a court, has behind it the force of politically organized society. It is this backing that gives the power of the administration such significance for private individuals. Administrative orders must be obeyed if the imposition of sanctions is to be avoided. "It is common experience that men conform their conduct to regulations by governmental authority so as to avoid the unpleasant legal consequences which failure to conform entails."[72]

In the American system administrative decisions are of two kinds in their immediate legal effect upon the individual. The first type is not self-operative, and suit for its enforcement must be brought by the agency concerned before the appropriate court. Before 1906, for example, no sanction was provided for securing obedience to orders of the Interstate Commerce Commission other than a suit by the Commission to compel obedience; and the same is still true of orders of the National Labor Relations Board. In other cases the administrative decision becomes effective immediately unless those affected take affirmative action to have it set aside by the courts. In cases of this type various sanctions are provided to ensure enforcement of the decision. The most usual is the criminal penalty for willful violation, but other means of enforcement are also common. They include civil penalties and forfeitures, so-called statutory injunctions, and civil liability to injured parties.[73]

In the Anglo-American world administrative action depends for its enforcement on sanctions imposed by the courts. Even in instances in which the administrative decision becomes effective immediately it is not the administration itself that can penalize those who disobey it. Penalties for disobedience are imposed by the courts, which are thus the ultimate enforcers of administrative action.

In France there is nothing like the American distinction between administrative decisions that are effective immediately and those that are of no legal effect until the agency concerned petitions the appropriate court for enforcement. All decisions of the French administration are effective at once, and those to whom they are directed must comply with them or suffer the legal consequences entailed by failure to comply.

These consequences are not, however, limited, as in the Anglo-

[72] Columbia Broadcasting System v. United States, 316 U.S. 407, 418 (1942).
[73] See Davis, *op. cit. supra* note 16, at 750.

American world, to the imposition of sanctions by the courts. In France, as in most Continental countries, the administration has always been vested with authority directly to execute its own decisions, by force if need be. It is true that administration in the common-law world may also proceed to forced execution of its decisions in certain cases. "Where immediate action is absolutely necessary in order to avoid disastrous results, as in the case of a nuisance prejudicial to the public health and in the case of the payment of taxes, the administration may proceed directly to enforce its orders, and in case of resistance to the execution of the law may, without application to the courts, apply force to overcome such resistance."[74] But in the Anglo-American world this type of case has remained the striking exception to the usual procedure for the enforcement of administrative decisions. In France, on the other hand, the normal rule is that "the administration, in principle, has the privilege of having its decisions directly executed by its agents, without having to resort to the courts for enforcement."[75]

The leading authority on this point is the *Saint-Just* case, decided by the Court of Conflicts in 1902.[76] It arose out of a law regulating religious associations that prohibited the formation of religious congregations without special legislative authorization. A ministerial decree rendered in execution of the law ordered the immediate closing of a particular unauthorized congregational establishment. Neither the law nor the decree provided any penalty for noncompliance, and the members of the congregation refused to comply with the order. The prefect then ordered the local police to evict them and to keep the premises closed under seal; and his action in thus himself forcibly executing the administrative order was upheld by the Court of Conflicts.

French students themselves have not been slow to recognize the dangers involved in the *Saint-Just* decision. "That the recognition in the administration of such a power of direct execution *manu militari* is dangerous for public liberties seems obvious: the abuse by the administration of so great a power is to be feared."[77] The *Saint-Just* decision itself has, however, normally been approved, because of fear of the consequences of not providing any enforcement for a law for the violation of which the legislator has failed to provide a penalty.

The French view with regard to the need for direct execution by

[74] I Goodnow, Comparative Administrative Law 126 (1893).
[75] Waline, *op. cit. supra* note 12, at 424.
[76] December 2, 1902.
[77] Waline, *op. cit. supra* note 12, at 426.

the administration in this type of case was well stated by the government commissioner in the *Saint-Just* case. "We start with the propositions that it is not admissible for a law to be unenforced or for public authority to be disobeyed; that an error in draftsmanship, an omission, a lacuna on the part of the legislature cannot make its prescriptions sterile; that, in the relations between public authority and individuals, obligation and coercion are indissolubly linked together; that obedience to an order legally given by competent authority, if it is not obtained voluntarily, must be obtained by compulsion. Here it is the private interests, the rights of individuals, that must yield to the necessity of having the law enforced."[78]

It should not, however, be thought that the French administration has in every instance the power forcibly to execute its own decisions. It is only where the enforcement of the decision cannot be otherwise legally compelled that resort may be had to direct administrative enforcement. Thus, if a penalty is provided by the legislature for failure to comply with the administrative decision, proceedings must be instituted to obtain an imposition of the penalty. "To allow the administration the right to substitute administrative execution for the penal sanction would be to recognize a right to choose between the sanction decreed by the legislature and an administrative execution that has no legal justification; it would be arbitrary anarchy, the negation of the basic principles of our public law."[79] Only if the legislature has failed to provide a penalty for violation, as in the *Saint-Just* case, may the administration proceed directly, by force if need be, to execution of its decision.

Even with this limitation, the power of the French administration directly to execute its own decisions remains a very significant one. "Direct execution by the administration constitutes a procedure that endangers the public order, a practice somewhat disquieting to individuals."[80] The dangers inherent in allowing such an administrative power, even if it is sought to be confined within narrow limits, is shown by the French experience with administrative requisitions since the Liberation.

One of the means by which the French Government has sought to deal with the grave housing crisis caused by the war is a scheme of

[78] I Hauriou, La Jurisprudence administrative de 1892 à 1929, 88 (1929).
[79] *Id.* at 91.
[80] Dupond, "Les Conditions de legalité de l'éxecution par la voie administrative" Revue du Droit Public 347, 353 (1924).

administrative requisitions of houses and apartments. If a dwelling were insufficiently occupied and the owner could not be persuaded to rent it, the administration was authorized to order its requisition in the interest of one in need who came within certain specified classes. Although the law authorizing such requisitions did not expressly provide for means of enforcement, the practice has grown up for the French administration itself to execute its requisition orders, by force if need be, if they were not obeyed voluntarily. This extension of administrative authority, as analyzed by one commentator, "is to be explained by the totalitarian tendency of new administrators who admit only with reluctance that they are subject to legal limitations. They have used the pretext of technical difficulties to liberate themselves from legal principles that they feel should be inapplicable. And they have arrogated to themselves the right themselves to execute requisition orders, opening doors by force to do so."[81]

Under the *Saint-Just* case, as we have seen, such direct execution by the administration itself is valid, but only if the legislature has failed to provide penalties for noncompliance with the administrative decision. As interpreted by the Court of Conflicts, the legislation authorizing administrative requisition of dwellings does not provide any penalties for the violation of requisition orders. And this omission, says the Court, authorizes direct execution by the administration, by force if need be, where its requisition orders are disobeyed. "In the absence of any penal sanction the prescriptions of the law cannot remain a dead letter, and in these conditions the administration can legally proceed forcibly to execute its requisition order."[82]

In the French system, then, there is the spectacle of a whole host of post-Liberation administrative orders executed directly by the use of administrative force. Certainly this situation strikes the Anglo-American—who feels that resort to the judge should be necessary before the force of politically organized society is directed against one who refuses to comply with an administrative decision—as somewhat extreme. Yet the Anglo-American should realize that the system in a country like France has had a different starting point from that with which he is familiar. French administrative law begins with an administration whose powers are virtually absolute. Its powers came to be rigorously curtailed with the establishment of republican government

[81] Fréjaville, "Les Palliatifs juridiques de la crise du logement" (1946) Dalloz, Chronique 85, 87.

[82] Dumont, May 12, 1949.

in the last century. But vestiges of the early absolutism still remain in the inherent power of the French administration to promulgate rules and in its authority directly to execute its own decisions where a penal sanction has not been provided.

It is these vestiges of absolutism that make the authority of the French administration greater than that of its counterpart in the common-law world. And it is they that make the need for judicial control of administration even more pressing in the French than in the Anglo-American system. Thus, "it is this privilege of the *action d'office*, the right of the administration to enforce its own decisions without the intervention of a judge, . . . which make[s] the possibility of a challenge of an administrative decision in an independent Court a paramount necessity for the preservation of individual liberties."[83] It is to the question of the means by which, in the French system, such challenge can be made that we must now turn our attention.

[83] Sieghart, *op. cit. supra* note 3, at 215.

Chapter Five

PROCEEDINGS FOR REVIEW OF ADMINISTRATIVE ACTION

Both the Anglo-American and the French systems of administrative law have as their basic principle that one adversely affected by improper administrative action may have such action set aside by a competent court. The need for such judicial control of administration is clear from the very nature of administrative authority and the possibilities of its abuse. There is danger of arbitrariness in all exercise of power, and only through constant control can illegality be minimized. The good faith of the administration—administrative desire to conform to the legislative mandate—is in this connection irrelevant. Legal rules, unlike those in the physical sciences, do not have fixed areas of strains and stresses. There is a tendency to stretch legal rules to the breaking point permitted by expediency—to carry out the desired action even at the risk of illegality. As a noted French administrative lawyer has stated, in language that recalls Lord Acton's famous aphorism: "Public officers have a natural tendency to use the powers conferred upon them to attain objectives other than those directly aimed at by the enabling legislation: every man vested with power tends to abuse it."[1]

Judicial control of administration is one of the important balances of both the Anglo-American and the French constitutional systems. The historic role of the courts in the common-law world—to act as a brake on excursions by the executive beyond its lawful area of authority—has been assumed in France by the Council of State. That tribunal has taken for itself an administrative-law jurisdiction analogous to that exercised by the law courts in Anglo-American countries; to it and the courts subordinate to it the French citizen adversely affected by improper administrative action turns for his remedy.

[1] Jèze, "La Jurisprudence du Conseil d'État et le détournement de pouvoir" Revue du Droit Public 58, 59 (1944).

Proceedings for Review of Administrative Action

Principle of Legality

Judicial control of administrative action is essential to the efficacy of what has been termed the "most fundamental characteristic"[2] of Anglo-American political institutions: that is, the constitutional concept of the rule of law. That concept "means . . . the absolute supremacy or predominance of regular law as opposed to the influence of arbitrary power, and excludes the existence of arbitrariness, of prerogative, or even of wide discretionary authority on the part of the government. Englishmen are ruled by the law, and by the law alone."[3]

In essence the rule of law in the common-law world has meant the subordination of administration to the law of the land as administered by the ordinary courts. It is true that the law of the land is also made by the administration itself. But the concept of the rule of law in the Anglo-American system assumes that law made by the administration is not on the same plane of authority as that which issues from certain other lawmaking organs of the State. The rule of law thus presupposes a veritable hierarchy of lawmakers within the State.

At the apex is the constituent assembly or its equivalent, which alone has the authority to promulgate the organic instrument under which the State is governed. The provisions of the constitution enacted by it constitute the supreme law of the land. The law made by any other organ of the State is valid only so far as it does not conflict with the terms of the constitution.[4] Next in the lawmaking hierarchy come the elected representatives of the people, given authority to enact statutes the provisions of which are legally binding upon all, provided only that they are not inconsistent with the constitution. At the base of the lawmaking hierarchy is the administration. Strictly speaking, its only role is to execute the laws made by the legislature. But the effective performance of that role has required that it, too, be vested with substantial lawmaking authority. Thus, as we have seen, modern administration has the power to promulgate rules having the force of law and to render decisions in cases involving particular citizens.

The subordinate position of administration in the hierarchy of lawmakers means, however, that administrative exercises of lawmaking authority are valid only if they do not conflict with the constitution

2 Hewart, Introduction, in Amos, The English Constitution vi (1934).

3 Dicey, Law of the Constitution 202 (9th ed., 1939).

4 In Britain, of course, there is no organic instrument to limit the lawmaking authority of Parliament.

and with the statutes enacted by the legislature. Or, to put it another way, administrative action is valid only so far as it is *legal*. It is illegal if inconsistent with the prescriptions of an organ superior to administration in the hierarchy of lawmakers within the State.

This "principle of legality" has dominated the public law of France, just as it has that which has developed in the common-law world. Léon Duguit, whose writings have greatly contributed to the development of modern French public law, well expresses the doctrine when he states that it is "this principle essentially that protects the individual, and one can assert that there are not, cannot be, and ought not to be any exceptions to it. A State that does not recognize it or recognizes it only with reservations and exceptions does not truly live under a rule of law."[5]

In determining the meaning of the principle of legality, Duguit emphasized the subordination of the administration to laws that have general applicability. And this emphasis led him to state the principle in the following terms: In a State governed by law "there is no organ of the State that can render an individual decision not conforming to a general standard previously promulgated."[6]

If the principle as thus stated were valid, it would eliminate from the French legal system much of the retroactive creation of new law by adjudication that has been of such importance in both the administrative and judicial processes in the common-law world. It was essentially Duguit's principle condemning such retroactive lawmaking by adjudication that the United States Supreme Court refused to apply in the well-known second *Chenery* case.[7] The relevant administrative agency there, the Securities and Exchange Commission, in approving a reorganization plan under the Public Utility Holding Company Act, had refused to permit the management of a company that had purchased preferred shares during the period of reorganization to participate in the reorganization equally with other holders of preferred stock. The Commission's refusal was made under its statutory authority to determine whether the terms of a reorganization were "fair and equitable," even though the specific practice involved, the purchase by management of the securities of a corporation under reorganization, was not condemned either by statute or regulation. "The absence of a general rule or regulation governing management trading during reorganization," asserted Mr. Justice Murphy, "did not affect the Commission's

[5] 3 Duguit, Traité de droit constitutionnel 732 (3d ed.).
[6] *Ibid.*
[7] Securities and Exchange Commission v. Chenery Corp. 332 U.S. 194 (1947).

duties in relation to the particular proposal before it."[8] Or, to state the Court's holding in terms of the rejection of Duguit's principle, the Commission could proceed by individual decision even though the particular practice condemned by it was not outlawed by a general disposition in statute or regulation.

In France, too, the courts have refused to apply the principle asserted by Duguit. According to the outstanding recent work on the *droit administratif*: "Stated in these terms, the principle of legality represents only an ideal, Duguit's own, and it has no value as a rule of positive law."[9] Yet the fact that the French, like the Anglo-American, administration may thus in effect make law retroactively by its adjudications does not mean that it can make law in conflict with that made by organs superior to it in the French hierarchy of lawmakers. In France as in the common-law world the basic principle of public law is that "no act of legal consequence can be done validly unless it does not conflict with the rules laid down by an authority superior to the author of the act; for example, administrative authorities cannot make a valid decision not consistent with the Constitution, with statute law, and with decrees."[10]

French administrative law, like that with which the common lawyer is familiar, thus has at its foundation the principle of legality. Frenchmen, like Englishmen, are ruled by the law and by the law alone, in the sense that any act of the administration that does not conform to law is invalid.

It will doubtless be objected that there is more than the mere assertion of the principle of legality to the Anglo-American concept of the rule of law. The fact that the principle of legality is enforced by the ordinary courts is what makes it a thing of meaning in the common-law world. The rule of law in the Anglo-American system has consequently had two main aspects. The first is the assertion of the principle of legality—that only governmental acts in accord with law are valid. And of at least equal importance has been the enforcement of the principle of legality in particular cases by the ordinary law courts. To the common lawyer the aspect of judicial enforcement is of cardinal significance. Unless the courts can intervene in cases where it is violated,

[8] *Id.* at 201.
[9] Waline, Traité élémentaire de droit administratif 103 (6th ed., 1951).
[10] *Ibid.*

the principle of legality becomes but as sounding brass or a tinkling cymbal.[11]

French jurists, too, have insisted on the need for judicial enforcement to give substance to the principle of legality. "It is evident," writes Duguit, "that it is not enough to recognize the principle of legality in theory. There must be a strongly organized sanction behind it. And I can see no other feasible one than this: For a country to live under the rule of law, it is absolutely indispensable that it have a high court, with all possible safeguards of independence, impartiality, and competence, before whom can be brought an action to set aside any decision maintained to be contrary to law."[12]

The French system has in the Council of State, as we have seen, such a court. Thus, in the French as in the Anglo-American system, "the illegality of acts done in violation of a superior legal rule can always be determined, on petition of those adversely affected, by a judge who embodies all the guarantees of judicial impartiality and procedure."[13]

In both the French and the Anglo-American systems, then, the principle of legality is enforced by an independent judge. It is true, as we have throughout insisted, that the judge who has made the *droit administratif* is not the same as the judge who has made administrative law in the common-law world. In the Anglo-American system the principle of legality is enforced by the same courts that enforce the ordinary private law. In France the law courts are barred from exercising a significant role in this field, and the control of the legality of administrative action is vested in a separate order of administrative courts.

This difference does not, however, change the fact that in both systems the basic principle is the control of administrative action by a judge wholly independent of the active administration. This similarity in basis was well expressed by the greatest of modern French administrative lawyers in answer to those who urged "that our institution of administrative courts, which does not exist at all in Anglo-American countries, was an insurmountable obstacle to the establishment of the English rule of law, for it required the extension of the jurisdiction of the law courts to all cases, even those dealing with questions of administrative law. . . . This difficulty does not exist today. Since the law of

[11] The phrase used in National Labor Relations Board v. Robbins Tire & Rubber Co., 161 F. 2d 798, 804 (5th Cir. 1947).

[12] Duguit, Leçons de droit public général 280 (1926).

[13] Waline, *loc. cit. supra* note 9.

May 24, 1872, the Council of State, dispensing justice like the law courts, has been on an equal judicial level with them and can assume, vis-à-vis the law and administrative regulations, the same sovereign powers of interpretation. The essential requirement of the English rule of law is sovereign judges, *i.e.*, judges independent of the government. It matters little whether they are called law courts or administrative courts, provided that they are in fact independent."[14]

This similarity of basis between the French and the Anglo-American system should make a comparative study of control of administration in France of value to the common lawyer. Once the working of the French two-court system is understood, the details of judicial control of administration in France are not difficult to grasp. Indeed, the control exercised by the Council of State and other French administrative courts is not so different from that exercised by Anglo-American courts as one might presuppose. Nor, upon reflection, is this existence of numerous points of similarity in the French and common-law systems a matter greatly to be marveled at. Both systems have had to deal with essentially the same problems presented by the growth of administrative authority and by the need to keep such authority within the bounds of legality. There are, to be sure, important differences in detail and terminology in the solutions adopted by the two systems to resolve these problems; but if the Anglo-American administrative lawyer looks not at the form but at the substance of the French system of judicial control, he will find a great many useful points of comparison with his own system.

Forms of Action: Common-Law World

Review of administrative action in the Anglo-American world has been greatly influenced by the common lawyer's concern with the procedural aspects of justice. The result has been an undue emphasis on technicalities of pleading and forms of action in a field where there is little place for the overtechnical procedural niceties that have generally prevailed in our law.

In an ordinary case between two private citizens it may be difficult for the seeker after justice to comprehend why he has not prevailed in his righteous cause merely because his counsel has failed to frame his complaint within the proper form of action. But it is, after all, only he who is aggrieved if he has not observed the technical rules of the legal

[14] 1 Hauriou, La Jurisprudence administrative de 1892 à 1929, 47 (1929).

game. But in a case to which the administration is a party much more is at stake. Society as a whole has a very direct interest in ensuring administrative conformity to the principle of legality. If an individual adversely affected by illegal administrative action fails to have such action annulled, because of his inability to avoid the perilous pitfalls of legal procedure, it is not he alone who is aggrieved. An illegal act of the administration has been permitted to go untouched, and the interest of a democratic society in the vigorous enforcement of the principle of legality has thereby been left unvindicated.

Anglo-American courts have tended to lose sight of the need for simplicity of procedure in administrative-law cases. The forms of action available to one adversely affected by administrative action have developed from those available at common law in the Court of King's Bench for controlling the action of inferior courts. These have been the writs of certiorari, prohibition, mandamus, quo warranto, and habeas corpus—the so-called extraordinary or prerogative writs. As Lord Justice Atkin explained in a leading case, with regard to certiorari and prohibition, "both writs deal with questions of excessive jurisdiction, and doubtless in their origin dealt almost exclusively with the jurisdiction of what is described in ordinary parlance as a Court of Justice. But the operation of the writs has extended to control the proceedings of bodies which do not claim to be, and would not be recognized as Courts of Justice. Wherever any body of persons having legal authority to determine questions affecting the rights of subjects, and having the duty to act judicially, act in excess of their legal authority they are subject to the controlling jurisdiction of the King's Bench Division exercised in these writs."[15]

The extraordinary writs—or remedies, as they have more recently been termed—that have thus become the normal means whereby review of administrative action has been obtained in the absence of statutory provisions for review in the Anglo-American world, have not been immune from the archaic and cumbrous technicalities that have characterized all the forms of action at common law. "The extraordinary legal remedies . . . have accumulated so vast a cargo of technicalities that the citizen desirous of challenging an administrative power or privilege finds himself frequently engulfed in a procedural bog which bars him from his goal."[16]

[15] Rex v. Electricity Commissioners, [1924] 1 K.B. 171, 205.
[16] Borchard, Declaratory Judgments xv (2d ed., 1941).

That the extraordinary remedies are wholly incongruous in the field of administrative law seems almost self-evident to one who closely examines their workings. "An imaginary system cunningly planned for the evil purpose of thwarting justice and maximizing fruitless litigation would copy the major features of the extraordinary remedies," asserts a recent treatise on American administrative law. "For the purpose of creating treacherous procedural snares and preventing or delaying the decision of cases on their merits, such a scheme would insist upon a plurality of remedies, no remedy would lie when another is available, the lines between remedies would be complex and shifting, the principal concepts confusing the boundaries of each remedy would be undefined and undefinable, judicial opinions would be filled with misleading generalities, and courts would studiously avoid discussing or even mentioning the lack of practical reasons behind the complexities of the system."[17]

If a legal rule, institution, or method of procedure is not working satisfactorily, there are several courses for would-be reformers to advocate. The simplest is to abolish it and substitute something better.[18] That is clearly what should be done with the extraordinary remedies in the field of administrative law. "The cure is easy. Establish a single, simple form of proceeding for all review of administrative action. . . . Get rid of extraordinary remedies as means of review."[19]

It is, however, not often that the simple remedy of abolition is adopted for an unsatisfactory legal rule or institution. "It is natural that so straightforward a remedy should only be employed when there are men with vigour and courage to carry it out. It is apt to be characteristic of the great moments of the common law, therefore, rather than of those less heroic times when the system is in repose."[20]

The present may not be one of the heroic moments of the common law. But it is certainly not an era in which our legal system is in repose. Surely this is a time, then, when the abolition of the extraordinary remedies from the field of administrative law can be urged as a practical matter, with the hope that advocacy here will count for more than the usual panaceas proposed by the academic theorist.

Thus far, it must be admitted, not too much has been done on this score in the common-law world. The Committee on Ministers' Powers

[17] Davis, Administrative Law 718 (1951).
[18] Plucknett, A Concise History of the Common Law 351 (2d ed., 1936).
[19] Davis, *op. cit. supra* note 17, at 719.
[20] Plucknett, *loc. cit. supra* note 18.

appointed by the Lord Chancellor to investigate administrative law in Britain did conclude that "procedure by way of *certiorari, prohibition,* and *mandamus* is archaic and in some ways cumbrous and inelastic, and we would suggest the expediency of introducing a simpler, cheaper and more expeditious procedure."[21] But the Committee did not go so far as completely to repudiate the extraordinary remedies, and the Administration of Justice Acts, 1933 and 1938, which sought to give effect to its suggestion, provided only that simple orders of mandamus, prohibition, and certiorari be substituted for what had formerly been known as the prerogative writs. This change did mean a simplification in procedure for those seeking review of administrative action. It did not, however, in any way alter the legal effects of what had previously been the extraordinary remedies, and it did not eliminate from the field of administrative law the problem of forms of action.

Though the Acts of 1933 and 1938 did not thus deal squarely with the problem, it has been dealt with by the British Parliament in statutory provisions covering review of certain administrative agencies. The Housing Act of 1930, for example, provides that the legality of slum clearance and compulsory purchase orders made under it may be challenged by a simple application to quash in the High Court. And it is provided that such application is the only method by which judicial review may be obtained, for the use of certiorari, prohibition, or any other legal proceedings whatsoever is expressly precluded.

The Housing Act procedure does effectively substitute a simple petition for review for the extraordinary remedies. But it does so only in the cases covered by it. Though there is a tendency in Britain to re-enact the Housing Act type of statutory review in subsequent laws conferring authority upon the administration,[22] it is still too early to say that such statutory review provisions have completely taken over the field. In the absence of express provision in statutes for the Housing Act type of review—and there are still many such instances—judicial review of administrative action is still obtained essentially through the extraordinary remedies.

Nor should it be assumed that the situation in the United States is any better. Except for Illinois and New Hampshire, which have expressly abolished the extraordinary remedies as a means of reviewing administrative action and have substituted for them a simple uniform

21 Report of the Committee on Ministers' Powers 62 (Cmd. 4060, 1932).

22 For a list of such laws, see Schwartz, Law and the Executive in Britain 209 (1949).

action for review, the extraordinary remedies continue to dominate the procedural aspect of judicial review in our states.[23] And they do so even where the use of the extraordinary remedies has seemingly been repudiated by the legislature. The Civil Practice Act of New York, for example, provides: "The classifications, and writs and orders of certiorari to review, mandamus and prohibition are abolished. The relief heretofore obtained by such writs or orders shall hereafter be obtained as provided in this article."[24] Yet, as the highest court of New York has stated, this provision leaves untouched the technical distinctions involved in the extraordinary remedies. "The nature of the alleged grievance determines, none the less, the form of the hearing before the court to which the aggrieved party is entitled, the questions to be determined at such hearing, and the relief which the court has the power to grant."[25]

In the federal field the extraordinary remedies have not played so large a role, thanks in great part to a decision of the Supreme Court in 1913 which held that certiorari, the most commonly used of the extraordinary remedies in the administrative-law field, could not be employed to obtain review of an administrative order.[26] In its place the federal courts have relied mostly upon the injunction.[27] But injunction is an equitable remedy, and there has been insistence upon satisfaction of the requirements of equity jurisdiction in particular cases. The federal courts have thus avoided the technicalities connected with certiorari, only to find their review power encumbered with those involved in injunctions. And, indeed, it should not be assumed that the elimination of certiorari has meant the disappearance of the extraordinary remedies in the federal field. The complexities of mandamus, habeas corpus, and prohibition still put in their appearance in particular cases to plague those seeking review by the federal courts.

This multiplicity of forms of action appears hardly to be affected by the Federal Administrative Procedure Act. It provides that the form of proceeding to review administrative action shall be, in the absence or inadequacy of statutory provisions, "any applicable form of legal action (including actions for declaratory judgment or writs of prohibi-

23 See Davis, *op. cit. supra* note 17, chap. 17.
24 Section 1283.
25 Newbrand v. Yonkers, 285 N.Y. 164, 174 (1941).
26 Degge v. Hitchcock, 229 U.S. 162 (1913).
27 There has also been a growing use of the declaratory-judgment procedure in the federal courts.

tory or mandatory injunction or habeas corpus)"[28]—which, according to the Senate Committee on the Judiciary, "is an express statutory recognition of the so-called common-law actions as being appropriate and authorized means of judicial review."[29]

The situation just described has been substantially changed for the better with respect to many federal agencies, for the review of whose actions a simplified procedure has been provided by statute. The model here has been the Federal Trade Commission Act of 1914, which states that a person against whom the Commission has issued a cease-and-desist order may obtain review by filing a petition in the appropriate federal court of appeals. This simple procedure for review by petition has been copied in a large number of later statutes.[30] It is very similar to the review procedure provided for under the British Housing Act of 1930, and it is to be hoped that it, too, will tend to take over the field. Until it does so, however, review in the federal courts will continue largely to be dominated by the common-law forms of action.

Forms of Action in France

The common lawyer who has had to struggle constantly with the technicalities of the extraordinary remedies and their present-day equivalents before being able to obtain review of Anglo-American administrative action will doubtless be surprised to learn that such difficulties have never troubled the administrative lawyer in France. The French citizen who wishes to obtain judicial review of an administrative act that adversely affects him files a simple petition with the appropriate administrative court praying that the act in question be annulled or that the administration be ordered to take specified affirmative action if that is the relief requested.

The procedure for obtaining review in the *droit administratif* is, as we shall see, amazingly simple, inexpensive, and free of technicalities in comparison with that which prevails in Anglo-American administrative law. The French citizen who seeks review of administrative action has not had to worry about which among a number of possible forms of action he should choose. He has not had to concern himself with whether his action may be dismissed because another form of action affords an adequate remedy. Nor has he had to trouble himself about

28 Section 10(b).
29 Administrative Procedure Act, Legislative History 212 (1946).
30 For a list, see Davis, *op. cit. supra* note 17, at 726.

whether the action he is challenging comes within such concepts as judicial, nonjudicial, discretionary, or ministerial—not to mention all of these "only softened by a *quasi*."[31] In the *droit administratif*, in fine, there is no need for the litigant to label his pleading at his peril. He need only file with the appropriate administrative court a petition demanding the remedy he seeks. Thus, though the French litigant may, as we have seen, face problems not presented to an Anglo-American in determining whether to bring his case in an administrative court or a law court, once he correctly decides to bring suit in the appropriate administrative court he is not beset with the common-law litigant's procedural difficulties in choosing the proper form of action.

It should not, however, be imagined from this that all actions against the administration are treated alike in France. The French administrative lawyer has been accustomed to make a fundamental distinction that will be seen on reflection to inhere in the very nature of such actions. The private citizen adversely affected by illegal administrative action may, if permitted by the legal system in which he lives, seek either of two objectives in his recourse to the courts. He may be satisfied if the courts will order the administrative act that harms him to be annulled, and he will in effect, as under the common-law writ of certiorari, petition the reviewing court to set aside that act; or he may request affirmative action by the administration. As an example of the latter, the citizen whose property or person has been injured by illegal administrative action may ask the court to order the administration to pay him money damages to make him whole.

When the common lawyer refers to judicial review he normally has in mind only the first type of case. Review to him usually means a proceeding in the courts to have improper administrative action set aside. From the point of view of the citizen affected by administrative action the second type of case would certainly appear to be just as important. But, largely because Anglo-American law has refused in the past to allow the courts to entertain actions for damages against the administration, our administrative-law theory has concentrated almost entirely on the action-to-annul side of judicial control.

In France, as we shall see, there has been no hesitancy about allowing judicial control to extend to ordering the administration to make whole those damaged by its wrongful acts. The *droit administratif* has

[31] The famous phrase of Holmes, J., dissenting, in Springer v. Government of the Philippine Islands, 277 U.S. 189, 210 (1928).

consequently had to deal with both types of cases referred to above. French theorists have, however, treated them separately, as involving two different types of action.

The result has been two essentially different kinds of review actions in the French system. The first is the proceeding to annul an *ultra vires* administrative act (*recours pour excès de pouvoir*). The second is the proceeding to order the administration to take affirmative action, such as the payment of money damages (*recours de pleine juridiction*). Each is begun, as we shall see, by the filing of a petition in the appropriate administrative court, and the procedure is relatively simple and inexpensive. We shall, however, concentrate chiefly on the first, the proceeding to annul; for it is the more analogous to the type of direct review of administrative action on which Anglo-American administrative law has largely focused.

Review Pleadings

Petition—A suit to review administrative action in France is begun with the filing of a petition with the appropriate administrative court. That court has been the Council of State unless jurisdiction in the particular type of case was vested by statute in some other tribunal. Until 1934 only the Council of State could quash improper administrative action. At that time some jurisdiction to annul was vested in the Prefecture Councils. Under the 1953 decree conferring general original jurisdiction upon them,[32] it is the Prefecture Councils (under their new title "Administrative Courts"—*Tribunaux administratifs*) that are now to be competent in the great majority of such cases,[33] subject, of course, to the full appellate jurisdiction of the Council of State.

The one seeking review must file his petition with the clerk of the appropriate administrative court. Such filing is of great importance: it fixes the date at which the action is brought, thus establishing whether the relatively short statute of limitations (which, as we shall note, obtains in most cases) has run so as to bar the action. The petition must contain a summary statement of the facts, the ground on which relief is claimed, the relief sought, and the names and addresses of the parties.

[32] *Supra* p. 49.

[33] Under the September 30, 1953, decree vesting the "Administrative Courts" with the general jurisdiction formerly exercised by the Council of State, the basic procedural rules of the Council are to be applicable to those tribunals. Hence, whatever is said about proceedings in the Council of State is relevant as well to first-instance proceedings that will arise in the "Administrative Courts."

It must be signed by the petitioner or his attorney. If the validity of an administrative decision is attacked, a copy of the decision must be joined.

The petition is addressed to the administrative court from which review is sought or to its president. It must contain a demand for relief—either a request that an allegedly illegal administrative act be annulled or that the administration be ordered to take some affirmative action, such as the payment of money damages to the petitioner to repair an injury caused by an improper administrative act. The Council of State has in the past insisted on this demand for relief. It should not be supposed, however, that the French court has refused to consider a petition that did not state a cause of action in the technical sense in which that term has been used in the common-law world. One could rather say about a petition for review in a French administrative court what Mr. Justice Brandeis urged should be the rule with regard to a complaint in a proceeding in an American administrative agency like the Federal Trade Commission: "The function of the complaint is solely to advise the respondent of the charges made so that he may have due notice and full opportunity for a hearing thereon. . . . All that is requisite . . . is that there be a plain statement of the thing claimed to be wrong so that respondent may be put upon his defense."[34]

In recent years the Council of State has tended to be even more liberal about the matter of the petitioner's pleading. As one of its members states: "The only substantial rule is the filing of the petition with the Clerk of the Council within the period fixed by the statute of limitations."[35] In practice, a petition not containing what is required by the Council's rules is returned to its author for correction by the clerk or by the reporter to whom, as we shall see, the case is assigned.

Answer—Two copies of the petition must be filed with the appropriate administrative court. The petitioner must submit in addition what is known as an amplifying memoir. In this the facts on which the action is based are set out in greater detail, and there is a fuller specification of the legal grounds on which relief is sought and a discussion of the authorities on which the petitioner relies.

One copy of the petition and memoir is then sent to the administrative agency whose action is attacked in the petition. In the majority of cases in the Council of State this act is performed by the Council itself,

[34] Dissenting, in Federal Trade Commission v. Gratz, 253 U.S. 421, 430 (1920).
[35] Odent, Cours de contentieux administratif 225 (1949-50).

without expense to the petitioner. With petitioner's pleadings goes a notice to the agency to return them to the Council "with your observations" within a stated time. The time allowed varies; it is fixed by the reporter to whom the case is assigned. The notice states that failure to answer within the time given will lead to a decision on the petitioner's pleadings alone, though a request may be made for additional time if it is needed.

The administration's answer contains, like the petition, a summary of the facts and of the legal grounds—this time the grounds on which it is contended that the petition should be denied. Joined to the answer are normally (1) an amplifying memoir setting out the administration's side of the case in greater detail and (2) a copy of the administrative dossier, which contains all documents pertinent to the history of the case within the administration. This dossier, as we shall see, often plays a key role in the decision of the French reviewing court.

To examine the pleadings in cases before the Council of State is to be struck by their simplicity in comparison with the usual in proceedings in the law courts, whether in France or in the common-law world. The petition is rarely couched in legal language. In numerous instances petitions are filed without the assistance of counsel and are as unsubtle and straightforward as the statement that the average nonlawyer with a grievance against the State would normally make.

Counsel

Generally speaking, the legal profession in France is more like that of England than like that of the United States. Its members are divided much on the pattern of the barrister-solicitor (*avocat-avoué*) distinction familiar to the common lawyer. "In this system, the solicitor (*avoué*) is the true representative of the parties; he directs the proceeding and does all the acts necessary for that purpose. The barrister (*avocat*) pleads before the court or is consulted in writing. There is thus a sort of division of labor, traditional in France, between preparing a case and pleading it."[36]

The barrister-solicitor distinction does not, however, prevail in cases before the Council of State and the Court of Cassation. Before these, representation of the parties is by an attorney of the bar of the Council of State and Court of Cassation (*avocat au Conseil d'État et à la Cour*

[36] Morel, Traité élémentaire de procédure civile 164 (2d ed., 1949).

de Cassation),[37] who exercises the functions of both barrister and solicitor, much as an attorney does in the American system. To become a member of the bar of the two highest courts in France one must have been an ordinary member of the bar (*avocat*) for at least three years and be specially admitted before the Council of State and Court of Cassation.

In this respect, the bar of the two highest courts in France can be compared to that before the Supreme Court of the United States. There is, however, a fundamental difference. Membership in the bar of the French supreme courts is very rigorously restricted by law, and it consists of only sixty attorneys. This number was fixed by a royal ordinance of 1817 under which the bar of the two French courts is still largely organized. In practice this restriction has meant that the bar of the Council of State and Court of Cassation is a veritable closed guild. Newcomers can gain admittance to it only by, in effect, purchasing the place of a present member—a usage that strikes the outside observer as an anomalous survival from the age when even judges of the French courts had a vested interest in their positions, which could be inherited and sold like ordinary property. It should be noted, though, that it is an anomaly widespread in the French system, for it also applies to the solicitors (*avoués*) who represent parties before the French law courts. To become a solicitor in France one must in practice, besides passing a professional examination, purchase the position of an established solicitor.

To the American observer the solicitor in France appears to be in an enviable position wholly unlike that enjoyed by members of the legal profession in this country. Not only is he a member of what is substantially a closed guild—an advantage that in effect limits the professional competition encountered—but also, under French law, his services are obligatory in every case before the law courts. The parties in France cannot represent themselves. They must be represented in every case by a solicitor.

The position of members of the bar of the Council of State and Court of Cassation would seem to be even more advantageous. They belong to a closed guild whose limited number was fixed almost a century and a half ago when the *droit administratif* was in its very beginnings. The great increase in litigation in the past hundred years has not

37 Members of the bar of the two highest courts in France also represent parties before the Court of Conflicts.

led to any increase in their number. Moreover they fulfill the dual functions of both solicitor and barrister, so that there is no need to divide the fees received in any given case.

Article 41 of the ordinance of July 31, 1945, provides that a petition filed with the Council of State must be signed by a member of the Council's bar. This requirement means that the services of a member of that bar are obligatory in cases before the Council, as those of the ordinary solicitor are in other cases. One bringing an action in the Council of State must, in principle, be represented by a member of that tribunal's bar.

There is, however, a very important exception to this principle. If the petition filed seeks only to have administrative action annulled, the services of an attorney are not obligatory. In such cases the petitioner can appear for himself, just as he can, generally speaking, in most cases before courts in the United States.[38]

In this country the right to appear personally rather than through counsel is availed of in only a very small minority of cases. Litigants normally realize that the expense involved in being represented by professional counsel is a necessary one if they are to present their cases adequately—especially in the field of administrative law, where the opposite party is the administration with its veritable horde of attorneys. In France the right to appear without counsel in suits to annul administrative action is made use of much more frequently. The difference is largely due to the fact that the procedure before the French administrative courts is inquisitorial rather than, as in Anglo-American courts, adversary. Under the French procedure, as we shall see, the court itself plays an active part in developing the case, and there is much less scope for the attorney, whose role is reduced to an almost mechanical one. Thus the litigant who comes into the Council of State without counsel is not in the almost hopeless position of his counterpart in the common-law world. If his case is not presented adequately because of his lack of proficiency in pleading, the judge himself will seek to correct his errors.

[38] Article 5 of the decree of September 30, 1953, making the "Administrative Courts" (the former Prefecture Councils) the general courts of first instance, provides that cases before them must be brought through a member of the bar of the Council of State, an ordinary member of the bar, or a local solicitor. But, as is the case with the Council of State, the services of counsel are not to be obligatory for the bringing of actions to annul.

Cost of Litigation

The French citizen's right to have administrative action annulled without retaining counsel means that French administrative law has been able largely to solve a problem still very acute in the common-law world: the cost of litigation. Undeniably, the high cost of justice is one of the principal reasons why the Anglo-American courts are unable to play so effective a role as they might in the field of administrative law. The cost of going to law, though not so formidable in this country as in Britain—where the old adage still holds that the courts are "open to all, like the Ritz Hotel"—is here, too, a strong deterrent to the average citizen with a grievance, especially when the other party is the administration, with its well-nigh limitless resources.

The common lawyer who looks at the cost of litigation in the French administrative courts will find it difficult to persist in the belief, exceedingly common in the legal profession, that great expense is inherent in judicial justice. The French citizen seeking to have administrative action annulled is put to expense no more than nominal by Anglo-American standards. If he is not represented by counsel and his action succeeds, his total costs amount to about *one dollar*. If his petition to annul is denied, his expenses amount to a little less than *ten dollars*. Even though these figures must be doubled or tripled to express their real meaning to a Frenchman, whose income is only about one third that of the average American, they still represent amounts inconsequential for one seeking justice.

The result is that access to the Council of State has been available on the widest scale to all French citizens. In the common-law world the cost of litigation has meant the practical preclusion of judicial review of administration for those lacking financial resources. A look at the leading Anglo-American administrative-law cases quickly proves this point. For every case involving an indigent alien against whom a deportation order has been issued there are ten involving large corporations with the financial means to challenge illegal administrative action in the courts. In the common-law world the administration is all too often the only forum practically available to anyone adversely affected by its action. Even if review by the courts is theoretically available, the cost of courtroom litigation will normally deter the citizen from availing himself of the remedy.

Compare this with the situation under the *droit administratif*. Expense is no deterrent to the French citizen who seeks to have *ultra vires* administrative action set aside. He knows that at trifling cost he can bring in the appropriate administrative court an action to annul. And the records of cases in the Council of State demonstrate that most such actions have, in fact, been brought by ordinary citizens whose grievances were financially too trifling to justify the burden of expense connected with most litigation.

It should not be forgotten that in the field of administrative law the interest of the individual who brings the suit to annul improper administrative action is not the only interest vindicated by a favorable decision. The entire community has a vital concern in ensuring that illegal action of the administration shall not go untouched. If one private citizen has a grievance against another, his failure to take appropriate legal action because of his dread of the cost leaves no one but him victimized. But if his grievance is against the administration, whatever deters him from seeking judicial review has a much wider effect. An illegal administrative act has been left unchallenged, and the interest of society in enforcing unvarying conformity to the rule of law is left unvindicated.

A common lawyer solicitous for the improvement of his system of administrative law must not hesitate in his efforts to eliminate most of the expense of securing justice against the administration in Anglo-American courts. He must first seek to secure the establishment of a uniform review procedure by the filing of a simple petition of the type already discussed. And then he must turn his attention to the far more difficult problem of the costs not chargeable to cumbersome procedural technicalities: primarily the cost of retaining counsel. The *droit administratif* shows that more headway can be made on both problems than most common lawyers think possible.

The problem of the cost of administrative-law litigation will not be solved merely by enlarged programs of legal aid such as are being urged at present by the organized bar in the common-law world, however valuable these may be in coping with many of its aspects. Legal aid concerns the indigent litigant. It does not touch the case of the solvent citizen who, harmed by illegal administrative action, feels that his injury is not great enough to warrant the expense of judicial review. For the few Pyms and Hampdens that may emerge, ready to assume any burden to assert the principle of legality, there is a whole host of ordinary men willing to forgo that assertion if the cost is too great.

It is not suggested that the common-law world adopt on this point the solution of the *droit administratif*. The French system has, in fact, solved the problem of the cost of administrative-law litigation by making it so low that the administrative-court system has become the veritable forum for all citizens with legal grievances against the administration, no matter how small they may be measured financially. But the French method, under which actions to annul administrative action can be brought successfully even though the petitioner be not represented by counsel, is practicable only because the procedure in the French administrative courts is inquisitorial rather than adversary. Such procedure is wholly foreign to common-law concepts, and for an Anglo-American to urge its adoption in his own system is almost unthinkable. It is only where the judge himself plays an active part in developing both sides of the case, as in the French system, that the litigant will avail himself of the right to come into court without counsel. In the common-law world, where the judge decides solely on the basis of the case as developed by the parties, to appear without counsel is to risk almost certain loss of one's case.

What is needed in the Anglo-American system is an attempt to achieve the virtues of the French review system without importing bodily the inquisitorial procedure on which it rests. Something in this direction could be done by the establishment in the common-law world of an Office of Public Prosecutor in administrative-law cases. A citizen adversely affected by administrative action he holds to be illegal would file a petition with this Office. It would look into his case and, finding it meritorious, would initiate suit to have the action annulled. The proposal, in other words, is to place the prosecution of cases against the administration in the hands of a public official, just as their defense is now in the hands of public officials.

The State has as great an interest in ensuring administrative observance of the principle of legality as it has in ensuring the enforcement of the criminal law. And, just as the State intervenes actively in criminal-law enforcement, so it should take affirmative steps when complaint is made of illegal administrative action. The Public Prosecutor in administrative-law cases should be an independent public officer; his compensation should be ample; he must be a competent lawyer of high repute; he should have the necessary assistants and investigators; he should be as powerful and have the same official standing as the district attorney.[39] An analogy in this country is the public

[39] Compare Goldman, The Public Defender 6 (1919).

defender appointed in a certain number of jurisdictions for criminal cases.

In criminal law it is the State that prosecutes, and a public defender has to be provided to equalize the position of the private individual who cannot employ counsel. In administrative law it is the State that defends: should it not also appoint a public prosecutor to equalize the position of the individual injured by administrative action?

The Office of Public Prosecutor in the common-law world would perform part of the role undertaken in the French system by the court itself; that is, the active development of the plaintiff's case. For this role the Prosecutor would have to be given a discretion like that vested in a district attorney to determine whether a sufficient case of administrative illegality existed to warrant his bringing an action. His position would be essentially that of legal watchdog of the administration, though, it should be noted, he would be able to act only on complaint of one adversely affected by its action. Nor would his role be exclusive. Individuals who chose to bring on their own motion suits to annul administrative action would still be able to do so.

Statute of Limitations

Article 49 of the Ordinance of July 31, 1945, under which the Council of State is today set up, provides: "Unless there is a statutory provision to the contrary, the petition in the Council of State against the decision of an authority or court subject to its control must be filed within two months from the date of such decision." Since, under the 1953 decree vesting them with general original jurisdiction, a similar time limit is to apply to actions in the "Administrative Courts" (as the Prefecture Councils are now to be termed), there is in the French system, for cases involving actions to annul illegal administrative action, a uniform two-month statute of limitations.

The comparative shortness of the period is explainable by the upsetting effect on administration of judicial invalidation of administrative action that has been in effect for some time. The Council of State "has a very clear understanding of the confusion caused within the administration by judicial decisions that overturn a settled legal status. This consideration does not lead the Council to renounce its task of controlling the legality of administrative action, but it does feel that at the end of the short period the stability of administration should be strictly guaranteed."[40]

[40] Odent, *op. cit. supra* note 35, at 209.

The problem of administrative stability with which the short statute of limitations in France tries to deal is one that exists likewise in the common-law world. "The confusion which would arise if [an administrative] scheme were suddenly to be ruled illegal after it had been in operation for any length of time can readily be appreciated," asserts a British report. "In fact it would be impracticable to set up a Board with extensive powers of holding property, incurring liabilities, and, perhaps, of trading if the courts could hold at any time that the scheme and, indeed, the very existence of the Board had been a nullity from the start."[41]

The administrator feels, it is true, that the only way to achieve real stability is to vest his decision with conclusive finality. To his mind, even judicial review with a strict time limit introduces a harmful uncertainty. "If you take a Town Planning Scheme or a Slum Clearance Scheme, and you say that the Order comes into force unless it is challenged within so many days or weeks or whatever it is, that means that the Scheme will be held up for that period, and of course we have constant criticisms and complaints of the time which it takes to carry out Slum Clearance Schemes. For years we have been trying to expedite that procedure. It is difficult, and the time spent is long, and one hesitates to recommend something which would have the effect of adding X days to that time."[42] Such an objection clearly goes too far: it would bar all review by the courts. Administrative convenience must give way, at least for a limited period, to the need for judicial control. As a member of the British Committee on Ministers' Powers pointedly remarks: "If Utopia is worth having, it is worth waiting for, is it not?"[43]

The French solution, of making suits to annul administrative action available on the widest possible basis but at the same time providing that they must be brought within a two-month period, represents a necessary compromise between the administrative desire for finality and the individual interest in the right of unbounded access to the courts. It may be urged that a two-month time limit will in many cases prove too short. It should be noted, however, that under the British

[41] Report of the Ministry of Agriculture on the Agricultural Marketing Act, 1931, p. 17, quoted in Willis, The Parliamentary Powers of English Government Departments, 104 n. 2 (1933).

[42] Robinson, in Committee on Ministers' Powers, Minutes of Evidence 134 (1932).

[43] Fisher, *id.* at 113.

Housing Act of 1930, which, as we have noticed, has become the model for statutory review provisions in Britain, only six weeks are allowed for the bringing of review actions. And a relatively short period is also provided under many American statutory provisions for review. In these cases the need for administrative stability may well cause the individual interest in unlimited recourse to the courts to give way, after being fully protected for the short statutory period. A system such as the French, under which judicial review of administrative action is available on the widest possible basis but which fixes a short time limit for review actions, leaves open to the public, as Lord Justice Scott has expressed it, "the right of saying 'the Minister has exceeded the powers that Parliament intended him to have,' while on the other hand . . . [it makes] it necessary for the public affected to be reasonably expeditious in bringing their grievances before the Court."[44]

[44] *Id.* at 134.

Chapter Six

REVIEW PROCEDURE

Every petition filed with the clerk of the judicial section of the Council of State receives an identification number. These numbers continued without interruption from August 1, 1806, when the judicial section of the Council first began to function, until 1900, when petition No. 100,000 was filed. Then a second series of 100,000 was begun, which in turn lasted until 1927. Petition No. 100,000 of a third series was filed on November 12, 1948. A fourth series instituted on that day is now current.

The Council of State is thus well on the way toward dealing with its 400,000th petition—a number that shows how that tribunal has come to be regarded by Frenchmen as their forum for legal grievances against the administration. It is interesting to note in the figures how the number of petitions has grown by geometric progression. The judicial section of the Council was in existence ninety-four years before petition No. 100,000 was filed. It took only twenty-seven years before petition No. 100,000 of the second series was reached, and only twenty-one years for the third series of 100,000 to run its course. It is this constant growth in the case load that made it impossible for the Council to decide cases without a substantial time lag and rendered the reallocation of much of its original jurisdiction imperative if it was to keep abreast of its work.

Each petition, after receiving its identification number, is referred by the president of the judicial section to an appropriate subsection. We have already seen that the judicial section is divided into nine subsections, which are in most cases the organs of decision. They are designated by number. The first four are preparatory organs that work on cases until they are ready for judgment. The cases are then decided by two of these subsections combined. The last five subsections have the authority to decide cases by themselves, and they deal exclusively with certain less important, though numerous, types of cases.

The subsection to which a petition is referred is not at all like the normal judicial organ with which the common lawyer is familiar. With us the court before which a case is brought for judgment does not play a very active part in developing the case. The issues are defined by the parties, and the decision of the court is based solely on materials that the parties present. If one of them has been deficient in his pleadings or presentation, the court will not ordinarily seek to aid him. Above all, with us, the key part of any case is the public trial. Here, especially, the essentially adversary nature of our justice is emphasized. Everything that has gone before—the pleadings and pretrial incidents—are seen to be only preparations for the public battle. And it is largely a trial by verbal battle, with the court restricted to the role of referee between the parties and their champions.

In the French administrative-court system the decision of a case follows a wholly different pattern. To the common lawyer courtroom procedure is synonymous with an oral adversary trial, and that whether or not the administration happens to be involved in the case. In the French tribunals the procedure is essentially written and inquisitorial. Both aspects of French administrative-law procedure are so different from those to which the common lawyer is accustomed that it is worth while to emphasize them in some detail.

Inquisitorial Procedure

Largely for historical reasons, the procedure in the French administrative courts has always been, like procedure in the criminal courts in the civil-law world, inquisitorial rather than adversary. In civil cases between two private citizens the civil lawyer has thought it unnecessary for the judge to be more than an inactive referee between the parties. The State has no interest in such cases, except as it provides an impartial tribunal to which the parties can resort for justice. In criminal proceedings, on the other hand, the State has been seen to have a more direct interest, for due enforcement of the criminal law is of clear concern to the community. In criminal cases, therefore, civil-law countries have tended to adopt inquisitorial procedure, with the judge playing an active part in the development of the case. But the considerations that make the State assume a more positive role in criminal cases exist as well in cases involving questions of administrative law. Here, too, society as a whole has a direct interest in ensuring observance by the administration of the principle of legality. It is not surprising, therefore, that procedure in the administrative courts in France has come to be patterned on the inquisitorial type that prevails in the French criminal courts.

The outstanding contrast of inquisitorial procedure as compared with the adversary type familiar to the common lawyer is the assumption by the judge of an active role. His job is not solely that of an umpire: he has a duty actively to inquire into the law and the facts, and his inquiry is not limited to materials presented by the parties. In practice this latitude means that there must be an investigatory stage in which the facts and the legal issues are inquired into by the court. Only after this preparatory stage in which the affair is actively investigated by a member of the court is it actually submitted for argument and decision.

In the Council of State the investigatory work on cases is normally assigned to the junior members of the Council—the auditors and the *maîtres des requêtes*. After a petition has been referred to the appropriate subsection of the Council, it is assigned by the subsection's president to a reporter, usually an auditor or a *maître des requêtes*. "The reporter examines the petition and the challenged decision and, bearing in mind the way the case is presented, determines the preparatory measures that seem to him necessary to throw light upon the matter, to notify the interested parties and permit them to present their views."[1]

As soon as the case is assigned to the reporter, his is the primary responsibility for preparing it for the stage of decision. It is henceforth his case, and in fact the folder in which the record is contained is now labeled with his name and kept at his disposal with other cases assigned to him, in a room reserved for the purpose. The record itself is largely worked up through his efforts. When he first receives the case the record contains the petition and the answer. To the answer is often joined the administrative dossier. It is the reporter's job to go over this material and determine, first of all, whether the record contains all the

[1] Odent, Cours de contentieux administratif 228 (1949-50).

Since, under the 1953 decree vesting them with general original jurisdiction (*supra* p. 49), the basic procedural rules followed by the Council of State are to be applicable to review actions in the "Administrative Courts" (*Tribunaux administratifs*), as the Prefecture Councils are to be called, whatever is said about Council of State procedure is relevant as well to proceedings in the latter tribunals. It is, therefore, felt to be unnecessary to treat their procedure separately in this chapter.

information necessary to decide the case. If he feels that some vital information is lacking, it is his responsibility to see that it is forthcoming.

It should be emphasized that the reporter, in performing this task, is not limited by anything like the common-law world's restrictions on judicial investigatory power. He may get at the relevant materials in any way he deems fit. He may, and usually does, conduct personal ex parte investigations for the purpose. The reporter will normally first seek information from the parties. If the administrative dossier appears to lack some necessary papers, he will communicate with the defendant agency and request it to explain the omission. Nor need his communication follow any formal pattern. A letter, a telephone call, a personal visit—all ex parte—are admissible means.

Information from the parties alone may often not suffice. The reporter may then communicate with others who appear to be informed. Administrative agencies other than the one whose act is challenged by the petition will very often be consulted. Thus, in requisition cases the reporter frequently seeks the views of the Ministry of Justice, which is deemed to have a general interest in all matters affecting private property or personal liberty. But whether there shall be such consultation and what form it shall take depend entirely on the reporter.

From this analysis of the reporter's role it can be seen that the Anglo-American concept of exclusiveness of the record, and cases like *Errington v. Minister of Health*[2] and the second *Morgan* case,[3] can have no application to the decision process within the French Council of State. Not only is the reporter not limited to the record as made by the parties, but it is his duty actively to complete that record, and he may do so by ex parte consultation or in any other way he sees fit. His role is, indeed, in many ways more that of a prosecutor than of a judge in the Anglo-American sense. Like the prosecutor, he has the task of securing, by private investigation if need be, the information necessary for the presentation of the case. The analogy should not, however, be carried too far. The reporter may have some of the prosecutor's freedom of action, but he does not have his biased outlook. His task is to develop both sides of the case, not merely to sustain a prosecution. Thus he approaches the case as a judge, not caring which

[2] [1935] 1 K.B. 249.

[3] Morgan v. United States, 304 U.S. 1 (1938). It should be noted that the *Errington* and *Morgan* cases concerned organs of the active administration, rather than a court like the French Council of State.

side will prevail, but seeking only to prepare the case for decision by the Council of State in a manner that will ensure a just decision.

The reporter, when he feels that the case has been sufficiently investigated, will prepare a report on it. His report sets forth the issues of law and of fact in the case, examines their legal aspects, and recommends a decision, with supporting reasons. The record then goes back to the clerk of the judicial section of the Council. When its turn arrives it comes before a session of the subsection to which the reporter belongs. Here he discusses his report, and especially his recommended decision. The various members present their views on the matter, which most of them now hear formally for the first time. After this meeting the decision advocated by the reporter may be adopted by the subsection as its recommended decision, with any changes that it has seen fit to make. The entire record, including the report and the tentative decision, is now transmitted to a member of the Council known as the government commissioner. His role is even more important than that of the reporter and will have to be gone into more fully. But first a word must be said about the almost exclusively written form of French administrative-court procedure.

Written Procedure

To the common lawyer the decision of a case by a court means decision after an oral adversary hearing before the judge, in which both parties present their evidence and arguments. It is, indeed, difficult for him to think of courtroom procedure as other than oral. A nonoral system of judicial procedure is unacceptable to one nurtured in Anglo-American traditions. In such a system, in his view, "right of access to courts . . . is reduced to the right to file one's claim—to drop it, so to speak, into the governmental slot. This manner of dealing with the claims of persons who assert injury or threatened injury is . . . foreign to our system of law."[4]

From the Anglo-American point of view the French administrative courts do admittedly present something of the aspect of judicial slot machines. The French citizen aggrieved by improper administrative action drops his petition and amplifying memoir into the proper governmental slot and then sits back to await the decision. The inquisitorial

[4] WJR v. Federal Communications Commission, 174 F. 2d 226, 236 (App. D.C. 1948).

procedure followed enables his case to be decided even if he does not play an active role.

In such a case the French court will reach its decision without hearing evidence and arguments at an oral hearing of the type preliminary to judicial decision in the common-law world. True, a public hearing is held by the court before it decides a case. But this, as we shall see, is not at all like the hearing before Anglo-American courts. Its main purpose is to enable the government commissioner to present his conclusions. The parties are limited in their right of oral argument, and in fact the right to make an oral statement at the hearing is not availed of in most cases.

The procedure in the French administrative courts is, then, almost entirely written. The case is normally decided solely on the pleadings and the memoirs in support submitted by the parties, plus any materials that the reporter may, on his own motion, have included in the record.

One familiar with Anglo-American judicial techniques will immediately wonder how the evidence on both sides can be properly presented to the court under a procedure almost exclusively written. To the common lawyer the resolution of disputed issues of fact requires the judge personally to hear the testimony of witnesses and to seek the true facts from a consideration of the testimony heard. How, it will be asked, can the administrative courts decide cases in which the facts are disputed if they do not hear the oral testimony of those who have witnessed the facts?

This question, it must be admitted, cannot be answered adequately by a common lawyer, even one who has spent many months in analyzing the work of the French tribunals. He is too prone to approach the procedure of a body like the Council of State with the strong bias in favor of oral procedure derived from training in his own system.

Various sources of evidence are open to the reporter to whom a case is assigned in the Council of State. In the first place, there is the administrative dossier itself. This, we have noted, is normally joined to the answer to the petition filed by the administrative agency whose action is challenged. This dossier is in effect the administrative file or record of the case; it contains the materials on which the agency concerned has acted—the relevant correspondence, investigators' reports, inter- and intra-agency instructions and memoranda, statements of what occurred at any administrative hearings that may have been held, and other documents of the sort. This dossier is shown to the petitioner, and he is asked for his comments. If he contends that a vital document is missing, the reporter will seek to obtain it from the agency concerned.

The use of the administrative dossier as a primary source of evidence does not appear to an outside observer to be the best way to obtain an unbiased view of the case. To rely for decision on the administrative record where there is no enforceable formal requirement[5] that the record contain all relevant materials, is to risk placing the private citizen at a serious disadvantage in his at best unequal contest with the administration. There are, however, other sources of information that may enable the Council of State to obtain a more complete picture.

Though the Council does not itself hear the testimony of witnesses,[6] it will receive the deposition of anyone who can shed light on a case. In a proceeding to annul an administrative order requisitioning the petitioner's apartment, for example, he will normally submit with his pleadings depositions of persons who, knowing him, state that the apartment is needed for his own personal use; for in that situation requisition orders may not be issued. The parties may also submit any additional documentary evidence that they deem relevant. In one case examined the petitioner sought the setting aside of a prefectoral order directing him to demolish his dam because it caused flooding in the adjoining area. He joined to his petition letters from expert engineers upholding his position. In support of the prefect, however, there were submitted a map and photographs of the area that clearly showed the flooding. The petitioner not being able to explain away this evidence, the Council had no difficulty in upholding the challenged administrative order.

Where the facts are particularly difficult to determine the Council of State may order what is known as an *expertise*. This is the general means by which expert evidence is received in the French courts when it may help clarify a disputed issue of fact. Each French court, including the Council of State, has its own list of experts in particular professional fields. When an *expertise* is ordered each party chooses one

5 Such as is contained, for example, in section 7(d) of the Federal Administrative Procedure Act.

6 The Prefecture Councils—now to be the "Administrative Courts"—may order what is known as an inquest, under which oral testimony is received before one of their members. Utilization of the inquest procedure has, however, been relatively rare by these tribunals.

expert from the list, and a third is chosen by the court.[7] These experts may do anything that they feel will aid them in getting at the facts. They may even examine witnesses and receive other forms of evidence. They then submit a report stating to the judge their views of the disputed facts. This report is not binding, but it is ordinarily given great weight.

The Government Commissioner

After a case is reported on and the recommended decision of the reporter examined by his subsection the record is transmitted to the government commissioner. This official plays a cardinal role in the decision process of the French administrative courts. It is his job to go over the record as it has been worked up thus far and to determine on his independent judgment how the case should be decided. He will state his conclusions for the benefit of the court at the public hearing held prior to decision.

There are twelve government commissioners in the judicial section of the Council of State. They are commonly appointed from among the *maîtres des requêtes*, from the point of view of seniority the intermediate echelon in the Council. They are so few that the burden on them is very great, for they must state their conclusions in every case decided by the Council.

It has been stated that in the Council of State the office of government commissioner is second in importance only to that of the president of the judicial section.[8] To measure the significance that his work has for the French administrative lawyer one must realize that his is, in effect, the only reasoned decision publicly rendered by the Council. There is, indeed, the recommended decision by the reporter, but that is not made known to the public. And the final decision by the judicial section of the Council itself is, as we shall see, hardly an adequate reasoned decision by Anglo-American judicial standards.

The statement by the government commissioner is the closest analogy in the *droit administratif* to the reasoned decisions customarily rendered by Anglo-American judges. In his conclusions at the public hearing he goes fully into the legal and factual issues. "He sets forth

[7] The relevant court may, in particular cases, decide that the *expertise* is to be conducted by only one expert chosen by it.

[8] Hamson, "Rule of Law in France: II. Form and Function of the Conseil d'État," The Times (London), February 21, 1951, p. 5.

the entire case; he analyzes and criticizes all the possible grounds of decision, he does the same for all the legal rules that may be applicable; very often he indicates the direction followed by the case law, the stages already reached by it, and a foreshadowing of the stages yet to come. Finally, he recommends that the petition be granted or denied. All this he does orally, without ever filing written conclusions. All this he does in his own name, without having to follow the advice of the subsection . . . or of any hierarchical superior."[9]

Though he is still called the government commissioner, that name is today a pure misnomer, for he does not in any way represent the government in cases before the Council of State. "The *commissaire* represents nothing if not the law itself; he is the embodied conscience of the court. It is his business to see that every relevant consideration, and in particular every material previous decision, is before the court. It is his duty to appraise those decisions, and if necessary to declare his dissent from them."[10]

To anyone interested in the *droit administratif* the conclusions of the government commissioner are at least as important as the decision of the Council of State itself. For his conclusions alone give a full public picture of the law and the facts in cases decided by the Council. "In important cases the *commissaire's* arguments are reported in full, and when accepted by the court they form perhaps the chief authorities of the Conseil's jurisprudence."[11] In the great majority of cases the government commissioner's recommended decisions are followed by the Council. They are treated with almost as much respect as if they were part of the Council's decision, especially if the commissioner has been able to persuade the Council to embark on a new course of jurisprudence. His reasoning is then of vital importance to one who seeks to understand the significance and consequences of the skeleton-type decision that is normally rendered by the Council.

The Hearing

The seat of the Council of State is the Royal Palace, one of the celebrated monuments of Paris. Constructed for Cardinal Richelieu in 1629, it was later used as a residence by members of the Orléans branch

9 Sauvel, "Les Origines des commissaires de gouvernement auprès du Conseil d'État statuant au contentieux" Revue du Droit Public 5 (1949).

10 Hamson, *loc. cit. supra* note 8.

11 *Ibid.*

of the royal family. The building is divided into two parts, one used by the four administrative sections of the Council of State, the other by its judicial section. In the center is the Council's library, in which the major part of that tribunal's judicial business is prepared.

Also in the Council building are various meeting and hearing rooms. Article 66 of the Ordinance of July 31, 1945, under which the Council operates today, provides for the holding of a public hearing in every case before decision by the judicial section. Such hearings are held in a large room designated as the public-hearing room. (It is elaborately decorated, as befits a chamber in a former royal residence, with paintings and other works of art.) Most of it is occupied by a large horseshoe-shaped bench. Around this are normally about ten members of the Council. The president of the judicial section sits in the center, the other members at either side in decreasing order of seniority. At the end of the room opposite the president is a bench for counsel, and beyond is a relatively small space for the public.

It should be emphasized that the hearing held before decision by the judicial section is not at all similar to that commonly held in advance of judicial decision in the common-law world. "The English observer will misapprehend the judicial methods of the Conseil if he considers only the public hearing."[12] That hearing is nothing like the detailed presentation of evidence and arguments in Anglo-American courts. Largely formal, it is intended primarily as a means of enabling the government commissioner to present his public conclusions. A score of cases may be heard in one afternoon, for it is the rare case that takes as much as half an hour.

The hearing of a case is begun by the calling of its name by the clerk of the judicial section.[13] The reporter then reads, usually almost inaudibly, what is essentially a summary of the procedure in the case thus far. It is then that counsel for the parties have their opportunity to make an oral statement. One who visits the Council for the first time cannot help being impressed by the formidable appearance of counsel in the stately robes that distinguish members of the bar in France, as they sit at their bench facing the court, whose members are in ordinary street clothes. The visitor is therefore somewhat taken aback when counsel, asked for their observations after the reporter's

[12] *Ibid.*

[13] The hearing calendar is prepared in advance, largely by the government commissioners, and posted at the entrance to the office of the clerk of the judicial section.

remarks, merely rise one after another, bow, and sit meekly down without saying anything beyond the formal statement that they refer the Council to their written pleadings.

The observer realizes after he has visited several hearings that this is the normal order of things in the Council of State. Even if counsel is retained in a case, he usually does not take advantage of his opportunity to argue orally. Oral statements are sometimes made by counsel, but even they are tame by Anglo-American standards of advocacy. Under the Council's rules an attorney may not raise in his oral argument any point not referred to in his written memoirs. Partly this and partly the traditional emphasis on exclusively written procedure make counsel generally feel that there is little to gain from an oral argument.

The stage is now set for the concluding part of the hearing, the statement by the government commissioner of his conclusions. He is seated behind a podium at one side of the horseshoe-shaped bench at which members of the Council sit. After counsel have had their opportunity to make their oral statement the government commissioner rises and places his notes on the podium. "Gentlemen," he begins, in a deliberate voice, looking at the other members of the court. His conclusions, which ordinarily take about ten minutes, end with his recommendation that, for the reasons he has just stated, the petition be granted or denied. His conclusions stated, he sits down, and the hearing on that case is at an end.

The Decision

After all the cases on the calendar for the given session have been heard in the manner just described, the public is barred from the hearing room and there is held what is known as a deliberative session. Each case heard is gone over in some detail by the members of the Council. The reporter reads the recommended decision that he has prepared. If it differs from that suggested by the government commissioner, the latter presents his point of view.[14] Other members may raise questions and state opinions. The discussion in close cases may, indeed, become pretty heated. Eventually a decision is reached by a majority vote.

It should be noted that before the actual decision the case has already been gone over three times by members of the judicial section. We can take as an example the average case, decided by two of the

14 The government commissioner does not, however, participate in the actual vote on the decision.

first four subsections combined. First it is examined by the reporter. His report is debated in the subsection of which he is a member. The entire matter is then examined afresh by the government commissioner. Only after his examination does the case come for judgment before the two subsections combined. In the deciding organ itself half of the judges have come to a definite conclusion as a result of considering in their subsection the reporter's recommendations. The other half formally hears the details of the case for the first time at the public hearing. "The Conseil attaches great importance to a matter being decided partly by persons who have already debated it and partly by persons who come to it with a fresh mind, prepared if necessary to resolve a difference between colleagues."[15]

The decisions rendered by the judicial section of the Council of State are required by law[16] to be read in public. Because of the number of cases decided at any one session, in actual practice the president of the judicial section merely makes a statement at the beginning of a later hearing session that the decisions disposed of in the earlier session are on file with the clerk's office and may on request be examined.

The decisions themselves are not at all like those that the common lawyer expects from a court. In the first place, there is only the one decision rendered in the name of the Council. No matter how close the question may be, how heated the discussion, or how small the majority, there is only the one expression of opinion by the court. Any dissenting members must hold their peace. There is nothing in the *droit administratif* like the dissenting opinion that plays so important a role in the jurisprudence of Anglo-American courts.

Nor are the decisions reasoned ones in the sense of those rendered by Anglo-American courts. The Council's decisions contain nothing like the detailed exposition of the facts and legal issues that the common lawyer has come to expect from his courts. There is merely a statement of the names of the parties, the briefest description of the administrative act attacked, the relief sought, citation of the relevant statutes, a bare statement of the legal considerations involved, and then the Council's disposition of the case. The whole decision, and especially the legal reasons that motivated it, may occupy three short paragraphs. It is the exceptional Council of State decision that occupies as much as two printed pages.

[15] Hamson, *loc. cit supra* note 8.
[16] Ordinance of July 31, 1945, article 68.

The skeleton pattern of the decisions being perhaps best gathered from an example, the Council's decision in an important case decided in 1944[17] is supplied in Appendix B.[18] In that case, which will be discussed in detail at a later point,[19] the Council held that one who is adversely affected in his individual property rights by an administrative decision must be afforded an opportunity to be heard before the decision can be made. In so doing it altered the whole course of the previous case law in the *droit administratif*, for the French cases had uniformly refused to impose any procedural requirements on the administration in the absence of express legislative provision. The Council's decision was thus one of the most important it had ever delivered. In effect it imported into the *droit administratif* something very much like the doctrine of due process or, more accurately, the British doctrine of "natural justice."

But anyone who reads the Council's decision alone will look in vain for the reasons that prompted such a fundamental change in the Council's jurisprudence. All that the decision states on this point is that "in consideration of the significance that the revocation of the permit carried in these circumstances and of the gravity of that penalty, such a measure could not be taken legally without [petitioner's] having been given an opportunity to be heard." This much, it is submitted, does not tell the student of French administrative law a great deal; yet it is all that the Council's skeleton decision gives us.

One who seeks the equivalent of a reasoned decision in the Anglo-American sense must look instead to the conclusions of the government commissioner. To enable the necessary comparison to be made, these conclusions are contained in Appendix B, just after the Council's decision.[20] In reading them the common lawyer will feel that he is on familiar ground. He will find a detailed discussion of the facts and legal issues, analysis of the case law, and extension of the principles of the precedent cases by analogy, so that ultimately the new principle of "no adverse effect on individual rights without opportunity to be heard" is formulated as a logical consequence.

It cannot be denied that the skeleton-type decision rendered by the Council of State tends to make difficulties for the student of the *droit administratif*. If the conclusions of the government commissioner are

17 Dame veuve Trompier-Gravier, May 5, 1944.
18 *Infra* p. 342.
19 *Infra* pp. 208-9.
20 *Infra* p. 342.

not published, it is often not easy to divine the meaning of a decision of the French tribunal. The common lawyer who tends to criticize the overexpansiveness of the judges in his courts should bear this in mind. The American administrative lawyer is naturally disturbed when the five Justices of the United States Supreme Court who concur in an important administrative-law decision[21] deliver a separate opinion each, and another is rendered for the three dissenting Justices. "What is the rule of the case?" is the natural query of the common lawyer after an important decision. It must be admitted that it cannot be answered with full certainty after such a Supreme Court decision. But let the Anglo-American who finds fault with the prolixity of his judges place himself in the situation of a student of the jurisprudence of the French Council of State. For that tribunal gives little more in its decisions than a bare statement of the rule of the case to enlighten those affected by its work.

The decisions of the Council of State themselves are published, together with those of the Court of Conflicts, in an official report known as the Report of the Decisions of the Judicial Section of the Council of State and the Court of Conflicts.[22] First issued in 1821, it is often referred to as the Lebon Report,[23] after its founder. Until recently it contained all the decisions of the judicial section of the Council. Since the Liberation, however, the great increase in the number of decisions has made it necessary for some to be left unreported. All such decisions are briefly noted in the topical index contained at the end of each volume. The decisions are reported in chronological order, and it is customary to cite them by the name of the petitioner and the date.

In addition to the official Lebon Report there are also the two unofficial reports published by the two great legal publishing houses in France, Sirey and Dalloz.[24] These contain the decisions of all French courts that the editors feel warrant publication, including those of the Council of State, the Court of Conflicts, and, to a lesser extent, those of the Prefecture Councils. They do not include more than a small minority of those tribunals' decisions, but they try to cover all im-

21 Joint Anti-Fascist Refugee Committee v. McGrath, 341 U.S. 123 (1951).

22 Recueil des arrêts du Conseil d'État statuant au contentieux et du tribunal des conflits. To an American, this seems to be more or less an official report since it is sponsored directly by the Council of State. French jurists, however, tend to treat it as unofficial. See David, French Bibliographical Digest: Law 5 (1952).

23 Recueil Lebon.

24 Recueil Sirey and Recueil Dalloz. Other unofficial reports which contain administrative-court decisions are the Gazette du Palais, Gazette des Tribunaux, and Semaine Juridique et Jurisclasseur Périodique.

portant cases. With the decision in these reports is usually published a critical note by an authority in the field and, where they are deemed significant, the conclusions of the government commissioner.[25]

Institutional Decisions

The procedure before a French administrative court like the Council of State is so different from the judicial procedure to which the common lawyer is accustomed that it is almost impossible for him to criticize it fairly by reference to his own experience and background. To him, active participation in the investigation and development of a case by a member of the court, such as occurs in the inquisitorial procedure of the Council of State, is the very negation of judicial procedure. As he sees it, the type of procedure followed by the Council would be more appropriate to a decision by an agency of the active administration than to one rendered by a court petitioned to review the legality of administrative action.

Decision of a case by a court in the common-law world means decision by the judge as an individual, as well as by him as a member of the deciding tribunal. The opinion explaining an Anglo-American court's decision normally bears the seal of the individual judge who wrote it, and those members of the court who do not agree are quick to dissent or concur. The decision of the French court stands on an entirely different footing. It is rendered, not by the individual judge, but by the tribunal itself as an institutional entity.

The type of institutional decision made by the Council of State is one that the common lawyer has come to associate with the performance of adjudicatory functions by an administrative agency rather than by a court. The normal decision made by an American administrative agency, for example, is the product of that agency as an institution, rather than the work of a designated individual within it. To aid in the decision each of the various specialists among the agency's employees contributes his skills as needed.

In the institutional decision there are undeniable elements of strength not present in the personal decision by a judge which is characteristic of the Anglo-American judicial process. "The strength springs from

[25] Most Prefecture Council decisions have not until the present been published. However, now that they are to become (under their new title of "Administrative Courts") the tribunals of original jurisdiction in the *droit administratif*, it seems essential that their decisions be published in a report comparable to the Recueil Lebon.

the superiority of group work—from internal checks and balances, from cooperation among specialists in various disciplines, from assignment of relatively menial tasks to low-paid personnel so as to utilize most economically the energies of high-paid personnel."[26]

But the institutional decision also has its special weaknesses, whether rendered by the Council of State or by an administrative agency of the type with which the common lawyer is familiar. The institution "is one great obscure organization with which the citizen has to deal. It is absolutely amorphous. He pokes it in one place and it comes out another. No one seems to have specific authority. There is someone called the commission, the authority; a metaphysical omniscient brooding thing which sort of floats around the air and is not a human being. That is what is baffling. . . . There is an idea that Mr. A heard the case and then it goes into this great building and mills around and comes out with a commissioner's name on it but what happens in between is a mystery. That is what bothers people."[27]

One should not, however, overemphasize the analogy between the procedure in the French Council of State and that followed in decisions by an Anglo-American administrative agency. In both cases, it is true, the particular affair is actively investigated and developed by a member of the deciding organ, and the decision, when made, is made by that organ as an institutional entity rather than by one or more of its members as individuals. But there is a fundamental difference that goes far toward destroying the analogy. The administrative agency with which the common lawyer is familiar cannot decide disputes with the virgin mind of a judge. An administrative agency is created to accomplish certain purposes, and it would be derelict in its duty if it were not biased in favor of those objects for which it was created. In many cases, indeed, the "bias" of the agency is even more direct, for the case decided by it has been investigated and prosecuted by its own employees.

In the Council of State there is nothing like this "departmental bias" that characterizes Anglo-American administrative agencies. The judicial section of the Council is today separated from the active administration, and it is wholly uninfluenced by a tendency to decide cases in the administration's favor. If anything, there is a bias in favor of individuals seeking review, and this the inquisitorial procedure followed helps to foster. The Council's procedure and its institutional type of decision

[26] Davis, Administrative Law 330 (1951).
[27] Dean Acheson, quoted in *id.* at 357.

are not used, then, to help it carry out particular administrative policies. Like the courts in the common-law world, it has no ax to grind in the cases decided by it. The keynote of its work is that "the Conseil considers itself as corporately charged with the duty of doing justice. . . . The Conseil believes itself to have as great an interest in due administration as the aggrieved subject himself."[28]

Critique of Administrative-Court Procedure

That the procedure followed by a French administrative court like the Council of State is not subject to all the defects inherent in that followed by Anglo-American administrative agencies does not mean that it is one that the common lawyer would deem appropriate in a court. It is, to be sure, not wholly fair to judge the use of the inquisitorial type of procedure by Anglo-American standards. In the French system, as we have seen, that procedure is followed in criminal cases. If the French jurist considers it proper in that kind of case, it would be difficult for him to understand why it should be unfair in administrative-law cases. If anything, he would say, that is the type of case in which the inquisitorial procedure is the most completely justified. In cases involving review of administrative action the petitioner is at best engaged in an unequal struggle with a far more powerful opponent. What could be more fair then, the French lawyer would ask, than to have the court seek to equalize the parties by actively participating in the case in an impartial manner?

There are many Anglo-Americans who feel that the present fighting method of conducting trials in the common-law world is carried to excess, especially in noncriminal cases. They would like to see our trial judges play a more active part in cases and to have the State assume more responsibility for seeing that all practically available important evidence is introduced at a trial.[29] It is to be assumed that no common lawyer would go so far as to advocate the importation into our courts of the inquisitorial procedure followed by the administrative courts in France. But the fact that "trial by battle" can be almost wholly eliminated from the workings of the French tribunals does furnish strong practical support for those who urge its minimization in the Anglo-American judicial system.

28 Hamson, *loc. cit. supra* note 8.

29 See, e.g., Frank, "Short of Sickness and Death: A Study of Moral Responsibility in Legal Criticism" 26 N.Y.U. L. Rev. 545, 631 (1951).

A more difficult question is that of the effectiveness of a wholly written procedure such as that followed by the French administrative courts. Here, too, some Anglo-Americans have felt that the almost exclusive reliance on oral evidence and argument is overdone in common-law courts and even in our administrative agencies that utilize judicial procedural techniques. They have felt that much can be gained from the substitution, in appropriate situations, of written evidence for oral. But that is a far different posture from urging the usc of written evidence exclusively as in the French administrative courts. The common lawyer is too convinced of the benefit to the judge of oral testimony to feel that disputed factual issues can be properly resolved in a system that puts practically no reliance on it.

Members of the Council of State, when asked whether they do not feel the need to have the testimony of those familiar with the facts of cases before them, have confessed that at times they do regret the lack. The example given was that of an action against the State to recover damages for injuries caused by a State-owned automobile, with the facts hotly disputed. But, say these members of the French tribunal, cases of this type are so comparatively rare as not to require the abandonment by the administrative-court system of its exclusive reliance on written evidence.

It should not, however, be assumed that the French themselves have been unanimous in their approval of the procedure followed by the administrative courts. In a famous article of 1903 on the evolution of their procedure[30] it was asserted that the inquisitorial, written, and secret elements with which it had become stamped had totally overshadowed the prime objective of safeguarding individual rights. "With their purely written and secret procedure, the administrative courts could with ease arbitrarily smother the petition or paralyze the defense."[31] This result, said the author, is impossible under the oral adversary procedure followed in civil cases in French as in Anglo-American law courts. That type of procedure arises from the "need for maintaining the equal balance between the parties. Meeting that need, it seems on the whole clearly preferable, despite its undeniable faults, to the procedure followed by the administrative courts."[32]

This criticism of the written inquisitorial procedure of the adminis-

[30] Jacquelin, "L'Évolution de la procédure contentieuse administrative" Revue du Droit Public 373 (1903).

[31] *Id.* at 400.

[32] *Id.* at 403.

trative courts in France is one that strikes a responsive chord in the Anglo-American ear. But it would be a mistake to assume that it has met an equal responsiveness from French administrative lawyers. It cannot be denied that most French commentators have not only not criticized, but have even excessively praised, the procedure followed by the Council of State and the tribunals subordinate to it. Their view was well stated by a prominent administrative lawyer over a generation ago:

"The direction of the procedure by the judge and its written form present undeniable advantages. If the control of procedure is taken away from the parties and given to the judge, he ceases to be the mere spectator of the forensic duel and becomes its actual director with the duty of carrying it through by the most expeditious means to the necessary solution: the judgment. In effect, if the direction of procedure is left to counsel, they, representing only their client, do not seek so much to throw light on the case as to establish the correctness of their side; and to that end they utilize as weapons every possible procedural device. This tactic leads only to pettifoggery. There is, on the contrary, no pettifogging under the administrative-court procedure; an impartial judge presides whose sole concern is the truth. As for the written aspect, it is both a guarantee against surprise and a guarantee that the case will be seriously studied by the judge before decision. By obliging the parties to state all their conclusions and arguments in writing the procedure makes a clear and fair discussion certain. There is no surprise in the administrative-court procedure, as there is in law-court procedure, where it all too frequently happens that counsel save for the opportune moment their decisive argument—that which will win the triumph of the court's decision, and for which the opposing side has not prepared a reply."[33]

The common lawyer need not necessarily agree with this point of view, but he should certainly recognize and understand it if he hopes to comprehend how the administrative courts in France have developed a procedure so foreign to his notions of proper judicial procedure.

[33] Font-Réaulx, Les Pourvois devant le Conseil d'État contre les décisions des autres tribunaux administratifs 20 (1930). For more recent expressions of this view, see Duez and Debeyre, Traité de droit administratif 321-23 (1952); Méjean, La Procédure devant le Conseil de Préfecture 31 (1949).

Chapter Seven

AVAILABILITY OF REVIEW

Every case involving judicial review of administrative action presents two questions that must be answered by the reviewing court before its decision can be reached. The first is whether review is available. If the court decides that it is, it must then define the extent of its reviewing power on the merits—as it is usually expressed, the scope of review.

Discussions of judicial review in this country have mostly centered on the second question. Indeed, until a comparatively recent time the proper scope of review was one of the most hotly debated issues in our administrative law. It is often overlooked, however, that the availability of review is in some ways an even more important question. Unless it is answered in the affirmative, the case is at an end and the question of scope never comes up. Only if the judge decides that review is available is he called upon to determine the extent of his reviewing power.

In deciding the availability of review the judge steeped in common-law traditions naturally starts with a strong predilection in favor of review. This predilection does not mean, of course, that he must answer in the affirmative the question of availability in every case in which administrative action happens to be challenged. As Mr. Justice Frankfurter has reminded us, in the Anglo-American world "courts are not charged with general guardianship against all potential mischief in the complicated tasks of government."[1] The judicial function is, with us, a more limited one. Judicial power, however large, has an orbit more or less strictly defined.[2] It "could come into play only in matters that were the traditional concern of the courts at Westminster and only if they arose in ways that to the expert feel of lawyers constituted 'Cases' or

[1] Federal Communications Commission v. Pottsville Broadcasting Co., 309 U.S. 134, 146 (1940).

[2] Frankfurter and Fisher, "The Business of the Supreme Court at the October Terms, 1935 and 1936" 51 Harv. L. Rev. 577, 621 (1938).

'Controversies' . . . . even as to the kinds of questions which were the staple of judicial business, it was not for courts to pass upon them as abstract, intellectual problems but only if a concrete, living contest called for the arbitrament of law."[3]

Our courts, emphasizing as they have done the importance of judicial self-limitation, have been cautious in their approach to cases presenting problems of judicial review of administrative action. In the common-law world the proceeding for review has been anything but the *actio popularis* of the Roman law, whereby any citizen could petition to have improper administrative action annulled, regardless of whether he was adversely affected thereby. Our courts have constantly insisted on the need for a direct personal interest in the petitioner before they will consider his review action. If the petitioner is not adversely affected in his individual person or property, his action will be dismissed, no matter how improper the administrative act of which he complains.

To our courts the insistence on a direct interest in the individual bringing the review action is of fundamental significance. "One of the greatest sources of strength of our law is that it adjudicates concrete cases and does not pronounce principles in the abstract."[4] It is only when there is a real case between the administration and a citizen adversely affected by its action that our courts will take cognizance of the matter. To do otherwise would be to concern themselves with abstract disputation rather than with actual living controversies.

But even judicial fear of abstraction can be carried too far. In the *droit administratif* as in our own system, we shall see, the basic principle has been to require a direct interest in the individual bringing the review action. But the Council of State has been able to interpret this requirement so as to make it, in some cases, a less formidable hurdle for would-be petitioners than it is in the Anglo-American world.

The common lawyer has justified rigid insistence on a direct personal interest in seekers of judicial review by fear of the consequences that might otherwise result. To permit review on a wider scale would be to open the floodgates of litigation and hopelessly to clog both the administrative and judicial processes. It is this danger that has led the common lawyer to suffer some stifling of review despite his ingrained predisposition in favor of making review available on the widest pos-

[3] Coleman v. Miller, 307 U.S. 433, 460 (1939).
[4] New York v. United States, 326 U.S. 572, 575 (1946).

sible scale to ensure effective enforcement of the principle of legality. The existence in another country of a system of judicial control of administration in which review is available on a wider scale should, however, give the Anglo-American reason to reflect. If the French administrative courts feel able to grant review somewhat more freely than common-law courts, is it likely that our restrictions on the availability of review really inhere in the very nature of judicial power?

Legislative Silence

To determine whether judicial review of particular administrative action is available in the Anglo-American world, one must look first to the applicable statutes. Availability in a given case depends primarily on the provisions that the legislature has seen fit to make. It is clear, as was stated in a leading English case, that appeals from administrative decisions cannot be taken in the absence of statutory provisions. "An appeal is the creature of statute. . . . If a person desires to appeal from one tribunal to another, be the former a judicial tribunal in the ordinary sense of the term, or a tribunal such as the Minister of Health and his department, for purposes such as I am considering in this case, he can only do so if a statute has given him the right, and only within the limits which the statute giving him the right lays down."[5]

The absence of statutory provisions for appeal, however, does not mean that access to the judiciary is barred. Even in the absence of statute the Anglo-American courts have developed means for controlling administrative officers in their relation to private right.[6] An administrative tribunal, as Farwell, L.J., has affirmed, "is not an autocrat free to act as it pleases, but is an inferior tribunal subject to the jurisdiction which the Court of King's Bench for centuries, and the High Court since the Judicature Acts, has exercised over such tribunals."[7]

In the United States, too, the mere fact that one starts in a particular case with a statute that makes no provision for judicial review is not decisive. "For the silence of Congress as to judicial review is not necessarily to be construed as a denial of the power of the federal courts to grant relief in the exercise of the general jurisdiction which Congress has conferred upon them."[8]

[5] In re Bowman, [1932] 2 K.B. 621, 633.

[6] Report of the Attorney General's Committee on Administrative Procedure 80 (1941).

[7] Rex v. Electricity Commissioners, [1924] 1 K.B. 171, 205.

[8] Estep v. United States, 327 U.S. 114, 120 (1946).

The review power of the American courts in these cases is an inherent one that arises out of the delegation to them of *the* judicial power. "When Congress passes an Act empowering administrative agencies to carry on governmental activities, the power of those agencies is circumscribed by the authority granted. This permits the courts to participate in law enforcement entrusted to administrative bodies only to the extent necessary to protect justiciable individual rights against administrative action fairly beyond the granted powers. The responsibility of determining the limits of statutory grants of authority in such instances is a judicial function entrusted to the courts by Congress by the statutes establishing courts and marking their jurisdiction."[9]

The Anglo-American situation just described is also that under the *droit administratif*. The French administrative lawyer, when faced with the question of availability of review, looks first, like his common-law confrere, to the relevant statutes. If there is an adequate statutory provision for review by an administrative court, then the petition must be filed with it. It should be noted that such specific statutory provisions governing the review of particular administrative action are much less common in France than in the Anglo-American world.

The failure of the French Parliament to make express provision for review of administrative action does not, however, mean that in a given case access to the administrative courts is barred. The French judge, like his Anglo-American counterpart, has felt that the search for significance in the silence of the legislature is too often the pursuit of a mirage.[10] Legislative silence, in the French as in the common-law system, does not indicate a legislative intent to preclude review. It means merely that a nonstatutory action for review must be brought in the appropriate court of general jurisdiction.

In the French administrative-court system that court has been the judicial section of the Council of State. Under the 1953 decree, discussed at the end of Chapter Two, the court of general original jurisdiction in the *droit administratif* is to be the appropriate "Administrative Court" (*Tribunal administratif*), as the Prefecture Council is to be called, and it is to have competence in most cases in which the citizen is not given an adequate remedy in some other administrative court. Legislative silence in France will thus signify only that the challenged administrative action is to be subject to review by the appropriate

9 Stark v. Wickard, 321 U.S. 288, 309 (1944).

10 Paraphrasing Scripps-Howard Radio v. Federal Communications Commission, 316 U.S. 4, 11 (1942).

Tribunal administratif in the exercise of its general jurisdiction over administrative-law cases, subject to full review in the Council of State.

The authority of the French administrative courts even in the absence of statutory review provisions is, like the similar power exercised by courts in the common-law world, almost entirely the handiwork of the courts themselves. It dates from a leading decision of 1889,[11] when the principle was laid down that the Council of State was henceforth the tribunal of general jurisdiction in the field of administrative law. "Whenever an administrative authority vested with powers of decision renders a decision that affects private citizens," asserted the government commissioner, whose conclusions were followed by the Council in that case, "a review action can be brought, and the Council of State can be vested directly with jurisdiction; all that is necessary for the case to arise is the adverse effect produced by the administrative decision."

The rule that judicial review of administrative action is not precluded by mere legislative silence on the subject—a rule that prevails in both France and the common-law world—is clearly the proper starting point for a system based on the principle of legality. To hold otherwise would mean that, in the absence of statutory review provisions, an administrative order is conclusive and not reviewable by any court, even though entered arbitrarily, without substantial supporting evidence, and in defiance of law. "Such a sweeping contention for administrative finality is out of harmony with the general pattern of administrative and judicial relationships."[12]

The need for judicial control such as that exercised by both the French administrative courts and the Anglo-American judiciary has been emphasized in strong language by a federal court. "If the judiciary had no power in such matter, the only practical restraint would be the self-restraint of the executive branch. Such a result is foreign to our concept of the division of the powers of government."[13] As the same principle was pithily phrased by Napoleon Bonaparte: "I do not see how there could be property owners in France if a man could be irrevocably deprived of his field by a mere administrative decision."[14]

[11] Cadot, December 13, 1889.
[12] United States v. Interstate Commerce Commission, 337 U.S. 426, 433 (1949).
[13] Fleming v. Moberley Milk Products Co., 160 F. 2d 259, 265 (App. D.C. 1947).
[14] Quoted in Goldenberg, Le Conseil d'État: juge du fait 130 (1932).

Legislative Preclusion

In particular cases the legislature may not only fail to make specific provision for review of administrative action, but may expressly provide that judicial review is precluded. The most striking example in the common-law world is the so-called "conclusive-evidence" clause that has found its way into certain British statutes. Such clauses generally provide that the particular administrative order itself "shall be conclusive evidence that the requirements of this Act have been complied with, and that the order has been duly made and is within the requirements of this Act."[15]

Such provisions for administrative conclusiveness must, of course, be given effect by the English courts, because of the doctrine of parliamentary supremacy. Parliament may, in Lord Hewart's words, "provide that the decision of the Minister shall be final and conclusive. When this is the case, the Courts are powerless to intervene, however unjust and absurd a decision may appear to be, and even though it is obviously based upon an erroneous view of the law."[16]

In the United States, too, statutory provisions for administrative conclusiveness have been not uncommon, though they have not generally been so extreme as the British "conclusive-evidence" clause. An example of the type of conclusiveness provision in American statutes is in the Immigration Act of 1917. That law authorizing the deportation of aliens who come within its provisions states that the administrative decision in particular deportation cases "shall be final." Interpreted literally, such a provision for administrative finality would place the administrative decision in a conclusive position and bar all recourse to the courts.

The courts in this country have, however, consistently refused to give literal effect to such provisions for administrative conclusiveness. As a federal court stated in 1948: "Nevertheless and in spite of such language, it is perfectly clear that it [*i.e.*, the administrative decision] is not final in the sense that courts cannot do anything about it."[17] It has long been established that an alien against whom a deportation order has been issued could obtain a judicial decision on the legality of that order in a habeas corpus proceeding. Thus, "while it might look as though judicial review were precluded by the giving to the deportation

15 For a discussion of such clauses, see Schwartz, Law and the Executive in Britain 188 *et seq.* (1949).

16 Hewart, The New Despotism 49 (1929).

17 United States ex rel. Trinler v. Carusi, 166 F. 2d 457, 460 (3d Cir. 1948).

order the air of finality, in practice such finality never existed because of the availability of habeas corpus."[18]

It may be objected that the courts in this country, in refusing literally to interpret a provision such as that in the deportation statute, are violating the correct canons of statutory construction. Yet, as Justice Frankfurter has aptly pointed out, "It is true also of Acts of Congress that 'The letter killeth.' . . . in enacting legislation Congress is not engaged in a scientific process which takes account of every contingency. Its laws are not to be read as though every *i* has to be dotted and every *t* crossed."[19]

Rigid literal construction in these cases would be to free administrative agencies from all judicial control. Such complete preclusion of review, if objectionable anywhere, would seem to be so particularly in deportation proceedings, where the result may be "loss of both property and life; or of all that makes life worth living,"[20] and "where we frequently meet with a voteless class of litigants, who not only lack the influence of citizens, but who are strangers to the laws and customs in which they are involved, and who often do not even understand the tongue in which they are accused."[21]

In the French system, too, there have been statutory provisions for administrative conclusiveness that suggest a legislative intent to preclude review. But the Council of State, like the courts in this country, has refused to give literal effect to such provisions. The approach of the French tribunal on this point is basically similar to that followed by the United States Supreme Court in *Estep v. United States*.[22] In that case the Court held that a provision that the administrative order at issue should be "final" did not place it beyond judicial control. "It is only orders 'within their respective jurisdictions' that are made final,"[23] Mr. Justice Douglas asserted, and the jurisdictional question is a judicial question. To hold otherwise would be to impute an intent to the legislature to depart drastically from our normal tradition of judicial control of legality in a case in which the legislative intent has not been

[18] *Id.* at 461. Heikkila v. Barber, 345 U.S. 229 (1953), is not to the contrary. It held only that review of a deportation order was not available under the Federal Administrative Procedure Act. The Court expressly recognized, however, that the legality of such order could be attacked by habeas corpus.

[19] United States ex rel. Knauff v. Shaughnessy, 338 U.S. 537, 548 (1950).

[20] Ng Fung Ho v. White, 259 U.S. 276, 284 (1922).

[21] Wong Yang Sung v. McGrath, 339 U.S. 33, 46 (1950).

[22] 327 U.S. 114 (1946).

[23] *Id.* at 120.

unequivocally expressed. "We cannot readily infer that Congress departed so far from the traditional concepts of a fair trial when it made the actions of the local boards 'final.' "[24]

The French high court has taken a similar view. In a case decided by it in 1950,[25] involving the administrative licensing power, the relevant statute provided that the administrative action in particular cases "shall not be subject to any review either administrative or judicial." This seemingly strong provision for administrative conclusiveness was held by the Council of State not to bar review. The statutory language, reads the Council's decision, "does not have the effect of precluding the action to annul the grant of the license before the Council of State, an action available even in the absence of legislative provision therefor, the goal of which action is to ensure, in accordance with the general principles of our law, respect for the principle of legality."[26] Thus, even in a system based on the absolute sovereignty of the written law, the dangers inherent in administrative conclusiveness have led the courts to refuse to give literal effect to provisions precluding review.

The result in these cases, in both the French and the American systems, is not unlike that already noted in situations where the legislature has been silent about judicial review. In both instances the courts refuse to find a legislative intent to preclude review. To hold otherwise might, indeed, raise a difficult constitutional question, at least in cases arising in this country. A statutory provision for administrative conclusiveness, as the highest court of Maryland recently declared, "cannot override the basic principle that the Legislature cannot divest the courts of their inherent power to review the actions of administrative agencies which are illegal, arbitrary, or unreasonable and which impair personal or property rights."[27]

"Privilege" Cases

It should be noted, however, that the principle of availability, seen to be basic to both French and American administrative law even in the face of seemingly preclusive statutory provisions, has not been applied in this country in an important category of cases. These are the cases involving so-called grants, benefits, or "privileges," in which the State

[24] *Id.* at 122.
[25] Lamotte, February 17, 1950.
[26] See, similarly, Société Dourlet, Walder, Lejeune et Cie., Council of State, April 30, 1948; d'Aillières, Council of State, February 7, 1947.
[27] Johnstown Coal & Coke Co. v. Dishong, 84 A. 2d 847, 850 (Md. 1951).

accords to the individual something to which he has no pre-existing legal right. In these "privilege" cases a statutory provision for administrative conclusiveness is given effect by our courts in a way to exclude judicial review.

As good an example as any of a provision for conclusiveness in the field of State benefits is the statute applicable to the Veterans' Administration. It provides, in language approaching that of the British "conclusive-evidence" clause, that the decisions of this agency on claims for benefits under the statutory schemes administered by it "shall be final and conclusive and no other official or any court of the United States shall have power or jurisdiction to review any such decision."[28] The purpose of this provision appears to have been to remove the possibility of judicial relief in the cases covered.[29] And, in the words of one federal court, "the authority of Congress to withhold judicial review here is now beyond question. Veterans' benefits are mere gratuities and 'the grant of them creates no vested right.' "[30] In these cases, Mr. Justice Stone has asserted, "The United States is not, by the creation of claims against itself, bound to provide a remedy in the courts. It may withhold all remedy or it may provide an administrative remedy and make it exclusive, however mistaken its exercise."[31]

Another important class of "privilege" cases recently before the Supreme Court is that involving government contractors. In these, too, provisions for administrative conclusiveness are so interpreted by the courts as completely to bar review.[32] The government contractor, like the applicant for a veterans' benefit, is held to have only the "privilege" of dealing with the government. He is placed in a different position from that of the private citizen whose property or personal "rights" are adversely affected by administrative action. Provisions for administrative conclusiveness will be given literal effect by the courts in the contractor's case.

That administrative conclusiveness is explainable legally in these cases because in this country a government contract is considered as a "privilege," not a "right," does not, however, mean that the legal result is the desirable one. "The rule we announce has wide application and a

[28] 54 Stat. 1197 (1940), 38 U.S.C. § 11a-2; 48 Stat. 9 (1933), 38 U.S.C. § 705.
[29] Lynch v. United States, 292 U.S. 571, 587 (1934).
[30] Slocumb v. Gray, 179 F. 2d 31, 34 (App. D.C. 1949). See, similarly, Hahn v. Gray, 203 F. 2d 625 (App. D.C. 1953).
[31] Dismuke v. United States, 297 U.S. 167, 171 (1936).
[32] United States v. Wunderlich, 342 U.S. 98 (1951); Moorman v. United States, 338 U.S. 457 (1950).

devastating effect," asserted Mr. Justice Douglas in dissenting from the Court's upholding of administrative conclusiveness in the most recent of the government contractor cases. "It makes a tyrant out of every contracting officer."[33]

It is unrealistic today to treat the applicant for a pension or a government contract, whose financial well-being may be wholly dependent on the government grant, any differently from one declared to be injured in his personal or property "rights." With regard to the availability of judicial review, is there, for example, any adequate reason for differentiating a veteran seeking a pension from an alien being deported, simply because a veteran's benefit is termed a privilege instead of a property right? As far as the effect on the individual is concerned the veteran's pension case, regardless of the tag used, involves a need for judicial control just as great as that in any other administrative proceeding. And the same is true of other cases involving the grant of so-called privileges or benefits by the State. The power of the State altogether to deny such privileges should not mean that they can be denied by the administration to particular individuals without the latter's being entitled to judicial decisions on the legality of the denials.

The American administrative lawyer, if he feels that there is little justification for using the privilege-right distinction as a basis for determining whether judicial review is available in a particular case, finds strong support for his views in the jurisprudence of the French administrative courts. The field of State benefits has certainly been of at least as great importance in France as in this country. Yet the Council of State has never seen the need to draw a distinction between cases involving grants or benefits from the State and those in which administrative action affecting personal or property rights is at issue.

In benefit as in "right" cases, judicial review is not precluded in the French system, whether or not there is an applicable statutory provision apparently barring review. Indeed, some of the French cases of statutory preclusion referred to above dealt with administrative action affecting grants or concessions from the State that might well be treated as mere "privileges" under the American case law.[34] But the Council of State treated these cases just like those affecting personal or property rights, holding that the statutory provisions were ineffective to preclude the exercise of its inherent review power.

33 United States v. Wunderlich, 342 U.S. at 101.

34 Lamotte, Council of State, February 17, 1950; Société Dourlet, Walder, Lejeune et Cie., Council of State, April 30, 1948.

Acts of Government

Absence of the "privilege-right" distinction from the French law on availability of review means in effect that under the *droit administratif* recourse to the administrative courts is available in every case unless there is a statutory provision precluding review in terms so blatant as to be positively indecent.[35] And the cases referred to show that provisions that may appear at first glance to indicate an express legislative intent to bar review are not taken at face value by the Council of State. As one commentator puts the point, the parliamentary will to preclude review "must never be presumed, for we must suppose that a democratic legislator will not sin against the spirit of his system of government."[36]

The basic principle of availability on the widest scale has, however, given way in the French system in relation to one important class of administrative acts. "Precious though this principle may be for the protection of citizens against administrative abuses of power, it contains, in France, one lacuna: there are acts known as 'acts of government' that are not subject to any review."[37]

According to an English observer, French law has always recognized an indefinite class of acts which, "as they concern matters of high policy or of public security or touch upon foreign policy or the execution of treaties, or concern dealings with foreigners, must be left to the uncontrolled discretion of the government, and lie quite outside the jurisdiction of any court whatever."[38] The nonreviewability of these acts of government has its legal basis in a provision of the law of May 24, 1872, the organic instrument of the Council of State under the Third Republic. It authorized Cabinet ministers to have cases before the Council of State involving measures not inherently in the category of reviewable acts transferred to the Court of Conflicts for decision as to reviewability. This law expressly recognized that there were administrative acts the legality of which the Council of State could not review —those since termed acts of government.

But if the law thus recognized that acts of government were not subject to any review, it supplied no definition, no list of the measures

[35] Paraphrasing Willis, The Parliamentary Powers of English Government Departments 103 (1933).

[36] De Soto, Revue du Droit Public 710 (1950).

[37] Waline, Traité élémentaire de droit administratif 103 (6th ed., 1951).

[38] Dicey, Law of the Constitution 346 (9th ed., 1939).

comprised in this category of nonreviewable acts. The silence of the statute on this point has had to be filled in by subsequent case law.[39]

The early cases on the subject held that the act of government was an act characterized by pursuit of a "political end."[40] "What makes an act of government," wrote the leading doctrinal writer of the early period, "is the end that its author has in view. The act that has as its goal the defense of society, taken as an entity or personified in government, against its enemies foreign and domestic, avowed or hidden, present or future—that is an act of government."[41]

The test of "political end" could be applied in a great many cases. If the motive that inspired its authors were the criterion, any transaction on the part of the government could be treated as an act of government, provided that it was carried out bona fide with the object of furthering the interest or security of the country.[42] "Every act of the executive and its agents can become an act of government, because of the motive which inspired it—defense of the State or of the political system. This conception is clearly dangerous for legality, for it contains within it the germ of an indefinite expansion of the act of government, under the pretext of reason of State."[43]

The political-end criterion, because of the dangers inherent in it, was ultimately abandoned by both the Council of State and the Court of Conflicts. Contemporary theory looks to the nature of the act at issue, rather than to the motives that inspired its authors, in determining whether it is an act of government and, as such, immune from judicial control. And French jurists have been coming more and more to recognize that a mathematical definition of acts of government cannot be devised, and to conclude, with the foremost of them, that "there is only one way out of the difficulty, that of proceeding by enumeration. . . . the act of government is that which is contained in a list of political acts laid down in the case law under the direction of the Court of Conflicts."[44]

What acts would a list such as that referred to contain? It would include acts in the following categories:

1. Acts of the executive in its relations with the legislature;

[39] Bonnard, Précis de droit administratif 259 (3d ed., 1940).
[40] Rokham and Pratt, Studies in French Administrative Law 22 (1947).
[41] Dufour, quoted in Duez, Les Actes de gouvernement 31 (1935).
[42] Compare Dicey, *loc. cit. supra* note 38.
[43] Duez, *loc. cit. supra* note 41.
[44] Hauriou, Précis de droit administratif 418 (12th ed., 1933).

2. Acts involving the relations of the French Government with a foreign power, in which by far the greatest number of cases falls; and
3. Certain acts related to the conduct of war and the national defense.[45]

Comparison with Political Questions

The common lawyer who seeks to understand the French concept of acts of government has a ready basis of comparison in the doctrine of political questions or acts of State developed by his own courts.

In 1460 the Duke of York brought suit to have himself declared the rightful heir to the throne. But the judges decided that they "durst not enter into eny communication thereof, for it perteyned to the Lordes of the Kyngs blode and th'apparage of this his lond, to have communication and medle in such maters."[46] Ever since, Anglo-American courts have refused to exercise jurisdiction in cases in which the exercise of judicial power was felt to be inappropriate. These cases have involved what the American courts have come to term "political questions."

"What are these political questions?" asks one observer. "To what matters does the term apply? It applies to all those matters of which the court, at a given time, will be of the opinion that it is impolitic or inexpedient to take jurisdiction."[47] As Chief Justice Hughes affirmed in an important case: "In determining whether a question falls within that category, the appropriateness under our system of government of attributing finality to the action of the political departments and also the lack of satisfactory criteria for a judicial determination are dominant considerations."[48]

Like the French act of government, action of the American executive that relates to political questions is wholly immune from judicial control. The "decision of a 'political question' by the 'political department' to which the Constitution has committed it 'conclusively binds the judges, as well as all other officers, citizens and subjects of . . . government.' "[49] And the doctrine of political questions, like the French

[45] These are discussed more fully in Duez, *op. cit. supra* note 41, at 38 *et seq.*

[46] The Duke of Yorke's Claim to the Crown, 5 Rotuli Par. 375 (1460), quoted in Weston, "Political Questions" 38 Harv. L. Rev. 296, 303 (1925).

[47] Finkelstein, "Judicial Self-Limitation" 37 Harv. L. Rev. 338, 344 (1924).

[48] Coleman v. Miller, 307 U.S. 433, 454 (1939).

[49] *Id.* at 457.

concept, has never been defined adequately by either courts or doctrinal writers. "The decision that a question is political in this sense is inferred from its essential nature," states one text. "There exists no very definite test for determining when that inference is permissible with respect to any particular act."[50]

An analysis of the case law does, however, enable one to draw up a list of such matters as our courts have considered to be political questions not subject to judicial control. Such a list would contain a certain number of matters relating to the government of our internal affairs. For example, under the constitutional provision that the United States shall guarantee to every state a republican form of government[51] it has been held that it rests with Congress to decide what government is the established one in a state and whether or not it is republican in form.[52] Our list would also include questions involving the government and the conduct of the relations of the executive with the legislature, as well as matters involving the command and disposition of the military forces.[53]

The doctrine of political questions has, however, been employed the most widely in the field of foreign affairs. "The conduct of the foreign relations of our Government is committed by the Constitution to the Executive and Legislative—'the political'—Departments of the Government, and the propriety of what may be done in the exercise of this political power is not subject to judicial inquiry or decision."[54]

One cannot but note that the categories contained in a list of political questions are roughly similar to those covered by the French concept of acts of government. Both include certain acts relating to domestic government, such as those touching upon the acts of the executive in its relations with the legislature. And both the French and the American doctrines emphasize the autonomy of the political departments in the field of foreign affairs. In both countries most of the cases in which the courts have applied the doctrines of acts of government and of political questions to bar judicial review have dealt with the conduct of foreign relations, which involves "considerations of policy, considerations of extreme magnitude, and certainly, entirely incompetent to the examination and decision of a court of justice."[55]

[50] Rottschaefer, Handbook of American Constitutional Law 69 (1939).

[51] Article IV, §4.

[52] Luther v. Borden, 7 How. 1 (U.S. 1849).

[53] Goodnow, The Principles of the Administrative Law of the United States 49 (1905).

[54] Oetjen v. Central Leather Co., 246 U.S. 297, 302 (1918).

[55] Ware v. Hylton, 3 Dall. 199, 260 (U.S. 1796).

That there must be some judicial self-limitation in cases bearing directly on the transaction of the country's foreign affairs cannot be denied. At the same time, one wonders whether American courts have not gone too far in this direction. In the recent jurisprudence of our Supreme Court one can note a tendency to hold that judicial review is barred, not only when the conduct of foreign affairs is immediately involved, but also whenever the administrative act at issue is seen to have any repercussions at all upon our international relations.

As good an illustration as any of a case exemplifying this tendency in the highest tribunal is *Chicago & Southern Air Lines v. Waterman Steamship Corp.*[56] It concerned the power of the Civil Aeronautics Board to license those seeking to engage in aerial transport. The Board is authorized to grant licenses to engage in both domestic and foreign air transportation, though in the latter field its decision is subject to the approval of the President. The relevant statute provides for review of any order of the Board "except any order in respect to any *foreign* air carrier subject to the approval of the President."[57] This statutory exception did not expressly cover the particular case, which concerned an application by a citizen carrier to engage in overseas transportation. Despite this, the Court held that review of the Board's decision was precluded because of the possible effect on our foreign affairs.

Although Mr. Justice Jackson, who delivered the opinion, conceded that a literal reading of the statute would subject the administrative decision to re-examination by the courts, he asserted that the letter need not govern here. Because of the impact of the Board's order on foreign relations, the courts should not intervene. Decisions such as this "are wholly confided to the political departments of the government. . . . They are decisions of a kind for which the judiciary has neither aptitude, facilities nor responsibility and which has long been held to belong in the domain of political power not subject to judicial intrusion or inquiry."[58]

In the *Chicago & Southern Air Lines* case the Court held that it could not exercise jurisdiction even though the challenged administrative action clearly affected adversely the property of the individual seeking review. Even in such a case review is precluded because of the foreign-affairs aspects of the Board's decision. As the dissenting Justices stated, "no matter how extreme the action of the Board, the courts are

[56] 333 U.S. 103 (1948).
[57] Emphasis added.
[58] 333 U.S. at 111.

powerless to correct it under today's decision."[59] The individual affected may doubtless find it difficult to comprehend why he is in a worse position than if he were applying only for a license to engage in domestic transport. The effect on him of a refusal by the Board is essentially the same whether he is applying for a domestic or an overseas license; yet, so far as judicial review is concerned, the Court's decision does make for a substantial difference in his rights. If his license relates to overseas traffic, the administration can act in a lawless way[60] without fear of restraint by the courts.

Here, indeed, is the great weakness of both the American and the French doctrines of political questions and acts of government. It is all very well to assert that the executive should be free from judicial interference in its conduct of foreign affairs. But when executive action has immediate effect on the person or property of particular citizens, is it not opening the door to administrative lawlessness wholly to free such action from judicial control? "If you make just one exception to the principle of legality," a consistent French opponent of the act-of-government doctrine has declared, "you cannot tell where it may lead you. . . . To make a single exception to the principle of legality is to take the fatal first step toward the German doctrine and say . . . with Jellinek: 'The State is above every particular rule of law.' "[61]

To a student of the *droit administratif* it appears that the doctrine of acts of government as a bar to judicial review is tending to become of lessened importance. It may be premature to say, with a distinguished councilor of state, that that doctrine is now "scarcely more than a historical souvenir, an episode in the evolution of the administrative case law."[62] But it is undeniable that the list of acts of government has been consistently growing smaller in the jurisprudence of the French administrative courts. The earlier test of "political end," under which almost any act could become an act of government, has, as we have seen, been abandoned. And more recently the Council of State has been asserting jurisdiction to review acts formerly thought to be beyond its review power. To take a 1949 case as an example: In that case the French tribunal held that the validity of administrative action imposing an exit tax on rubber destined for export from Indo-China could be considered in a review action. Whatever may have been the gravity of the political

[59] *Id.* at 118.
[60] The term used by Douglas, J., dissenting, *id.* at 117.
[61] 3 Duguit, Traité de droit constitutionnel 738 (3d ed.).
[62] Odent, Cours de contentieux administratif 73 (1949-50).

events leading to the administrative action, the decision states, it cannot be maintained that the challenged order comes within the class of orders that cannot be referred to the Council of State on a petition to annul.[63]

This recent French tendency should be compared with decisions of the United States Supreme Court that have followed the approach outlined above in the *Chicago & Southern Air Lines* case.[64] To one concerned with the effective enforcement of the principle of legality the trend of French jurisprudence is surely the more desirable. One can, indeed, hope with the outstanding contemporary treatise on the *droit administratif* for the complete disappearance of judicial refusal to exercise the review power that is based on doctrines like that of acts of government.[65] "One should not shut one's eyes to the extent to which the preclusion of all review under this doctrine contravenes liberal principles and endangers private citizens. . . . To preclude all judicial review of certain acts, all possibility of scrutinizing the legality of certain administrative decisions, the conformity to law of certain actions on the part of executive authorities—this amounts to proclaiming that in certain cases the administration is, for practical purposes, freed from respect for law and that it can engage in the most arbitrary conduct toward citizens without any fear of judicial control."[66]

Reviewable Acts

The courts in the common-law world, swayed by their strong feeling that the judiciary is not charged with the minute supervision of everything done by the administration, have been careful to limit the types of agency action that could be reviewed. Their approach to the question of what kinds of administrative action are reviewable is not, however, a formalistic one. So much has been clear in this country ever since *Rochester Telephone Corp. v. United States*,[67] the famous deci-

[63] Société Comptoir de l'Industrie Cotonnière et Autres, December 23, 1949. Compare Société des Etabl. Ricalens, Council of State, March 28, 1952.

[64] See, e.g., United States ex rel. Knauff v. Shaughnessy, 338 U.S. 537 (1950); Ludecke v. Watkins, 335 U.S. 160 (1948); United States v. Bush & Co., 310 U.S. 371 (1940). Cases like these are classified as act-of-government cases by a French observer. Pinto, La Crise de l'état aux États-Unis 147-48 (1951).

[65] Waline, *op. cit. supra* note 37, at 108. See, similarly, Mignon, "Une Emprise nouvelle du principe de légalité; Les Actes de gouvernement" (1951) Dalloz, Chronique 53, 60.

[66] Waline, *op. cit. supra* note 37, at 104.

[67] 307 U.S. 125 (1939).

sion of our highest Court that struck down the so-called "negative order" doctrine, a limitation on the availability of review based solely on the form of administrative action. In the view of the Supreme Court today a formalistic concept such as that of negative orders has served, not to clarify the relations between administrative bodies and the courts, but rather to obscure them. "Negative has really been an obfuscating adjective in that it implied a search for a distinction—non-action as against action—which does not involve the real considerations on which rest . . . the reviewability of Commission orders within the framework of its discretionary authority and within the general criteria of justiciability."[68]

The *Rochester Telephone* case formulated the principle that the availability of review does not depend on the form of particular administrative action. Since that case it has been clear that reviewability of a challenged act depends not on its form but on its effect. If the administrative act has a direct adverse effect on the person or property of the individual bringing the review action, then it is subject to review regardless of its form. As the principle is usually expressed in this country, whether administrative action is reviewable depends on whether it is "final."

Administrative "action is 'final' in the sense here involved when at no future time will its impact on the petitioner become more conclusive, definite, or substantial."[69] If the challenged agency order is merely preliminary or procedural, the review proceeding will be dismissed as premature. According to the Supreme Court in an important case, the review action will not be entertained when the "so-called order here complained of is one which does not command the [petitioner] to do, or to refrain from doing, anything; which does not grant or withhold any authority, privilege or license; which does not extend or abridge any power or facility; which does not subject the [petitioner] to any liability, civil or criminal; which does not change the [petitioner's] existing or future status or condition; which does not determine any right or obligation."[70]

This requirement of "finality,"[71] or ripeness for review, which must

[68] *Id.* at 141.

[69] Frankfurter, J., in Joint Anti-Fascist Refugee Committee v. McGrath, 341 U.S. 123, 154 (1951).

[70] United States v. Los Angeles R.R., 273 U.S. 299, 309 (1927).

[71] It is important to note that the term "finality," in addition to the sense in which it is used here, is also employed in a different sense with which we are not

be met before particular administrative action may be subjected to challenge in our courts, has received equal emphasis in the *droit administratif*. "The petition to annul administrative action," states a leading treatise, "is not available except with regard to decisions having adverse effect. The petitioner must not complain merely of administrative tendencies; he must not allege mere idle threats; he must refer to an act that directly injures him."[72]

It is true that in the French system, as in the Anglo-American, the form of the challenged act is today of no importance. "The form of the act matters little. Accordingly the Council of State allows the review action, provided only that the act challenged before it has a clear existence."[73] The French tribunal has, indeed, gone so far as to hold that review was available for merely oral administrative orders, provided only that they had a direct adverse effect upon the petitioner.[74]

Investigation and Preparation

In both the French and American systems, then, reviewability of particular administrative action depends on whether it is "final" agency action with a direct adverse effect. But, as the United States Supreme Court has aptly pointed out in a decision dealing with a related matter,[75] no self-enforcing formula defining when an order is final can be devised.[76] One point is clear in the Court's approach to the problem. If its decisions appear sometimes unduly to restrict the availability of review, it is motivated by what it believes to be the practical necessities of judicial administration. "The considerations that determine finality are not abstractions but have reference to very real interests—not merely those of the immediate parties but, more particularly, those that pertain to the smooth functioning of our judicial system."[77]

Every administrative act passes through two principal stages, that of investigation and preparation and that of decision. Only when the

---

at present concerned, in reference to executive action not subject to any judicial review. Cases involving such use of the term have been considered earlier in this chapter.

[72] Alibert, Le Contrôle juridictionnel de l'administration 85 (1926).

[73] *Id.* at 94.

[74] E.g., Cabo, November 28, 1913; Neveu-Roux, August 2, 1912; Bruant, July 8, 1900.

[75] Whether a judgment was "final" within the meaning of §237 of the Judicial Code (now §1257 of the Revised Code of 1948).

[76] Republic Gas Co. v. Oklahoma, 334 U.S. 62, 67 (1948).

[77] *Id.* at 69.

administrative agency concerned has gone through the second can its action have a direct adverse effect on particular citizens. "As long as it is in the stage of preparation, the petitioner's complaint is premature, for nothing has as yet been decided."[78] This distinction, indeed, is the basis for American cases like *Myers v. Bethlehem Shipbuilding Corp.*,[79] in which our courts have refused to act before the administrative agency concerned has arrived at a decision with regard to the matter before it, even though it were contended that the agency was proceeding without jurisdiction. In our system an agency that assumes jurisdiction in a given case is entitled to proceed to a conclusion without judicial interference. If in the end it is found to have mistaken its authority or its competence, correction must come by way of judicial review.[80] But the courts will not intervene before the agency has reached the stage of "final" decision.

Like the courts in this country, the French administrative courts have refused to entertain review actions while the agency concerned was still in the stage of preparation. Thus, the Council of State has consistently held that an administrative order prescribing an inquiry or hearing is not subject to review. The reasoning of the French tribunal on this point is basically similar to that of the United States Supreme Court in cases like the *Myers* case. The hearing is something preliminary to the taking of the administrative action, reads a postwar decision of the Council of State. As such a merely preparatory measure it does not have an adverse effect on the petitioner.[81]

Closely related to these cases in which an administrative order prescribing a hearing is at issue are those that involve orders directing particular individuals to appear at the hearing. Here, too, the Council of State has refused to intervene. In a case decided by it in 1945 petitioner had been ordered to appear at a hearing before a tax commission and to bring with him a statement of his property and income. This, said the Council, was not an act that had a direct adverse effect. It was only the first stage of the procedure fixed by law to enable the commission to obtain the information needed to impose taxes.[82]

78 Waline, *op. cit. supra* note 37, at 116.

79 303 U.S. 41 (1938).

80 McFarland and Vanderbilt, Cases and Materials on Administrative Law 663 (2d ed., 1952).

81 Cazaubon, October 27, 1948. See, similarly, Commune de Corps, November 3, 1950; Rousseau, November 14, 1947; Anthoinoz, April 10, 1946.

82 Thomas, March 23, 1945. See, similarly, Dewavrin, July 11, 1947; Vuillermet, February 19, 1947; Charles Messance, May 30, 1945.

Such cases should be compared with recent American decisions on administrative exercise of the subpoena power. In this country administrative subpoenas do not, to be sure, generally have legal effect unless and until they are enforced by the courts. The role of our courts in subpoena enforcement proceedings has, however, been tending ever to diminish in importance, though the tendency may not yet have reached the stage at which they are merely "automata carrying out the wishes of the administrative."[83]

Under the recent jurisprudence of the United States Supreme Court the defense of lack of statutory jurisdiction cannot be raised in a subpoena enforcement proceeding.[84] This restriction tends to approach the view of the Council of State, which refuses to review an order of the French administration directing a citizen to appear at a hearing. And the reasoning of the American court is essentially like that of the French tribunal. The administrative issuance of a subpoena is seen to be only a preliminary to later action. For the courts to interfere at this stage would "stop much if not all of investigation in the public interest at the threshold of inquiry."[85]

Administrative Advice

Unlike the legislature, which is normally empowered solely to enact laws, the modern administration is vested not merely with the authority to promulgate rules and regulations having the force of law, but also to interpret the law that it has made as well as the statutes under which it operates. Such "interpretative service bulks large in the work of the present-day administrative agency"[86] on both sides of the Atlantic.

Administrative interpretations of the law are made known not only through agency exercises of rule making and adjudicatory authority. The administration may also render what amounts to an advisory ruling or opinion for a particular individual. Such advice enables those subject to administrative authority to learn how the agency concerned will interpret the law in cases involving them. "The value to the public of

[83] The phrase used by Frankfurter, J., dissenting, in Penfield Co. v. Securities and Exchange Commission, 330 U.S. 585, 604 (1947).

[84] Oklahoma Press Publishing Co. v. Walling, 327 U.S. 186 (1946); Endicott Johnson Corp. v. Perkins, 317 U.S. 501 (1943).

[85] Oklahoma Press Publishing Co. v. Walling, 327 U.S. at 213.

[86] Blair-Smith, "Forms of Administrative Interpretation under the Securities Laws" 26 Iowa L. Rev. 241 (1941).

this means of guidance in advance of action is apparent,"[87] and the practice of issuing advice has become widespread in present-day administration.

In most instances advice given by an administrative agency is not subject to judicial review. "The correctness of administrative advice cannot be reviewed by the courts."[88] Even if it is clearly incorrect, it does not of itself adversely affect the individual. True, it may as a practical matter involve a certain degree of hardship for those subject to administrative authority. The citizen will normally comply with the advice given him by the administration even if he believes it to be erroneous. The alternative is to risk a later administrative proceeding against him, which may involve great expense, loss of time, and often the imposition of a penalty if the administrative advice proves to have been correct. Yet, under the requirement of ripeness for review, which is basic in both French and Anglo-American administrative law, it seems clear that the giving of advice is not usually "final" action which the courts will review.

As good an American case as any to illustrate this point is *Hearst Radio v. Federal Communications Commission.*[89] The Commission had issued its so-called "Blue Book," a 59-page report entitled *Public Service Responsibility of Broadcast Licensees.* It discussed comprehensively the broadcast practices that the Commission approved and disapproved under its interpretation of its enabling legislation—the practices that would guide it in granting and renewing licenses. This report was in the nature of interpretative advice to the broadcast industry as a whole, and in the particular case a member of that industry sought a declaratory judgment as to the validity of certain portions of the Blue Book which, it claimed, applied directly to it. The court, however, had no difficulty in holding that the publication of the Blue Book did not come within the concept of reviewable agency action.

The French Council of State, like the courts in the common-law world, has normally refused to review administrative advisory rulings or interpretations. It declined to review, for example, the letter of a prefect stating the conditions under which an individual could be authorized to take water by means of a canal from a public fountain.[90]

[87] Benjamin, Administrative Adjudication in New York 262 (1942).

[88] Employers Group of Motor Freight Carriers v. National War Labor Board, 143 F. 2d 145, 151 (App. D.C. 1944).

[89] 167 F. 2d 225 (App. D.C. 1948).

[90] Gueyffier, July 10, 1946.

And the same result was reached about a ruling of the Minister of Finances stating his interpretation of a particular section of the tax laws in its application to a petitioner.[91] In cases of this type, the French tribunal has said, the administrative act does not of itself have any adverse effect. It constitutes the mere giving of advice or the statement of its policy by the administration, and it does not require the petitioner to do, or to desist from doing, anything.

Declarations of Status

The questions as to which an administrative advisory ruling may be sought can be divided into two general categories: (1) those touching jurisdiction or "coverage" and (2) those bearing on the legal effect of contemplated action by a person with regard to subject matter indisputably within an agency's jurisdiction.[92] In the first an individual is seeking essentially a declaration of his status by the administration. He wishes to learn, for example, whether his relationship with certain individuals is employment, bringing him within the status of employer and hence within the operation of the Unemployment Insurance Law or of the Workmen's Compensation Law or of a minimum wage order, or whether it is rather a partnership or independent contractor relationship. The administrative declaration of status does not usually have by itself any adverse effect. The individual concerned will not be aggrieved unless and until further administrative action is taken, based on a determination that he is within the agency's jurisdiction.

There are, however, cases in which an administrative determination of status immediately subjects the individual found to come within the agency's jurisdiction to obligations imposed by the statutory scheme administered by the agency. In that event there is direct adverse effect, and the declaration of status itself is subject to judicial review. This type of case is illustrated by *Shields v. Utah Idaho Central R. Co.*,[93] in which the plaintiff carrier had been found by the Interstate Commerce Commission not to be within the exceptions contained in the Railway Labor Act, and hence to be subject to that statute. In this case, said the Court, there is more than a mere abstract declaration of status. The administrative determination "has the effect, if validly made, of sub-

[91] Fédération Nationale des Commissionaires de Transports, Commissionaires de Douanes Agréés, Transitaires, Agents Maritimes et Assimilés de France, February 1, 1950. See, similarly, Syndicat des Propriétaires Viticulteurs de Chateauneuf-du-Pape, February 10, 1950; Société Minière de Sarladais, January 29, 1947.

[92] Benjamin, *loc. cit. supra* note 87.

[93] 305 U.S. 165 (1938).

jecting the respondent to the requirements of the Railway Labor Act, which was enacted to regulate the activities of transportation companies engaged in interstate commerce. The Mediation Board has ordered the posting of the prescribed notice that disputes between the carrier and its employees will be handled under the Railway Labor Act. Disobedience is immediately punishable and it is made the duty of the United States Attorney to institute proceedings against violators."[94]

The jurisprudence of the Council of State on this point is similar. The French tribunal, like the American Court, treats an administrative determination of status as it does the mere giving of advice by the administration, *unless* the determination of itself imposes obligations on the petitioner, as in the *Shields* case. A case of this type was decided by the Council of State in 1946. The administration had determined that the petitioner's apartment was subject to the requisition laws. This determination, like that involved in the *Shields* case, had the effect of requiring the petitioner to comply with certain orders, such as one forbidding him to dispose of the furniture in his apartment. In such a case, said the Council of State, the administrative determination was immediately subject to review.[95]

Internal Administration

An important class of cases in which there is no immediate adverse effect on private individuals, and hence no reviewable act, is that involving measures of internal administration. The heads of an agency may, for example, send out instructions to their subordinates to govern their conduct in specified cases. These instructions serve as a guide to civil servants in their application of the law administered by the agency. The instructions may be binding on those receiving them, but by themselves they ordinarily have no adverse effect on private individuals. "They therefore do not concern the public, are not in most cases even brought to its knowledge, and in any event do not directly affect it, since the public, not being within the administrative hierarchy, does not have to obey orders not addressed outside the administrative hierarchy, but must only conform to rules or individual decisions made"[96] in reliance on the instructions.

[94] *Id.* at 183. A similar case is Rochester Telephone Corp. v. United States, 307 U.S. 125 (1939).

[95] Sebban, November 29, 1946.

[96] Waline, *op. cit. supra* note 37, at 118.

That such instructions are not of themselves reviewable is the settled jurisprudence of the Council of State. It is thus that that tribunal has dealt, for example, with the instruction sent by a minister to a prefect giving his interpretation of the law prescribing maximum hours of labor. This, said the Council, was not an act that adversely affected employers, and it could not be the object of a petition to annul.[97] And the same has been held more recently with regard to a letter from the Comptroller-General to the Treasury's disbursing officer, giving his views on the application of certain provisions of a retirement pay law to a former civil servant.[98]

But, as with the administrative declaration of status, the measure of internal administration may of itself have a direct adverse effect on the person or property of particular citizens. Perhaps the best example of this type is *Joint Anti-Fascist Refugee Committee v. McGrath*,[99] decided by the United States Supreme Court in 1951. It involved the so-called loyalty program of the Federal Government. Under Executive Order 9835, promulgated by the President in 1947, the Attorney General was to furnish the Loyalty Review Board with the name of each organization that he, after appropriate investigation and determination, designated as subversive. The Board was directed to disseminate such information to all departments and agencies to guide them in employing and discharging employees. In the case referred to, the plaintiff organization sought injunctive relief against the Attorney General's designation of it as subversive in a list furnished by him to the Loyalty Review Board and distributed by it to executive departments and agencies.

It seems clear that the administrative action at issue in this case was primarily a measure of internal administration. "The employment and discharge of its civil servants, and the establishment of terms and conditions which must be met by employees or applicants for employment are internal administrative matters," the Court of Appeals for the District of Columbia has stated.[100] Yet it is unrealistic to hold, as that court held,[101] that it had no adverse effect on the plaintiff. As Mr. Justice Burton declared: "It is unrealistic to contend that because the respond-

[97] Carsault, December 10, 1909.

[98] Campana, September 19, 1945. See, similarly, Syndicat des Marchands Ambulants d'Eure-et-Loire, Council of State, April 9, 1951.

[99] 341 U.S. 123 (1951).

[100] International Workers Order v. McGrath, 182 F. 2d 368, 371 (App. D.C. 1950).

[101] Joint Anti-Fascist Refugee Committee v. Clark, 177 F. 2d 79 (App. D.C. 1949); International Workers Order v. McGrath, 182 F. 2d 368 (App. D.C. 1950).

ents gave no orders directly to the petitioners to change their course of conduct, relief cannot be granted against what the respondents actually did. We long have granted relief to parties whose legal rights have been violated by unlawful public action, although such action made no direct demands upon them."[102]

The touchstone of justiciability is injury to a legally protected right; and the right of an allegedly bona fide charitable organization to carry on its work free from the defamatory implications in the listing of it as subversive is a right that the law will protect.[103] The direct adverse effect on this right of the plaintiff organization led the Court to hold that review was available, even though the challenged administrative action was mainly intended as an internal administrative matter.[104]

Contingent Effect

Mr. Justice Frankfurter in his opinion in *Rochester Telephone Corp. v. United States*[105] referred to cases in which an administrative order did not in itself affect the petitioner, but only affected his rights adversely on the contingency of future agency action. "In view of traditional conceptions of federal judicial power," he said, "resort to the courts in these situations is either premature or wholly beyond their province."[106]

The type of case referred to can be illustrated by the *Banque de France* case, decided in 1925 by the French Council of State.[107] Review was sought by a trade union of a letter addressed to it by the president of the Bank of France, a government corporation, in which he declared that employees of the Bank who were union members would not be promoted unless they resigned their membership. This declaration, said the Council of State, was not an administrative act that could be reviewed by it. The challenged act, as it was explained by one com-

102 341 U.S. at 141.
103 *Ibid.*
104 French examples of cases involving matters of internal administration, such as instructions given to subordinates by agency heads, that are reviewable because of their direct adverse effect on private individuals include the following Council of State decisions: Chaveneau, April 1, 1949; Union des Véhicules de Transport Privé, February 4, 1949; Chassant, June 23, 1948; Fabre, November 24, 1916; Fédel, July 22, 1910.
105 307 U.S. 125 (1939).
106 *Id.* at 130.
107 July 17, 1925.

mentator, would have no adverse effect until it was applied to a particular employee. "The union should have waited until a promotion was made in accordance with the directive. Then the employee or employees who had been told of the proposed promotion and who, not having been willing to resign from the union, were not promoted, could attack the promotion actually made."[108] Adverse effect of the declaration was thus dependent on the contingency of future administrative action applying it in individual cases.

A similar case of mere contingent effect was presented, according to the majority of the United States Supreme Court, in *Eccles v. People's Bank.*[109] The respondent bank had been granted membership in the Federal Reserve System, subject to a condition that provided for withdrawal from membership within sixty days after written notice from the Board of Governors if a named corporation or any of its affiliates thereafter acquired any interest in the bank without the approval of the Board. Respondent contended that the imposing of the condition was beyond the powers of the Board of Governors and sought a declaratory judgment to that effect. Mr. Justice Frankfurter, speaking for the majority of the Court, held that the bank's action was premature. His analysis is not unlike that of the French commentator discussed above. Respondent could not be affected by the administrative action at issue until the Board of Governors commenced revocation proceedings for a violation of the condition. "The Bank seeks a declaration of its rights *if* it should lose its independence or *if* the Board of Governors should reverse its policy and seek to invoke the condition even though the Bank remains independent. . . . The concurrence of these contingent events, necessary for injury to be realized, is too speculative to warrant anticipatory judicial determinations."[110]

One wonders, though, whether cases of the type of *Eccles v. People's Bank* should be treated as involving merely the possibility of adverse effect on the contingency of future administrative action. In the words of the dissenting Justices on the effect of the condition imposed by the Board of Governors: "It seems obvious that the requirement was a restriction on the market for respondent's stock and therefore detrimental to the conduct of its business, a continuing threat of the Board to exclude respondent from the benefits of the System."[111] It is all very

108 2 Hauriou, La Jurisprudence administrative de 1892 à 1929, 95 (1929).
109 333 U.S. 426 (1948).
110 *Id.* at 432.
111 *Id.* at 437.

well to argue, as the majority of the Court does, that the bank is not actually injured until the Board moves to revoke its membership for a violation; but in a practical sense does not that position make it inordinately difficult for the respondent to obtain a judicial determination of the *vires* of the condition? At that later stage it could secure that determination only at the risk of losing its membership if the condition were held to be within the Board's authority.

These considerations apply with equal force to the *Banque de France* case, discussed above. There, too, if review is not made available at this stage it may, as a practical matter, never be obtained. Unless the union can secure a judicial decision now on the validity of the announced administrative policy not to promote union members, it may never be able to obtain a decision. True, its members may challenge the policy on which the administration acts if it is applied in a particular case involving one of them. But is it not more likely that there will never be such a challenge by an individual member? The individual members will probably resign from the complaining union rather than risk their promotions.

An American case directly in point here is *Columbia Broadcasting System v. United States*.[112] The appellant sought review of the Chain Broadcasting Regulations promulgated by the Federal Communications Commission. The regulations provided that no licenses were to be granted to stations or applicants having specified contractual relationships with broadcasting networks. Appellant was a network organization whose business depended on the maintenance and renewal of contracts such as those against which the particular regulations were directed. It was argued that the order promulgating the regulations was not reviewable, for in and of themselves they did not purport to affect the contract rights of the appellant or of its affiliate stations. They merely laid down principles to govern future action of the Commission. Their effect was thus contingent on F.C.C. action in future license-application or renewal cases, and, it was asserted, it was only when the Commission acted in such a case in conformity to the regulations that its action was reviewable.

This argument was rejected by the majority of the Court. It loses sight, said Mr. Chief Justice Stone, of the regulations' immediate effect on appellant's contractual relations with its affiliates. Knowledge that contracts such as theirs with the appellant would result in a refusal to

[112] 316 U.S. 407 (1942).

renew their station permits would lead the affiliates to repudiate the contracts rather than run the risk of losing their licenses. "If the regulations are valid they alter the status of appellant's contracts and thus determine their validity in advance of such [renewal] proceedings. By striking them down by a determination proclaimed in advance that licenses shall be cancelled or refused because of a previous failure to comply with the regulations, they impose a penalty and sanction for non-compliance far more drastic than the fines customarily imposed for breach of reviewable administrative orders."[113]

Appellant's rights were affected more immediately than by the mere contingency of future administrative action. It may be true enough that licensees who regarded the regulations as invalid were free to continue their existing contracts and to challenge the regulations when the Commission refused to renew their licenses, and that the network could intervene in the renewal proceeding. But is it not more probable that there would never be such a challenge by a licensee in a renewal proceeding? For to make the challenge would be to chance losing its license. The licensees were "free only in the sense that all those who do not choose to conform to regulations which may be accepted to be lawful are free by their choice to accept the legal consequences of their acts. Failure to comply with the regulations entails such consequences to the station owner and to appellant. These are the loss of the affiliated stations' licenses if they adhere to their contracts, and disruption of appellant's network through the declared unlawfulness of the contracts, if the regulations are valid."[114]

The decision of the Court in the *Columbia Broadcasting* case is to be preferred to its decision refusing review in *Eccles v. People's Bank* or that of the Council of State in the *Banque de France* case. This has, indeed, been recognized in other decisions by the French tribunal in which review is granted despite the contention that adverse effect is dependent on the contingency of future administrative action.[115] The answer in any given case must, of course, depend on its particular fact pattern. But if adverse effect is clear, even though eventual, review should be available, especially if, as in the cases discussed, future challenge of the administrative action appears unlikely. As Justice Frankfurter has recently stated: "Finality is not . . . a principle inflexibly applied. If the ultimate impact of the challenged action on the peti-

[113] *Id.* at 418.
[114] *Id.* at 419.
[115] E.g., Groffe, July 15, 1927.

tioner is sufficiently probable and not too distant, and if the procedure by which that ultimate action may be questioned is too onerous or hazardous, 'standing' is given to challenge the action at a preliminary stage."[116]

Standing

The analysis just given shows that the *droit administratif* is not unlike our own administrative law in its requirement of ripeness for review. In both systems administrative action is not reviewable unless it is "final" in the sense of having by itself a direct adverse effect. And the cases discussed show that French and American courts have not been too far apart in their application of the requirement of finality.

The same is also true, though to a lesser extent, of the interest deemed necessary in the individual who seeks to bring the review action. Here, too, the starting point of both systems has been similar. Both the Council of State and the courts in this country have begun with the proposition that the petitioner must have, before his review action will be entertained, a direct personal interest in the administrative action challenged. "A petitioner does not have standing to sue," Mr. Justice Frankfurter has asserted, "unless he is 'interested in and adversely affected by the decision' of which he seeks review. His 'interest must be of a personal and not of an official nature'."[117]

Similar statements are often made by French writers. "The action to annul," reads a leading text, "is not the *actio popularis* of the Roman law; citizens cannot bring it in the interest of the community as a whole to make sure that the rule of law is respected"[118] by the administration. The French citizen who files a petition to annul an administrative act must show that he has a personal interest in having it annulled. "The Council of State applies the well-known procedural principle: 'No interest, no action.' It does not mean to deal with the petitions of persons who, not having any personal interest in the annulment of the challenged act, may have acted out of pure chicanery."[119]

The requirement of a personal interest in the petitioner has been imposed by the Council of State more or less as a rule of convenience.

[116] Joint Anti-Fascist Refugee Committee v. McGrath, 341 U.S. 123, 156 (1951).
[117] *Id.* at 151.
[118] Alibert, *op. cit. supra* note 72, at 96.
[119] Waline, *op. cit. supra* note 37, at 116. For a recent case, see Morin, Council of State, January 17, 1951.

In this country, on the other hand, the requirement is based on the Supreme Court's interpretation of the Federal Constitution. "By the express terms of the Constitution, the exercise of the judicial power is limited to 'cases' and 'controversies'. Beyond this it does not extend, and unless it is asserted in a case or controversy within the meaning of the Constitution, the power to exercise it is nowhere conferred."[120]

The judicial power in this country in the field of administrative law, as in other branches of the law, extends to the resolution of actual controversies arising between adverse litigants. In the view of our courts there can be no real "case" or "controversy" in the sense required by the Constitution if the individual bringing the review action does not have a personal interest in getting the challenged administrative act set aside. Unless adversely affected as an individual, he is seeking only a judgment in the abstract on the legality of the administrative act. Such an objective is insufficient to call for the exercise of federal judicial power. Its exercise "is legitimate only in the last resort, and as a necessity in the determination of real, earnest and vital controversy between individuals."[121]

As Mr. Justice Frankfurter has phrased the principle: "The jurisdiction of the federal courts can be invoked only under circumstances which to the expert feel of lawyers constitute a 'case of controversy.' The scope and consequences of the review with which the judiciary is entrusted over executive . . . action require us to observe these bounds fastidiously."[122] It is this feeling on the part of the American courts that has led them to construe the requirement of personal interest in the petitioner somewhat more strictly than, in certain cases, the Council of State has construed it. If they did not do so, it has been feared, they might encroach beyond the bounds of judicial power imposed by the Constitution.

Collective Interest

Among the most difficult cases involving standing in the field of administrative law are those in which the person bringing the review action relies on injury, not alone to himself as an individual, but to a larger group or collectivity of which he is a member. The most obvious case, of course, is that in which the petitioner alleges only that he is a

120 Muskrat v. United States, 219 U.S. 346, 356 (1911).
121 Chicago & Grand Trunk Railway Co. v. Wellman, 143 U.S. 339, 345 (1892).
122 Joint Anti-Fascist Refugee Committee v. McGrath, 341 U.S. at 150.

member of the community, interested as such in ensuring the enforcement of the principle of administrative legality. In such a case he is seeking to vindicate not so much a personal interest adversely affected as the collective interest in proper administration that every individual has as a member of society.

If the only interest alleged is that of a citizen concerned with good administration, the review petition will not be entertained in either the French or the American system. A recent decision of the Council of State involved just such a petition. Petitioner, a doctor, sought review of a prefectoral decision refusing to change a public poster about anti-diphtheria vaccination that referred to the law of November 24, 1940, enacted by the Vichy regime, so as to read the "so-called law of November 24, 1940." The petition cannot be entertained, reads the Council's decision, because petitioner, "who has based his petition on his position as a citizen and could not in the circumstances rely on any other interest, does not show that he has a direct personal interest in having the challenged act set aside."[123]

Taxpayers' Suits

The case of the individual who alleges merely his interest as a member of the community is relatively easy to dispose of. Unless the requirement of personal interest is to be wholly done away with, a petition that alleges only such an interest must be dismissed.

A more difficult type of case in which the individual bringing the review action relies on a collective interest that is injured as a member of some group or collectivity occurs when the petitioner alleges that he is a taxpayer whose interest arises from the fact that the administrative act challenged as illegal involves an expenditure of public funds. Does the petitioner *qua* taxpayer have the interest required to give him standing for a review action?

In this country the answer is probably in the affirmative if the case concerns only the level of local government. The resemblance between private and municipal corporations has led to a treatment of the local taxpayer as the counterpart of the stockholder whose proprietary interest is sufficient to maintain an action for relief from misconduct by corporate officials. "From the nature of the powers exercised by municipal corporations, the great danger of their abuse and the necessity of

[123] Faveret, February 11, 1949. For a similar American decision, see Elliott v. White, 23 F. 2d 997 (App. D.C. 1928).

prompt action to prevent irremediable injuries, it would seem eminently proper," the Supreme Court has asserted, "for courts of equity to interfere upon the application of the tax-payers of a county to prevent the consummation of a wrong, when the officers of those corporations assume, in excess of their powers, to create burdens upon property-holders."[124]

Although the corporate analogy is not specifically used, an increasing majority of the state courts in this country have extended the principle of the municipal-corporation cases to suits involving the acts of state administrative officers.[125] But the federal courts have consistently refused to apply it in cases involving the acts of federal officers.

The leading case is the decision of the Supreme Court in *Frothingham v. Mellon.*[126] The Court admitted that a municipal taxpayer had been held to have a sufficient interest to bring an action to review the legality of acts of municipal officers. "But," said Mr. Justice Sutherland, "the relation of a taxpayer of the United States to the Federal Government is very different. His interest in the moneys of the Treasury—partly realized from taxation and partly from other sources—is shared with millions of others; is comparatively minute and indeterminable; and the effect upon future taxation, of any payment out of the funds, so remote, fluctuating and uncertain, that no basis is afforded for an appeal to the preventive powers of a court of equity."[127]

The early decisions of the Council of State on this point are even narrower than those of the American Court. In 1893, in a case whose fact pattern was not unlike that presented in *Frothingham v. Mellon,* the French tribunal refused to entertain a petition to annul brought by one who relied solely on his interest as a taxpayer of the City of Paris.[128] This decision of the Council was strongly attacked by students of the subject, and not the least strongly by Hauriou, pre-eminent among modern French administrative lawyers. It is clear, he wrote in 1894, that the Council's decision presents a serious problem, and that the growth of democracy will only accentuate it. Taxpayers are no longer sufficiently protected against the lapses of their administrators.[129]

124 Crampton v. Zabriskie, 101 U.S. 601, 609 (1879).
125 See Note, 50 Harv. L. Rev. 1276, 1278 (1937).
126 262 U.S. 447 (1923).
127 *Id.* at 487. The doctrine of this case has constantly been reaffirmed by the American Court. For a recent case, see Doremus v. Board of Education, 342 U.S. 429 (1952).
128 Bied-Charreton, February 10, 1893. A similar case is Poisson, March 10, 1893.
129 Hauriou, *op. cit. supra* note 108, at 208.

The way out is to give them access to the Council of State to control the legality of the acts of the administration. And, he concluded on a prophetic note, the failure of previous petitioners should not discourage taxpayers. "Let them continue to knock on the door; ultimately it will open."[130]

This prophecy bore fruit in 1901, when the Council of State abandoned its earlier case law in one of the most famous decisions it has ever rendered. In that case, which bears the suggestive name of *Casanova*,[131] the French tribunal held that a municipal taxpayer had standing to bring an action to review the legality of a governmental act that might involve the illegal expenditure of municipal funds. His interest as a taxpayer alone, reads the decision, is sufficient to give him standing.

The principle of the *Casanova* case has been constantly reaffirmed by the Council of State. That case involved merely a municipal taxpayer. In later decisions the Council has extended its principle to a departmental taxpayer[132] and to a taxpayer of an overseas territory.[133] But it has thus far refused to allow a national taxpayer to challenge the acts of the central administration, holding that in such a case the interest of the taxpayer was not enough to give him standing to sue.[134]

The Council of State's refusal to extend the principle of the *Casanova* case to a national taxpayer has been criticized. To allow him to bring such an action, writes one authority, "would contravene no legal principle and would in practice be highly beneficial."[135] The position of the Council has nonetheless been supported by the need to limit the number of review actions. "To allow actions by national taxpayers who rely only on their interest as such would lead to a great increase in the number of petitions to annul; annulments on the ground of illegality would probably be very few; the advantage that would result would thus be hardly appreciable."[136]

This is essentially the argument used by Mr. Justice Sutherland to justify his decision in *Frothingham v. Mellon*. "If one taxpayer may champion and litigate such a cause, then every other taxpayer may do the same. . . . The bare mention of such a result, with its attendant

130 *Id.* at 210.
131 March 29, 1901.
132 Richemond, January 27, 1911.
133 Galandou Diouf, June 24, 1932.
134 Dufour, February 13, 1930; Le Doussal, June 25, 1920.
135 Alibert, *op. cit. supra* note 72, at 105.
136 (1933) Dalloz, Critique, part 3, p. 14.

inconveniences, goes far to sustain the conclusion which we have reached, that a suit of this character cannot be maintained."[137]

The fear of the consequences involved in allowing all taxpayers to bring review actions has motivated both the Council of State and the United States Supreme Court in their affirmation that a taxpayer of the national government does not have standing. In both countries the interest of a local taxpayer is deemed sufficient to allow him to bring the review action. Though the trend is perhaps clearer in the French system, in this country too it is manifest. In both systems, however, a line is drawn at the national level. The reasoning of Justice Sutherland in *Frothingham v. Mellon* is applied to bar actions by anyone who asserts only the interest arising from his payment of taxes to the national government.

Consumer Interest

Closely related to the taxpayer cases are those in which the person bringing the review action relies on his interest as a consumer using the product or service regulated or operated by the administration. In these cases, as in those involving taxpayers' suits, the petitioner is a member of a group or collectivity affected by the administrative action, and his suit, if successful, vindicates not only his personal interest but even more a collective interest.

The United States Supreme Court has been most reluctant to allow suits by individuals who allege only the interest of a consumer. An outstanding example of the Court's attitude is found in *City of Atlanta v. Ickes*.[138] In that case a city that was a large consumer of coal sought review of the validity of an administrative order fixing minimum coal prices. The district court, after a full treatment of the issues, decided against the city on the merits. The Supreme Court, in a one-sentence *per curiam* opinion, held that the reviewing court need not have gone into the merits at all. "The judgment is affirmed on the ground that the appellant has no standing to maintain this suit." *Atlanta v. Ickes*, Mr. Justice Frankfurter has explained in a later case, stands for the proposition that a consumer has no standing to challenge a minimum price order.[139]

What is true of minimum price orders has also been true, in the

[137] 262 U.S. at 487.
[138] 308 U.S. 517 (1939).
[139] Dissenting, in Stark v. Wickard, 321 U.S. 288, 319 (1944).

jurisprudence of the Supreme Court, of orders fixing public-utility rates.[140] The Court, in holding that a consumer of the service furnished by a utility has no standing to challenge rate orders fixing the price he has to pay for the service, has asserted that in rate-making proceedings there are only two necessary parties: the regulatory agency and the public utility. As for the public that subscribes to the service, its interests are represented by the administration. On this point, Mr. Justice Sutherland has asserted, "it is only necessary to say that the commission represents the public and especially the subscribers."[141] The administration itself is thus considered to be the representative of the consumer interest, and individual consumers are deemed to be sufficiently protected by its representation. It may well be, as one commentator has affirmed, that "to a considerable extent, this principle may not reflect the practical situation."[142] But it is used nonetheless by the Supreme Court to justify its holding that consumers have no standing to bring review actions.

In the *droit administratif* there has been no hesitancy, such as that just noted in the jurisprudence of the United States Supreme Court, over review actions by consumers of a product or service regulated or operated by the administration. The leading case is a noted decision of the Council of State rendered in 1906.[143] Petitioners there were the inhabitants of an outlying section of the City of Bordeaux. They were dependent for transportation on a tramway line connecting their section with the main part of the city. The company that operated the line discontinued the portion of its service leading to petitioners' section, although the law provided that continuation of such service could be compelled by the prefect if it were necessary in the interest of the

140 Wright v. Central Ky. Natural Gas Co., 297 U.S. 537 (1936); City of New York v. New York Tel. Co., 261 U.S. 312 (1923).

141 Smith v. Illinois Bell Tel. Co., 270 U.S. 587, 592 (1926).

142 Gellhorn, Administrative Law: Cases and Comments 426 (2d ed., 1947). Lower federal courts have had less hesitancy in upholding the standing of consumers. See, e.g., Reade v. Ewing, 205 F. 2d 630 (2d Cir. 1953); National Coal Association v. Federal Power Commission, 191 F. 2d 462 (App. D.C. 1951); United States v. Public Utilities Commission, 151 F. 2d 609 (App. D.C. 1945); Associated Industries v. Ickes, 134 F. 2d 694 (2d Cir. 1934). More recent Supreme Court cases may foreshadow a change, as yet inarticulated, in that Court's jurisprudence. See Public Utilities Commission v. Pollak, 343 U.S. 451 (1952); Parker v. Fleming, 329 U.S. 531 (1947). Compare Chapman v. Federal Power Commission, 345 U.S. 153 (1953), where a consumer organization was held to have standing, though differences of view precluded a single opinion of the Court on the point.

143 Syndicat des Propriétaires du Quartier-Croix-de-Seguey-Tivoli, December 21, 1906.

public, even though the particular service did not pay its own way.[144] The petitioners, acting on the advice of Léon Duguit, at that time dean of the Law Faculty at Bordeaux University and, next to Maurice Hauriou, the outstanding public lawyer in France, sought to have the local prefect exercise his power to compel continuance. On his refusal to do so they brought an action in the Council of State to have his refusal set aside as illegal. On the merits, the Council held for the prefect. But in doing so it expressly held that petitioners, as users of the tramway line, had sufficient interest to bring an action to review the legality of an administrative act affecting the service they used.

Since this decision the standing of a consumer for bringing a review action has been clear in France. A more recent illustration is a 1936 decision of the Council of State. That case, too, involved a company that operated a tramway line. Under the French system at that time the fares charged by such companies were fixed by prefectoral decrees. Such a decree had been promulgated raising the fares charged by the particular company in the City of Nancy. Petitioner brought an action to have the fare increase set aside by the Council of State, relying only on his interest as a user of the tramway. In holding that review was available at the instance of petitioner, the French tribunal stated: "Since it is clear that [petitioner] lives in the City of Nancy and is a user of the tramway line operated in that city by the Company . . . he consequently has a personal interest in demanding that the challenged decree be set aside."[145]

The Council of State's readiness to allow review actions to be brought by consumers surely has more to commend it than the reluctance of the United States Supreme Court in analogous cases. It is difficult to see why a consumer does not have a direct personal interest in administrative action affecting the product or service that he purchases. If the price he has to pay is increased by administrative order, is it not to deal in abstract legal learning rather than in the realities of the record[146] to hold that he does not have a personal interest in getting the order reviewed?

In both the French and the American systems of administrative law the case law has recognized that the economic interest of a competitor

144 There is a similar power in American regulatory agencies like the Interstate Commerce Commission. See, e.g., Alabama Public Service Commission v. Southern R. Co., 341 U.S. 341 (1951).

145 De Roche du Teilloy, December 4, 1936.

146 Paraphrasing Indianapolis v. Chase National Bank, 314 U.S. 63, 69 (1941).

is sufficient to allow him to bring a review action.[147] If this is true of a competitor, why is it not also true of a consumer, whose economic well-being may likewise be wholly dependent on the service he uses, especially in the field of public utilities? The answer that the United States Supreme Court has sometimes given, that in cases of this type there are only two parties involved, the administrative agency and the company regulated, simply does not square with the facts. It rests on the proposition that the consuming public is adequately represented by the administration, which can be wholly relied upon to defend the public interest—a proposition that may often be, at the best, a pious fiction.

In cases of the type under discussion, unless a consumer is permitted to challenge the administrative action it is unlikely that its legality will ever be reviewed. In a practical sense, then, such action would be placed in a conclusive position, for it would never be challenged by the only other parties involved, the agency and the company regulated by it. If the administrative action is beneficial to the company—e.g., an order raising the price of its product or services—it is only the consumer who is adversely affected and who will seek to challenge its validity.

In view of the role of the courts in enforcing the principle of administrative legality, it is of the utmost importance that agency action should not be placed in a position of conclusiveness. In these cases review should be made available at the suit of the consumer, the one party who may have an interest in challenging the administrative action. As the Supreme Court stated in the well-known *Sanders* case, with regard to the standing of one injured economically by the grant of a license to a competitor: "Congress had some purpose in enacting §402(b)(2). It may have been of opinion that one likely to be financially injured by the issue of a license would be the only person having a sufficient interest to bring to the attention of the appellate court errors of law in the action of the Commission in granting the license."[148]

The Supreme Court, in its reluctance to hold that a consumer has the personal interest required to bring a review action, tends to lose sight of the need to make sure that someone shall in fact be able to secure review of administrative action. It is this need more than any

147 Federal Communications Commission v. Sanders Radio Station, 309 U.S. 470 (1940); Chambre Syndicale des Propriétaires de Bains, Council of State, February 2, 1906.

148 Federal Communications Commission v. Sanders Radio Station, 309 U.S. 470, 477 (1940).

other that has led the French Council of State so to broaden its conception of the interest required to bring a review action as to include the interest of a consumer. It may well be that the American Court's narrow approach on this point has been induced by its fear of unduly broadening the concept of standing, in view of the constitutional limitations on the exercise of federal judicial power already referred to. Such fear would, however, seem to be unjustified so far as the cases under discussion are concerned. The interest of a consumer in the product or service that he purchases appears to be direct enough to eliminate the danger of judicial decision in the abstract, which the framers of the judiciary Article of the Federal Constitution sought to avoid.

Actio Popularis?

It cannot be denied that the jurisprudence of the French Council of State has been somewhat more liberal than that of the United States Supreme Court on the question of the standing required to bring a review action. The cases just discussed, on the standing of petitioners alleging only the interest of a consumer, serve to show this liberality. At the same time the French tribunal has been careful not to do away entirely with the requirement that the petitioner bringing the review action have a personal interest in the setting aside of the challenged administrative act. If his interest is so slight as to be negligible, his petition must be dismissed for lack of standing. Thus, in the taxpayer cases a local taxpayer is seen to have enough of an interest in local administration to justify allowing him to seek review, whereas a national taxpayer is held to have too inconsequential an interest in the national treasury to require him to be permitted, *qua* taxpayer, to challenge the legality of acts of the central administration.

The basic principle with regard to standing in the *droit administratif* is still that stated by the government commissioner in his conclusions addressed to the Council of State in a case decided by it in 1944. "To be admitted to challenge an administrative act before you it is not enough, according to your case law, for the petitioner to rely on any interest whatsoever. His interest must have an individual, direct, and legitimate reality. Though you may be inclined to make the review action both a safeguard of such interests and a powerful instrument of administrative morality, you never intended to make of it a popular action, available to anyone at all."[149]

[149] Conclusions delivered in Robert, January 7, 1944.

The Council of State has consequently continued to insist on the requirement of a personal interest, although, as in the cases involving review actions by consumers, it may have been more liberal than the United States Supreme Court in its interpretation of that requirement. The insistence on a personal interest in would-be petitioners has been induced primarily by the fear that any other rule might unduly hamper judicial administration. To permit review by anyone, regardless of whether he is personally interested in the proceeding, might be to open the floodgates of administrative-law litigation. Mr. Justice Frankfurter aptly expressed this risk in a case involving the radio broadcast industry: "So much by way of limitation seems necessary to prevent . . . mass appeals by the industry at large, with resulting hopeless clogging of the administrative process by judicial review."[150]

One wonders, however, whether this fear, which seems to underlie both French and American law on the subject, is not more theoretical than real. Such at least was the conclusion of one federal court in a case involving review of a price-fixing order at the suit of a consumer. The administration contended that to allow a consumer to bring a review action would open up the possibility of separate lawsuits by hundreds of thousands of individual consumers attacking agency orders, with the result of impairing effective administration. "But," said Judge Frank in dealing with this contention, "there are no such horrendous possibilities."[151] A decision by one court, he said, would normally have a *stare decisis* effect, and the filing of a review petition with one court should prevent other courts from entertaining a petition with respect to the same order subsequently filed by other aggrieved persons. It is recognized that this reasoning of Judge Frank may be contrary to the approach of the Supreme Court in the consumer cases discussed. All the same, as one commentator has pithily expressed it, it satisfactorily explodes the notion that permitting all those with interests as consumers to get review will flood the courts with countless cases.[152]

To assume an inevitable congestion of the judicial and administrative processes if judicial review is made more freely available is to make an unwarranted assumption. Widespread availability of review will not necessarily lead to a plethora of cases, for the right of review is rarely resorted to for its own sake. "Nobody outside Bedlam sup-

150 Dissenting, in Federal Communications Commission v. National Broadcasting Co., 319 U.S. 239, 260 (1943).

151 Associated Industries v. Ickes, 134 F. 2d 694, 707 (2d Cir. 1943).

152 Davis, Administrative Law 716 (1951).

poses that the reason why Courts of law exist in a civilized community is that the founders of the State have believed happiness to consist in the greatest possible amount of litigation among the greatest possible number of citizens. The real triumph of Courts of law is when the universal knowledge of their existence, and universal faith in their justice, reduce to a minimum the number of those who are willing so to behave as to expose themselves to their jurisdiction. . . . The knowledge that the machinery exists, and that when it is employed it is employed with skill and without favour, has the effect of rendering its employment unnecessary save only in the exceptional case."[153]

It is unrealistic to assume that the individual who seeks judicial review of administrative action is vindicating only his personal interest. It may, indeed, be to his benefit to have an illegal administrative act adversely affecting him set aside. But, even more important, he is also vindicating the public interest just as truly as a district attorney does when he institutes a criminal prosecution. It is clearly in the interest of the community that illegal administrative action be not left untouched. The individual who brings a review action is thus vindicating the public interest in the enforcement of the principle of administrative legality in addition to any personal interest he may happen to have.

In administrative-law cases the individuals bringing review actions are not merely in the position of ordinary parties plaintiff. They are also, to use an apt characterization, "private Attorney Generals."[154] If the action for review is entrusted to private individuals, "it is to transform them into overseers of the Administration; they doubtless have a personal interest, but at the same time they act in the public interest; in this type of case, they are not merely parties defending their own right: their position approaches that of a district attorney pursuing the prosecution of a crime."[155]

If one so construes the suit to obtain judicial review of administrative action, one can easily conclude that it ought to be treated as the *actio popularis* of the Roman law was treated, with no restrictions on the standing of those who seek to bring it. If such actions vindicate the public interest by preventing administrative officers from acting in excess of their authority, is it not in the public interest that they should be able to be brought as freely as possible?

[153] Hewart, *op. cit. supra* note 16, at 155.

[154] The term used in Associated Industries v. Ickes, 134 F. 2d 694, 704 (2d. Cir. 1943).

[155] Hauriou, *op. cit. supra* note 108, at 408.

It should, however, be recognized that neither the French nor the American system of administrative law has gone so far as to allow review actions to be brought by anyone who asserts no more than his interest as a member of the public. Our discussion of the citizen and taxpayer interest cases will have made this limitation clear. Nor does it seem likely that the courts, at least those in this country, will ever go so far. The constitutional requirement of "case or controversy" will probably continue so to be construed as to demand some personal interest in review petitioners. One can, all the same, venture to hope that our courts will become at least as liberal as the French Council of State in their determinations in particular cases on the question whether the required personal interest does or does not exist.

Chapter Eight

SCOPE OF REVIEW

The reviewing court, after it has determined that review is available in the given case, must then examine the merits of the arguments advanced against the legality of the challenged administrative act. We must now measure the scope of such judicial inquiry into the merits.

This question, the scope of review, has been a crucial one in American administrative law. Until a comparatively recent time, indeed, the issue of proper scope was a highly controversial one. But now, as Professor Davis puts it: "The long debate about de novo review versus restricted review is about ended; the Ben Avon and Crowell cases[1] are of little interest except as history; extremists have moved from both ends toward the middle; and the substantial-evidence rule now dominates nearly all judicial review of administrative action in the federal courts."[2]

The fact that present-day discussions of the scope of review in this country are no longer dominated by the heat of partisan controversy does not, however, mean that that question is now of only academic importance. The revelation by Professor Davis of his own mental processes in writing up the subject for his treatise on administrative law is highly significant in this respect. "The easy supposition," he has stated, "was that the book . . . would include a mere summary of the law concerning scope of review. But the preparation of what started out to be such a summary has led to the surprising discoveries that the heart of the scope-of-review problem as of 1950 is inadequately treated by the literature and that few branches of administrative law are more challenging."[3]

The basic importance of scope of review lies in the fact that the

[1] Ohio Valley Water Co. v. Ben Avon Borough, 253 U.S. 287 (1920); Crowell v. Benson, 285 U.S. 22 (1932).

[2] Davis, Administrative Law 868 (1951).

[3] Davis, "Scope of Review of Federal Administrative Action" 50 Col. L. Rev. 559 (1950).

extent of judicial inquiry in particular cases may determine whether or not full effect is given to the legislative purpose in creating administrative agencies. "One of the principal reasons for the creation of such agencies is to secure the benefit of special knowledge acquired through continuous experience in a difficult and complicated field."[4] If the review of administrative determinations were to be very broad, with the reviewing court deciding the case *de novo* on its independent judgment, "administrative tribunals would be turned into little more than media for transmission of the evidence to the courts. It would destroy the values of adjudication of fact by experts or specialists in the field involved. It would divide the responsibility for administrative adjudications."[5]

We should not forget that "in the whole of administrative law the functions that can be performed by judicial review are fairly limited."[6] The role of the courts in this field "is to serve as a check on the administrative branch of government—a check against excess of power and abusive exercise of power in derogation of private right."[7] The judicial function is thus one of control: we can expect judicial review to *check* —not to *supplant*—administrative action.[8] The province of the judge is to confine the administrator within the bounds of legality, not to determine for himself the wisdom of challenged administrative action.

At the same time the limitations imposed on the scope of inquiry of the reviewing court must not go so far as to prevent full judicial scrutiny of the question of legality. If that question cannot be properly explored by the judge, the right to judicial review can become but an empty form. "It makes judicial review of administrative orders a hopeless formality for the litigant. . . . It reduces the judicial process in such cases to a mere feint."[9]

Investigatory Powers of Reviewing Court

Before we go into the scope of review itself in detail, we should say a word about the powers of investigation and decision possessed by the

4 Securities and Exchange Commission v. Associated Gas & Electric Co., 99 F. 2d 795, 798 (2d Cir. 1938).

5 Report of the Attorney General's Committee on Administrative Procedure 91 (1941).

6 *Id.* at 76.

7 *Ibid.*

8 *Id.* at 77.

9 Jackson, J., dissenting, in Securities and Exchange Commission v. Chenery Corp., 332 U.S. 194, 210 (1947).

reviewing court. In this country the law of the judge's authority in this respect is relatively simple and clear. The basic proposition developed with regard to the court's power of inquiry is that it must in general be limited to the administrative record. The judge may not go behind the record and seek to probe the mental processes of the deciding officials within the administration.

This proposition has been settled ever since the decision of the United States Supreme Court in the fourth *Morgan* case, in which that tribunal asserted in vigorous language the principle that administrative officers may not be interrogated before the reviewing court to aid the court in determining the process of decision that led to challenged agency action. "Such an examination of a judge would be destructive of judicial responsibility. . . . Just as a judge cannot be subjected to such a scrutiny . . . so the integrity of the administrative process must be equally respected."[10]

The French law is similar so far as interrogation of administrative officers before the reviewing court is concerned, although there have been no French cases like the fourth *Morgan* case to call for the judicial articulation of this principle. "Without doubt," states a leading doctrinal writer, "it is not for the Council of State to summon administrators before its bar to demand an accounting."[11] The French tribunal has, however, as we shall see,[12] assumed for itself the authority to inquire into the motives behind an administrative act in a way that Anglo-American courts have refused to do. If the purpose that motivated the challenged act is other than that which the legislature intended, the act will be set aside on review for what is termed "abuse of power." But even in such cases, we shall note, the inquiry into motives by the French court is limited to inquiry into the record.

In the *droit administratif* as in the American system the fundamental principle is that the power of investigation of the reviewing court is restricted to the record. The record itself in cases before the administrative courts is, as has already been seen,[13] wholly written. The French, like the American, reviewing court does not normally have the authority to hear oral testimony to supplement the written record. The proof of illegality must be found in the written record, or the review action

10 United States v. Morgan, 313 U.S. 409, 422 (1941).
11 Alibert, Le Contrôle juridictionnel de l'administration 258 (1926).
12 *Infra* pp. 216-19.
13 *Supra* pp. 136-37.

must be dismissed. "Such proof cannot consist of oral testimony. . . . It must result from evidence in the record."[14]

It should, of course, be borne in mind that the record in a case before a French administrative court is not precisely the same thing as the record before an American reviewing court. With us the record on review is essentially the administrative record, which, according to the Federal Administrative Procedure Act,[15] consists of the transcript of testimony and exhibits, together with all papers and requests filed in the proceeding. In the French system, too, the administrative dossier becomes part of the record for decision.[16] But this dossier is not nearly so complete as the record made in adversary administrative proceedings in this country. Even if a hearing is held by the administration, the dossier contains, not a stenographic transcript, but only a digest by an agency official of what occurred at the hearing. This incompleteness by American standards of the administrative dossier will help explain the relative freedom allowed the reporter to whom a case is assigned in developing the record on which the French court's decision will be based.

Powers of Decision

One can also note a basic similarity between the powers of decision exercised by the French administrative courts in review actions and those wielded by American reviewing courts. It should be remembered that French administrative lawyers are accustomed to divide review actions into two categories, the action to annul an illegal administrative act (*recours pour excès de pouvoir*) and the action to compel an affirmative act on the part of the administration, such as the payment of money damages (*recours de pleine juridiction*).[17] It is the first of these that is more or less analogous to the review action in the American system, and it is in respect to it that the powers of decision of the reviewing court are essentially alike in both France and this country.

The United States Supreme Court has often asserted that in reviewing administrative action the federal courts created under Article III of the Constitution exercise only the "judicial power" delegated to them by that Article and are not in the position of hierarchical supe-

14 Jèze, "La Jurisprudence du Conseil d'État et le détournement de pouvoir" Revue du Droit Public 58, 60 (1944) (emphasis omitted).

15 Section 7 (d).

16 *Supra* p. 136.

17 See *supra* p. 120.

riors of the agency whose action is being reviewed. These courts may not be required, then, to exercise a delegated legislative or administrative power of review in rate making or licensing cases, and thereby to revise administrative orders and enter such substitute orders as they may deem appropriate.[18]

The French Council of State has adopted a similar view as to powers of decision in actions to annul illegal administrative action. "Vested with a review petition," asserts the authoritative contemporary treatise on the *droit administratif*, "the Council of State can only dismiss it or set aside the challenged act; it cannot amend the latter."[19] The only question before the French reviewing tribunal in such cases is the legality of the challenged administrative act. If it answers that question in the affirmative, the review petition will be dismissed; if in the negative, the administrative act will be annulled. But the power of the French tribunal in these cases is limited to upholding or setting aside the challenged act. If it determines that an administrative decision is illegal, it cannot enter the substitute decision that it thinks the administration should have made.[20]

This alternative does not, of course, mean that the French reviewing court must uphold or set aside as a whole the administrative act that is challenged. Like the American courts, the Council of State quickly asserted a power of partial annulment—*i.e.*, the authority to set aside only that portion of the challenged act which is illegal, or only that portion which adversely affects the petitioner.[21]

Moreover, though the French reviewing tribunal has refused, as has been pointed out, to assert the authority to substitute for an administrative decision set aside as illegal the decision that it deems the proper one, it has often followed the practice of remanding the case to the administration "so that there may be taken the measures required by the present decision." A similar power to remand "for proceedings not inconsistent with this opinion" has also been exercised, it should be noted, by American courts. Although the remand power does not go so far as the authority to enter a substitute decision, it does enable the reviewing court to indicate clearly to the administration the course on which it

[18] Report of the Attorney General's Committee, 79. See Keller v. Potomac Electric Co., 261 U.S. 428 (1923).

[19] Waline, Traité élémentaire de droit administratif 146 (6th ed., 1951).

[20] See, e.g., Lourador, Council of State, May 14, 1948.

[21] See, e.g., Syndicat des Filateurs, Retordeurs de la Coton de Lille, Council of State, November 24, 1944.

should proceed in the given case if it wishes its action to be legal.[22] As a distinguished councilor of state has declared, the remand "formula does not give a direct order to the agency concerned; but it does draw the agency's attention to the fact that the legal solution given by the reviewing court's decision implies an administrative follow-through, and it notifies the agency that the decision will not be completely carried out so long as the necessary administrative measures are not taken."[23]

Intermediate Relief

The proceeding for judicial review of administrative action may, because of its very nature, take a great deal of time. Such delay is inherent in all litigation. Judicial justice is dispensed ever so slowly, though it may be dispensed exceedingly well.

Unless the reviewing court has the power to stay the effects of challenged administrative action pending decision on its legality, the right of judicial review may well become devoid of practical content. The problem here was well put by a French jurist. If the bringing of the review action does not stay the effects of the challenged act, "the delays in procedure and the congestion in the Council of State's docket may permit an illegal decision to remain in effect for two or three years; that is an undeniable advantage for the administration, especially when it is borne in mind that certain decisions produce their entire effect in a matter of hours. In setting aside the refusal of a mayor to permit a procession on the public way one does not resuscitate the demonstration that was to have taken place two years ago. The satisfaction obtained by the petitioner here corresponds to an award for nominal damages in a private-law case: it is the *pretium doloris*, or rather the *pretium injuriae*."[24]

The reviewing court's need of the authority to stay the effects of administrative action pending its decision in the review proceeding has been recognized in both French and American administrative law. "No court can make time stand still," reads the leading opinion on the matter by the United States Supreme Court. "The circumstances surrounding a controversy may change irrevocably during the pendency of an appeal, despite anything a court can do. But within these limits it is

[22] For a good example, see Pech, Council of State, June 19, 1929.
[23] Odent, Cours de contentieux administratif 364 (1949-50).
[24] Goldenberg, Le Conseil d'État: juge du fait 25 (1932).

reasonable that an appellate court should be able to prevent irreparable injury to the parties or to the public resulting from the premature enforcement of a determination which may later be found to have been wrong."[25] For this reason the stay power has always been held to be a part of the traditional equipment of the American courts. "If the administrative agency has committed errors of law for the correction of which the legislature has provided appropriate resort to the courts, such judicial review would be an idle ceremony if the situation were irreparably changed before the correction could be made."[26]

According to article 48 of the ordinance of July 31, 1945, the organic instrument under which the Council of State is at present constituted, the filing of a review petition with the Council does not of itself stay the effect of challenged administrative action. But the French tribunal may issue a stay order if requested to do so by the petitioner in an appropriate case.[27] This provision, it should be observed, is essentially similar to that contained in American statutes like the Interstate Commerce Act.

In what cases will a stay order be granted by the French reviewing court? According to the conclusions of M. Detton, the government commissioner in the principal case on the subject,[28] three conditions must exist before a stay order will be granted. The essential condition is irreparable injury to the petitioner if intermediate relief be not afforded him. The application of the challenged administrative act must cause the petitioner damage that cannot be redressed by the reviewing court's ultimate setting aside of that act. It should be noted that this is also the fundamental requirement in the American system. As is stated in section 10(c) of the Federal Administrative Procedure Act, the reviewing court may postpone the effective date of agency action "to the extent necessary to prevent irreparable injury."

The United States Supreme Court has, however, declared: "A stay is not a matter of right, even if irreparable injury might otherwise

[25] Scripps-Howard Radio v. Federal Communications Commission, 316 U.S. 4, 9 (1942).

[26] *Id.* at 10.

[27] This has been true ever since a decree of July 22, 1806, the language of which is very much like that in article 48 of the 1945 ordinance. A similar provision is contained in article 9 of the September 30, 1953, decree, *supra* p. 49, vesting the "Administrative Courts," as the Prefecture Councils are now to be called, with general first-instance jurisdiction.

[28] Mouvement Social Français des Croix de Feu, Council of State, July 17, 1936. The conclusions of M. Detton are printed in (1936) Dalloz, Critique, part 3, p. 77.

result."[29] And that is the reason why other factors besides irreparable injury must be present before the stay order will be granted. The second indispensable condition, said M. Detton in the case referred to, is that the review petition must be based on serious grounds. If it appear obvious from the pleadings that the challenged administrative act is legal, a stay will not be ordered, for to grant it in such a case would be to allow the petition for a stay to be made use of as a purely dilatory device. There are American cases that impose a similar condition,[30] though it seems that the Council of State has been stricter in applying it. "Although the stay order does not prejudge the legal solution that the Council of State will adopt when it examines the case on the merits," a member of the French tribunal has stated, "the Council will only consent to order a stay if convinced that the petition rests on good grounds."[31]

The third condition required before the French reviewing court will grant a stay, according to M. Detton, is that there be a public interest of a sort to supersede the normal rule that the bringing of a review action does not have a suspensive effect. This last condition has not, per se, been required in American cases, though our courts have indicated that they may, in cases involving petitions for a stay order, balance the public interest in having the administrative act take effect immediately against the private interest of the petitioner in having its effect stayed.

It should be pointed out that the French administrative courts have been much more reluctant to exercise authority to stay the effects of administrative action, pending decision on its legality, than the American courts have been. Thus, in a recent study of the Council of State's procedure it is admitted that the case law on intermediate relief is very narrow. The grant of a stay by the Council is stated to be "exceedingly rare."[32] Complaints have been heard against the French tribunal's reluctance in this field for at least two generations.[33] One can perhaps detect a recent abatement of the Council's overcaution, for a number of stay

[29] Virginian Railway Co. v. United States, 272 U.S. 658, 672 (1926).

[30] E.g., North Carolina v. United States, 56 F. Supp. 606 (E.D. N.C. 1944).

[31] Odent, *op. cit. supra* note 23, at 229.

[32] *Ibid.* It should be noted that the 1953 decree provision referred to, *supra* note 27, declares that the "Administrative Courts" are to issue stays in "exceptional cases."

[33] See, e.g., 2 Hauriou, La Jurisprudence administrative de 1892 à 1929, 6 (1929). The vice-president of the Council of State, M. Cassin, has recently asserted a doubt as to the efficacy of the stay power, characterizing it as a mere "palliative." Conseil d'État, Études et documents 11 (1948).

orders have been granted since the Liberation.[34] In view of the importance of the stay power it is to be hoped that these cases foreshadow a liberalization of the Council of State's attitude. Though some American courts may in the past have exercised too freely their authority to afford intermediate relief, it would seem that the French tribunal has erred equally in the opposite direction.

Ultra Vires

The law of judicial review of administrative action in the common-law world has been largely developed as a branch of the law of *ultra vires*. Review in the Anglo-American system is based on the theory "that every public officer has marked out for him by law a certain area of 'jurisdiction.' Within the boundaries of this area he can act freely according to his own discretion, and the courts will respect his action as final and not inquire into its rightfulness. But if he oversteps those bounds, then the courts will intervene. In this form, the law of court review of public officers becomes simply a branch of the law of *ultra vires*. The only question before the court is one of jurisdiction, and the court has no control of the officer's exercise of discretion within that jurisdiction."[35] Under this theory judicial review of administrative action is focused primarily on the issue of jurisdiction. If the administration acts within its jurisdiction, its action is not subject to judicial correction.

In France, too, the control of administrative action exercised by the Council of State has been based on something very like the doctrine of *ultra vires*. The petition to annul in the *droit administratif*, like the review action in the common-law world, is aimed against administrative action deemed to be beyond the authority conferred on the agency involved. The very name of the French review action, *recours pour excès de pouvoir*, indicates this *ultra vires* basis of review: taken literally, it means the petition against action in excess of the power possessed by the administration.

The French law of judicial review, like that with which the common lawyer is familiar, is focused on the question of jurisdiction. "The basis of the petition to annul is the lack of jurisdiction of the adminis-

[34] Among these cases are Rousset, May 13, 1949; Chambre des Métiers de la Vienne, November 14, 1948; Ville de Paris, July 26, 1946; Compagnie générale Française des Tramways, May 18, 1945.

[35] Dickinson, Administrative Justice and the Supremacy of Law 41 (1927).

trator or of the administrative authority that made the decision."[36] Thus much is, indeed, clear from the language of the law of October 7-14, 1790, from which the authority of the administrative courts to entertain petitions to annul is today considered to be derived. "Claims of lack of jurisdiction with regard to administrative bodies," it reads, "are not in any event within the competence of the law courts, but must be addressed to the king, the head of the administration." This authority conferred on the head of the executive branch to decide cases in which it was asserted that an administrative agency had acted beyond its jurisdiction was transferred to the Council of State when that organ was created by Napoleon Bonaparte.

Extension of Ultra Vires

The review power of the Council of State, based on the law of 1790 just quoted, was exercised at the outset only in cases involving lack of jurisdiction in the narrow sense. "The first application of the petition to annul for excess of power was the case of lack of jurisdiction, and it is to that, indeed, that the petition owes its name, for 'to exceed one's powers' is above all to go beyond one's competence or beyond the competence possessed by the administration."[37]

But the doctrine of *ultra vires* is not necessarily limited to the bare question of jurisdiction. Liberally construed, the judicial authority under it extends to the correction of administrative abuses committed within the area of jurisdiction. Thus, procedural matters may be gone into by the reviewing court, for conformity to the procedural requirements imposed by law is essential to the proper exercise of jurisdiction. "It was very quickly seen," states Hauriou, "that the notion of *ultra vires*, thus introduced for the particular case of lack of jurisdiction, could be extended to other cases, notably to that of procedural defects, for the procedural requirements prescribed by the law are limits that the administrator must defer to, and he exceeds his powers if he does not observe them."[38]

Subsequent developments in France have seen the extension of the *ultra vires* concept by the Council of State to include error of law and what has been termed "abuse of power." The reasoning behind such extension has been similar to that noted with regard to procedural de-

[36] Hauriou, Précis de droit administratif 405 (12th ed., 1933).
[37] *Id.* at 407.
[38] *Ibid.*

fects. Administrative action based on an error of law or involving an abuse of power by the administration cannot be said to be within the authority conferred. To put it another way, the notion of *ultra vires* has been expanded from its starting point of lack of jurisdiction to embrace cases involving improper exercises of jurisdiction.

The common lawyer can more readily understand this development in the *droit administratif* if he realizes that an analogous process has taken place in the law of judicial review in his own system. In the Anglo-American world, too, the starting point of the law of judicial review was the concept of lack of jurisdiction. Only if the administration acted in excess of its authority would our courts set aside its action on review. But the common-law courts soon saw, as the French Council of State saw, that review limited to the bare question of jurisdiction was not sufficient to control administrative illegality. "It must be apparent to anyone," an American court asserted almost a century ago with regard to the scope of its review power in an action for a writ of certiorari, "that if the superior court could only examine into the right of the inferior one to enter upon an inquiry, without reference to the manner in which that inquiry is conducted, this remedy would be of small account."[39]

That the scope of review in our system has indeed expanded beyond the mere consideration by the reviewing court of the jurisdictional question is evident to anyone at all familiar with Anglo-American administrative law. It is shown clearly by an important recent English case that involved the reviewing power in an action for certiorari, which is still the basic review action in Britain as in most of the American states, in the absence of statutory provisions for review. In the case referred to it was admitted that the administrative agency concerned had made an error of law in reaching its decision, but it was maintained that the Court of King's Bench could not intervene in such a case. "No one has ever doubted," stated Lord Justice Denning, "that the Court of King's Bench can intervene to prevent a statutory tribunal from exceeding the jurisdiction which Parliament has conferred on it; but it is quite another thing to say that the King's Bench can intervene when a tribunal makes a mistake of law. A tribunal may often decide a point of law wrongly whilst keeping well within its jurisdiction. If it does so, can the King's Bench intervene?"[40] If the court should interfere

[39] Jackson v. People, 9 Mich. 111, 118 (1860).

[40] Rex v. Northumberland Compensation Appeal Tribunal, [1952] 1 K.B. 338, 346.

when the administrative tribunal makes a mistake of law, it was urged, the court itself would be exceeding its own jurisdiction.

This argument loses sight of the role of judicial review in controlling the legality of administrative action. "The answer to this argument, however, is that the Court of King's Bench has an inherent jurisdiction to control all inferior tribunals, not in an appellate capacity, but in a supervisory capacity. This control extends not only to seeing that the inferior tribunals keep within their jurisdiction, but also to seeing that they observe the law. The control is exercised by means of a power to quash any determination by the tribunal which, on the face of it, offends against the law. . . . When the King's Bench exercises its control over tribunals in this way, it is not usurping a jurisdiction which does not belong to it. It is only exercising a jurisdiction which it has always had."[41]

Grounds of Review

French jurists, in dealing with the scope of the review power exercised by the administrative courts today, are accustomed to state that those tribunals can set aside challenged administrative action on the following grounds when a petition to annul is filed with them:

1. Lack of jurisdiction;
2. Failure to observe procedure required by law;
3. Abuse of power; and
4. Error of law.

Apart perhaps from the third, these are also the grounds on which administrative action can be set aside on review by courts in the common-law world. In both the French and Anglo-American systems the starting point has been, as has been mentioned, the first ground, lack of jurisdiction. The others have developed as the courts have come to see that inquiry into them was essential if judicial control were to be more than a mere form. As the Attorney General's Committee on Administrative Procedure stated, judicial review is generally limited to the inquiry whether the administrative agency acted within the scope of its authority. "But the narrow inquiry into the agency's authority to act as it did covers a wide field."[42] It embraces the agency's interpretation of the law and all the requirements of fairness derived from the Constitution and from statute law.

[41] *Ibid.*
[42] Report, 87.

Procedural Requirements

Enough has been said thus far with regard to the jurisprudence of the French Council of State to indicate that that tribunal has not been unsympathetic to claims based on the need for effective administration. But the very recognition of the administrative role and the need of broad authority to enable that role properly to be performed have led in recent years to increasing emphasis on the way administrative power is exercised. Of especial significance in this respect is the growing insistence by the Council of State on the development of adequate procedural safeguards by the administration. This insistence by the French tribunal, which, as we shall see, has become articulate only since the Liberation, is of particular interest to the common lawyer, for the emphasis on administrative observance of the fundamentals of fair play[43] has been one of the outstanding characteristics of the administrative-law jurisprudence of Anglo-American courts.

According to section 10(e) of the Federal Administrative Procedure Act, which merely restates a principle already uniformly applied, a reviewing court shall hold unlawful and set aside administrative action, findings, and conclusions found to be "without observance of procedure required by law." The same principle has been applied by the Council of State almost from the beginning of its exercise of the authority to review the legality of administrative acts. The procedural ground of review, a leading French treatise informs us, "is the second in chronological order. It corresponds to the primitive notion of *ultra vires* in its literal sense. It is contemporary with the ground of lack of jurisdiction; it can even be directly likened to it, for he who uses his power without complying with the legal procedure imposed for the safeguarding of individual rights commits a usurpation comparable to that which consists of encroaching on the authority of another. . . . Thus it has sprung in an almost spontaneous manner from the very notion of *ultra vires*."[44]

It should not be supposed, however, that the approach of the *droit administratif* to the procedural ground of review has necessarily been the same as that followed in the Anglo-American system. In fact, there has been until recently a basic difference in approach—one that has prevented the Council of State from being as effective a controller of

[43] The term used in Federal Communications Commission v. Pottsville Broadcasting Co., 309 U.S. 134, 143 (1940).

[44] Alibert, *op. cit. supra* note 11, at 218.

administrative procedural regularity as the courts in the common-law world have been.

The procedural ground of review, an important French article stated in 1941, "should ensure the respect of that outer legality which is the legality of procedure, and which results from the forms and procedures imposed by legal provisions touching the performance of administrative acts."[45] In the French system it is only the procedural requirements imposed by specific legal provisions that the administration has been obliged to follow. The Council of State, in its jurisprudence on this subject, has started from the proposition that its control of the procedural aspect of administrative law is limited to ensuring compliance with the procedure made mandatory by the legislature or by the relevant agency itself. "The procedural defect in the *droit administratif* is a defect that arises from the failure to follow the procedures prescribed by statutes and regulations."[46]

As is well known, American administrative law in its procedural aspect has had a wholly different point of departure: the constitutional doctrine of due process of law. "The dominant factor in the development of the procedural aspect of American administrative law has been the provision of federal and state constitutions that no person may be deprived of life, liberty or property without 'due process of law.' While the consideration of whether an administrative body must give notice and an opportunity to be heard to interested individuals frequently involves difficulties of statutory interpretation, the ultimate legal problem is whether the procedure utilized satisfies the guarantee of due process of law."[47]

The due-process concept as interpreted by the courts in this country imposes certain procedural demands on the American administration, whether or not they are made mandatory by any statutory or regulatory provision. Due process in its application to administrative action is essentially a requirement of notice and hearing.

"Notice and opportunity to be heard," Mr. Justice Douglas has recently reminded us, "are fundamental to due process of law."[48] The concept of due process and its employment in the field of administrative law have ensured to the procedural aspect of that subject in this

[45] Berlia, "Le Vice de forme et le contrôle de la légalité des actes administratifs," Revue du Droit Public 370, 371 (1941).

[46] Alibert, *op. cit. supra* note 11, at 221.

[47] Gellhorn, Administrative Law: Cases and Comments 229 (2d ed., 1947).

[48] Joint Anti-Fascist Refugee Committee v. McGrath, 341 U.S. 123, 178 (1951).

country a development different from that of its counterpart in France. The Council of State has tended to set aside administrative action for procedural defects only where the procedural requirements not observed were imposed by statute or regulation. The American courts, on the contrary, have gone much farther and have held the administration to the fundamentals of fair play, regardless of whether the applicable statutes or regulations have exacted any procedural demands.

"*Natural Justice*"

It will be objected that it is not quite fair to compare the procedural aspect of the *droit administratif* with that of the system that prevails in this country. The American courts have been able to hold the administration to the observance of basic procedural requirements, even in the absence of legislative provision, because of the due-process clause in the Constitution and because of our courts' successful assertion of their authority to declare invalid any governmental action that conflicts with the provisions of the organic instrument. In France, on the other hand, the fundamental principle has been the supremacy of statute law, even in the face of contrary constitutional provisions. The French courts have never sought to assume the power to invalidate governmental acts on the ground of unconstitutionality. It is therefore not surprising that they have refused to enjoin procedural prerequisites on the administration beyond those demanded by the legislature.

It is, however, a mistake to assume that nonstatutory procedural requirements can be imposed only by judicial enforcement of an express constitutional provision such as the due-process clause. There are certain fundamentals of just procedure demanded by man's inherent sense of fair play. They antedate the constitutional provision for due process, and upon them that provision is based. As an American court averred almost eight decades ago: "It is a rule founded upon the first principles of natural justice, older than written constitutions, that a citizen shall not be deprived of his life, liberty, or property without an opportunity to be heard in defense of his rights; and the constitutional provision that no person shall be deprived of these without due process of law has its foundation in this rule."[49]

It is this realization that has led the courts in Britain, like those in the United States, to hold that the administration must comply with certain basic procedural requirements, regardless of whether they are

[49] Stuart v. Palmer, 74 N.Y. 183, 190 (1878).

demanded by the relevant enabling legislation. British experience in this respect is particularly significant for one interested in the *droit administratif,* for in Britain, as in France, there are no constitutional procedural requirements that the courts can enforce. But the British courts have endeavored to ensure administrative fair play through the concept of "natural justice." "It has been truly said," reads the well-known Report of the Committee on Ministers' Powers on this point, "that, however much a Minister in exercising such [*i.e.*, judicial] functions may depart from the usual forms of legal procedure or from the common law rules of evidence, he ought not to depart from or offend against 'natural justice.' "[50]

The principles of natural justice can be said to be as much a part of British administrative law as the procedural demands that the United States Supreme Court has held are required of the American administration under the due-process clause. These principles are implied as a condition precedent to the lawful exercise of adjudicatory authority by the administration—an implication well shown by the language of Lord Justice Bowen in an important opinion on the employment of such authority by bodies other than the ordinary courts. The relevant enabling statute merely prescribed that the particular decision should be made after due inquiry. "The statute says nothing more," the opinion states, "but in saying so much it certainly imports that the substantial elements of natural justice must be found to have been present at the inquiry. The accused person must have notice of what he is accused. He must have an opportunity of being heard, and the decision must be honestly arrived at after he has had a full opportunity of being heard."[51]

Natural Justice in France

The procedural starting point of the *droit administratif* was, as we have seen, the principle that the administration was held to observance of only those procedural requirements that were imposed by some legal text. The Council of State would annul administrative action for procedural defects only if the agency concerned failed to follow a procedure demanded expressly by statute or regulation. The British experience shows, however, that the courts can impose upon the administration the fundamentals of fair procedure, even in the absence of a

50 Report of the Committee on Ministers' Powers 75 (Cmd. 4060, 1932).
51 Leeson v. General Council of Medical Education (1889), 43 Ch. D. 366, 383.

judicially enforceable constitutional provision like the due-process clause. And since the Liberation the Council of State has, indeed, in one of the most significant changes in its jurisprudence that has ever occurred, imported into the *droit administratif* something very much like the British concept of "natural justice."

The change in the attitude of the French tribunal was clearly shown for the first time in a case decided in 1944,[52] just before Allied troops were to land on French soil. The administration had summarily revoked the petitioner's permit to operate a stand from which she sold newspapers on one of the main Parisian boulevards. Under the pre-existing case law there was clearly no procedural question that could be raised on judicial review, for there was no requirement imposed by statute or regulation for notice and hearing in such a case. But M. Chenot, the government commissioner, in his conclusions addressed to the Council, urged a wholly new approach, and it was followed by the tribunal in its decision.

After admitting that the general rule did not require an opportunity to be heard unless a legal text demanded it, M. Chenot went on to say: "In certain cases, however, this practical rule gives way to a higher principle. Certain decisions, by virtue of their nature and their object, must be preceded by a hearing, or at the very least they must not be rendered before those affected have had some opportunity to present their point of view. So much is true of all judicial decisions and of disciplinary matters involving civil servants. Only a legal text could exempt the administration from following an adversary procedure in these two fields."

In actual fact the principle of a required hearing in the absence of a legal text demanding it had been applied by the Council of State, when M. Chenot rendered his conclusions in 1944, only to the decisions of lower administrative courts.[53] He was thus in effect proposing a very great extension of the Council's jurisprudence, which he stated in the following terms: "When an administrative decision assumes a penal quality and has a sufficiently serious adverse effect on the situation of an individual, your jurisprudence requires that the individual be given an opportunity to present his point of view on the measure affecting

[52] Trompier-Gravier, May 5, 1944. Both the decision of the Council and the conclusions of the government commissioner are contained in Appendix B, *infra* p. 342.

[53] Cases involving the disciplining of civil servants, the other case referred to by M. Chenot, had been held to require a hearing because of a 1905 statute giving the civil servant the right to be informed of the case against him.

him. . . . The victim of a penalty must be given notice and enabled to present his defense."

Few cases are better fitted to illustrate the key role of the government commissioner in the decision process of the Council of State. Though careful to leave the impression that he was merely restating existing case law, M. Chenot was actually pointing the way to an audacious step forward—one that would revolutionize the approach of the French tribunal to review of the procedural aspect of administrative action. And that step was taken by the Council; for its decision in the case agreed with the conclusions of its government commissioner. ". . . in consideration of the significance that the revocation of the permit carried in these circumstances," reads the decision, "and of the gravity of that penalty, such a measure could not be taken legally without the Widow Trompier-Gravier's having been given an opportunity to be heard."

A great many cases since the Liberation have applied the principle of this case. Most of them have involved attempts by the administration to purge itself of those civil servants who had collaborated too closely with the government of Vichy. The statute that authorizes the dismissal of such collaborationists does not expressly provide any procedural guarantees. The Council of State has, however, applied the principle of its 1944 decision and annulled dismissals in cases in which the individual was not given an opportunity to present his views to the commission charged with carrying out the law. As the Council stated in one of these cases in language analogous to that used in M. Chenot's conclusions cited above, "it results . . . from the general principles of law that are applicable even in the absence of a legal text that a penalty cannot be pronounced legally unless the individual concerned has been given an opportunity adequately to present his defense."[54]

This language of the French tribunal is of primary significance, for it shows us the basis for its holding that an opportunity to be heard must be afforded even though no statute or regulation requires it. Such opportunity, asserts the Council of State, is demanded by *the general principles of law.* "We consider," the president of the Council's judicial section has recently asserted, "that certain unwritten rules of law exist which have legislative status, and which consequently must be followed by those exercising administrative authority, so long as they

[54] Avanne, October 26, 1945.

have not been contradicted by a positive provision of the statute law."[55] Among these general principles is that of the right to be heard. "It requires the administration to institute an adversary procedure and to call forth the views of the individuals affected, before serious measures that modify their legal positions are taken, where the agency concerned bases such measures on certain grounds of complaint against such individuals."[56]

It should not be supposed that the jurisprudence of the Council of State on the right to be heard, even in the absence of statutory provisions, has as yet developed in any of the detail that has characterized the case law of the Anglo-American courts on the subject. The assertion by the French tribunal of the basic principle is still too recent for that. But the Council's decisions have undeniably begun to evolve in a manner that permits one to hope for an early development analogous to the Anglo-American law of administrative procedure.

Soon after laying down the principle of the right to be heard the French tribunal held that implicit in that right was the requirement of due notice as a condition precedent to the proper exercise of administrative authority.[57] And the Council has held that the mere giving of notice was not necessarily enough. The adequacy of the notice under the circumstances of the case was a question open to the court on review. In one case in which the petitioner was given notice of hearing by a letter mailed the previous day, the Council decided that she was not given sufficient time to prepare her case.[58]

The French tribunal has also dealt with the conduct of the hearing and with the process of decision. In a decision recalling that of the United States Supreme Court in the second *Morgan* case[59] the Council annulled an administrative decision in which the petitioner was not given any information of the concrete claims of the administration during the hearing.[60] And the French tribunal, like the American Court in the first *Morgan* case,[61] has insisted that the administrative officers in whom is vested the authority to decide cases affecting the rights and

[55] Address of M. Bouffandeau, June 10, 1950, on the occasion of the one hundred and fiftieth anniversary of the Council of State.

[56] *Ibid.* For a good discussion, see Letourneur, "Les Principes généraux du droit dans la jurisprudence du Conseil d'État," Conseil d'État, Études et documents 19 (1951).

[57] Clary, November 4, 1946. Compare Servant, March 14, 1947.

[58] Descieux, May 3, 1946. See, similarly, Séraffon, July 10, 1946.

[59] Morgan v. United States, 304 U.S. 1 (1938).

[60] Brois, July 16, 1947.

[61] Morgan v. United States, 298 U.S. 468 (1936).

obligations of private citizens have a personal duty to decide such cases, which duty cannot be delegated to others.[62]

Of perhaps even more significance is a recent Council of State judgment dealing with the requirement of reasoned decisions. Like the courts in Britain, the French tribunal has consistently refused to require that the administration give the reasons for its decisions in the absence of a statutory provision imposing that requirement. In 1950, however, the Council rendered a decision[63] that, in the words of one commentator, may "open a first breach in the established jurisprudence under which, in the absence of a legal text requiring it, the decisions of administrative authorities need not be reasoned ones."[64] In the case referred to, the Council of State annulled an administrative decision in which reasons were not given. M. Letourneur, the government commissioner, advocating in his conclusions a bold departure from the precedent case law, stated that the Council should require reasoned decisions in every case in which the administration was exercising quasi-judicial functions, even though the legislature did not expressly impose such requirements. Otherwise, he asked, how could the Council really determine the validity of a challenged decision?[65]

The obligation to give reasons, as expressed in the Council's decision, is imposed "in order to enable the reviewing court to be able to determine whether the directions and prohibitions contained in the law have been followed." This, it should be noted, is at bottom the reason why American courts have required administrative decisions to contain findings that show their basis. It is to be hoped, in the words of the commentator already referred to, that the Council's decision "is only the cornerstone of a jurisprudential edifice that will give citizens a new safeguard by ensuring a more effective control by reviewing courts."[66]

Natural-Law Aspects

The common lawyer who examines the recent jurisprudence of the Council of State, under which the right to be heard must be afforded by the administration even though not provided for by the legislature,

[62] Cattin, March 30, 1949. Compare Pradère, June 4, 1947; Ruche, April 23, 1948 (commission that heard accused of different composition from that which rendered decision); Drouard, March 21, 1947 (absence of member of commission during testimony of witnesses).

[63] Billard, January 27, 1950.

[64] (1950) Sirey, part 3, p. 41.

[65] M. Letourneur's important conclusions are printed in *ibid.*

[66] *Ibid.*

will immediately perceive that what the French tribunal has done is to import into the *droit administratif* something very much like the concept of natural justice. Just as the courts in Britain have held that administrative adjudicatory procedure must conform to the principles of natural justice, so the Council of State has held that it must not violate the "general principles of law," which include that of the right to be heard. And in both countries, it should be noted, the courts have acted without the aid of an express constitutional provision such as the due-process clause in American constitutions.

The present view of the French tribunal is summarized thus by a leading administrative lawyer:

1. There exists a body of general principles of French public law.

2. These principles have positive legal value. They have the effect of law, and the judge is bound to enforce respect for them, just as he does for the written law.

3. The bases of the authority that these principles are thus recognized as possessing are not to be found in the statute law; the principles are applicable even in the absence of any statute.

4. The judge does not create these principles. He refers to them as objective rules of whose existence he takes cognizance, and which do not at all depend upon his pleasure.[67]

The review power that the Council of State has asserted over administrative procedure since the Liberation is thus seen to depend on certain unwritten legal principles required by man's sense of fair play, to which principles the administration must conform. The use by the French tribunal of such a concept, resting on an inherent unwritten law applied by the judge, may, however, lead to difficulties, for it has moral as well as legal connotations. The same is true, it should be noted, of the concept of natural justice that the British courts use. That concept, the Report of the Committee on Ministers' Powers affirms,[68] "must be regarded as belonging to the field of moral and social principles and not as having passed into the category of substantive law, so as necessarily to make every act obnoxious to its canons a transgression of a legal rule recognised and enforced as such by our Courts."

The weakness of legal analysis based exclusively on ethical precepts has been evident ever since Austin. "With the goodness or badness of laws," said he, general jurisprudence "has no immediate con-

[67] Rivero, "Le Juge administratif français: un juge qui gouverne?" (1951) Dalloz, Chronique 21, 22.
[68] P. 75.

cern."[69] It is not enough merely to choose some moral principle and then to formulate it in legal form. We must, with Dean Pound, "ask how far it has to do with things that may be governed by legal rules. We must ask how far legal machinery of rule and remedy is adapted to the claims which it recognizes and would secure. We must ask how far, if we formulate a precept in terms of our moral principle, it may be made effective in action. Even more we must consider how far it is possible to give the moral principle legal recognition and legal efficacy by judicial action or juristic reasoning, on the bases of the received legal materials and with the received legal technique, without impairing the general security by unsettling the legal system as a whole."[70]

The difficulties involved in deriving legal results from ethical principles led a British judge to go far toward rejecting the whole concept of natural justice in a famous passage in *Local Government Board v. Arlidge*, the leading British case on the exercise of adjudicatory authority by the administration. "The words 'natural justice,' " he declared, "occur in arguments and sometimes in judicial pronouncements in such cases. My Lords, when a central administrative board deals with an appeal from a local authority it must do its best to act justly, and to reach just ends by just means. If a statute prescribes the means it must employ them. If it is left without express guidance it must still act honestly and by honest means. In regard to these certain ways and methods of judicial procedure may very likely be imitated; and lawyer-like methods may find especial favour from lawyers. But that the judiciary should presume to impose its own methods upon administrative or executive officers is a usurpation. And the assumption that the methods of natural justice are ex necessitate those of Courts of Justice is wholly unfounded. This is expressly applicable to steps of procedure or forms of pleading. In so far as the term 'natural justice' means that a result or process should be just, it is a harmless though it may be a high-sounding expression; in so far as it attempts to reflect the old jus naturale it is a confused and unwarranted transfer into the ethical sphere of a term employed for other distinctions; and in so far as it is resorted to for other purposes, it is vacuous."[71]

A similar criticism of the recent jurisprudence of the Council of State is contained in an article by Professor Rivero that has attracted a great deal of notice in France. Significantly enough, its title is "The

69 Austin, Jurisprudence 1107 (4th ed., 1873).
70 Pound, Law and Morals 63 (2d ed., 1926).
71 [1915] A.C. 120, 138, per Lord Shaw.

French Administrative Judge: A Judge Who Governs?"[72] This is intended as a paraphrase of a famous French study of judicial review of the constitutionality of laws by the United States Supreme Court, entitled *Government by Judiciary*.[73]

The Council of State, Professor Rivero asserts, in invalidating administrative action that violates the "general principles of law," is in effect arrogating to itself a power analogous to that of the American Court—the power to judge governmental action in the light of certain broad principles that are almost wholly of judicial creation. "Believing itself the servant of these principles, the Council of State is in fact their creator. More exactly, it is the Council's action that chooses which elements among the complex mass that make up the national conscience shall be given the legal effect that it alone can give them, and that makes them, by that means, a part of the positive law."[74]

Here, it must be admitted, lies one of the great weaknesses in a natural-law concept like natural justice or its French counterpart. The judge must himself determine the content of the general principles that he holds the administration obligated to follow, however earnestly he may assert that he is only finding, not making, the law. "Is there not in these general principles an element of serious uncertainty, a temptation to judicial arbitrariness? Is there not more security, more stability for the individual, in the reign of statute-law, even though it be poorly made, than in the action of the judge, however benevolent?"[75]

To assume, however, that control of administrative procedure under a concept like that of natural justice must rest wholly on the unfettered discretion of the judge is to go too far. "Although 'natural justice' does not fall within those definite and well-recognised rules of law which English Courts of Law enforce, we think it is beyond doubt that there are certain canons of judicial conduct to which all tribunals and persons which have to give judicial or quasi-judicial decisions should conform. The principles on which they rest are we think implicit in the rule of law. Their observance is demanded by our national sense of justice."[76]

The vague contours of natural justice and of its French equivalent do not leave judges at large. They may not draw upon their merely

[72] *Supra* note 67.
[73] Lambert, Le Gouvernement des juges (1921).
[74] *Loc. cit. supra* note 67.
[75] *Id.* at 24.
[76] Report of the Committee on Ministers' Powers, 76.

personal and private notions and disregard the limits that bind judges in their judicial function. Even though the concept of natural justice is not final and fixed, these limits are derived from considerations that are fused into the whole nature of the judicial process.[77] "To practice the requisite detachment and to achieve sufficient objectivity no doubt demands of judges the habit of self-discipline and self-criticism, incertitude that one's own views are incontestable and alert tolerance toward views not shared. But these are precisely the presuppositions of our judicial process. They are precisely the qualities society has a right to expect from those entrusted with ultimate judicial power."[78]

In executing his responsibility to ensure that administrative procedure conforms to the fundamentals of fair play, "there is little reason to fear that a judge, relying on his own deliberate reflections and the call of his own conscience, will apply erratic, capricious, or idiosyncratic moral standards. Our judges are products of our society, and . . . they will generally think along with the beliefs of some substantial segment of the citizenry. A man who uses a moral standard that no one shares in a population of 150 million probably does not belong at large, much less on the bench."[79]

Judicial control of administrative procedure, such as is exercised by both Anglo-American courts and the French Council of State under its post-Liberation jurisprudence, is not to be derided merely as resort to a revival of "natural law."[80] Those who, like the critics already cited, assert that a concept such as natural justice is a matter of judicial caprice fail to distinguish between the forms of justice and its underlying inherent principles. "It is one thing to depart from the procedure adopted at common law, and another, and a very different thing, to adopt a procedure which is inconsistent with the principles of natural justice on which the English common law is based."[81] As Dean Pound has aptly pointed out, "there are certain fundamentals of just procedure which are the same for every type of tribunal and every type of proceeding."[82] It is for the courts to ensure conformance by the administration to these fundamentals—whether through the constitutional concept of due process or the ethico-legal device of natural justice or its French equivalent. "The heart of the matter," Mr. Justice Frank-

77 Paraphrasing Frankfurter, J., in Rochin v. California, 342 U.S. 165, 170 (1952).
78 *Id.* at 171.
79 Cahn, "Authority and Responsibility" 51 Col. L. Rev. 838, 850 (1951).
80 Paraphrasing Rochin v. California, 342 U.S. at 171.
81 Rex v. Local Government Board, [1914] 1 K.B. 160, 176.
82 Administrative Law 75 (1942).

furter has recently reminded us, "is that democracy implies respect for the elementary rights of men, however suspect or unworthy; a democratic government must therefore practice fairness; and fairness can rarely be obtained by secret, one-sided determination of facts decisive of rights."[83]

Abuse of Power

It cannot be denied that the authority assumed by the Council of State since the Liberation to set aside administrative action because the fundamentals of fair procedure have not been observed, even though procedural requirements have not been imposed by statute in the particular case, has greatly increased the scope of the French tribunal's reviewing power. A similar broadening of its authority on review took place almost a century ago when the Council developed the notion of abuse of power, today one of the most important grounds on which the setting aside of administrative action may be sought under the *droit administratif*.

"An administrative authority commits an abuse of power," a prominent councilor of state informs us, "when, though it performs an act within its jurisdiction, observes the proper procedures, and respects the provisions of statutes and regulations governing its actions, it uses its authority for purposes other than those that the one delegating the authority to it had in mind. The abuse of power is a violation of the spirit of the law."[84] Under the theory that the Council of State has developed, the administration's powers have been delegated to it by the legislature with certain goals in view. To deviate from these goals is to abuse the authority conferred. Abuse of administrative power, in the French theory, is thus the use by the administrator of his authority for an illicit purpose—a purpose other than that which the legislator intended.[85]

To determine whether an abuse of power has been committed the French reviewing court must necessarily inquire into the motives that prompted the author of the challenged act. It must search out what were his intentions, what was the result that he meant to effect; and it must then determine whether or not his objective was legitimate.[86] The Council of State, in its case law on the subject, started with the proposition that public authorities may exercise their authority only in

[83] Joint Anti-Fascist Refugee Committee v. McGrath, 341 U.S. 123, 170 (1951).
[84] Odent, *op. cit. supra* note 23, at 357.
[85] Waline, *op. cit. supra* note 19, at 142.
[86] Odent, *loc. cit. supra* note 84.

the general interest and that acts not intended to further that interest constitute illegal abuses of power. "However large may be the powers delegated to an administrator, they have never been given to him except in the public interest. Thus there is an abuse of power whenever the administrator has used his authority for a purpose clearly foreign to the public interest."[87]

The decisions in which the concept of abuse of power has been applied by the Council of State fall into certain defined categories. The first includes cases in which the author of the challenged act was motivated, not by the public interest, but by a personal one. A good example is a decision that involved the action of a mayor who regulated public dance halls to reduce their competition with his inn.[88] In other cases of this type the administrator acted against the petitioner out of personal enmity, in a spirit of spite or vengeance. For example, where a disciplinary measure taken against a police officer is motivated by personal vindictiveness the Council of State holds that the administrative officer concerned has "acted for a purpose other than the safeguarding of the interests confided to him, and he has consequently exceeded the powers conferred upon him by the law."[89] A like result is reached where the administrator has been motivated by a desire to favor the interest of third persons at the expense of petitioner.[90]

In these cases in which the administrator has been led to act by personal motives, it is clear that he has not acted in the public interest, and his action is annulled as an abuse of power. In other cases he may act for what he deems to be the public good, but his action is nonetheless held invalid because the good he intended is not that which the legislature, in conferring power upon him, sought to promote. This overzealousness is conspicuously manifest in cases in which exercises of administrative regulatory authority are inspired by motives primarily political. A recent example is found in a 1948 decision of the Council of State in which a prefect used his powers to requisition a gas company in order to realize by an indirect means his own policy in favor of nationalization of public utilities.[91]

Decisions of this kind often involve what has been termed a "fraud

[87] Waline, *loc. cit. supra* note 85.

[88] Rault, Council of State, March 14, 1934. For a more recent example, see Heuland, July 16, 1947.

[89] Maugras, November 16, 1900.

[90] Trapy, Council of State, October 29, 1948; Moreau, Council of State, March 28, 1945; Martin du Magny, Council of State, February 28, 1945.

[91] Société des Hauts Fourneaux de Rouen, May 14, 1948. See, similarly, Société des Aciéries du Nord, Council of State, July 25, 1947. Compare Hamon, Council of State, March 18, 1949.

upon the law." In these cases the administration uses its authority to promote the public interest, but by attaining an end not that for which the particular authority was delegated. The best examples are cases in which the administration uses its regulatory power to promote its own financial interests. The classic decision arose out of an 1872 statute that set up a state monopoly in the manufacture of matches. That law provided for the nationalization of privately owned match factories, the owners of which were to be paid a certain compensation. In order to make it unnecessary for the compensation to be paid the Minister of Finances ordered the various prefects to close these private factories under the pretext that they were dangerous to the public health. This order was set aside by the Council of State as constituting a flagrant abuse of power.[92]

As has already been stated, the Council of State, in its development of the concept of abuse of power, started with the proposition that all administrative authority must be exercised with the interest of the general public in view. If the administrative purpose is other than promotion of the general interest, its action will be annulled as an abuse of power. The cases cited indicate, however, that furtherance of the general interest is not all that must be aimed at. As one commentator expresses it: "In the French positive law of today, as seen in the decisions of the judicial section of the Council of State, no public agent ever has authority except to further, not merely a purpose in the general interest, but also the particular purpose for which the power was conferred on him by the enabling legislation."[93]

This requirement is clearly shown by the decisions dealing with administrative regulatory action motivated by the administration's own financial interest. In one of them[94] a landowner applied for a permit to build near a public way. The permit could be refused only if the proposed building would infringe on the public way or violate the local zoning laws. It was refused because the municipal administration was trying to force the applicant to sell his property to the municipality. The administrative decision here was, indeed, motivated by the public

[92] Paris et Laumonnier-Cariol, November 26, 1875. For recent examples of administrative acts motivated by financial considerations, see Bluteau, March 20, 1953; Giacobbi, March 26, 1947.

[93] Jèze, "La Jurisprudence du Conseil d'État et le détournement de pouvoir," Revue du Droit Public 58, 59 (1944) (italics omitted).

[94] Fleury, Council of State, May 22, 1942. See, similarly, Dupérier, Council of State, February 20, 1935.

interest, but it was manifestly not induced by the purpose for which the particular power was delegated.

Anglo-American Analogies

Administrative abuse of power under the concept developed in the *droit administratif* is, as one authority tells us, "an abuse of an agent's mandate, an abuse of right."[95] It is not surprising that nothing exactly like the French concept so defined has been articulated by Anglo-American courts as a separate ground of review. In the common-law world the notion of abuse of rights, which has been of ever-growing importance in civil-law countries like France, is almost completely rejected. "The theory of the abuse of rights is one which has been rejected by our law, with the result that the ancient brocard '*dura lex sed lex*' finds its most vivid illustration in the present-day decisions of the Anglo-American Courts."[96] The proposition that a legal right can be abused has not received the imprimatur of the common law, which merely asks what the defendant has done and not why he did it.[97]

Under the concept of abuse of power as developed by the Council of State the reviewing court must ask, not only what the administration has done in the particular case, but also why it did it. It must thus inquire into the motives that induced the challenged act and then determine whether the purpose that the administration had in mind squares with that of the legislature in delegating the given power. The question of abuse of power "presupposes an inquiry into the mind of the agent, into his secret intentions which he has probably made every effort to conceal."[98] It is precisely this type of inquiry into motives that the Anglo-American courts have refused to admit that they may make.

In investigating the question of abuse of power the reviewing court must probe into the mental processes of the administrator in order to lay bare the motives that induced the challenged act. This obligation the Anglo-American courts have consistently declined. It is not for our courts, in the words of Chief Justice Hughes in the second *Morgan* case,[99] to probe the mental processes of the administration. "Our duty is at an end," the American Court has stated, "when we find that the

[95] Alibert, *op. cit. supra* note 11, at 236.
[96] Gutteridge, Abuse of Rights, 5 Camb. L. J. 22 (1933).
[97] *Id.* at 30.
[98] Rokham and Pratt, Studies in French Administrative Law 37 (1947).
[99] Morgan v. United States, 304 U.S. 1, 18 (1938).

action of the Commission was based upon findings supported by evidence, and was made pursuant to authority granted by Congress."[100]

That the courts in the common-law world have not articulated a concept analogous to that of abuse of power, as developed in the *droit administratif*, does not, however, mean that they have not set aside administrative acts in cases that the French administrative lawyer would classify under the rubric: abuse of power. A well-known English case, that of *Rex v. Minister of Health;* ex parte *Davis*,[101] is as good an example as any. It involved the power given to the Minister of Health to confirm schemes submitted by local authorities for improving slum areas. Under the relevant statute such schemes were to provide for improving the slum area by rearranging and reconstructing the streets and houses therein. The scheme submitted by the local authority gave it the power to sell, lease, or otherwise dispose of the area in question. The authority was intending to acquire the particular area compulsorily and then to dispose of it as corporation property in whatever way it saw fit, "not, of course, for private profit or for any corrupt motive, but for what was deemed to be general municipal development and advantage, though not of the kind contemplated by this Act."[102] The court in the *Davis* case held that the scheme at issue was clearly *ultra vires*. "Under the name, and the agreeable name, of an improvement scheme," reads the decision of Lord Hewart, C.J., "this particular council is minded to acquire a slice of very valuable land in the heart of the city of Derby, not for any purpose of rearrangement or reconstruction, but for the purpose, if and when the local authority thinks fit, of resale, and of course, resale at the highest obtainable price."[103]

In setting aside the administrative action in the *Davis* case the court decided only that a scheme that did not provide for rearrangement and reconstruction was *ultra vires* the enabling statute. A French administrative lawyer might, however, well classify it under the concept of abuse of power. The administration was motivated, not by a desire to improve the slum area, which was the purpose for which the legislature had delegated the power to acquire land compulsorily, but by its own financial interest, as in some of the French decisions considered.

100 National Broadcasting Co. v. United States, 319 U.S. 190, 224 (1943).

101 [1929] 1 K.B. 619.

102 Allen, Law and Orders 135 (1945).

103 [1929] 1 K.B. at 624. See, similarly, Municipal Council of Sydney v. Campbell, [1925] A.C. 338.

An American case with similar characteristics is *Morrill v. Jones.*[104] The relevant statute provided that "Animals, alive, specially imported for breeding purposes, from beyond the seas, shall be admitted free [of duty] upon proof thereof satisfactory to the Secretary of the Treasury, and under such regulations as he may prescribe." Among the regulations issued under this section was one that required the official concerned, before admitting such animals free, to be "satisfied that the animals are of superior stock adapted to improving the breed in the United States." This proviso, said the Supreme Court, was in excess of the power of the Secretary. "This is manifestly an attempt to put into the body of the statute a limitation which Congress did not think it necessary to prescribe. Congress was willing to admit, duty-free, all animals specially imported for breeding purposes. The Secretary thought this privilege should be confined to such animals as were adapted to the improvement of breeds already in the United States."[105] Here, too, the French student might well find that the case involved an administrative abuse of power. The Council of State, if such a case were presented to it, might well annul the regulation at issue because the Secretary, however laudable his actual purpose, had used his powers for a purpose other than that which the legislature had in mind.

Most American cases of this type involve the authority that our courts exercise over the reasonableness of administrative exercises of the rule-making power. In this country the judicial power to pass upon the *vires* of administrative sublegislation carries with it the power to pass upon its reasonableness. "Not only must a regulation, in order to be valid, be consistent with the statute, it must be reasonable."[106] American courts, in exercising their authority to determine the reasonableness of regulations, look to see if there is a rational relationship between the particular regulation and the governing statute. This scrutiny permits our courts to exercise a control similar to that exerted by the French Council of State under its concept of abuse of power. For the required rational relationship clearly does not exist when a challenged regulation has been promulgated for a purpose other than that which the legislature had in mind. As one American court has stated: "Such rules and regulations must be reasonably appropriate and calculated to carry out the legislative purpose."[107]

[104] 106 U.S. 466 (1883).
[105] *Id.* at 467.
[106] Manhattan General Equipment Co. v. Commissioner, 297 U.S. 129, 134 (1936).
[107] Wallace v. Feehan, 206 Ind. 522, 533 (1934). For an interesting recent case

But even with thus much admitted there is still nothing like the French concept of abuse of power in American administrative law. In the first place, our courts will normally not make an inquiry into the reasonableness of administrative action except in the case of rules and regulations. And even where such administrative sublegislation is concerned, the notion of reasonableness is not nearly so clear as the concept of abuse of power. Although there are in our law cases similar to those involving abuse of power in France, the American courts have never worked out a definite concept such as the Council of State's. It seems clear, then, that abuse of power, as such, cannot be classified as a separate ground of review in Anglo-American administrative law.

Inquiry into Abuse of Power

The common lawyer who examines the concept of abuse of power as developed in the *droit administratif* is often prone to overestimate its importance for those seeking review of administrative action. He sees the administrative courts in France inquire into the motivation behind an administrative act in a manner in which Anglo-American courts have consistently refused to do, and his not unnatural response is to see in the concept of abuse of power a means of controlling administrative action far more effective than anything thus far devised by courts in the common-law world.

That control of administrative abuse of power represents a significant forward step in the direction of adequate judicial review cannot be denied. At the same time, one should not overlook the fact that its practical significance as a means of controlling administrative action tends to be reduced by the limitations on the powers of inquiry possessed by the French reviewing courts in cases of this type.

In cases involving asserted abuses of power the French tribunals must investigate, as has been pointed out, the motives behind the administrative act in order to determine whether the purpose was that which the legislature had in mind. The best way to conduct such an investigation would doubtless be by an interrogation of the administrative officers. But this type of interrogation by the reviewing court is, as we have already seen,[108] just as unauthorized in the French as in the Anglo-

involving particularized rule making, see Jones v. Harper, 98 F. Supp. 460 (W.D. Okla. 1951). The subsequent reversal of this decision, 195 F. 2d 705 (10th Cir. 1952), shows once more the reluctance of our courts to inquire into administrative motives.

108 *Supra* p. 194.

American system of judicial review. It is certain, states a leading text, that the administrative courts "cannot order an inquiry merely to scrutinize the motives that led [administrators] to act."[109]

In our discussion of the powers of inquiry of the reviewing court we saw that the investigation on review is limited to the record. This restriction means that an administrative act will not be set aside for abuse of power unless it appears from the record that the administration was motivated by a purpose other than that intended by the legislature. "The fact of abuse of power must be shown by the terms of the challenged decision itself or by materials contained in the record."[110] Under the jurisprudence of the Council of State as explained by a leading authority, the following principles are applied by the French tribunal in these cases: "1) It is not enough merely to allege an abuse of power; he who pleads it must produce evidence of it. 2) Such evidence cannot consist of oral testimony, at a trial in the proper sense of that term. It must be contained in materials in the record."[111]

If one bears in mind the composition of the record on which the French reviewing courts base their decision on review,[112] one will perceive the difficulty involved in inquiries by them into the question of abuse of power. "It is easily comprehensible, actually, that when an administrator uses his authority for an improper purpose, he is not so naïve as to admit it. He disguises the true motives of his act and officially gives some legal pretext. His ruse must be unmasked—not always an easy matter."[113]

The Council of State has itself recognized the difficulties inherent in inquiry into the motives behind an administrative act when inquiry is limited to the record before it. In its more recent jurisprudence it has sought to mitigate these difficulties by holding that evidence of abuse of power can be implied from all the circumstances of the case as they appear in the record, even with no express proof. Specifically, the French tribunal has considered the following as raising a presumption of abuse of power: the abnormal haste with which the particular

109 Alibert, *op. cit. supra* note 11, at 258.

110 Bonnard, "Le Pouvoir discretionnaire des autorités administratives et le recours pour excès de pouvoir," Revue du Droit Public 363, 392 (1923).

111 Jèze, *supra* note 93, at 60.

112 *Supra* pp. 136-37.

113 Waline, *op. cit. supra* note 19, at 144. For a recent case in which petitioner sought to prove the motives of the author of the administrative act by introducing excerpts from a book he had written, see Société des Automobiles Berliet, Council of State, July 22, 1949.

administrative decision was made;[114] in a case involving an application for a permit, the fact that the permit was denied only to petitioner while granted to all other applicants;[115] the failure of the record to show any act by petitioner that justified the imposition of a penalty;[116] events that preceded the challenged act;[117] and the nonexistence of the reasons given by the administration as the grounds for its action.[118]

One of the principal weaknesses in the application by the administrative courts of the concept of abuse of power has arisen from the fact that there has been no requirement in the *droit administratif* that the French administration give reasons for its decisions unless a statute has imposed that requirement. If the administrator does not give the reasons for his action, it is often most difficult to determine them, and the inquiry into whether there was the necessary correlation between his purpose and that of the legislature consequently cannot be made. In 1950, however, we saw, the Council of State took an important step toward holding that reasoned decisions are required in all cases involving administrative exercise of quasi-judicial powers.[119] If the French tribunal remains true to the principle of its 1950 decision and does apply the requirement of reasoned decisions to all administrative adjudications, it will be taking a step that should greatly improve the practical efficacy of its control based on abuse of power.

Even if one recognizes the limitations just discussed on the power of inquiry that the administrative courts exercise in these cases, one cannot but conclude that the French doctrine of abuse of power is a valuable adjunct to the reviewing authority of the judge. Nor is there any reason to assume that such a concept would not be as useful as French students assert it to be if it were imported into Anglo-American administrative law. It should, however, be realized that it is most unlikely that our courts will at present develop anything like the French concept. Under it the reviewing court must make an acknowledged inquiry into the motives behind an administrative act. This type of investigation into the mental processes of an administrator is, as has been emphasized, something that courts in the common-law world have consistently refused to engage in. "According to an early English judge,"

[114] Laurent, March 3, 1939.
[115] Société L'Eveil de Contres, December 23, 1932.
[116] Moreau, March 28, 1945. In this case, the court inferred that the power to impose the penalty was being used for a personal motive.
[117] Compagnie pyrénéenne de Transports par Taxis, February 10, 1928.
[118] Union Syndicat des Débitants de Nice, August 18, 1944.
[119] Billard, January 27, 1950, *supra* p. 211.

the United States Supreme Court has stated, " 'the devil himself knoweth not the mind of man,' and a modern reviewing court is not much better equipped to lay bare unexposed mental processes."[120]

Error of Law

We have thus far seen that the French reviewing court, in cases in which administrative action is challenged as illegal, inquires into the questions of lack of jurisdiction, procedural defects, and abuse of power. Judicial review limited to these three grounds would, however, hardly be adequate to ensure enforcement of the principle of administrative legality. Therefore the courts, in both the French and the Anglo-American systems of administrative law, have extended the scope of their review power to include inquiry into the question whether the administration has committed an error of law.

The Council of State, like the courts in the common-law world, has not hesitated to set aside administrative action as illegal when it has been based on an error of law. As the United States Supreme Court has said, in language as applicable to the French tribunal: "If the action rests upon an administrative determination—an exercise of judgment in an area which Congress has entrusted to the agency—of course it may not be set aside because the reviewing court might have made a different determination were it empowered to do so. But if the action is based upon a determination of law as to which the reviewing authority of the courts does come into play, an order may not stand if an agency has misconceived the law."[121]

An example of the similar attitude of the Council of State on this point is contained in a 1949 decision that involved a refusal on the part of the administration to reinstate the petitioner in his position as a harbor pilot, from which he had been summarily removed because of alleged collaborationist activities during the German occupation. The administrative action was based on the view that such a pilot, though a government employee, did not have the status of a civil servant under the relevant laws, and hence could be summarily dismissed. The Council of State held that harbor pilots did possess the status of civil servants as defined in the applicable statute. Hence the administrative decision

120 National Labor Relations Board v. Donnelly Garment Co., 330 U.S. 219, 229 (1947).

121 Securities and Exchange Commission v. Chenery Corp., 318 U.S. 80, 94 (1943).

was set aside, for, as the Council's decision puts it, it "rests on a ground erroneous in law and is consequently *ultra vires*."[122]

Administrative errors of law, the leading French text on judicial review informs us, are of two kinds. The first involves a clear-cut violation of the relevant statutory provisions—a situation in which the agency concerned refuses to recognize the terms of the statute. This is the most obvious type of error of law; "it is the simplest and clearest case. Almost always the illegalities that result from such errors of law are glaringly obvious, for they usually have a more or less flagrant quality."[123]

In this flagrant kind of error the relevant statute is simply not followed by the administration. But there is another kind, "more difficult to perceive, more hidden, more subtle, that results neither from refusal to recognize the statute nor from addition to its provisions: the erroneous interpretation of the law. This occurs when the author of the administrative act, though he recognizes and applies the controlling statutory provision, gives it an improper signification or meaning. In acting thus he violates the statute."[124] It is in this latter type of error that the student of administrative law is primarily interested, for it is in dealing with it that the most difficult problems concerning the scope of review are encountered.

Error of Fact

The foregoing shows that the French reviewing court, like the courts in the common-law world, will set aside administrative action on review when the agency concerned has committed an error of law. Is the same result reached by the French tribunal when the challenged action is based on an error of fact?

Here again, to be sure, one can argue that the administration is guilty of a false application of law. It ordinarily receives authority to take certain action, but only on the existence of a given legal and factual situation. If the required situation of fact does not really exist, can it not be said that the administration has misapplied the law just as truly as when it commits an error of pure law? "Must not the authority charged with ensuring respect for legality by setting aside errors of law also necessarily inquire into the facts?" asks a French

[122] Dilly, June 17, 1949.
[123] Alibert, *op. cit. supra* note 11, at 260.
[124] *Id.* at 276.

jurist. "Does not a false appraisal of the facts lead to an error of law? In separating the two, are we not unjustifiably mutilating the role of the reviewing court?"[125]

However valid this argument, it must be recognized that both the French and the Anglo-American systems of administrative law have started with the proposition that an administrative act should not be set aside by a reviewing court simply because it is based on an error of fact. In both systems appreciation of the facts in a given case rests with the administrator rather than with the judge.

That this principle is the established one on which the scope of review in the Anglo-American world rests is by now too clear to admit of any dispute. As early as 1896 the United States Supreme Court refused to substitute its judgment on a question of fact for that of the administration, asserting that "the question was one of fact peculiarly within the province of the Commission."[126] And ever since that time it has been recognized with us that it is primarily for the administration to determine the facts on which its action is based. "In sustaining the Commission's findings in these proceedings, as in related cases," asserted the American Court in 1950, "this Court has held that the point in time and space at which the carrier's transportation service ends is a question of fact to be determined by the Commission and not the courts."[127]

Like the courts in the common-law world, the French Council of State started with the proposition that the determination of questions of fact is primarily entrusted to the administrator rather than to the judge. Its early decisions, like those of the American Court just cited, consistently refused to set aside administrative action resting on alleged errors of fact. Where petitioner raises solely a question of fact, reads a 1925 decision of the French tribunal, his petition to annul cannot be granted.[128] In the words of the greatest of modern French administrative lawyers, "when the Council of State found itself for the first time in the presence of allegations of errors of fact, it recoiled before the obstacle and flatly refused to see in that type of error a basis of *ultra vires*."[129] A 1910 decision expresses this view categorically. "The only

125 Goldenberg, *op. cit. supra* note 24, at 13.

126 Cincinnati, N.O. & P. Ry. v. Interstate Commerce Commission, 162 U.S. 184, 194 (1896).

127 United States v. United States Smelting Refining Co., 339 U.S. 186, 193 (1950). For an important similar English case, see In re Bowman, [1932] 2 K.B. 621.

128 Mariani, March 27, 1925.

129 Hauriou, *op. cit. supra* note 33, at 381.

ground asserted by M. Huberson's petition against the decision of the special commission of Béthune is based on an alleged error of fact," it states, "and even if that be established, such an error would not constitute a ground for a finding of *ultra vires* or an error of law."[130]

Law-Fact Distinction

The scope of review of administrative action in both the French and the Anglo-American systems is thus based, as the above analysis indicates, on the distinction between "law" and "fact." The law-fact distinction is one that the common lawyer well knows to be fundamental in his jurisprudence; it has been, in fact, the keystone on which our entire system of appellate review is built. In its application to administrative law this separation of law and fact, as an English observer has pointed out, sounds attractively simple. The administrator would find the facts, and the judge would not interfere unless there had been an error of law.[131] In this field "it is generally agreed that the jurisdiction of superior courts should be invoked only on questions of law. . . . To re-open all disputed issues of fact might lead to endless litigation, with no very satisfactory conclusion in the end."[132]

The law-fact distinction, of such importance to the common lawyer, has been of equal significance to his French confrere. As we have already seen,[133] the control exercised over the decisions of inferior courts by the Court of Cassation—the apex of the judicial system in France—has been basically restricted to questions of law. The French "lawyer thus thinks naturally of the distinction between fact and law when he has to define the competence of a court. It consequently appears natural to him, at first glance, to assimilate the Council of State (supreme administrative court) to the Court of Cassation (supreme law court). Both will be judges of the law alone. The Council of State will in this way respect the independence of the administration, as the Court of Cassation respects the sovereign power of the lower courts to appreciate the merits."[134]

It should be borne in mind, however, that the Council of State has had more than the example of the Court of Cassation to guide it in fashioning the scope of review power. Intermediate appellate juris-

130 Huberson, March 18, 1910.
131 Carr, Concerning English Administrative Law 108 (1941).
132 Allen, *op. cit. supra* note 102, at 159.
133 *Supra* p. 55.
134 Goldenberg, *loc. cit. supra* note 125.

diction in the French judicial system is exercised by the Courts of Appeal, whose appellate authority extends to full review of both the law and the facts.[135] The example of the full review power of the Courts of Appeal has been of perhaps even greater importance to the Council of State than that of the limited authority of the Court of Cassation. For though, as has been pointed out, the French administrative tribunal started by limiting the scope of review power on the model of the Court of Cassation, it has more recently, as we shall see, been broadening review authority so as to approach that exercised by the Courts of Appeal.

Jurisdictional Facts

The power of the reviewing court in both the French and the Anglo-American systems of administrative law, it has already been stated, has been basically limited to questions of law. The reviewing court has had no power to examine administrative findings of fact to determine whether they are correct. The courts in the common-law world, it is true, have constantly asserted the authority to inquire into whether challenged findings of fact have some evidentiary basis; they have reasoned, in the words of an English judge, that to make a finding "which there is no evidence to support is to make an error of law."[136]

But the inquiry of Anglo-American courts into the question of evidentiary support clearly does not go so far as to authorize the judge to determine the correctness of administrative findings of fact on his independent judgment. "In such cases the judicial inquiry goes no further than to ascertain whether there is evidence to support the findings, and the question of the weight of the evidence in determining issues of fact lies with the legislative agency acting within its statutory authority."[137] The judicial function is exhausted when there is found to be a rational basis for the administrative fact findings.[138] "Such is the full limit of judicial review of the fact findings of an administrative tribunal when made within the scope of its jurisdiction."[139]

[135] *Supra* pp. 54-55.

[136] Bean v. Doncaster Amalgamated Collieries, Ltd., [1944] 2 All E.R. 279, 284. For a similar analysis in an American case, see Florida East Coast Railway Co. v. United States, 234 U.S. 167, 185 (1914).

[137] Hughes, C.J., in St. Joseph Stock Yards Co. v. United States, 298 U.S. 38, 51 (1936).

[138] Cardozo, J., in Mississippi Barge Line Co. v. United States, 292 U.S. 282, 287 (1934).

[139] Sunshine Anthracite Coal Co. v. Adkins, 31 F. Supp. 125, 129 (E.D. Ark. 1940).

But what if the fact in question is a *jurisdictional* one, in the sense that its existence is a condition precedent to the lawful exercise of the administrative power? "If the right of review is rested on the theory of *ultra vires*, and an administrative officer is given authority, for instance, to destroy infected articles or diseased animals, it is possible to argue that he is 'without jurisdiction' or authority over articles not actually infected or over animals not actually diseased."[140]

For the Anglo-American courts to apply the normal theory of limited review in such cases would seem to run counter to the general policy of our law against allowing inferior tribunals finally to determine the limits of their own jurisdiction. "An [administrative] agency may not finally decide the limits of its statutory power," the United States Supreme Court has asserted. "That is a judicial function."[141] Where the administrative jurisdiction depends on a finding of fact the reviewing court should be able to determine for itself whether or not that finding is correct. "The law is settled that where a jurisdiction is given to a tribunal in certain events, the jurisdiction only arises on the actual happening of those events. If they have not happened in fact, they cannot obtain jurisdiction by wrongly deciding they have happened."[142]

These considerations led in 1932 to the famous decision of the United States Supreme Court in *Crowell v. Benson*.[143] That case, which arose under the Longshoremen and Harbor Workers' Compensation Act, concerned a suit to enjoin the enforcement of a compensation award. The plaintiff alleged that the award was contrary to law for the reason that the claimant was not at the time of his injury an "employee" of the plaintiff and that his claim was consequently not within the jurisdiction of the agency concerned. "The fact of employment was thus made the decisive issue,"[144] and the Court had to determine the scope of the review available over the administrative finding of that fact.

First of all, according to Mr. Chief Justice Hughes, who delivered the opinion, the enabling statute contains two fundamental limitations

[140] Dickinson, *op. cit. supra* note 35, at 309.

[141] Social Security Board v. Nierotko, 327 U.S. 358, 369 (1946).

[142] Rex v. Local Government Board, [1922] 2 I.R. 76, 93. Compare the language of Farwell, L.J., in Rex v. Shoreditch Assessment Committee, [1910] 2 K.B. 859, 880.

[143] 285 U.S. 22 (1932).

[144] Dickinson, "Crowell v. Benson: Judicial Review of Administrative Determinations of Questions of 'Constitutional Fact,'" 80 U. of Pa. L. Rev. 1055, 1056 (1932).

on the right of compensation that it confers. "It deals exclusively with compensation in respect of disability or death resulting 'from an injury occurring upon the navigable waters of the United States' . . . , and it applies only when the relation of master and servant exists."[145] The administrative fact findings on these two issues, the opinion goes on, cannot be vested with the same finality as ordinary factual determinations. These "determinations of fact are fundamental or 'jurisdictional' in the sense that their existence is a condition precedent to the operation of the statutory scheme."[146] The existence of these facts is "indispensable to the application of the statute . . . because the Congress has so provided explicitly."[147]

What is the scope of review, then, with regard to these "fundamental" or "jurisdictional" facts? Clearly, says Chief Justice Hughes, the reviewing court may determine the question of their existence on its independent judgment. The court in determining whether a compensation order is in accordance with law may determine for itself the existence of the "jurisdictional" facts underlying the operation of the statute.[148]

Such, briefly stated, was the decision of the Supreme Court in *Crowell v. Benson.* As a leading critic has admitted, "the logical cogency of the court's reasoning is impressive."[149] The doctrine of "jurisdictional fact" is applied with almost mathematical exactness to reach the result of Chief Justice Hughes's opinion. The reasoning of the Court can be stated in syllogistic form as follows:

Major Premise: It is the function of the reviewing court to determine whether administrative agencies have exceeded their jurisdiction.

Minor Premise: The existence of the employment relationship is essential to administrative jurisdiction under the enabling statute.

Conclusion: The existence of the employment relation must therefore independently be found by the reviewing court in order for it to conclude that the agency concerned was acting within its jurisdiction; otherwise the agency would itself be finding the facts on which the very exercise of administrative power depends.[150]

145 285 U.S. at 37.

146 *Id.* at 54.

147 *Id.* at 55.

148 For a similar English case, see White and Collins v. Minister of Health, [1939] 2 K.B. 838. Compare Rex v. Fulham, Hammersmith and Kensington Rent Tribunal, [1951] 2 K.B. 1.

149 Dickinson, *supra* note 144, at 1059.

150 Compare Landis, The Administrative Process 127 (1938).

Jurisdictional Fact in France

The French Council of State, like the United States Supreme Court, has recognized that its general principle of finality for administrative findings of fact could not be applied uniformly to all factual determinations. For it, too, has come to see that there are cases in which the administrative power to act depends on the existence of certain facts. In such cases the French tribunal has asserted a theory of review similar to that enunciated by Chief Justice Hughes in *Crowell v. Benson.* Judicial review in such cases would lose much of its effectiveness if the administration could finally determine the issue of its own jurisdiction merely because that turned on a question of fact.

The first important step toward the articulation by the Council of State of a doctrine of "jurisdictional fact" analogous to that advanced by the American Court in *Crowell v. Benson* was taken in the *Gomel* case, decided in 1914.[151] It arose out of a law that authorized the prefect of the Seine to refuse to permit property owners to build on their land if he determined that the proposed construction would tend to affect adversely what the law called a "monumental perspective"; *i.e.*, a notable picturesque or historic view that should be preserved in the public interest. The prefect had refused to allow the petitioner to build in accordance with his plans, on the ground that the site constituted a monumental perspective that would be destroyed.

In its decision the Council of State set aside the order of the prefect. The administrative authority here, said the French tribunal, existed only if the place in question did indeed constitute a monumental perspective such as the law was designed to protect. And the administrative finding on that point could be reviewed by the Council on its independent judgment. "It is for the Council of State to verify whether the site of the proposed construction comes within an existing monumental perspective," the decision reads, "and, if it does, whether the proposed construction would affect it adversely." And the Council went on to find that the particular place was not part of a monumental perspective within the meaning of the statute. The prefect had consequently applied the statute incorrectly, and his order was annulled.[152]

It is clear that in the *Gomel* case the Council of State substituted

[151] Gomel, April 4, 1914.

[152] For more recent similar decisions of the Council, see Société Foncière Passy Mont-Blanc, March 19, 1948; Ploit, December 5, 1947.

its own judgment for that of the administration on a question of fact. To quote an astute commentator, the case involves an "ascertainment of the facts by the judge, or, if we prefer, an error of fact which the prefect may have committed, and which the judge corrects. . . . In our case, could Beauvau Square, in its *ensemble*, be considered as forming a monumental perspective? The prefect of the Seine had said Yes; the Council of State says No."[153]

Though it was thus clear that in the *Gomel* case the Council of State had set aside administrative action for error of fact, its decision did not really tell why it had fully reviewed the finding of fact in this case when it had consistently refused to do so in other cases. "Its all too concise decision did not at all explain why the error of fact committed by the prefect of the Seine in the determination of the monumental quality of Beauvau Square turned into an error of law in the application of the statute."[154] The American observer can readily see that the French tribunal's approach was grounded on the "jurisdictional fact" doctrine. But the failure of the Council to articulate that doctrine in its decision left French students somewhat confused about the true basis of the *Gomel* decision.

It was not until 1922, eight years after the *Gomel* case, that the Council of State expressly formulated a doctrine like that of "jurisdictional fact." At that time the French tribunal decided a case similar to the *Gomel* case in that the administrative finding of fact at issue was one whose existence was necessary before the administrative power to act could come into play. The Minister of the Interior had acted under a statute authorizing him to grant a leave to a prefect on the prefect's request. The Council of State held that it could fully review the question whether an application for leave had in fact been made by the prefect. On finding that it had not been made, the Council set aside the Minister's order placing the prefect on leave.

In reaching its decision the Council of State did not limit itself, as in the *Gomel* case, to stating merely that it would itself determine whether the particular fact existed. It also gave the reason why full review was available of the existence of the fact. The Minister, in acting under a statute that authorized him to place a prefect on leave on the prefect's request when in fact no such request had been made—so the Council's decision reads—had grounded his action on a fact that

[153] Hauriou, *op. cit. supra* note 33, at 377.
[154] Hauriou, *op. cit. supra* note 36, at 451.

actually did not exist and had thus given a "nonexistent legal basis" (*cause juridique inexistante*) for his action.[155]

As explained by Hauriou, the first really to appreciate the significance of the jurisprudence inaugurated by the Council of State's 1922 decision, the legal basis of an act is the factual situation that calls it forth. "It is the fact pattern into which an act interposes that the law considers as the basis of the act: it is thus both legal and factual in quality . . . for if there is a fact that did not really exist, and that fact has served as the basis of the act, there is an error of law because the act is grounded on a nonexistent legal basis."[156]

The common lawyer who is able to discount differences in terminology[157] will soon perceive that the doctrine of "nonexistent legal basis," which was laid down by the Council of State in its 1922 decision, is essentially like the doctrine of "jurisdictional fact" applied by the United States Supreme Court in *Crowell v. Benson*. Under both doctrines the correctness of facts on which the administrative power to act is based must be determined by the reviewing court for itself. "Correct fact findings must serve as the legal basis for administrative acts. There can thus be error of law through mistake of fact only if the particular fact were the basis prescribed in law for the act. The thread followed by this idea is thus the following: error of jurisdictional fact, error in the legal basis of the act; nonexistent legal basis; and hence error of law."[158] The end result under the French doctrine is thus much like that reached under the "jurisdictional fact" doctrine. If the existence of the particular fact is one on which the administrative jurisdiction depends, or, as the French jurist would express it, if the legal basis of the challenged act is the existence of the fact in question, then the normal rule of finality for administrative findings of fact does not apply. The reviewing court must determine for itself the existence of the jurisdictional fact or, to use the French terminology, whether the challenged act had the proper legal basis in fact.

155 Trépont, January 20, 1922. The principle of this case was applied soon thereafter by the Council in two other important cases that firmly established it in French law: Blanchard, March 23, 1923; Lefranc, January 22, 1926. The latter is usually referred to as the leading case, because it prompted a famous article by Hauriou explaining the doctrine. (1926) Sirey, part 3, p. 25, reprinted in Hauriou, *op. cit. supra* note 33, at 380.

156 Hauriou, *loc. cit. supra* note 154.

157 Especially those flowing from the fact that the French doctrine is based on the concept of *causa*, which is so important in civil-law countries.

158 Hauriou, *op. cit. supra* note 33, at 385.

The Challenge of Justice Brandeis

It can be argued that the decision of the United States Supreme Court in *Crowell v. Benson* does not go so far as to require full judicial review of all factual issues on which the administrative power to act under the enabling statute depends, but only of those facts whose existence is necessary to the constitutional operation of the particular statutory scheme.[159] It has, however, usually been thought that the Supreme Court's decision was intended to apply to review of all so-called jurisdictional facts, regardless of whether the particular fact was one on which constitutional or only statutory power to act depended. As one federal court has stated, under *Crowell v. Benson,* "upon a judicial review of administrative orders and decisions, a court may receive new evidence to determine whether the administrative official or body acted within the scope of the statutory authority conferred."[160]

It was this interpretation of the Court's decision in *Crowell v. Benson* that called forth in that case the vigorous dissent of Mr. Justice Brandeis. Under the enabling statute involved in *Crowell v. Benson* the administrative power to act was dependent on the finding that the claimant was an employee, for the authority to make a compensation award did not exist in the absence of such a finding. The existence of an employment relationship, said Justice Brandeis, is, however, but one of many facts on which the administrative power to award compensation depends.

Logically applied, Justice Brandeis asserted, the decision of the majority of the Court would leave the agency concerned "powerless to hear or determine any issue of asserted non-liability under the Act. For non-existence of the employer-employee relation is only one of many grounds of non-liability. Thus, there is no liability if the injury was occasioned solely by the intoxication of the employee; or if the injury was due to the wilful intention of the employee to injure or kill himself or another; or if it did not arise 'out of or in the course of employment'; or if the employer was not engaged in maritime employment in whole or in part; or if the injured person was the employee of a subcontractor who has secured payment of compensation; or if the proceeding is brought against the wrong person as employer; or if the

159 See Schwartz, "Does the Ghost of Crowell v. Benson Still Walk?" 98 U. of Pa. L. Rev. 163, 168-70 (1949).

160 United States v. Int. Freighting Corp., 20 F. Supp. 357, 358 (S.D. N.Y. 1937).

disability or death is that of a master or a member of the crew of any vessel; or if it is that of a person engaged by the master to load or unload or repair any small vessel under eighteen tons net; or if it is that of an officer or employee of the United States or any agency thereof; or if it is that of an officer or employee of any State, or foreign government, or any political subdivision thereof; or if recovery for the disability or death through workmen's compensation proceedings may be validly provided by state law. And obviously there is no liability if there was in fact neither disability nor death. It is not reasonable to suppose that Congress intended to set up a fact-finding tribunal of first instance, shorn of power to find a portion of the facts required for any decision of the case; or that in enacting legislation designed to withdraw from litigation the great bulk of maritime accidents, it contemplated a procedure whereby the same facts must be twice litigated before a longshoreman could be assured the benefits of compensation."[161]

Here, indeed, Justice Brandeis has issued a challenge to the very basis of the "jurisdictional fact" doctrine. Most statutory schemes imply a large number of facts on which jurisdiction turns, and full review over them could practically do away with the limitations imposed by the courts upon their review power over factual issues. In Justice Brandeis' view it would be both burdensome to reviewing courts and disruptive of administrative processes to hold that every fact-issue on which a claim of lack of statutory jurisdiction can be made to depend becomes thereby entitled to a full redetermination by the courts on review. The reason is that there are few factual questions of any importance that, if incorrectly decided by the administration, cannot be made the basis of a claim of lack of statutory jurisdiction.[162]

It must be recognized that Justice Brandeis, in his dissent in *Crowell v. Benson*, has put his finger on one of the great difficulties involved in the application of the jurisdictional-fact doctrine. If that doctrine is to be employed in the field of administrative law, it must be realized that it means a substantial change in the scope of review. Since statutory jurisdiction may depend on a great number of facts, the jurisdictional-fact doctrine, logically applied, can lead to the breakdown of the law-fact distinction, on which the scope of review has heretofore turned. These are the implications of the doctrine of *Crowell v. Benson* on which Justice Brandeis based his dissent in that case.

[161] 285 U.S. at 73.
[162] Compare Dickinson, *supra* note 144, at 1077.

The American Answer

Both the American and the French systems of administrative law have answered the challenge contained in Justice Brandeis' dissenting opinion in *Crowell v. Benson.* But they have done so in wholly different ways.

The United States Supreme Court itself soon became convinced of the logic of Justice Brandeis' dissent. With him, it has recognized that rigorous application of the jurisdictional-fact doctrine could lead to the practical nullification of the principle of narrow review of administrative findings of fact. And this perception has led the Court in effect to abandon the jurisdictional-fact doctrine; so that in its recent jurisprudence findings of fact on which administrative jurisdiction depends are reviewed no more broadly than ordinary findings of fact.

That the American Court has in truth all but abandoned the jurisdictional-fact doctrine is shown by a number of its recent decisions, involving both the agency whose action was at issue in *Crowell v. Benson* and other administrative agencies. An example of the first type is *South Chicago Coal & Dock Co. v. Bassett.*[163] Under the coverage section of the Longshoremen's Act no compensation shall be payable in respect of the disability or death of "a master or member of a crew of any vessel." The Supreme Court in the *Bassett* case held that the administrative finding that a particular employee was or was not "a member of a crew" was to be treated, for purposes of judicial review, as an ordinary finding of fact. "So far as the decision that this employee, who was at work on this vessel in navigable waters when he sustained his injuries, was or was not a 'member of a crew' turns on questions of fact," the Court's opinion reads, "the authority to determine such questions has been confided by Congress to the deputy commissioner. Hence the Court of Appeals correctly ruled that his finding, if there was evidence to support it, was conclusive."[164] The scope of review of the administrative finding was thus held to be a narrow one, even though the fact at issue was one on which the administrative power to award compensation depended.

Perhaps the best known of the non-Longshoremen's Act cases that illustrate the tendency of the American Court to discard the jurisdictional-fact doctrine is *National Labor Relations Board v. Hearst Publications.*[165] That case arose under the National Labor Relations Act,

[163] 309 U.S. 251 (1940).
[164] *Id.* at 257. For other cases under the Longshoremen's Act, see Schwartz, *supra* note 159, at 172-73.
[165] 322 U.S. 111 (1944).

whose operation is limited to cases in which there is an employer-employee relationship. The Court held that the Labor Board's finding that an employment relationship existed was to be given the same degree of conclusiveness as any other finding of fact. Resolving the question of who is an employee under the Act, asserted Mr. Justice Rutledge, " 'belongs to the usual administrative routine' of the Board. . . . the Board's determination that specified persons are employees under this Act is to be accepted if it has 'warrant in the record' and a reasonable basis in law."[166] And the above was true despite the fact that the finding at issue was similar to that involved in *Crowell v. Benson*, in that the administrative authority to act was dependent on the existence of the employment relationship.

It is difficult to see why the existence of an employment relationship was held "fundamental" to jurisdiction under the Longshoremen's Act in *Crowell v. Benson* but not under the Labor Act in the *Hearst* case. The answer to this inconsistency is, of course, to be found in the Supreme Court's present hostile attitude to the jurisdictional-fact doctrine. The Court's view on this point was well expressed in 1944 by Mr. Justice Frankfurter. "Analysis is not furthered," said he, "by speaking of such findings as 'jurisdictional' and not even when—to adapt a famous phrase—jurisdictional is softened by a quasi. 'Jurisdiction' competes with 'right' as one of the most deceptive of legal pitfalls. The opinions in *Crowell v. Benson* . . . and the casuistries to which they have given rise bear unedifying testimony of the morass into which one is led in working out problems of judicial review over administrative decisions by loose talk about jurisdiction."[167]

It seems clear, then, that the American Court has answered the challenge to the jurisdictional-fact doctrine contained in Justice Brandeis' opinion in *Crowell v. Benson* by abandoning that doctrine. In the words of Justice Frankfurter replying to the assertion of inherent authority in the courts to review jurisdictional questions, "this argument revives, if indeed it does not multiply, all the casuistic difficulties spawned by the doctrine of 'jurisdictional fact.' In view of the criticism which that doctrine as sponsored by *Crowell v. Benson* . . . brought forth and of the attritions of that case through later decisions, one had supposed that the doctrine had earned a deserved repose."[168]

[166] *Id.* at 130, 131. For the application of the doctrine of Crowell v. Benson in other non-Longshoremen's Act cases, see Schwartz, *supra* note 159, at 176-82.

[167] Yonkers v. United States, 320 U.S. 685, 695 (1944).

[168] Estep v. United States, 327 U.S. 114, 142 (1946).

The French Answer

Under the French counterpart of the doctrine of "jurisdictional fact," it will be recalled, "if an administrative decision is based on certain facts, it is not legal unless the facts as found by the administration are correct. When such findings fail to be correct, the decision lacks a legal basis; it must be set aside as *ultra vires*."[169]

Students of the *droit administratif* have been quick to realize the implications of this doctrine, which are similar to those that Justice Brandeis pointed out to the American administrative lawyer in his dissenting opinion in *Crowell v. Benson*. As perhaps the greatest of modern government commissioners declared, in his conclusions delivered to the Council of State in an important case: "Inquiry into error of law leads most of the time to the appraisal of the factual circumstances on which the legality of the challenged act depends; thus, the Council of State is constantly led to inquire if in fact the administration has used its authority so as not to infringe the rights of citizens and if a certain measure taken falls . . . within the class of those measures that the administration can take."[170]

Because every administrative decision presupposes certain facts that must be found before the authority delegated under the enabling statute can properly come into play, broad review of so-called "jurisdictional" facts could in effect make the reviewing court, rather than the administration, the true judge of the merits. Under the jurisdictional-fact doctrine, to arrive at a determination of the legal question of jurisdiction "the reviewing judge is obliged to substitute his own appreciation of the facts for that of the author of the challenged act. When the reviewing judge goes thus far he becomes in reality a judge of the merits. He becomes such, it is true, only to proclaim an error of law and to pronounce the setting aside of an administrative act. But it must be recognized that the powers assumed in such a case are analogous to those possessed by a judge of the merits. This analogy is true because the law flows from the facts, and the *ultra vires* act really consists here in an error of fact."[171]

Though French students have thus recognized that the logical application of the jurisdictional-fact doctrine can lead to a substantial broad-

[169] Alibert, *op. cit. supra* note 11, at 289.

[170] Conclusions of M. Romieu, later president of the judicial section of the Council of State, in Jacquin, November 30, 1906.

[171] Alibert, *op. cit. supra* note 11, at 289.

ening of the scope of review, they have not, like American jurists who recognized the implications pointed out by Justice Brandeis, urged that that doctrine be discarded. They have felt that the importance of judicial control on the question of jurisdiction outweighed any inconveniences to administration that might result from rigorous employment of the jurisdictional-fact doctrine. Nor has the Council of State followed the American Court in its abandonment of the doctrine. Though it, too, has recognized the validity of a challenge such as that issued by Justice Brandeis, it has answered the challenge by continuing to review fully all facts on which administrative jurisdiction is seen to depend, even though to do so has meant a substantial broadening in the scope of its reviewing power.[172]

The present attitude of the Council of State to the review of facts so far as they are the conditions on which the legality of an administrative act depends has been well stated by one of its members. "The judge of *ultra vires* asserts the authority to appreciate the facts of the case when such appreciation is necessary for the discovery of errors of law. The Council of State asserts the authority to inquire whether an act based on certain factual circumstances is or is not erroneous in law. In effect, judicial review of the given act depends on the factual circumstances in which it takes place. The judge, to determine if the act is correct in law, must determine these circumstances with some accuracy, but he makes this factual inquiry only so far as the facts are the conditions of legality. The powers of the Council of State over questions of fact thus depend on whether the law makes the existence of certain facts the condition for the challenged act."[173]

Mixed Questions of Law and Fact

Our discussion thus far has been based on the assumption that there is a clear-cut distinction between questions of law and questions of fact, with the former for the reviewing court and the latter primarily for the administration, unless the particular fact be one on which the administrative jurisdiction depends. Actually, as students of administrative law on both sides of the Atlantic have come to realize, the distinction between "law" and "fact," on which the scope of review is based, is not nearly so well defined as is often supposed. "The judges who have the

[172] A recent decision of the Council of State in which the language of "jurisdictional fact" is expressly used is Parayre, February 21, 1947.

[173] Odent, *op. cit. supra* note 23, at 353.

last word can confidently draw the line between law and fact; for the rest of us it is not so easy."[174] The extent of review depends upon which side of the law-fact dividing line the given administrative finding is seen to fall. Yet there is great difficulty in concrete cases in determining on which side of the line a particular finding does fall. The law-fact distinction, the United States Supreme Court has asserted, "is often not an illuminating test and is never self-executing."[175]

"Law" and "fact" are not necessarily two mutually exclusive kinds of question, so that the scope of review becomes a mere mechanical matter depending on the category in which the administrative finding at issue falls. The reviewing court itself has the final word on whether the particular finding is one of "law" or of "fact," and in deciding that question it practically determines whether the review of that finding is to be a broad or a narrow one. "The knife of policy alone effects an artificial cleavage at the point where the court chooses to draw the line between public interest and private right."[176]

The difficulty involved in applying the distinction between "law" and "fact" in concrete cases has led the Anglo-American administrative lawyer to term a large number of questions "mixed questions of law and fact." Perhaps the chief difficulty involved in applying the theory of review developed by our courts, Mr. Justice Jackson has stated in an important case, "lies in the want of a certain standard for distinguishing 'questions of law' from 'questions of fact.' This is the test Congress has directed, but its difficulties in practice are well known and have been the subject of frequent comment. Its difficulty is reflected in our labelling some questions as 'mixed questions of law and fact' and in a great number of opinions distinguishing 'ultimate facts' from evidentiary facts."[177]

The problem involved in these so-called "mixed questions of law and fact" is one that has arisen under the *droit administratif* just as in the Anglo-American system. "The judge of *ultra vires*," asserts the foremost French text on judicial review, "cannot separate the law from the facts and always proclaims the rule of law in the light of the facts."[178] In France as in the common-law world it has been recognized that the same question may have both legal and factual attributes. And

174 Carr, *loc. cit. supra* note 131.
175 Baumgartner v. United States, 322 U.S. 665, 671 (1944).
176 Dickinson, *op. cit. supra* note 35, at 55.
177 Dobson v. Commissioner, 320 U.S. 489, 501 (1943).
178 Alibert, *op. cit. supra* note 11, at 30.

the Council of State, like the Anglo-American courts, has been confronted with the problem of whether the legal or factual aspects of such questions shall be emphasized by the reviewing court for the purpose of determining the proper scope of review.

Application of Law to Fact

In the American system of administrative law the problem of so-called "mixed questions of law and fact" has arisen the most frequently in recent years in connection with the application of statutory language to particular states of fact.[179] "The heart of the problem of scope of review," asserts Professor Davis, "is now the extent to which the courts do and should review the application of legal concepts to undisputed or established facts."[180]

Though the administrative findings in these cases may be primarily findings of fact—e.g., whether the subjects of particular administrative determinations fall within a statutory concept or category may largely depend upon their factual characteristics—they also involve questions of statutory interpretation in the defining of the concept or category itself. "Every determination which refines the meaning of a legal concept is to that extent analytically a determination of law, even though the facts to which the concept is applied are unique and may never again occur."[181] Ultimately the scope of review in these cases depends on whether the application of the statutory concept or category to the particular factual situation, *i.e.*, the application of law to fact, is thought of as being primarily a judicial or an administrative function.

According to *Federal Trade Commission v. Gratz*,[182] which was decided by the United States Supreme Court in 1920, the application of law to fact is a judicial function. The *Gratz* case was the first important decision of the Court dealing with the application to specific business practices by the Federal Trade Commission of the standard of "unfair methods of competition" contained in its enabling statute. The Court reversed the conclusion of the Commission that the trade practices at issue constituted such unfair methods. In so doing the Court did not confine itself to the question whether there was an evidentiary basis for the administrative conclusion. "The Court instead conceived its

179 Stern, "Review of Findings of Administrators, Judges and Juries: A Comparative Analysis" 58 Harv. L. Rev. 70, 94 (1944).

180 Davis, *op. cit. supra* note 2, at 868.

181 *Id.* at 875.

182 253 U.S. 421 (1920).

function to embrace the right to determine independently what the appropriate rule of law should be. Its approach was identical with that which it would possess were it reviewing a legal ruling by a lower court."[183] The application of the statutory concept to the particular situation was thus treated by the Court primarily as a question of law. "The words 'unfair methods of competition,'" said Mr. Justice McReynolds, "are not defined by the statute and their exact meaning is in dispute. It is for the courts, not the commission, ultimately to determine as matter of law what they include."[184]

In Justice McReynolds' view a finding such as that at issue in the *Gratz* case is one involving a question of statutory interpretation, to be reviewed fully. An authority on statutory interpretation has divided the steps in the judicial process of interpreting statutes into three parts: (1) finding or choosing the proper statute or statutes applicable; (2) interpreting the statute law in its technical sense; (3) applying the meaning so found to the case at hand.[185] On the other hand, it has been urged that the interpretation and the application of statutes are two different things. In this view interpretation properly so called includes only the determination of the proper, sensible meaning of the statute. Application is the process of determining whether the facts of the particular case are within or without that meaning.[186]

The American Court in its more recent jurisprudence has shown that it is in accord with the second of these views on the meaning of statutory interpretation, at least so far as the law-fact classification for purposes of the scope of review is concerned. The leading case to illustrate this accord is *Gray v. Powell*,[187] decided in 1941. It involved the Bituminous Coal Act of 1937, which sought to fix minimum prices for the bituminous coal industry, though exempting from its provisions "coal consumed by the producer." The respondent company in *Gray v. Powell* asserted that it was a producer-consumer within this section and hence entitled to exemption from the act. The administrative agency concerned held that respondent was not a "producer" consuming its own product, and issued an order denying the claimed exemption.

This determination was sustained by the Court in language imply-

[183] Landis, *op. cit. supra* note 150, at 150.
[184] 253 U.S. at 427.
[185] De Sloovère, "Steps in the Process of Interpreting Statutes" 10 N.Y.U. L. Q. Rev. 1 (1932).
[186] *Id.* at 17.
[187] 314 U.S. 402 (1941).

ing that the question at issue was primarily within the administrative competence and not subject to wider review than administrative findings of pure fact. "Where as here a determination has been left to an administrative body," the opinion reads, "this delegation will be respected and the administrative conclusion left untouched. Certainly a finding on Congressional reference that an admittedly constitutional act is applicable to a particular situation does not require such further scrutiny. Although we have here no dispute as to the evidentiary facts, that does not permit a court to substitute its judgment for that of the Director."[188]

As explained by Mr. Justice Rutledge in a later case, *Gray v. Powell* stands for the proposition that "where the question is one of specific application of a broad statutory term in a proceeding in which the agency administering the statute must determine it initially, the reviewing court's function is limited."[189] In such cases the administrative determination is to be accepted if it has warrant in the record and a reasonable basis in law.[190] Under the Court's approach, unless the question at issue is seen to be wholly one of law the scope of review is not wider than that over administrative findings of fact. When the reviewing court cannot separate the elements of an administrative decision so as to identify a clear-cut mistake of law, said the Court in the well-known *Dobson* case, the administrative decision must stand.[191]

That such is indeed the present view of the American Court is shown by its most recent pronouncement on the subject, in a case decided in 1951. The administrative agency in that case had found as a "fact" that a deceased employee's death had arisen "out of and in the course of his employment" within the meaning of that term in the applicable compensation statute. Its doing so, stated Mr. Justice Frankfurter, "only serves to illustrate once more the variety of ascertainments covered by the blanket term 'fact.' Here of course it does not connote a simple, external, physical event as to which there is conflicting testimony. The conclusion concerns a combination of happenings and the inferences drawn from them. In part at least, the inferences presuppose applicable standards for assessing the simple, external facts. Yet the standards are not so severable from the experience of industry nor of

188 *Id.* at 412.

189 National Labor Relations Board v. Hearst Publications, 322 U.S. 111, 130 (1944).

190 *Id.* at 131.

191 Dobson v. Commissioner, 320 U.S. 489, 502 (1943).

such a nature as to be peculiarly appropriate for independent judicial ascertainment as 'questions of law.' "[192]

Application of Law to Fact in France

"Ultimately," writes the author of a study of the Council of State's review power over questions of fact, "and this is perhaps the most obdurate of all the difficulties—when it is a matter of qualifying a fact legally, of saying that a certain factual situation does indeed come within a given legal concept, that a particular act is a fault within the meaning of Article 1382 of the Civil Code or a fraud within the meaning of Article 1116 of the same Code, the appreciation of the facts and the interpretation of the law are indissolubly mixed together. How are we to say where one ends and the other begins?"[193]

When confronted with administrative findings that involved the application of a statutory concept to a particular state of facts the Council of State dealt with them much as the United States Supreme Court did in the *Gratz* case. The similarity can be seen in the Council's decisions dealing with the housing allowance accorded to schoolteachers under French law. By the terms of the relevant statute the various communes, which, as we have seen,[194] constitute the lowest level of administration in France, must procure for a teacher a "suitable dwelling" or grant the teacher an equivalent housing allowance. The allowance is due only if the dwelling placed by the commune at the disposition of the particular teacher is not suitable. The Council of State has often been petitioned by schoolteachers to annul the administrative refusal to grant them a housing allowance. In these cases, as one jurist has expressed it, "the Council of State, in order to determine the merits of the review petition, inquires whether the dwelling furnished is suitable or not; it must consequently substitute its own judgment for that of the administration on this issue of fact, for the hunting out of the facts by the judge is the sole way for him to determine whether or not the housing allowance should have been granted."[195]

In cases of this type the Council of State has decided on its own

[192] O'Leary v. Brown-Pacific-Maxon, Inc., 340 U.S. 504, 507 (1951). For a discussion of the English cases on "mixed questions of law and fact" see Schwartz, Law and the Executive in Britain 284-85, 293-97 (1949).

[193] Goldenberg, *op. cit. supra* note 24, at 15.

[194] *Supra* p. 83.

[195] Alibert, *op. cit. supra* note 11, at 296. The decisions of the Council include Commune de Quenza, May 21, 1920; Pille, June 24, 1910.

judgment whether the legal concept of "suitable dwelling" has been properly applied to the particular factual situation by the administration. Although the administrative determination here is based principally on the facts, the French tribunal, like the American Court in the *Gratz* case, has felt that the exercise of a broad reviewing power is justified by the need to ensure the proper application of the legal concept, which in its view is primarily a question of statutory interpretation.

Like the United States Supreme Court in the *Gratz* case, the Council of State has thus started with the proposition that so-called "mixed questions of law and fact" of the kind we have been discussing would be treated like questions of law for the purpose of determining the scope of review. But, unlike the American Court, the French tribunal has persisted in its adherence to this proposition, so that today, as a generation ago, full review is available in the *droit administratif* over administrative findings involving the application of statutory concepts to the facts of the particular case.

Some recent decisions of the Council of State can serve to illustrate its power of inquiry into administrative findings of this type. The law applicable to the licensing of doctors and pharmacists provides for the suspension of the right to practice if the licensee has been guilty of a "lack of probity." In cases involving petitions to annul such suspension orders the Council of State has fully reviewed the question whether there was actually a "lack of probity" in the circumstances of the case. Where, in its judgment, there had been no "lack of probity" the suspension order at issue was set aside.[196]

Similarly, where the relevant statute provided that the administration might take certain action in cities and communes in which there was a "serious housing shortage," the French tribunal has determined on its own judgment whether such a shortage existed in the given case.[197] And where the administration was authorized to act with regard to "abandoned plots" of land the Council has set aside an administrative act because in its opinion the particular plot was not "abandoned" within the meaning of the statute.[198]

In the decisions just referred to, all of which have been rendered since the Liberation, the Council of State has adhered to its view that questions involving the application of law to fact are to be treated like questions of law on review, with full inquiry into them by the review-

[196] Docteur Fécan, February 2, 1949; Roques, July 21, 1948.
[197] Commune de Veules-les-Roses, May 14, 1948; Barbedienne, January 9, 1948.
[198] Société Immobilière Suresnes-Washington, June 15, 1945.

ing court. The present approach of the French tribunal to such questions should be compared with that of the United States Supreme Court, which has, as has been noted, discarded the earlier view exemplified by its decision in the *Gratz* case, and tends now, so far as the scope of review is concerned, to treat questions involving the application of law to fact like questions of fact.

It is not intended to set up the *droit administratif* as an unalterable yardstick to which the American practice must conform or to judge the doctrine of *Gray v. Powell*,[199] as developed by the United States Supreme Court, by appealing to the superior moral jurisdiction of the French Council of State. Nevertheless it must be admitted that, under the doctrine of *Gray v. Powell*, the basic principle that questions of statutory construction are for the courts on review loses much of its force. This observation is true even though, strictly speaking, the administrative finding at issue in this type of case involves only the application of a statutory term to a particular state of fact. As Mr. Justice Frankfurter has aptly pointed out: "Meaning derives vitality from application. Meaning is easily thwarted or distorted by misapplication."[200]

Trend to Full Review

The cases dealt with thus far show that the Council of State reviews fully all questions of fact on which administrative jurisdiction in the particular case depends and all so-called "mixed questions of law and fact." This alone would make the scope of review in the *droit administratif* much broader than it is in the federal system in this country, for the United States Supreme Court has tended, as we have seen, to abandon both the jurisdictional-fact doctrine and its treatment of "mixed questions of law and fact" as questions of law for purposes of determining the scope of review.

But the French tribunal has not stopped with the cases cited, and in its most recent jurisprudence it has been tending to assert what amounts to a full review power over the law and the facts. Its approach in these cases has developed naturally from its application of the jurisdictional-fact doctrine. Under that doctrine, if a fact on which administrative jurisdiction depends has been found incorrectly by the agency concerned, the agency action will be set aside as *ultra vires*. Yet a look at any administrative decision will show that it is based on the entire fact

199 *Supra* note 187.
200 Trust of Bingham v. Commissioner, 325 U.S. 365, 380 (1945).

pattern in the given case. If the facts are not such as to justify the particular decision, can it not be argued that the administration has strayed beyond its competence, just as it has where the required jurisdictional fact does not exist? And if that is true, should not the reviewing court inquire fully into all the facts to determine whether they justify the particular decision?

Such, in any event, appears to be the reasoning followed by the Council of State in a number of recent cases. Thus, in a case decided in 1947 the petitioner's license as a captain in the merchant marine had been revoked. In setting aside the revocation the Council held that the facts of the case did not show any wrongful act on the part of the petitioner such as would justify the sanction of revocation. The Council appraised the facts on its independent judgment, for the agency concerned had found as a fact that the ship commanded by the petitioner had been lost through his fault and had revoked his license for that reason.[201]

Most of the decisions in which the Council of State has inquired fully into the facts to determine whether they justified the action taken by the administration have concerned dismissals of civil servants under the law authorizing the administration to purge itself of those who had collaborated too closely with the Vichy government. In these cases the French tribunal, almost from the very beginning, has inquired into whether the facts of the case warranted the penalty of dismissal. An early example is to be found in a decision rendered in 1946. The Council, after stating the key facts as it saw them, set aside the decision dismissing the petitioner on the ground that the facts "could not be regarded as being of such a sort as legally to justify the penalty imposed . . . and the decision was thus devoid of a legal basis."[202]

The control exercised by the Council of State in these cases, as one of its most distinguished members has recently declared, "goes very far; it extends, for example, to determining on its own judgment whether certain public functions were performed in an exceptionable manner, whether certain words were spoken on mere impulse or rather constituted an expression of considered opinion."[203] Cases in which the French tribunal has followed this approach are now almost too numer-

201 Di Dominico, February 28, 1947.
202 Bianquis, April 5, 1946.
203 Odent, *op. cit. supra* note 23, at 354.

ous to be cited.[204] In all of them the Council has determined for itself whether the facts justified the action taken by the administration. And in doing so the Council has in effect come very close to granting a full review of the facts on which the administrative action was based.

It seems clear, all things considered, that the trend in the *droit administratif* is now clearly in the direction of widening the scope of review. In this respect the tendency in France is wholly unlike that which prevails in the United States. Though both the French and the American systems have started with the law-fact distinction as the foundation stone of the law of review of administrative action, each system has built in a different manner. The American Court has more and more been broadening the domain of "fact" and limiting that of "law." The result has been a significant narrowing of the scope of review in this country. In France, on the other hand, it is the domain of "law" that has been broadened by the Council of State, with a resultant consistent widening of the scope of review. The ultimate outcome of the French development could well be full review on both the law and the facts—a stage that may not be too far off, in view of the Council's recent propensity for inquiring fully into the facts of a given case to determine whether they justify the challenged administrative action.

204 Recent Council of State decisions of this type include: Conquet, March 14, 1952; Bellières, July 7, 1949; Muffat, March 18, 1949; Hans, April 28, 1948; Martin, July 11, 1947; Parot, June 4, 1947; Bel, May 2, 1947; Contre-Amiral Seguin, January 17, 1947.

Chapter Nine

LIABILITY OF THE STATE AND OF PUBLIC OFFICERS

A system of administrative law is not adequate merely because it furnishes individual citizens adversely affected by administrative action with the right to judicial review. The effect of an administrative act is often immediate, and the damage caused cannot be undone by the mere judicial quashing of the act. The administration may, for example, be authorized to destroy food unfit for human consumption[1] or domestic animals afflicted with contagious diseases. If the administration acts improperly in a particular case and kills a horse that is not diseased,[2] can it be said that the owner is amply protected by having at his disposal only the right to seek judicial review? By a review action he can, it is true, probably obtain a judicial declaration that the administration has acted improperly. But the reviewing court can hardly, as a practical matter, set aside the administrative act found to be improper or, by setting it aside, restore to the petitioner his destroyed property.

In a great many cases an administrative act causes damage to an individual in circumstances that would make its author clearly liable if he were another private citizen. A vehicle negligently driven by a government employee may injure a pedestrian; or the administration may breach its contractual obligations, to the detriment of a private person. In these cases judicial review alone, though it result in the setting aside of an administrative act found to be unauthorized, is useless from a practical point of view to the injured citizen. Review is an adequate remedy only when the setting aside of the challenged administrative act by itself removes the possibility of any adverse effect on the individual affected. In the cases under discussion the mere setting aside of the administrative act cannot undo the damage already caused.

1 See North American Cold Storage Co. v. Chicago, 211 U.S. 306 (1908).
2 See Miller v. Horton, 152 Mass. 540 (1891).

Liability of the State and of Public Officers

What is needed in these cases is the redress of the injury inflicted by the action of administration. A system of administrative law that fails to provide the citizen with an action in damages to make him whole in such cases is actually but a skeletonized system. If individuals are to be protected adequately, an action for damages is the necessary complement of the action for review, which results only in the setting aside of improper administrative action.

A study of French administrative law would hardly be complete without some analysis of the way in which the French citizen who has suffered damage through an administrative act can obtain reparation. In the *droit administratif* as in the Anglo-American system the private individual injured by the administration has two possible sources of compensation for his damages: (1) the public officer who committed the act that caused the injury and (2) the State itself, on whose behalf the act was done. Largely for logical convenience, and also because of the order in which the law of liability developed in the Anglo-American system with which the common lawyer is familiar, our analysis of the subject will deal first with the liability of the public officer and then with that of the State.

Common-Law Liability of Officers

It is an ancient boast of the common law that public officers have no immunity from the sanctions of law applicable to the private individual.[3] In Anglo-American theory public officers have been regarded only as ordinary citizens who for the time being are serving the government, and who will fall back into the ranks of private citizens after their term of service has expired. The consequence has been that the same rules of law have been applied by our courts to officers as to private individuals. Under the common law public officers have not been placed because of their official status in any position of immunity.[4]

If the public officer is not vested with immunity greater than that of the ordinary citizen, it follows that he can be sued for the damages caused by his acts, just as a private individual can be, even if the acts were performed in the course of his official work. Here is, in fact, the starting point of the law of liability of public officers in the common-law world. "In England," states Dicey, "the idea of legal equality, or of the universal subjection of all classes to one law administered by the

3 Gellhorn, Administrative Law: Cases and Comments 298 (2d ed., 1947).
4 See 2 Goodnow, Comparative Administrative Law 163 (1893).

ordinary courts, has been pushed to its utmost limit. With us every official, from the Prime Minister down to a constable or a collector of taxes, is under the same responsibility for every act done without legal justification as any citizen."[5]

Thus, whereas the State in Anglo-American theory enjoys "sovereign immunity" from suit, its officers do not share in its immunity. They are answerable as ordinary citizens for wrongs committed even in the exercise of their official functions, just as a private agent is liable for a wrong done by him on behalf of or at the command of his principal. The officer may, to be sure, justify his conduct by referring to the statute under which he is acting. But that recourse raises precisely the question whether the law does actually authorize his conduct under the circumstances—the typical issue presented for judicial determination in these cases.[6]

What the common-law rule means in practice is shown by the famous case of *Miller v. Horton*,[7] decided by the highest court of Massachusetts in 1891. The defendants there were members of the board of health of a town. They were empowered by the relevant statute to destroy all animals infected with glanders, a contagious disease of certain domestic animals. Acting under this statutory authorization, the defendants had decided that the plaintiff's horse had glanders and had ordered it killed. In actual fact the horse had no disease. The plaintiff thus found himself deprived of his property because of the defendants' mistake, and he brought an action against them for the damages he had suffered; *i.e.*, the value of his horse.

The defendant health officers had been vested by the law only with the authority to destroy diseased animals. In killing a horse not infected they had clearly committed an act unauthorized by the enabling statute. And under the common-law theory public officers who act in a way not authorized by the law are personally liable for the consequences of their acts. "If during the period of their discharge of public functions they committed an act not justified by the law, such act was regarded as *coram non judice*—that is, an act of a purely private and personal character for which, like any citizen, they could be held responsible

[5] Dicey, Law of the Constitution 193 (9th ed., 1939). For a striking recent application of this principle, see Wade, Note, 29 Can. B. Rev. 665 (1951).

[6] Report of the Attorney General's Committee on Administrative Procedure 81 (1941).

[7] 152 Mass. 540 (1891).

before the ordinary courts."[8] Such, in fact, was the rule applied in *Miller v. Horton.* "We are of opinion," said Mr. Justice Holmes, "that the authority and jurisdiction of the commissioners to condemn the plaintiff's horse under section 13 was conditional upon its actually having the glanders. . . . The fact as to the horse having the disease was open to investigation in the present action, and on the finding that the horse did not have it, the plaintiff was entitled to a ruling that the defendants had failed to make out their justification."[9]

Immunity of Officers in America

It is not generally realized that the common-law rule of liability of public officers outlined above is one no longer followed by American courts. American law concerning liability of administrative officers for their torts is, according to one authority, today largely the antithesis of Dicey's proposition, already cited, that every official stands on the same footing as the ordinary citizen so far as the liability for his wrongful acts is concerned.[10]

It should be pointed out, indeed, that the strict common-law rule of liability has never been applied, either in Britain or this country, to one important class of public officers: namely, the judges of the law courts. "It is a general principle of the highest importance to the proper administration of justice," Mr. Justice Field has asserted, "that a judicial officer, in exercising the authority vested in him, shall be free to act upon his own convictions, without apprehension of personal consequences to himself. Liability to answer to every one who might feel himself aggrieved by the action of the judge, would be inconsistent with the possession of this freedom, and would destroy the independence without which no judiciary can be either respectable or useful."[11]

American courts have extended the immunity enjoyed by judges to administrative officers exercising judicial functions. There is a clear analogy between officers exercising such functions and judges who sit in the law courts.[12] They are vested with the authority to determine private rights and obligations by individual decisions, just as members of the judiciary are, and the considerations that have led our law to

[8] Goodnow, The Principles of the Administrative Law of the United States 397 (1905).
[9] 152 Mass. at 548.
[10] Davis, Administrative Law 801 (1951).
[11] Bradley v. Fisher, 13 Wall. 335, 347 (U.S. 1871).
[12] Gellhorn, *op. cit. supra* note 3, at 300.

confer immunity on judges have been seen to apply with equal force to administrators entrusted with judicial authority.

In particular cases the answer to the question whether the given officer is vested with immunity depends on whether his functions are seen to be of "judicial" or "administrative" quality. It is not surprising that our courts have not succeeded in formulating a mathematically precise criterion of "judicial" versus "administrative" functions for the purpose of determining whether a given officer is or is not liable for the damages caused by his acts. But however imperfect the case law on the subject may be, judicial affirmation of the principle of immunity for officers exercising "judicial" functions undeniably represents an important step away from the common-law rule—according to some, still basic in our system—under which all public officers are treated, so far as their tort liability is concerned, merely as ordinary citizens.

The present tendency in this country is, in fact, to go even further away from the common-law rule. The federal courts, for example, have extended the principle of immunity of public officers exercising judicial functions to officers vested with discretionary powers. "The rule as now declared in many cases," the Court of Appeals for the District of Columbia has stated, "has been applied, not only to officials judicial and quasi-judicial, but to executive officers generally."[13] Under recent American jurisprudence it would appear that the principle of personal liability now applies only to an officer exercising ministerial functions.[14] If he is entrusted with discretionary authority, he is placed in the same position of immunity as an officer exercising judicial functions, unless he "so palpably exceed[s] the scope of his authority as to remove himself from the protective coverage of the rule."[15] If one bears in mind the extent to which, under modern statutes, discretionary powers are conferred on administrative officers, one will soon realize that a rule relieving the public officer of personal liability for damages that result from the exercise of his discretionary powers goes far toward conferring full immunity.

To the common lawyer complete abolition of the personal liability of public officers appears intolerable, because it would eliminate an important incentive for them to conform strictly to the law in the performance of their duties. "No one can doubt the value of this rule," writes Professor Laski with regard to the principle of personal liability,

[13] Cooper v. O'Connor, 99 F. 2d 135, 141 (App. D.C. 1938).

[14] Harper, A Treatise on the Law of Torts 669 (1938).

[15] Gibson v. Reynolds, 77 F. Supp. 629, 634 (W.D. Ark. 1948). See Taylor v. Glotfelty, 201 F. 2d 51 (6th Cir. 1952).

"for it constitutes the fundamental safeguard against the evils of bureaucracy."[16] The foregoing analysis shows, however, that the strict rule of responsibility of officers, as applied in *Miller v. Horton*,[17] is now a thing of the past in American law. Personal liability, the starting point for the American system, has been giving way to immunity whenever the officer concerned is vested with judicial authority and, more recently, whenever he exercises discretionary powers. All this means the virtual replacement of responsibility by immunity for a large category of public officers.

Immunity of Officers in France

In the *droit administratif* there has never been anything like the rule of strict personal liability of public officers that was developed under the English common law. The starting point of the French system was, indeed, the principle of complete immunity for such officers. And even today personal liability remains the exception rather than the rule. "With us," wrote Hauriou in 1919, "liability for wrongful acts committed in the exercise of official functions has become the normal rule so far as the administration is concerned, but it is the exception so far as personal liability of officers is concerned."[18] This distribution of liability, he said, should be contrasted with that in the common-law world. There "the situation is the opposite: personal liability of officers is the rule, that of the administration, when it exists, is the exception."[19]

Under Article 1382 of the French Civil Code everyone is obligated to repair the damages caused by his faults. French administrative lawyers have always felt, however, that this basic principle of liability for fault should not be applied with the same rigor to public officers as to ordinary citizens. Although, according to the pre-eminent modern treatise on the *droit administratif*, the principle of personal liability of the officer whose act causes injury to private individuals is of natural, almost instinctive development, "there exists a danger of harassing or vexatious actions, of abuses of the right to bring such suits, that would disorganize the administration. Precautions have to be taken. In countries in which the judicial power is very great and is imbued with a sense of responsibility it has apparently been able, by itself, to deal with

[16] Laski, "The Responsibility of the State in England" 32 Harv. L. Rev. 447, 458 (1919).
[17] *Supra* note 7.
[18] 1 Hauriou, La Jurisprudence administrative de 1892 à 1929, 649 (1929).
[19] *Ibid.*

harassing actions, and the administration has felt no need to protect its officers.[20] But the administration in centralized countries like France—where, it must be admitted, it has been stronger than the judiciary—has always claimed for its officers an immunity that it itself could define and that would entitle it alone to appraise the consequences of their misdoings."[21]

Immunity of public officers in France dates from pre-Revolutionary times. Under the *Ancien Régime*, when officers of the administration were sued for damages in the law courts a practice developed whereby the king, as supervisor of the administration of justice, had the case transferred to his Council for decision—a transference that in effect made public officers immune from actions in the ordinary courts. It was natural for this system to be maintained in its essentials by the men of the Revolution, who were, as we have seen,[22] distrustful of the law courts and hostile toward them.

Article 75 of the Constitution of the year VIII of the Revolutionary era (1800) provided that "Public officers . . . may not be sued for acts performed officially, except by virtue of a decision authorizing such suit by the Council of State, and, in such case, suit may be brought in the ordinary courts." Since the Council of State at that time was primarily an administrative agency rather than a court, what this provision meant in practice was that a private citizen who wished to bring an action against a public officer had first to obtain the consent of the administration. That necessity was a serious obstacle for individuals seeking to bring such suits.[23] It gave the administration "an arbitrary power of determining whether to protect the officer being sued, and the abuse of such a power is to be feared. In effect, the administration always tends systematically to protect its agents."[24] Actually, consent to bring actions under Article 75 was very rarely given.

The immunity bestowed under Article 75 was constantly criticized during the Second Empire by the republican opposition, and when it came into power on the fall of Napoleon III one of its first acts was the abrogation of Article 75 by a decree of September 19, 1870: "Article 75 of the constitution of the year VIII is repealed. All laws whose object is to hamper actions against public officers of any kind are similarly repealed."

20 Anglo-American countries are cited in a footnote as an example.
21 Hauriou, Précis de droit administratif 520 (12th ed., 1933).
22 *Supra* p. 6.
23 Hauriou, *op. cit. supra* note 21, at 521.
24 Waline, Traité élémentaire de droit administratif 355 (6th ed., 1951).

The intention of the 1870 decree, according to Léon Blum, himself a distinguished government commissioner in the Council of State before embarking on his well-known political career, "was to confer on the law courts jurisdiction in all actions for damages caused by a wrongful act committed in connection with the exercise of a public function. This jurisdiction of the ordinary law seemed the surest safeguard of individual liberties. It was desired that, as for example in England, in the event of an arbitrary arrest, an illegal seizure, or a manifest irregularity of any kind, the officer who had given or executed the order should be subject to personal liability."[25]

If it were the intent of the 1870 decree to lay down a broad principle of liability of public officers, similar to that under the English common law, the intent was defeated by the jurisprudence of the Court of Conflicts in the cases after 1870. In the celebrated *Pelletier* case[26] (1873) that tribunal held that, despite the decree of 1870, the law courts were not competent to entertain all actions for damages against public officers based on faults committed by them while acting within the scope of their public functions. This incompetence, the court ruled, followed from the doctrine of the separation of administrative and judicial powers, which has been, as we have noted,[27] the basic principle of French public law since the Revolution. Under the doctrine of the separation of powers as applied in France the law courts may not question the regularity of administrative acts. If they judge a public officer sued because of an act done in connection with his functions, they must necessarily judge the regularity of the act. For it is only if the act is improper that there can be any liability. Since the French law courts cannot question administrative acts, it follows, said the Court of Conflicts, that they cannot judge the liability that public officers may have incurred by acts connected with their official functions.

Under the *Pelletier* case, now firmly established in French jurisprudence despite the decree of 1870, the law courts may not exercise jurisdiction when a public officer is sued before them for a fault committed in the exercise of his functions. If the law court refuses to decline jurisdiction, the administration may raise the question of conflict, which is resolved, as has been shown,[28] by the Court of Conflicts. It is thus ulti-

[25] Conclusions in Lemonnier, Council of State, July 26, 1918. M. Blum's important conclusions are printed in (1918-19) Sirey, part 3, 41, and Hauriou, *op. cit. supra* note 18, at 637.

[26] July 26, 1873.

[27] *Supra* pp. 6-7.

[28] *Supra* p. 64.

mately for the Court of Conflicts to determine (with all the difficulties for the litigant that adjudication by this tribunal entails) whether a particular public officer can be sued before the French law courts. If he cannot, he is in effect clothed in absolute immunity, for the administrative courts are not vested with the authority to render personal judgments against public officers in favor of private citizens.

In its *Pelletier* jurisprudence the Court of Conflicts acted, as M. Blum pointed out,[29] much as the United States Supreme Court has often done. It refused to give effect to the literal meaning of the decree of 1870, inasmuch as that conflicted with what it considered to be a more fundamental principle of French law: that is, the separation of powers. The jurisdiction of the law courts in these cases it recognized only so far as judicial examination of the public officer's fault would not involve a critical examination of the particular administrative service. And the court was thus led to the notion of what it called "personal fault" of the officer concerned; *i.e.*, a fault sufficiently separable from his official functions to be examined by the court without any need to inquire into the way such functions were performed.

Liability of Officers for Personal Faults

The Court of Conflicts, in its decision in the *Pelletier* case, emphasized that the act of the officer sued was clearly performed in the exercise of his official functions.[30] And the court went on to say that "aside from that act the plaintiff does not allege any personal acts on the part of defendants of such a sort as to involve their individual liability."

Relying on this language in the *Pelletier* decision, the subsequent case law has consistently employed the distinction between "personal fault" (*faute personnelle*) on the part of the public officer and what has been termed "service-connected fault" (*faute de service*); *i.e.*, a fault committed in connection with the functioning of the particular public service that the officer is administering. Only if he has committed a personal fault is he personally liable. If the damage be caused by a service-connected fault, the fault is seen to be that of the public service itself, and the administration rather than the officer is held liable.

The basis for this distinction has been well stated by Léon Duguit. "If there must be a fault on the part of the public officer for him to be held liable, not *every* fault will make him liable. There must be a

[29] *Loc. cit. supra* note 25.

[30] The act at issue was the seizure of copies of a newspaper on the order of a prefect.

personal fault; if there is a fault committed directly in the exercise of the official function, the administration may be liable, but the officer is not. The reasons for this solution are easily seen. When there is only a service-connected fault the identity of the officer is in a sense merged into the public service. It is entirely pertinent to say that it is not so much that the officer has acted as that the public service has functioned amiss."[31]

The *Pelletier* decision may, as has been pointed out, have defeated the intent of the decree of September 19, 1870, to enact a broad principle of personal liability of public officers similar to that developed under the English common law. But it should not be overlooked that it did constitute an important step forward. For it established the principle that French public officers could be sued in the law courts for the damages caused by their personal faults. The principle of complete immunity that had governed the French law until 1870 thus at least gave way so far as the personal misfeasances of officials were concerned.

Personal Fault Defined

The first and probably still the most famous attempt to state more precisely the distinction between personal faults and service-connected faults, on which the personal liability of French public officers is based, was that of Laferrière, who, more than anyone else, was the founder of the modern *droit administratif*. "If the wrongful act is impersonal," he stated in an oft-quoted passage, "if it reveals an administrator more or less subject to error rather than a man with his weaknesses, his passions, his imprudences, the act remains administrative and cannot entail the personal liability of the officer."[32]

As one commentator has pointed out, Laferrière's formula is elegant, but hardly precise.[33] Jèze, an outstanding twentieth-century administrative lawyer, sought to lay down a more exact test. According to him such personal fault as was necessary to make a public officer liable existed when there was willfulness or malice or gross negligence on the officer's part. In his view, unless there were willful or malicious intent or unless the officer's negligence exceeded the normal, the fault remained connected with the service.[34]

[31] 3 Duguit, Traité de droit constitutionnel 300 (3d ed.) (emphasis added).
[32] 1 Laferrière, Traité de la juridiction administrative et des recours contentieux 648 (2d ed., 1896).
[33] Duguit, *op. cit. supra* note 31, at 301.
[34] Jèze, cited in Duguit, *loc. cit. supra* note 33.

Jèze's test does not, however, wholly resolve the problem, for it does not deal adequately with the public officer who has no malicious intent and commits no gross negligence, but who is not acting within the scope of his official functions. This omission has led other writers, notably Hauriou, to assert the test of separability from official functions. "The act becomes personal to the officer," states Hauriou, "when there is a circumstance manifestly separable from the exercise of the function which places it outside the ordinary practices of the agency and makes one feel that the officer has been motivated by a desire not to act as an administrator."[35]

To the common-law observer the problem of determining whether the fault of a public officer is personal, so as to make him liable, or service-connected, so as to leave only the administration liable, is essentially similar to that met with in the Anglo-American law of agency in connection with the liability of a principal for the torts of his agent. In our law of agency the basic problem is also to determine whether the principal[36] or the agent alone is liable. And our courts have resolved the problem by deciding whether the act of the agent in the particular case was a "personal" act or one attributable to the principal.

It is interesting to note that the Anglo-American law of agency, in determining whether an act was "personal" to the agent or not, started with something very much like Jèze's test of willfulness or malice. It used to be said by our courts that a principal was not liable for the willful act of his agent. "The dividing line," it was declared in an early New York case, "is the wilfulness of the act."[37] It has come to be recognized by common-law courts, however, that willfulness alone is not enough of a criterion. The agent may have acted willfully, but his principal should still be held liable if the agent were acting within the scope of his employment. The test of scope of employment has consequently been adopted by our law. If the agent's fault was committed with reference to an act or matter "within the scope of his employment," his principal is liable. If the agent was acting outside the scope of his employment, then his act was "personal," and he alone is liable.

The test of scope of employment is fundamentally similar to that of separability from official functions as advocated in France by Hauriou and other recent writers. According to their view a public officer is personally liable only if his act be separable from his official functions,

[35] Hauriou, *op. cit. supra* note 21, at 525 (italics omitted).
[36] Of course, the agent is also liable, in these cases, in Anglo-American law.
[37] Wright v. Wilcox, 19 Wend. 343, 345 (N.Y. 1838).

or, to use the terminology familiar to the common lawyer, only if the officer were acting outside the scope of his public employment.

The Council of State and the Court of Conflicts, in their more recent jurisprudence, appear to have adopted the test urged by Hauriou, separability from official functions, although there appears still to be weight given to the factors of willfulness, malice, and gross negligence —those proposed by Jèze as the determinative elements. It can be stated, then, that in the *droit administratif* of today a public officer is liable personally only if he has acted willfully, maliciously, with gross negligence, or outside the scope of his official functions. If he has acted within that scope, he is normally not liable, for he has committed, not a personal fault, but a service-connected fault for which the administration alone is liable.

Examples of Personal Fault

The way the courts in France have applied the test of separability from official functions can perhaps best be gathered from some examples. In the following cases it was held that an official was acting outside the scope of his employment and had consequently committed a personal fault for which he alone was liable:

Use of a government vehicle for purely personal business;[38]

Burning down of plaintiff's house by soldiers in revenge for the murder of one of their comrades by plaintiff;[39]

Use of excessive brutality to restrain disorderly conduct by a policeman off duty and out of uniform;[40]

Use of the facilities of a municipal laboratory by its director to make analyses for a private individual.[41]

In such cases Anglo-American courts too would probably hold that the individual concerned was acting outside the scope of his employment if the case involved a private principal-agent relationship. In other decisions, however, the French courts appear to construe the concept

38 Salah ben Larbi Bezine, Court of Conflicts, July 10, 1947; Pastor, Council of State, November 28, 1947; Senoussi, Council of State, October 5, 1945. Under a recent decision, Mimeur, Council of State, November 18, 1949, State liability is not necessarily eliminated in such a case.

39 Bartholozzi, Council of State, October 12, 1945.

40 Clautour, Court of Conflicts, December 14, 1946. Under French law, defendant could intervene in such a case, but was under a duty to use only reasonable force.

41 Ville d'Amiens contre Marchand, Cour d'Appel d'Amiens, December 29, 1931.

of scope of employment more strictly. For example, they tend to hold that the public officer has acted outside the scope of his employment and committed a personal fault if he has acted in a manner manifestly improper, even though still acting on behalf of the administration. It has been held that a personal fault was committed when a policeman sought to frighten a child by shooting a pistol that he thought was not loaded;[42] when a public doctor vaccinated without taking the elementary precaution of cleansing himself;[43] when a government vehicle was driven in violation of traffic regulations;[44] and when the act committed constituted a crime.[45]

In cases of this sort, common-law courts would probably hold that the agent's act did not constitute such a departure from his service as to put his fault outside the scope of his employment. It should be realized, however, that the purpose of the French test is wholly different from that of the Anglo-American one, though the tests themselves have elements of similarity. The Anglo-American test, scope of employment, is used in the law of agency to determine whether a private principal is liable for the torts of his agent. It is to be expected that our courts would construe the test strictly against the principal, for it is felt to be just that he, as the one who appointed the agent and derived the benefits of his work, should be liable for the agent's torts unless the latter has departed completely from his duties.

The French test of separability from official functions has an altogether different purpose. It is used in the field of public law to determine whether a public officer is liable for his torts. Not unnaturally, the French courts interpret this test strictly against the officer, for it is considered undesirable that he should completely escape personal responsibility for his improper acts. Such escape is, of course, the outcome under the French test if his act is found to have been within the scope of his employment, unless he has been willful, malicious, or grossly negligent, for he has then committed only a service-connected fault for which he is not personally liable.

Critique of Personal Liability

"The liability of the individual official for wrongdoing committed in the course of his duty," Professor Robson has asserted, "on which

[42] Cornu, Court of Conflicts, December 6, 1937.
[43] T., Court of Cassation, February 11, 1941.
[44] Fox-Girard, Court of Conflicts, December 12, 1938.
[45] See Mestre, "Faute administrative et faute penale" (1935) Dalloz, Chronique 57. But compare Beauvalet, Court of Conflicts, January 20, 1945.

so much praise has been bestowed by English writers, is essentially a relic from past centuries when government was in the hands of a few prominent, independent and substantial persons, so-called Public Officers, who were in no way responsible to ministers or elected legislatures or councils. . . . Such a doctrine is utterly unsuited to the twentieth-century state, in which the Public Officer has been superseded by armies of anonymous and obscure civil servants, acting directly under the orders of their superiors, who are ultimately responsible to an elected body. The exclusive liability of the individual officer is a doctrine typical of a highly individual common law. It is of decreasing value today."[46]

Many administrative lawyers, both French and Anglo-American, have come to see that it is not wholly desirable for the personal liability of public officers to be treated on exactly the same footing as that of private individuals. The ordinary citizen commonly acts only in his own interest, and it is he who derives the benefits of his acts. The officer acts in the public interest, and it is the community as a whole that profits from his action. The considerations that, in Mr. Justice Field's phrase, have led "all countries where there is any well-ordered system of jurisprudence"[47] to confer complete immunity on judges have been seen by many to apply with equal force to officers of the administration. If a rule of strict liability of judges would jeopardize the independence and effectiveness of the judicial system, cannot the same be said with regard to the administrative process? A too heavy liability would paralyze the initiative of public officers; and one of the chief complaints directed at administration is that it is already too lacking in initiative.[48]

The danger of such paralysis of administration is clearly present under American decisions, like *Miller v. Horton*,[49] which inexorably apply the common-law rule of strict personal liability. In that case the owner of the horse destroyed as diseased by defendant health officers recovered damages from them when the court found that they had acted improperly, the horse being in fact not infected. The possible effects of *Miller v. Horton* on the zeal of the public officer are not difficult to imagine. An officer personally liable for torts committed in the exercise of his functions, who can be sued for damages by individuals

46 Quoted in Gellhorn, *op. cit. supra* note 3, at 299.
47 Bradley v. Fisher, 13 Wall. 335, 347 (U.S. 1871).
48 Waline, *op. cit. supra* note 24, at 355.
49 *Supra* note 7.

injured by such torts, is likely to be timid and irresolute in his administration of the law that exposes him to such risks. The health officer will hesitate before ordering the killing of a horse infected with glanders, though the law requires that that be done, if he knows that a court may decide that the animal was not diseased, that the killing was consequently illegal, and that he is therefore personally liable for the value of the horse to its owner.[50]

A strict rule of personal liability in such cases can, as Professor Gellhorn has pointed out, greatly impede effective administration. "If an officer knew that his exercise of judgment in doubtful cases might expose him to the payment of heavy damages, he might be disinclined to act at all in such cases. In a thoroughly individualistic society it might be regarded as a desirable thing that the doubtful cases should produce no governmental action. But when whole communities may be exposed to the spread of contagious disease unless the action of officers imposing quarantines is prompt, or where the herds of an important dairying state . . . may be afflicted with disease because an officer having [*Miller v. Horton*] in mind decided not to destroy an animal he believed but did not know to be afflicted, one may wonder whether the imposition of personal liability upon the officer produces desirable consequences."[51]

Furthermore, it seems unjust to impose on a minor public officer, who is generally poorly paid, the risks inherent in his functions and the duty of indemnifying from his meager personal resources the victims of his tortious acts. To assimilate the position of the public officer to that of the private citizen may often lead to unjust results. In the public service, faults in themselves exceedingly venial can often have extremely grave pecuniary consequences. It is hardly fair to make the public officer liable for the consequences in every such case.[52]

It will be objected that, even if these considerations be valid, there is still an overriding constitutional need for the principle of personal liability of officers. "If from an administrative point of view," states Hauriou in language paralleling that often heard from Anglo-American administrative lawyers, "it may be advantageous that one who suffers damage be prone to sue the administration rather than the public officer, from a constitutional point of view one may still wish that the practice

[50] Garner, "La Conception anglo-américaine du droit administratif" in Mélanges Maurice Hauriou 377 (1929).

[51] Gellhorn, *op. cit. supra* note 3, at 302.

[52] Waline, *op. cit. supra* note 24, at 354.

of suing officers personally before the law courts shall not be completely abandoned, for the possibility of personal liability is still the best method that has been found to prevent improper action by public officers."[53]

The English common law may have placed all too much emphasis on the value of the rule of personal liability of officers as a constitutional safeguard. Still, it cannot be denied that a public officer who knows that he will have to respond with his own resources if he commits a personal fault in the French sense of the term is less likely to act maliciously or outside the scope of his official functions than one who feels that he is acting only as an impersonal agent of administration. "The best way of keeping the public officer in check, of inspiring him with a sense of duty, is to warn him that there is a certain point at which he loses the status of impersonal cogwheel in a large public service, at which he becomes a human being with duties and responsibilities, and at which, as such, he finds himself confronted by the average citizen to whom he will be declared personally liable."[54]

The proper approach here may well be by the route followed by the *droit administratif* in these cases. Instead of the wholesale rule of strict personal liability developed by the English common law, which has proved unworkable under modern conditions, the French system has substituted a rule of personal liability for only so-called personal faults. But it is precisely these personal faults, as defined by the French courts, that from the constitutional point of view must be ensured against. Even if it be felt that the common-law rule of personal liability cannot be inexorably applied today, it must not be replaced by a principle of broad immunity such as that by which, as we have seen, it is tending to be replaced in the United States. There is still a constitutional need for personal liability for personal faults as the most effective means of eliminating them.

It must be admitted, then, that such a tendency as has recently prevailed in the American law of public officers is removing an important safeguard against their abuse of power. Of even greater importance, however, for those adversely affected by administrative action is the fact that the abandonment of the common-law rule of strict personal liability means elimination of the assets of the public officer as a possible source of reparation for any damages suffered. For those subject to administrative action the grant of immunity to the public officer is

[53] Hauriou, *op. cit. supra* note 18, at 649.
[54] Duguit, *op. cit. supra* note 31, at 295.

tolerable only if they are given some other source of reparation. This substitute source can be only the State itself, in whose name the officer who caused the damage was acting. It is to the questions of whether and to what extent such liability is imposed upon the State in the Anglo-American and the French systems that we must now turn.

The King Can Do No Wrong

If Anglo-American law started with the proposition that the public officer is personally liable for the damages caused by his wrongful acts, its starting point was a wholly different one as to the liability of the State. The basic principle here has been sovereign immunity, under which an action cannot be brought against the State without its consent.

As Mr. Justice Frankfurter has stated: "Though this immunity from suit without consent is embodied in the Constitution, it is an anachronistic survival of monarchical privilege."[55] It rests on the well-known historical maxim according to which the King can do no wrong. "The King," reads a famous passage from Blackstone, "is not only incapable of doing wrong, but even of thinking wrong; he can never mean to do an improper thing; in him is no folly or weakness."[56]

These words do nothing if they do not surprise a student of history. For he quickly discovers that at the relevant dates of English history the King was always doing wrong. "It is not too much to say," writes an acute English observer, "that the whole Constitution has been erected upon the assumption that the King not only is capable of doing wrong but is more likely to do wrong than other men if he is given a chance."[57]

In Anglo-American law the infallibility attributed to the King in the days when he was personally sovereign has been more recently recognized in the State, which the English Crown now merely personifies. Thus, even today, and even in the American democracy, the basic principle of public law is that the King can do no wrong.[58]

The anomaly of adoption by the American courts of the English historical maxim is almost self-evident. "That the English doctrine should have been introduced into the United States," comments the

[55] Dissenting, in Kennecott Copper Corp. v. Tax Commission, 327 U.S. 573, 580 (1946).

[56] 1 Blackstone's Commentaries 254 (1813 ed.).

[57] Herbert, Uncommon Law 292 (1935).

[58] Davis, *op. cit. supra* note 10, at 797.

author of an article seeking to explain Anglo-American administrative law to a French audience, "where there was no king, where the chief of State was never sovereign, where from the beginning sovereign power resided in the people, has appeared a mystery to certain American jurists themselves, and it is difficult to comprehend, in fine, how in a democratic republic, where the rights of the individual against the State are fundamental legal principles, people could have accepted the doctrine of sovereign immunity of the State and its nonliability for damages inflicted by its agents on private individuals."[59]

In accepting the doctrine of sovereign immunity the American courts have relied to some extent on the reasons given for the doctrine by the English courts. "It seems most probable," Mr. Justice Miller has affirmed, "that it has been adopted in our courts as a part of the general doctrine of publicists, that the supreme power in every State, wherever it may reside, shall not be compelled, by process of courts of its own creation, to defend itself from assault in these courts."[60] What is that if not essentially a restatement of the English principle that the King cannot be sued in his own courts?—a principle derived in turn from feudal days when a lord could not be sued in his own courts.[61]

But the American courts have gone farther and defended the doctrine of sovereign immunity with reasons that have much broader implications. "A sovereign is exempt from suit," reads a celebrated statement by Mr. Justice Holmes, "not because of any formal conception or obsolete theory, but on the logical and practical ground that there can be no legal right as against the authority which makes the law on which the right depends."[62] In other words, since the State is the creator and the source of all law it is consequently above the law. Hence no one may vindicate a right against the State before its courts without its consent.

These attempts to justify sovereign immunity have been strongly criticized, not the least emphatically by some members of the present

[59] Garner, *supra* note 50, at 364.

[60] United States v. Lee, 106 U.S. 196, 206 (1882).

[61] Wade and Phillips, Constitutional Law 309 (4th ed., 1950).

[62] Kawananakoa v. Polyblank, 205 U.S. 349, 353 (1907). Writing in 1926 to Harold J. Laski, Justice Holmes declared: "I can't understand how anyone should think that an instrumentality established by the United States to carry out its will, and that it can depose upon a failure to do so, should undertake to enforce something that *ex hypothesi* is against its will. It seems to me like shaking one's fist at the sky, when the sky furnishes the energy that enables one to raise the fist." 2 Holmes-Laski Letters 822 (Howe ed. 1953).

United States Supreme Court. "Whether this immunity is an absolute survival of the monarchical privilege, or is a manifestation merely of power, or rests on abstract logical grounds, . . . it undoubtedly runs counter to modern democratic notions of the moral responsibility of the State," Mr. Justice Frankfurter has asserted.[63] It must, however, be emphasized that the doctrine of sovereign immunity has never been expressly repudiated by an American court. Our courts have, indeed, consistently confirmed whenever occasion has arisen the principle that the State cannot be sued without its consent. If, as Maitland put it half a century ago in an oft-quoted sentence, "it is a wholesome sight to see 'The Crown' sued and answering for its torts,"[64] it is still a sight that, because of the persistence of the doctrine of sovereign immunity, was until recently comparatively rare in the common-law world.

The State Is an Honest Man

Before the Revolution, French public law, like the English common law, was governed by the maxim *le Roi ne peut mal faire*. "Under the *Ancien Régime* the public law of France reflected the theory of the absolute monarchy, a blend of the Roman *imperium* and feudal lordship for which the royal lawyers, such as Bodin and Loyseau, outlined the doctrine that sovereignty or the public power was delegated or attached to the monarch. As the fountainhead of power and justice, the monarch was invested with a type of sovereignty which excluded responsibility as to his acts or those acting on his behalf."[65]

Under the French system, then, as in Anglo-American law, the starting point of the law of State liability was the principle of complete irresponsibility. What it meant in practice, if we bear in mind that the French public officer could not be personally sued in any case without administrative consent before 1870, was well expressed by Léon Blum in his conclusions before the Council of State already referred to.[66] "In a relatively recent state of our law," he said, "the citizen injured by the faulty working of a public service possessed no remedy that permitted him to obtain redress for the damage suffered. If he wanted to sue the public officer who had ordered or committed the illegal or tortious act, he was met with a dismissal because of Article 75 of the Constitution of

[63] Dissenting, in Great Northern Ins. Co. v. Read, 322 U.S. 47, 59 (1944). Compare Street, Governmental Liability 8-10 (1953).
[64] 3 Maitland, Collected Papers 263 (1911).
[65] Rokham and Pratt, Studies in French Administrative Law 69 (1947).
[66] *Supra* note 25.

the year VIII. . . . If he wanted to sue the State . . . as a moral person responsible for its acts . . . the Council of State dismissed again, this time on a theory analogous to that of *force majeure*. It was the established law that the State was not liable to private citizens. The damage suffered from the faulty working of public services was a risk they had to run. They had to endure the possibility of lapses, to pay this premium for lapses, in return for the services, the benefits of all sorts, that they obtained from the administrative organization of the nation and the exercise of public authority."

The men of the French Revolution were impregnated with the theory of sovereignty that permeated the writings of Rousseau, and it was not to be expected that they would abandon the principle of State irresponsibility. But they were also strong believers in the sanctity of private property. And this belief led them to assert in Article 17 of the Declaration of the Rights of Man of 1789: "Property being an inviolable and sacred right, none may be deprived of it except where the public necessity, established according to law, clearly demands it and on condition that just compensation be paid beforehand." Thus, though the men of 1789 firmly believed in the principle of absolute national sovereignty, they believed even more firmly, if that be possible, in the right of private property. They themselves were for the most part property owners, and they asserted the need to protect the right of property against all attack. Their doctrine of absolute sovereignty led them, it is true, to concede that even private property could be taken by the State where the public necessity demanded it. But in that event, they said, the owner must be paid a just indemnity for his loss.

This provision for fair compensation in eminent-domain cases was, as one commentator has expressed it, the opening in the door through which the entire modern system of State liability was to work its way into French law. "It is easy to understand how this happened. In actuality, if one decides that when a property owner is directly dispossessed by the regular procedure of eminent domain, he has the right to a just indemnity from the State, one is perforce quickly led to the proposition that such indemnity is due when the owner's rights in his property are denied, not simply by eminent-domain proceedings, but by any other administrative action that adversely affects his property."[67]

During the first half of the nineteenth century the principle of State liability was firmly established in cases of private property injured by

[67] Duguit, *op. cit. supra* note 31, at 464.

public works. "There is doubtless no dispossessing of the owner, strictly speaking, in these cases. But if property is an absolute intangible right to which the sovereignty of the State itself must give way, it must be protected, not only when it is taken away from its owner, but also when a decrease in its value is caused."[68]

From the cases involving damage caused by public works the evolution has been a rapid one. Very quickly the principle of those cases was extended to all in which private property was injured by administrative action. And from there it was not far to the assertion of a principle of liability in cases involving other than purely property rights. "If we admit that when private property is involved the doctrine of irresponsibility must give way, it can be vigorously maintained that it should do the same whenever the private individual is injured in his person and, generally speaking, in his rights other than the right of property."[69]

The upshot of the evolution just traced has been the replacement in France of the principle of State irresponsibility by a broad rule of State liability in all cases of the private citizen injured by improper administrative action. "Irresponsibility has in practice become the exception, and the liability of the State has, on the contrary, become the rule."[70] The maxim that "the king can do no wrong" has been superseded by the saying that "the State is an honest man." As such it will seek to repair the damages caused by its wrongful acts and will not attempt to avoid liability by taking refuge behind the fictitious dogma of sovereignty.

The French evolution described has been made possible in large part by obsolescence of the notion of sovereignty on which the doctrine of State immunity was based. "Close analysis suggests that sovereignty and responsibility are mutually exclusive notions. . . . That which creates law by its sovereign will clearly cannot violate it. Just as in an absolute monarchy the king can do no wrong, and is therefore irresponsible, so the democratic state, which is no more than the nation sovereignly organised, can do no wrong and escapes responsibility."[71]

It is only because the classical notion of sovereignty, accepted without question by the men of the Revolution, has been coming to be repudiated by French legal theory that the principle of State liability has been able to extend itself over the entire field of public law. "The sacred dogma of national sovereignty, as set forth by J. J. Rousseau in

[68] *Id.* at 465.
[69] *Id.* at 466.
[70] Odent, Cours de contentieux administratif 257 (1949-50).
[71] Duguit, Law in the Modern State 199 (tr. Laski 1919).

magical terms that were long accepted without question, is today considered as a mere sophism. It is the divine right of the people substituted for the divine right of kings. . . . Since the beginning of the twentieth century that dogma, subjected to ever stronger criticism, has been discarded by legal thinkers."[72]

It should be emphasized that the fundamental change in the *droit administratif* which has replaced the doctrine of State irresponsibility by an ever-widening principle of State liability has been brought about almost entirely by the jurisprudence of the Council of State. "This evolution has occurred without the aid of statute; it was wholly the work of the judge."[73] Even today there is no law that decrees the liability of the French State. But the lack has not prevented the Council of State from developing and applying a broad principle of State responsibility.

A fundamental difference must therefore be noted between the French and the Anglo-American systems in their development of the law of State liability. Mr. Justice Frankfurter has recently referred to "the natural, even if unconscious, pressure to escape from the doctrine of sovereign immunity which—whatever its historical basis—is hardly a doctrine based upon moral considerations. The trend of deep sentiment . . . has looked askance at the doctrine."[74] But if the rising sentiment against State irresponsibility has been the same in France and in the common-law world, the way in which the doctrine of irresponsibility has been dealt with has differed in the two systems. In France, as we have just seen, the law of State liability has been largely the work of the judge: it is the Council of State that has replaced the original doctrine of irresponsibility by a broad rule of State liability. In the common-law world, on the contrary, the judge has done little to supplant the doctrine of sovereign immunity by one more suited to modern needs. What changes there have been are the work of the legislature rather than of the courts. A student of Anglo-American administrative law who is interested in the liability of the State will consequently look primarily to the statutes that have modified the doctrine of sovereign immunity. His counterpart in France, on the other hand, will focus his attention largely on the case law, for the French law on the subject has been almost entirely the handiwork of the Council of State.

[72] Jèze, "Réparation du préjudice spécial causé par une loi générale impersonelle," Revue du Droit Public 366, 368 (1945).
[73] Odent, *loc. cit. supra* note 70.
[74] Dissenting, in Snyder v. Buck, 340 U.S. 15, 29 (1950).

Federal Tort Claims Act

It will, however, be objected that it is no longer accurate to differentiate between the Anglo-American and the French systems on the ground that with us the law of State liability is wholly dominated by the doctrine of sovereign immunity, whereas in France the fundamental principle is State responsibility. It will be said that an analysis based on such a dichotomy overlooks the fact that recent legislation has profoundly modified the situation in the common-law world. For both the British Parliament and the American Congress have enacted statutes aimed at eliminating the abuses involved in the doctrine of sovereign immunity. It is these statutes that have sought to eliminate the "lacuna in the rule of law"[75] that previously existed because of the privileged position of the State as litigant.

As the United States Supreme Court has pointed out, in voting the passage of the Federal Tort Claims Act of 1946, the Congress showed "that it was ready to lay aside a great portion of the sovereign's ancient and unquestioned immunity from suit."[76] That law provides: "The United States shall be liable, respecting . . . tort claims, in the same manner and to the same extent as a private individual under like circumstances." There is, it should be noted, basically the same provision in the English Crown Proceedings Act, 1947, which establishes against the Crown liability in tort as if it were a private person of full age and capacity.[77]

"The Federal Tort Claims Act," according to one commentator, "is clearly a major step in the process of laying to rest the doctrine of sovereign immunity."[78] Even so, it is a mistake to assume that with the passage of a statute like the Tort Claims Act the problems arising from the doctrine of sovereign immunity have been completely solved, or that the law of State liability in the common-law world is now based on a broad principle of responsibility analogous to that developed in France by the Council of State.

In the first place, under the Tort Claims Act and its English counterpart the State is liable for its torts only on the same basis as private individuals. This limitation, we shall see, does not apply today in the *droit administratif*. Under the jurisprudence of the Council of State the liability of the State is no longer governed solely by the principles of the private law of torts as applied in cases involving ordinary citizens.

[75] Report of the Committee on Ministers' Powers 112 (Cmd. 4060, 1932).
[76] United States v. Spelar, 328 U.S. 217, 221 (1949).
[77] Wade and Phillips, *op. cit. supra* note 61, at 312.
[78] Comment, 56 Yale L. J. 534, 561 (1947).

Even if the principle of State liability laid down by the Federal Tort Claims Act were applicable in every case, the American law of State liability would not be the same as that developed by the Council of State. But the federal statute, by its own terms, does not apply in every case, for it ends with a long list of exceptions to the principle of State responsibility.

Exceptions to Tort Claims Act

"With whatever liberality the courts may interpret the waiver of immunity thus broadly defined in the first parts of the Act, the position of the Government is carefully protected by twelve specific exceptions."[79] Most of these exceptions exempt specific administrative functions or agencies, in addition to all claims arising in a foreign country. Moreover the Act expressly provides that there is to be no liability of the United States for *intentional* torts; for jurisdiction to the courts is denied over "any claim arising out of assault, battery, false imprisonment, false arrest, malicious prosecution, abuse of process, libel, slander, misrepresentation, deceit, or interference with contract rights." We have here a substantial weakening of the principle of State liability imposed by the federal statute: the principle that the State is liable in the same way as a private individual, for the individual would clearly be liable under American law for these intentional torts, as a private employer would be if they were committed by his employees within the scope of their employment.

The most important exception in the Federal Tort Claims Act is that providing that the principle of State liability shall not apply to "Any claim based upon an act or omission of an employee of the Government, exercising due care, in the execution of a statute or regulation, whether or not such statute or regulation be valid, or based upon the exercise or performance or the failure to exercise or perform a discretionary function or duty on the part of a federal agency or an employee of the Government, whether or not the discretion involved be abused."

This exception in effect exempts from the principle of State liability all administrative acts done under a statute or regulation unless the public officer who committed the act was negligent, and all acts done in connection with the exercise of discretionary powers. If one bears in mind the types of cases in which private citizens are damaged by acts of the administration, one will realize that the State still enjoys immunity for the most important kinds of administrative action. Only where the officer whose act has caused the injury has been negligent, in circum-

[79] *Id.* at 542.

stances in which a private employer would be liable if the officer were his employee, is the State liable under the federal law. In the absence of negligence the State is still not liable, provided only that the act causing the damage was done in execution of a statute or regulation or that the administrative function at issue involved the exercise of discretionary authority. And it matters little that the law or regulation itself is invalid or that the delegated discretionary power has been abused.

This exception has the effect of leaving the State irresponsible in most cases in which the act causing the damage is not committed by a negligent public officer, for it is only in the rare case that the officer has not acted in the execution of a statute or regulation or in the exercise of his discretionary powers. And if discretionary powers are involved, the Supreme Court has recently held, recovery against the State cannot be had even though the act causing the damage were done negligently.[80]

It is particularly important to note that the exception under consideration has the effect of leaving the private individual without a remedy under the Tort Claims Act where he has suffered damage from an illegal administrative act. Even if the act causing the injury were *ultra vires*, the exception to the principle of State liability is operative, provided only that the act was performed in application of a statute or regulation or in the exercise of a discretionary power.

If we now take a case like *Miller v. Horton*,[81] with which we began our analysis of administrative liability, we can see how this exception to the Tort Claims Act works in practice. In *Miller v. Horton* health officers vested with the authority to destroy diseased animals killed plaintiff's uninfected horse. *Miller v. Horton* was a Massachusetts decision involving local officials, and we discussed it with reference to the personal liability of the officials. What would happen if a case with a similar fact pattern arose today under federal law and the plaintiff horse owner decided to bring an action against the United States under the Tort Claims Act, rather than against the individual officials? His action would not meet with success unless the plaintiff could prove that the officers concerned had acted negligently. If they acted reasonably on the belief that the horse was diseased, there would be no liability under the Federal Act of 1946; for it is clear that the health officers acted in execution of the statute authorizing them to destroy diseased animals.

[80] Dalehite v. United States, 346 U.S. 15 (1953). See, similarly, Coates v. United States, 181 F. 2d 816 (8th Cir. 1950); Olson v. United States, 93 F. Supp. 150 (D.N.D. 1950).

[81] *Supra* note 7.

Clearly, then, the liability provided for by the Tort Claims Act is far from an extensive system of State responsibility comparable to that which, as we shall see, has been developed by the Council of State in France, or even to that set up under the English Crown Proceedings Act, 1947, which is not honeycombed, as the American statute of 1946 is, with exceptions to its basic principle of State liability. A student of American administrative law must, indeed, conclude that the failure to apply the principle of liability to all wrongful State acts causing damage still constitutes the most serious lacuna in the American system.[82]

It has been asserted by one commentator that the exceptions contained in the Federal Tort Claims Act are "for the most part well taken."[83] American observers tend to feel that there must be some limitations on the tort liability of the State. If the State were to be put only on the same level as the private citizen, the strain on the public treasury might, it has been feared, prove very great. "Realistically speaking," an American judge has stated, "the state should be free from the vexatious suits based on fictitious grounds which might spring into abundance were the immunity removed."[84]

Britain, which is certainly as solicitous about drains on the public fisc as we are in this country, has seen fit, in the Crown Proceedings Act, 1947, to enact a general principle of State liability in tort without the many exceptions contained in the American Tort Claims Act; and this fact suggests that the dangers involved in complete abandonment of the doctrine of sovereign immunity are not so great as many Americans have feared. Even more important, perhaps, is the fact that in France a system of general State responsibility has been able to function effectively for half a century—the reason why it is important for the American observer to understand the French law on this subject. The doctrine of sovereign immunity, as the American judge just quoted has remarked, "cannot be defended in any case on ethical grounds."[85] If it can be justified at all, it is only because it is felt to be unwise for practical reasons to abandon it and open the public purse to all who may have claims against the State. That the *droit administratif* has been able to function with success though it has discarded the principle of State

82 Some American states, notably New York, do apply a general principle of public liability without the exceptions contained in the Federal Tort Claims Act. See MacDonald, The Administration of a Tort Liability Law in New York, 9 Law & Contemp. Prob. 262 (1942).

83 *Loc. cit. supra* note 78.

84 Wolfe, J., concurring in Niblock v. Salt Lake City, 111 P. 2d 800, 804 (Utah, 1941).

85 *Ibid.*

irresponsibility contributes powerfully to the refutation of this supposedly practical argument.

State Liability for Fault in France

We have seen that in the French system the public officer himself is personally liable if he has committed what has been termed a "personal fault"; *i.e.*, if he has acted willfully, maliciously, with gross negligence, or outside the scope of his official functions. If he has acted within the scope of his employment, then he has normally committed only a "service-connected fault" for which he is not personally liable. But ever since the abandonment by the Council of State of the general doctrine of State irresponsibility the State itself has been liable for damage caused by such service-connected faults.

"The notion of service-connected fault," one of the best-known councilors of state informs us, "is almost impossible to define precisely. Service-connected faults are multiform. There is such a fault whenever the administrative service has functioned improperly, has functioned too early or too late, or has not functioned at all; whenever its officers have failed to conform to the limits of their jurisdiction, or to the rules governing its functioning, or have committed wrongful or negligent acts."[86]

The service-connected fault for which the State is liable in the *droit administratif* need not necessarily have any connection with the fault of a particular, identifiable public officer. "For a service-connected fault to come to light," as the leading French treatise on State liability puts it, "it is not necessary that individual public officers, designated by name, be at fault. It is enough to show a general anonymous improper operation of the administrative service, to which the damage can be imputed; to establish that the service is at fault either in its organization or its operation, and that the damage is attributable to this fault. . . . it is the service and not the officer that is being judged."[87]

Misfeasance

The French jurist is accustomed to divide the cases involving service-connected faults into three categories: (1) that in which the particular administrative service has functioned improperly; (2) that in

[86] Odent, *op. cit. supra* note 70, at 282.
[87] Duez, La Responsabilité de la puissance publique 21 (2d ed., 1938).

which the service has failed to function; and (3) that in which the service has functioned too late.[88] Of these, the first, that in which the administration has been guilty of misfeasance, is the most common and the easiest for the Anglo-American observer to comprehend. It is the case in which damage has been caused to a private individual by the positive fault of the administration.

The French conception of fault is not unlike that developed in the Anglo-American law of torts. All that the Civil Code provides is that everyone is obliged to make good the damage caused by his faults, and it goes on to say that negligence comes within the concept of fault.[89] Since this much is substantially all that the legislator has provided, the actual definition of the fault that leads to liability has had to be worked out by the French courts in the tort cases which have arisen since the promulgation of the Code Napoléon. It is not surprising to find that the concept of fault has been worked out by them in terms of deviation from a duty to observe a standard of reasonable conduct—a close parallel to what Anglo-American courts have done in analogous cases.

"Fault," a recent text on the French law of torts states, "is the nonperformance of a duty that the individual should have known of and been able to perform."[90] And the duty involved is to act according to the normal standard of a careful and prudent man. The individual is at fault when such a man would have foreseen and avoided the act that caused the damage. "Fault is the act or the failure to act that would not have been committed by a diligent man, a prudent man, a careful man"[91]—all of which, it should be noted, is not too far from the standard of the "reasonable man" applied in the Anglo-American law of torts.

If an administrative officer in France has deviated from the standard of a careful and a prudent man while acting in the scope of his official functions, then he has ordinarily committed a service-connected fault for which the State is liable. There is, for example, little doubt but that the French State is liable if one of its agents performs his duty negligently and in a manner that causes damage to a private citizen. Cases of this type, in which there is misfeasance on the part of a public officer acting within the scope of his employment, are almost too numerous to be cited.[92] They occur whenever injury is caused by the failure of a

[88] *Id.* at 27.
[89] Articles 1382 and 1383.
[90] 1 Savatier, Traité de la responsabilité civile en droit français 5 (2d ed., 1951).
[91] *Id.* at 7.
[92] For an illustrative list, see Duez, *op. cit. supra* note 87, at 28.

public officer to conform to the standard of conduct imposed on a reasonably prudent man by the circumstances of the case, unless he has so deviated from his employment that only he, and not the State, is liable.

But under the French theory of State liability the administration has more than the duty of ensuring that its officers conform to the standard of the "reasonable man." It must also see that they do not deviate from what may be called the standard of the "reasonable officer." In this respect the duty imposed on the French administration is to ensure that its agents respect the principle of legality by acting within the limits of the authority conferred on them by law, as the "reasonable officer" would do. If a public officer acting within his official functions does an *ultra vires* act, he has committed a service-connected fault, just as if he had acted negligently. If that act causes damage to a private citizen, that citizen may bring an action against the State under the general French rule of liability of the State for service-connected faults.

The Council of State has applied this principle of State responsibility for *ultra vires* acts to the four grounds of illegality which, as has been shown,[93] have been developed in the *droit administratif*. Where administrative officers have acted beyond their jurisdiction,[94] or failed to observe the procedures required by law,[95] or their action constituted an abuse of power,[96] or was based on an error of law[97]—in all these instances the French State is liable for any damage their acts may have caused, unless the officers so deviated from their functions that there is no longer a service-connected fault.

It may be seen, then, that in the *droit administratif* an *ultra vires* administrative act can be the subject both of an action to annul and of an action for damages. In both, the action is decided on the basis of the court's answer to the question of the legality of the act. In the action to annul, the challenged act is set aside if the court determines that it is *ultra vires*. In the action for damages against the State the determination of the illegality of the act causing the injury leads to a judgment against the State on the basis of the fault it has committed in not making sure that its officers respect the principle of legality while performing their functions—a fault that involves its tort liability.

[93] *Supra* p. 203.
[94] Ministre du Travail, Council of State, October 21, 1949.
[95] Torregrosa, Council of State, March 24, 1950.
[96] Société des Concerts du Conservatoire, Council of State, March 9, 1951; Compagnie anonyme des Sablières de la Seine, Council of State, June 30, 1944.
[97] Chami, Council of State, December 9, 1949.

This outcome should be compared with that under an American statute such as the Federal Tort Claims Act of 1946. As we have already seen, the exceptions to that law tend to eliminate State liability if the plaintiff shows merely that the act causing the damage was *ultra vires*.[98] It appears, then, that in American law an *ultra vires* administrative act can still be only the subject of a review action. The private individual adversely affected by it can only petition to have it set aside. He cannot recover from the State any damages suffered because of it. In this respect the citizen's protection certainly seems to be more nearly adequate under the *droit administratif*.

Nonfeasance

According to the classic modern work on French private law, "fault can be a positive act, the commission of a deed, or a negative act, the omission of a measure that should have been taken."[99] It was only natural that the same distinction should be applied in the field of State liability for fault. And since French law has not suffered from the reluctance to impose liability for failure to act that has characterized Anglo-American law, it is not surprising that State liability for nonfeasance has been greatly developed in the *droit administratif*.

The French theory with respect to liability for nonfeasance has been well stated in an important treatise on State responsibility. "To recognize that the administrative service, by not acting, can commit a fault is to say that the service was under a duty to act and that it must repair the pecuniary consequences resulting from its inaction. This is a substantial step forward in the law of State liability, and this development is due to the progress of ideas concerning the functioning of public services: the exercise of authority is not a privilege, but a duty imposed upon the administration."[100]

Examples of State liability for nonfeasance in France are by now legion. Such liability may arise when a private citizen has been injured by the administrative refusal to enforce a statute or regulation. As the foremost contemporary authority on the *droit administratif* states, "however great may be the discretion of the administration as to choosing the opportune time for executing the laws, it commits an illegal act involving the responsibility of the State if it systematically

[98] See, e.g., Chournos v. United States, 193 F. 2d 321 (10th Cir. 1951).

[99] 2 Ripert, Traité élémentaire de droit civil de Marcel Planiol 325 (3d ed., 1949) (italics omitted).

[100] Duez, *op. cit. supra* note 87, at 29.

refuses to enforce a statute."[101] A recent illustration of the application of this principle is contained in a 1948 decision by the Council of State. A regulation had forbidden doctors employed by the State to engage in private practice, but this regulation was not enforced. The plaintiff was a private practitioner who alleged that he had suffered damage because of the competition of doctors employed by the State—competition permitted by the administration's failure to enforce its regulation. The Council's decision held that in failing to enforce the regulation the administration had committed a fault and was obliged to repair whatever damage the plaintiff had suffered from the improper competition of the public doctors.[102]

The administrative abstention on which State liability is based often consists in the failure to take the precautions felt to be necessary in the particular public service. In a 1945 case in which the plaintiffs had been injured in a riot because the police had neglected to take the precautions necessary to maintenance of order, the Council of State held that their injury "was the consequence of an administrative lack of surveillance constituting a fault of such a kind as to involve the liability of the State."[103] Similarly, a city that had organized a gymnastic festival without providing for adequate medical and first-aid service in the vicinity was held liable to the extent that plaintiff's injuries were aggravated by the failure to provide such facilities.[104]

Among the most interesting of the French decisions applying the principle of State liability for nonfeasance are those involving an administrative failure to execute decisions rendered by courts of justice. In these cases, as in those involving the refusal to enforce statutes or regulations, the administration is held to have committed a fault that makes the State liable for any damages caused. The leading case is the *Couitéas* case, a famous decision of the Council of State in 1923.[105] The

[101] Waline (1937) Dalloz, part 3, 43.

[102] Vié et Gouverneur général de Madagascar, February 27, 1948. For interesting similar cases see Syndicat générale de Défense des Grands Vins de la Côte d'Or, Council of State, July 24, 1936; Bohler, Council of State, December 10, 1937; Van Outryve et Cie., Council of State, July 6, 1934. Compare Maurel, Council of State, April 25, 1941. There are, of course, no analogous cases in Anglo-American law.

[103] Ville de Saint-Rémy de Provence, Council of State, January 19, 1945. Compare Société La Séquanaise, Council of State, February 29, 1952.

[104] Lorain, Council of State, April 20, 1934. The most common cases of this type involve a lack of proper surveillance over the administrative officer whose act caused the damage. Hay, Council of State, July 29, 1949; Montégut, January 7, 1949; Bourret, Council of State, December 10, 1947; Arnaud, Council of State, October 24, 1947.

[105] November 30, 1923.

plaintiff was the owner of a large area of land in Tunisia, then as now a French protectorate. A considerable number of natives had established themselves on this land, and they refused to leave it. The plaintiff obtained a judgment in the French equivalent of ejectment and sought to have it executed. But the authorities charged with execution refused to eject the natives, largely because they feared serious local disturbances if the natives were dispossessed. The plaintiff then brought an action for damages in the Council of State, and that tribunal held in his favor. Even though the administration could refuse to act for reasons of public order, plaintiff still had the right to be made whole for the damages he had suffered from the administrative inaction. As the Council's decision expressed the principle, a litigant who has obtained a judicial decision in his favor has the right to rely on the assistance of public authority to obtain execution of the judgment. If such assistance is not forthcoming, the State has committed a fault and is liable for whatever damages may result.

The most striking cases in which the *Couitéas* decision has been followed are those that grew out of the rash of sit-down strikes that broke out in France, as in the United States, in the mid-thirties. How to deal with the situation presented by such strikes was one of the most difficult problems presented to American law a generation ago. Under common-law concepts of ownership and of remedies in vindication of it, employers whose plants were in the possession of employees engaged in a sit-down strike were clearly entitled to the expulsion of such strikers. As a practical matter, however, it was usually most difficult for the law of ejectment to be enforced in these cases. The result often was that the employer was vested with a paper judgment of eviction that could not actually be enforced.

The same outcome occurred in France in the sit-down strike cases. French employers whose plants were occupied by sit-down strikers were usually able to obtain judgments ordering expulsion. But the administrative authorities charged with execution of the judgments mostly refused to use force because of the fear of aggravating the already tense labor situation. The principle of the *Couitéas* case has, nonetheless, enabled French law to reach a more satisfactory result than that attained by the American system. For though overriding considerations of public order may justify the administrative refusal to execute *manu militari* the judgments of expulsion, it is hardly fair to require the employers to suffer alone the pecuniary consequences resulting from the administrative failure to enforce the law. And in these sit-down strike cases, as in the *Couitéas* case, the Council of State has held that those vested with a judgment in their favor are entitled to rely on public force to execute it.[106] If the State refuses to enforce the judgment, it must indemnify the holder of it for any damages he may suffer from the nonexecution.[107]

Late-Feasance

Closely related to the above cases of administrative nonfeasance are those in which the administration acted too late. Here, a prominent treatise on State liability in France informs us, "we are in the presence of a more recent conquest of the theory of service-connected fault: liability for administrative slowness. The operation of the public service can now be declared to be defective, and hence faulty, when it is too slow. The administration has the general duty of being diligent, and the lack of a certain degree of administrative diligence will lead to liability."[108]

The result in particular cases of this type depends, of course, on the Council of State's answer to the question whether the administration has acted with "reasonable" diligence in the circumstances. The application of the standard of reasonableness will vary as much here as it does in the misfeasance and nonfeasance cases, in accord with variations in the fact pattern of the cases at issue.

In some, administrative delay can lead to very serious consequences. A well-known case involved the enlistment of a minor in the Foreign Legion without parental consent. Such enlistment was null under French law, and the minor should have been discharged as soon as the military authorities were made aware of the facts. But several months elapsed after the minor's father asked for his son's release; and during this administrative lag the son was killed in combat. The Council of State held that the administration's delay in acting constituted a fault for which the State was liable.[109] Not all administrative tardiness will have such unfortunate consequences; but in all situations where damage is caused by the administration's failure to act with reasonable diligence the State is liable under the French concept of fault.[110]

[106] Société de Cartonnerie et d'Imprimerie Saint-Charles, June 3, 1938; Société des Brasseries de la Meuse, May 7, 1947; Barthélémy, November 21, 1947.

[107] For other recent applications by the Council of State of the *Couitéas* case, see Héritier, February 23, 1951; Peyriguey, February 27, 1948.

[108] Duez, *op. cit. supra* note 87, at 34.

[109] Brunet, July 18, 1919.

[110] For an illustrative list of cases, see Duez, *op. cit. supra* note 87, at 36.

Liability of the State and of Public Officers

In holding the State liable for the consequences of nonfeasance and late-feasance the French system has, of course, gone much farther than the Anglo-American law of State liability, even if one takes into account the recent statutory modifications of the doctrine of sovereign immunity in the common-law world. True, Anglo-American courts have often, by mandamus and its modern equivalents, ordered the administration to perform duties imposed on it by law. But liability for nonfeasance or tardy-feasance is quite another thing. In view of the normal reluctance of the common law to impose liability even on ordinary citizens for failure to act or for late action, it is difficult to see how the Anglo-American State could be held liable, even if it were uniformly to be held to the same degree of responsibility as a private individual; and it is far from being so held, it should be borne in mind, under a law like the American Tort Claims Act of 1946. It is clear, then, that even in responsibility for fault State liability under the *droit administratif* is much more extensive than in the common-law world, even under our recent statutes providing for State liability in tort.

Combination of Faults

We have seen thus far that the French law on administrative liability is based on a distinction between so-called personal faults and service-connected faults. The theory on this point has been well summed up by the leading contemporary work on the *droit administratif*. "We know that public officers are personally liable to third persons only for their personal faults, and not for so-called service-connected faults, in accordance with the distinction established by the case law of the Court of Conflicts. The 'service-connected' fault was considered as imputable, not to the officer, but directly to the administrative service. . . . On the contrary, the personal fault of the officer could not make the public collectivity liable. The liability of the State and the personal liability of the public officer were mutually exclusive."[111]

With the abandonment by the French system during the nineteenth century of the doctrine of sovereign immunity, it came to be felt that it was not right for the State to be absolved of liability in every case in which the official concerned happened to commit a personal fault that rendered him individually liable. It will be recalled that under the French case law a personal fault has been committed whenever the official has acted willfully or maliciously, with gross negligence, or out-

111 Waline, *op. cit. supra* note 24, at 588.

side the scope of his official functions. If the damaging act was done in the scope of his official employment, was the State to be freed of liability merely because the official had acted willfully or with extreme lack of care?

In these cases the result was often most illogical. "Was there a personal fault of the officer?" asks one author. "The victim secured a damage claim against the officer, for the payment of which the personal resources of the officer were answerable. Was there only a service-connected fault? The public treasury was answerable; the victim of the injury thus had a much more substantial guarantee of payment than in the first case. What was shocking in this arrangement was that the soundness of the victim's claim was in inverse ratio to the gravity of the fault committed: the victim of an injury brought about by the willful intention of the public officer, by his gross fault, had less chance of being paid than the victim of a lesser fault for which the public treasury would be answerable."[112]

This consideration has led the *droit administratif* more recently to abandon its earlier rule under which the State was absolved of liability in every case in which a personal fault had been committed. Under the present jurisprudence of the Council of State it is recognized that a given damage can be caused both by a personal fault of the officer concerned and by a fault of the administrative service, if the officer is acting within the scope of his official functions.

This principle was firmly established in the *Lemonnier* case, decided by the Council of State in 1918 in accord with the noted conclusions of government commissioner Léon Blum, already cited.[113] That case arose out of a local carnival held each year by a small southern commune. Its principal attraction was an afternoon-long shooting contest aimed at a target fixed on a small plank floating in the local river. The plaintiffs, husband and wife, when walking toward the river about 6 P.M. to see the carnival, were struck by bullets fired in the contest. It was found that some hours earlier several persons walking in that area had almost been hit, and they had hastened to inform the local authorities. But the mayor did not order the shooting stopped until after the plaintiffs had been injured.

In the *Lemonnier* case the mayor had acted with gross negligence in not ordering a halt to the shooting. Under the French theory he had thus committed a personal fault for which he was personally liable. Yet

[112] Duez, *op. cit. supra* note 87, at 94.
[113] *Supra* note 25.

his fault, said government commissioner Blum, did not mean that the State was absolved. If the officer's fault "has been committed in the administrative service or because of the service, if the means and the instruments have been put at the officer's disposition by the service, if the victim has been put into a position to be injured by the effect of the working of the service, if, in a word, the service has provided the conditions for the commission of the fault or its injurious consequences to a given individual, the administrative-court judge will then have to say: The fault may be separable from the service; that is for the law courts to decide; but the administrative service is not separable from the fault." As M. Blum put it at a later point in his conclusions: "State liability is the rule; the State is only relieved of its responsibility if the administrative service can be held to be a complete stranger to the fault."

The acceptance by the Council of State of M. Blum's conclusions was of cardinal significance to the French law of administrative liability, for it meant the renunciation of the old rule that the existence of personal fault by an officer necessarily excluded State liability. Henceforth, it was recognized, there could be what French students have termed a combination of faults—a coexistence of personal fault and service-connected fault in the same case. And this possibility means that in most cases the existence of a right of personal action against the public officer for damages for his personal fault no longer removes from the individual concerned the right to bring an action against the State. Under present-day French law it is only if the officer's wrongful act is wholly unconnected with his official employment that he alone, and not the State, is liable.[114]

Liability of Officer to State

Under the principle of the *Lemonnier* case, the State is now liable in most cases in which damage has been caused by the fault of an administrative officer. It is only where the officer concerned has so deviated from his official functions that his act is in effect that of a private individual unconnected with the administration that the State is absolved of responsibility. The result is that the French citizen injured by the personal fault of an administrative officer now has in most cases a

[114] For a recent example of a case involving a combination of faults, see Delville, Council of State, July 28, 1951 (automobile accident caused by both drunkenness of driver of government vehicle and poor condition of its brakes).

choice between remedies. He may either sue the officer personally or bring an action against the State. In practice, of course, the citizen will almost always choose the second course, for execution of a judgment against the State need never run the hurdle of the defendant's possible impecuniousness.

The availability of the remedy against the State in the *droit administratif*, even in connection with most personal faults, has naturally led to the virtual elimination of suing public officers personally for their personal faults. And this change has in turn occasioned increasing concern among French jurists. Even if, as we have seen, most administrative lawyers in France have looked unfavorably on a wholesale rule of strict personal liability of public officers, they have still felt that it is most desirable that such officers should be liable if they have committed a personal fault, as that term is understood in French law. "The fear of personal liability," as M. Blum himself pointed out in his conclusions in the *Lemonnier* case,[115] "is a much more powerful brake on the officer than the possible liability of the agency to which he belongs."

French jurists have been keenly aware that the practical effect of the *Lemonnier* decision was to free public officers from personal liability for most of their personal faults, inasmuch as the citizen with a choice of remedies would always tend to sue the State. They have often suggested that the needed check on the public official that was formerly supplied by his personal responsibility can be obtained by making the officer personally liable to the State under a theory of subrogation, where the State has been compelled to pay damages caused by the officer's personal fault.[116]

The Council of State had, however, consistently held that administrative officers are not personally liable to the State even though they have committed personal faults that have led to the State's being adjudged liable in actions brought by those who may have been injured by such faults.[117] Despite widespread criticism of this rule of nonliability of the officer to the State, it seemed to be firmly established in the French tribunal's jurisprudence. But the situation on this point has now been completely changed by a decision rendered in 1951.

A private individual injured by a government vehicle driven by a

[115] *Supra* note 25.

[116] See, e.g., Waline, "De l'Irresponsabilité des fonctionnaires pour leurs fautes personnelles et des moyens d'y remédier," Revue du Droit Public 5 (1948).

[117] Poursines, March 28, 1924; Morin, October 29, 1926; Dizier, December 14, 1934; Préour, August 1, 1942; Caisse de crédit municipal de Strasbourg, June 20, 1947.

drunken officer had brought an action against the State and recovered a judgment on the theory that there had been a fault connected with the administrative service involved. The State then sought indemnity in an action against the officer, maintaining that his personal fault in driving while drunk had really caused the injury. The Council of State, repudiating its earlier case law on the nonliability of officers to the State, held that it could recover from the officer the damages it had paid. "Although public officers and employees are not liable to the State for the damageable consequences of their service-connected faults," the Council's decision reads, "the same cannot be true when the damage that they have caused the State is due to their personal faults."[118]

With this 1951 decision the Council of State has in effect completed its construction of the system of liability for fault in the *droit administratif*. Undeniably, in comparison with the Anglo-American law the system worked out by the French tribunal is remarkably complete and logically consistent. Under the Council's jurisprudence the State is now liable in every case in which damage is caused by the faulty functioning of its services, unless the official concerned has so deviated from the scope of his employment that he has acted as a private citizen rather than as a man vested with official authority. From the point of view of those injured by administrative action this is, of course, the ideally practical solution, for a judgment against the State is one that will be paid.

But there remains the need for a check on the commission of personal faults by public officers—a check no longer furnished by the possibility of personal liability to those damaged by their acts. Such liability becomes a matter of academic theory where, as in the French system, the State is also liable, for the victim of administrative action will almost always sue the State rather than the officer. And it is here that the 1951 decision of the Council of State comes in to complete the picture. If the damage were caused by the personal fault of the officer, he is now personally liable, not only to the citizen injured, but also to the State, which, as a practical matter, has actually had to make the citizen whole for his damages.

The effectiveness in operation of this check of liability of the officer to the State, thus developed by the *droit administratif* to take the place

[118] Laruelle, July 28, 1951. Compare Delville, decided the same day (apportionment of liability between officer and administration where damage was caused by fault of both). For a case in accord with the *Laruelle* holding, see Carion, June 19, 1953.

of his liability to private citizens, remains, of course, to be seen. It is to be feared that the administrative agency concerned may not be overzealous in seeking to hold its own employees personally liable. This laxity can perhaps be overcome if the duty of enforcing personal liability is vested in an independent organ rather than in the agency that employed the officer whose act caused the damage—a measure apparently not as yet adopted in the French system.

Aside from this aspect of its effectiveness the French answer to the problem of State and officer liability for fault certainly seems more nearly adequate than that delivered by Anglo-American law. To the question of State liability for fault the *droit administratif* has responded with a broad principle of liability instead of with one honeycombed with exceptions as has been done under the Federal Tort Claims Act of 1946 in this country. And to the question of officer liability the French system has not given the Anglo-American answer of a wholesale principle of personal liability, which has proved unworkable under modern conditions. Instead, it has imposed personal responsibility only for so-called personal faults; *i.e.*, those involving willfulness, malice, gross negligence, or undue deviation from the scope of official employment. But these are precisely the faults against which, from a constitutional point of view, one most wishes to be safeguarded. And even where they are in question French law has recognized that the extension of State liability has tended to remove the personal remedy against the officer from its position as a check of any practical value. Hence it has recently evolved the principle of liability of the officer to the State where it has had to pay damages occasioned by the officer's personal fault. By this addition the *droit administratif* has completed its structure of liability for fault.

Liability without Fault

Under Article 1382 of the French Civil Code "every act that causes damage to another obliges him by whose fault the damage has occurred to make redress." This provision, on which most of the private law of torts in France has been based, makes fault a prerequisite of liability, and if it were applicable in the field of administrative law, it would seem that the responsibility of the French State, too, would be basically limited to liability for fault. The rules just discussed governing liability for fault would in that event be all that would have been developed in the *droit administratif*.

This limited result has, however, been obviated through the decision of the Court of Conflicts in the *Blanco* case in 1873[119]—a decision probably still the most famous in the case law of French administrative law. In the *Blanco* case the court held that an action for damages against the State or one of its agencies could be brought only in the administrative courts, just as a personal action against a public official could be brought only in the law courts in the French system. In the course of its decision the tribunal made the following statement, since repeated in innumerable cases: "The liability that the State incurs for damages caused to private individuals by the acts of persons employed by it in the public service cannot be governed by the principles laid down in the Civil Code for the regulation of the relationships of private individuals. Such liability . . . has its own special rules, which vary according to the needs of the administrative service and the necessity of reconciling the rights of the State with private rights."[120]

Rendered at a time when the private law of torts in France was based almost entirely on liability for fault, the *Blanco* decision had the effect of emancipating the French law of State responsibility from the restrictions imposed by the concept of fault. And, acting under it, the Council of State has been able to develop a system of risk liability that has supplemented, and is now tending to take over, the field occupied by fault liability. In its jurisprudence on this point the Council of State has shown the way to the French private law of torts and has extended the principle of State liability to a point beyond any even imagined as possible by most Anglo-Americans who have considered the subject.

Fault or Risk?

Absolute liability is characteristic of the formative period of a legal system. The primitive mind, unable to differentiate between varying degrees of the same type of conduct, brands all equally and metes out similar consequences to those concerned. "The indiscriminate liability of primitive times stands for an instinctive impulse, guided by superstition, to visit with vengeance the visible source, whatever it be—human or animal, witting or unwitting—of the evil result."[121] As the law grows more mature, differentiations are made and liability comes

119 February 8, 1873.

120 This is the form given in Waline, *op. cit. supra* note 24, at 576; it slightly differs from the original decision.

121 Wigmore, "Responsibility for Tortious Acts: Its History" 7 Harv. L. Rev. 315, 316 (1894).

to be measured according to the individual culpability of the actor. Liability becomes a corollary of fault instead of being attached indiscriminately to all acts causing injury. The common lawyer has seen this development in most fields of his law; he has seen so much of it that "no liability without culpability" has come to be considered a maxim of Anglo-American law. As Dean Ames has expressed it, the earlier "unmoral standard of acting at one's peril" has been replaced by the question, "Was the act blameworthy?"[122]

Under the French Civil Code, too, as we have seen, the basic principle is that of liability for fault. And it may well be that that principle, in its application to cases arising between private citizens, is essentially sound as the foundation of the law of torts, even though it may be yielding more and more on both sides of the Atlantic, even in the field of private law, to a system grounded on absolute liability.

In cases arising only between two private individuals it can rightly be asserted that there should be liability only if there is fault, or, to put it another way, that there should be only subjective liability. Both parties are, legally speaking, in equal positions; their freedom of activity is circumscribed by the same legal limits. As long as neither of them violates the standard of care imposed by the law, no obligation to make reparation should be imposed on either. It is only where there is fault on the part of one that he may be ordered to pay damages. For it is only when fault exists that the two are no longer on an equal footing. In cases between two ordinary citizens the basic principle cannot be that of objective liability; *i.e.*, liability without fault. If the conduct of neither party were culpable, why should not the loss remain where it has fallen?[123]

It will be objected, though, that this approach ignores the great development of liability without fault that has occurred in recent years in the private law of torts. This approach overlooks, it will be said, a branch of the law such as that governing the relations between employers and employees. The liability of an employer to his employees is today clearly based more on risk than on fault. Indeed, so far as injuries suffered by employees in the course of their employment are concerned the tendency is to eliminate the concept of fault entirely through schemes such as workmen's compensation laws.

If one looks to the basis for the rule of absolute liability in such cases as those between employers and employees, one will see that it

[122] Ames, "Law and Morals" 22 Harv. L. Rev. 97, 99 (1908).
[123] See Duguit, *op. cit. supra* note 31, at 467.

is not inconsistent with our reasoning above for cases arising only between two private citizens. In such cases, since both parties are in equal positions there can be, we have said, no liability unless one of them has committed a fault. But between the employer and his employee there is no such equality of position. To paraphrase a famous statement of Mr. Chief Justice Stone of almost a generation ago, there is grim irony in speaking of the equal position of those who, because of their economic necessities, may give their service for less than is needful to keep body and soul together.[124] It is precisely because there is no equality of position between employer and employee that the principle of liability solely for fault has proved unworkable in cases between them. In employer-employee cases the law has had to redress the inequality between the parties by applying the rule of absolute liability.

The application of a risk or fault theory of liability is thus seen to depend on the relative equality of the parties' positions. If only two equal individuals are involved, there is no liability unless one of them is at fault. If the parties are not in a position of equality, as in the employer-employee cases, there is more justification for abandoning the criterion of fault.

Risk Liability of State

The factors noted above with regard to employer-employee cases, which make for the inapplicability of the rule of liability only for fault, appear to operate with greater force in cases arising between the State and private citizens. In these cases, even more than in those between employers and employees, there is no equality of position between the two contesting parties. The private citizen here is not opposed merely by another citizen who, in both law and fact, is only his peer. The opposite party in these cases is the State, the collective entity that represents all the citizenry, endowed with all the attributes and all the authority that inhere in the sovereign organ of society.

Administrative law differs from a branch of private law such as the law of torts, a councilor of state has recently informed us, because "it governs the legal relations between parties who are unequal by their very nature: on the one side, the public power whose action is dictated by the necessities of the general interest, and which engages in operations wholly beyond the scope of those that private persons can carry out; on the other side, the ordinary individuals whose private interests

[124] Morehead v. New York ex. rel. Tipaldo, 298 U.S. 587, 632 (1936).

must yield before the public necessity. This inequality is one of the principal bases of the theory of liability without fault."[125]

There is, however, more than this inequality of the parties to make for an abandonment of the principle of liability only for fault in the field of public law. Strong moral considerations militate against a blanket rule of absolute liability in the private law of torts. "If it is just," state the authors of the leading treatise on French tort law, "that one whose fault has caused damage should be obliged to make redress, equity requires that he alone be liable. How can he who has acted without negligence or imprudence, who has behaved as a prudent and careful man, incur liability? If his activity has caused damage, it is only the result of chance. It is by chance that the injury has happened to someone. Why overturn this fact situation when the author and the victim are equally innocent and the conduct of each is equally blameless? That would be a 'social injustice.' "[126]

The moral argument, these authors tell us, is not so relevant in the law of State liability. "When, in effect, it is the State or one of its agencies that has caused the damage by the act of its officers, there is nothing immoral in requiring it to make reparation, even though no fault has been committed. It is here no longer a question of impoverishing a private individual, against which equity protests when his conduct is free from fault: it is a question of determining whether one citizen alone, the victim, should bear the cost of the functioning of the administrative service that has injured him, or whether all the citizenry, represented by the State, shall share the cost."[127]

Looking at the problem from this point of view has enabled the *droit administratif* to view the basis of State liability in a new light. The Council of State has for many years assumed that one of the fundamental principles of French public law, derived from the equalitarian ideal that inspired the men of the French Revolution, was that which provided for an equal distribution among the citizenry of the costs of government, in the absence of a legislative disposition to the contrary. If a particular citizen is damaged by the operation of an administrative service, even if there is no fault, the principle of equality in sharing the expense of government is violated. The victim of the administrative act that caused the damage is in effect asked to assume a burden not

[125] Odent, *op. cit. supra* note 70, at 292.

[126] 1 H. and L. Mazeaud, Traité théorique et pratique de la responsabilité civile 368 (4th ed., 1947).

[127] *Ibid.*

imposed on other citizens—a burden thrust upon him by the operation of a public service that functions for the benefit of the community as a whole. In such cases, it has been asked by French jurists, is not the State, even though it has not committed a fault, under an obligation to vindicate the principle of equality before the costs of government by removing the additional burden that has fallen upon the one injured and, by assuming it itself, distributing it among the entire body of the citizenry?

Such, indeed, is the master principle that tends more and more to govern the jurisprudence of the French Council of State.[128] The law of State liability is thus seen as aimed at restoring the equality of the citizenry before the costs of government whenever such equality has been upset at the expense of a particular individual. "In the absence of fault on the part of the administration," stated the government commissioner in his conclusions in an important case before the Council of State, "the basis of State liability is to be found in Article 13 of the Declaration of the Rights of Man.[129] That article laid down the principle of the equality of citizens before the costs of government. It is, in actuality, not permissible for a public activity, even though it be legal, to cause certain individuals damage that they alone must bear; that would be to make them carry more than their share of the costs of the State. All public activity is intended to benefit the community as a whole. It must therefore be paid for by the entire community. Consequently, individual damage caused by such activity, which, by upsetting the balance sought by the Declaration of Rights, destroys the equality of the citizenry before the costs of government, should lead to reparation. Such reparation, which, by means of the tax system, is actually made by the whole body politic, restores the equality thus destroyed."[130]

Social Insurance

The implications of this theory of State liability, which has dominated the post-Liberation jurisprudence of the Council of State, are far-reaching. The doctrine means in effect that the responsibility of the State is now grounded on the rule of absolute liability. As one observer

128 Waline, *op. cit. supra* note 24, at 579.

129 It reads: "For the maintenance of public power, and for the expenses of administration, a common contribution is indispensable; it must be equally divided among all citizens, in accordance with their capacities."

130 Conclusions in Société des Produits Laitiers "La Fleurette," January 14, 1938.

has pointed out: "We must now assume as a new principle of French public law, the application of which is general and no longer limited to certain types of cases, that every administrative act that causes injury involves the obligation to make pecuniary redress."[131]

The law of State liability in France is today based not only on a theory of fault but also on a theory of risk. "Each activity involves risks for third persons as well as for him who acts," states a councilor of state in explaining risk liability. "It is just that the latter make reparation for damages caused by his action, even though no fault can be imputed to him. Whoever creates a risk for his own profit should suffer the consequences of the risk; since he obtains the eventual profit from his activity, he should in return endure its disadvantages."[132]

This theory of liability has the effect of making him for whose benefit an activity is carried on an insurer against damage to those who come in contact with the activity. In the field of private law such a risk theory is unworkable unless supported by some scheme guaranteeing the solvency of the party liable.[133] Such a guarantee can in most cases be secured only by a scheme of liability insurance (until now normally voluntary save in the fields of workmen's compensation and automobile insurance) by which the one for whose benefit the activity is conducted can feasibly provide for the satisfaction of his liability. But even if such liability insurance be made compulsory in every field of activity, there is still the question of what risks are peculiar to the particular activity and hence calculable and insurable.

These difficulties do not arise in the field of public law. Governmental activities are carried on for the benefit of the entire community, and the risks of injury involved should also be borne by the citizenry as a whole. Nor is there the problem, met with in the field of private law, of compulsory as against voluntary insurance or insurable risk. For there is here no need of insurance in the normal use of that term. The State itself is the insurer of its own activities. The risk that for a private individual is spread by liability insurance is apportioned by the State among the community as a whole by the working of the tax system.

That State liability without fault really involves a scheme of social

[131] Mignon, "La Socialisation du risque" (1947) Dalloz, Chronique 37, 40. In 1938, the leading French treatise on State liability was already able to assert that this was the principle toward which the law in France was tending. Duez, *op. cit. supra* note 87, at 213.

[132] Odent, *op. cit. supra* note 70, at 256.

[133] See Ehrenzweig, Negligence without Fault 41 (1951).

insurance far removed from the normal operation of the law of torts was acutely seen over a generation ago by Léon Duguit. "The activity of the State," he wrote in his monumental treatise on constitutional law, "is carried on in the interest of the entire community; the burdens that it entails should not weigh more heavily on some than on others. If, then, State action results in individual damage to particular citizens, the State should make redress, whether or not there be a fault committed by the public officers concerned. The State is, in some ways, an insurer of what is often called social risk, i.e., the risk arising from social activity, which, in practice, is carried on by the intervention of the State."[134]

The law of State liability in the *droit administratif* is thus grounded on what amounts to a scheme of social insurance, supported by the public treasury, for the benefit of those damaged by administrative action performed in the interest of society as a whole. The situation in France is in many ways like that which would exist if the State were operating a system of mutual insurance for those subject to administrative accidents.[135] A citizen injured by State action is, in effect, compensated out of a mutual insurance fund supported by premiums paid in the form of taxes. This is, in practice, the way the law of State liability is tending to operate today in France. It is indeed a far cry from the doctrine of sovereign immunity with which the French, like the Anglo-American, system of administrative law began.

Development of Risk Theory

A study of the *droit administratif* written before the Second World War would have had to contain a detailed analysis of the case law applying the theory of risk in the field of State liability. Fault, asserted a leading treatise on the subject in 1938, "remains—and we cannot insist too emphatically on this point—the fundamental element that produces State liability."[136] It is true that French jurists had by that time begun to realize that the jurisprudence of the Council of State was coming to include an ever greater number of cases in which liability was imposed on the State although there was clearly no evidence of fault. But these were still seen to be only exceptions to the general rule of liability for fault, and the cases involving such exceptions had to be

134 Duguit, *op. cit. supra* note 31, at 469.
135 See Hauriou, *op. cit. supra* note 18, at 684.
136 Duez, *op. cit. supra* note 87, at 58.

closely analyzed in order to determine precisely the types of situations in which absolute liability would be imposed.

With the acceptance by the Council of State since the Liberation of the theories of risk and social insurance outlined above, such detailed analysis of the risk-theory cases is no longer important. The rule in France today is the blanket rule that anyone injured by administrative action is entitled to compensation, and there is little to be gained by attempting to classify the countless variety of cases in which that rule can be applied. Of course, even under the present French rule the would-be plaintiff must still show that he has suffered actual damage[137] and that such damage was caused by an administrative officer acting within the scope of his official functions, under the rules of causation that are applied in the French law of torts.

As the principle of absolute State liability actually developed in the *droit administratif*, it was first applied in a few specific cases in which it was felt that the administration was imposing an abnormal risk on those with whom it came into contact. The most important early cases involved what has been called an "abnormal risk of the neighborhood." The leading case of this type concerned the explosion of a munitions dump in a fort on the outskirts of Paris, with considerable personal and property damage in the area. In awarding compensation to those injured the Council of State declared that the administrative activity that caused the damage "entailed risks exceeding those normally met with in the neighborhood. Such risks, even without any fault, could, in the event of an accident, involve the liability of the state."[138] The reasoning of the French tribunal here is similar to that used in the celebrated English case of *Rylands v. Fletcher*.[139] Here, too, absolute liability is imposed on one who uses his property in such a way as to increase unduly the normal risks of those living in the neighborhood.

The Council of State was soon able to extend the principle of this type of case beyond the *Rylands v. Fletcher* situation of a landowner

[137] It should, however, be noted that French law has been much more lenient than Anglo-American law on the question of what type of damage is necessary for a tort action to be maintained. For example, there has been a greater readiness on the part of French jurisprudence to allow recovery for so-called moral damages. On the calculation of damages, see Morange, "L'Évaluation du préjudice par les juridictions administratives" (1951) Dalloz, Chronique 61.

[138] Regnault-Desroziers, March 28, 1919. For a more recent case of this type, see Société Nationale des Chemins de Fer Français, March 16, 1945. Compare Dalehite v. United States, 346 U.S. 15 (1953), where recovery was denied in an analogous case.

[139] (1868) L. R. 3 H.L. 330.

who creates an abnormal risk for the property of his neighbors. The principle of absolute liability was extended to any administrative act that imposed an exceptional risk upon the community. Most of these cases involved uses by the administration of dangerous instruments or means of action, such as a cannon that announced midday in a town in Morocco[140] or a flare dropped from an airplane.[141] And, more recently, this principle has been applied to the use of any firearms by public officers.[142]

Among the most interesting cases that deal with the administrative use of so-called dangerous instruments are the automobile-accident cases. In a well-known 1924 decision the Council of State asserted that in cases where an individual has been injured by a government vehicle "the particularly dangerous conditions of traffic at the present time make for a presumption of fault on the part of the driver of the automobile that caused the damage."[143] This posture amounted to the establishment of a doctrine like that of *res ipsa loquitur*—a doctrine which, as a practical matter, went far to eliminate the principle of liability only for fault in automobile-accident cases. In two post-Liberation cases the Council of State has taken the next step of expressly applying the rule of absolute liability, thus placing the automobile in the category of the dangerous instruments mentioned above.[144]

With the application of the rule of absolute liability extended thus far, it was not difficult for the Council of State to adopt broadly the risk theory of State responsibility already outlined. More and more the decisions of the French tribunal allowing recovery against the State are coming to use language like that contained in a 1947 decision: that administrative action "has made the plaintiff company suffer in the general interest individual damage that cannot be regarded as an expense normally falling upon it, and for which it is justified in demanding pecuniary reparation."[145] In such a case, as we have already seen, the French theory requires the State, as the representative of the community for whose benefit the act was done, to make redress to the citi-

140 Société des Arts Marocains, Rabat, January 21, 1928.

141 Chayet, Council of State, March 1, 1933.

142 Lecomte, Council of State, June 24, 1949. See Aubergé et Dumont, Council of State, July 27, 1951.

143 Société d'Assurances Mutuelles "Les Travailleurs Français," December 22, 1924.

144 Capot et Denis, July 9, 1948; Beschon, October 18, 1946. See Société La Mutuelle Richelieu, Council of State, July 17, 1950.

145 Société Boulenger, November 21, 1947.

zen who has been forced to assume more than the normal share of the burdens connected with the operation of government.

Liability for Legislative Acts

Before concluding the subject of State liability in France we should say a word about an aspect that French jurists consider to be of great importance: the liability of the State for legislative acts. Cases involving this problem occur when a law is enacted that causes special damage to particular individuals. The legislature passes, say, a statute that prohibits the sale of colored oleomargarine. Such a law clearly causes injury to the manufacturers of oleomargarine. But are they entitled to compensation if the statute does not provide for it?

To the Anglo-American the answer must undoubtedly be No. The very notion of State liability is, to us, wholly out of place in this type of case. To enact a law is one of the prime attributes of sovereignty, and to hold the sovereign liable for the exercise of the attribute would be considered a complete *non sequitur* by common-law courts. The injury that an individual may suffer from the passage of a statute is considered by us to be part of the social burden of living under government.[146]

Until recently the same was true in the French system. "Until just lately," states the leading treatise on State liability in France, "the rule was certain and absolute: if the legislative act was silent, the courts held that they did not have the authority to accord compensation to those who might have suffered damages from the passage of that act."[147] A leading case arose out of a law of 1915 that prohibited the sale of absinthe, an alcoholic liquor universally associated with the Bohemian way of life for which Paris has become celebrated. In denying compensation for the damages suffered by an absinthe manufacturer who was forced out of business by this law, the Council of State asserted in very strong terms that the State was not liable for damages caused by the enactment of a statute.[148]

The rule of nonliability was, however, changed by the French tribunal in its decision in the now famous *Fleurette* case, rendered in 1938.[149] That case arose out of a newly enacted law that forbade the

[146] Paraphrasing Petroleum Co. v. Public Service Commission, 304 U.S. 209, 222 (1938).
[147] Duez, *op. cit. supra* note 87, at 204.
[148] Société Premier et Henry, April 29, 1921.
[149] *Supra* note 130.

manufacture and sale of cream substitutes that looked and tasted like cream but were not made from milk. Such substitutes were not in any way injurious to the public health, and the sole purpose of the law was to protect the French dairy industry, as has been the case with regard to the many oleomargarine laws enacted in this country. The plaintiff company, which had made a cream substitute prohibited by this law, brought an action against the State for the damage caused it by the law, and the Council of State allowed recovery, although there was no provision in the statute for the compensation of those injured. In its decision the Council stated that "it cannot be thought that the legislator intended to impose upon plaintiff a burden that does not normally fall upon him; and . . . this burden, imposed in the general interest, must be borne by the community as a whole."

State liability for the damages caused by the enactment of a law is thus recognized under the *Fleurette* decision—which, it should be noted, has been followed in a subsequent case[150]—on the same basis as that on which the responsibility of the French State is today generally considered to be grounded; namely, the duty of the State to maintain the equality of the citizenry before the burdens imposed upon them by government. "When a statute causes special damage to one specific individual or to several, equality before the burdens of government is upset. Now, such equality appears to our jurisprudence to be so fundamental a principle of modern public law that it considers itself unable to interpret the silence of the legislator as a refusal of compensation."[151] Here, too, then, the basis of State liability is ultimately that section of the 1789 Declaration of the Rights of Man that provides for the equality of the citizenry in the assumption of the costs of government.[152]

To the American student this provision of the French Declaration of 1789 is analogous to the provisions in the Fifth and Fourteenth Amendments to our Federal Constitution, guaranteeing due process of law and the equal protection of the laws. Those amendments, in effect, provide for the equality of American citizens in the assumption of the burdens of government except as the right to such equality is taken away by other provisions of the organic instrument, such as the Sixteenth Amendment. A statute that unjustly destroys such equality in

150 Caucheteux et Desmont, Council of State, January 21, 1944. Compare Caumont, Council of State, May 16, 1941.

151 Waline, *op. cit. supra* note 24, at 605.

152 *Supra* note 129.

this country would violate our Constitution, just as a similar law in France violates Article 13 of the Declaration of the Rights of Man.

What, then, would be the situation in the United States with regard to a statute such as that which gave rise to the *Fleurette* case in France, if it were passed by our Congress? Such a law forbidding the manufacture of a product that presents no danger to the public health or morals, enacted solely for the benefit of those making competing products, could be declared unconstitutional by our courts if there is no provision for just compensation. It may well be that the American courts have been overhesitant in cases of this type, notably in those involving the validity of statutes restricting the sale of oleomargarine. But they clearly have the power to declare statutes like that in the *Fleurette* case invalid, if they would only choose to exercise it. It is the existence of such authority in our judiciary that makes a principle such as that laid down in the *Fleurette* case not so necessary in the United States as it is in France. The question presented in the *Fleurette* case can be avoided in this country by the exercise by our courts of their authority over the constitutionality of statutes. It is the absence of such authority in the French judiciary that induced the decision of the Council of State in the *Fleurette* case.

That case thus seeks in an indirect way to accomplish what the American courts can do directly through their authority to declare statutes unconstitutional. In both systems the end result is a power in the judiciary to avoid the possibility of statutes whose practical effect is the taking of private property without just compensation. This identity holds despite the great difference in the methods used by the judiciary in the two systems. "There is a great difference," as an acute French observer has pointed out, "between judicial control of the constitutionality of laws and award of compensation for the special damage caused by a law. Judicial control of constitutionality results in the invalidation of laws by the courts or in their refusal to apply them because they violate a superior constitutional principle. The French courts have neither the will, nor the social force, nor the support of public opinion to exercise control over the constitutionality of laws. They do not stand up against the legislator. They do not censure him. They seek first of all to determine whether the legislator himself has settled the question of compensation. It is only after the Council of State has decided that the legislator has not done so that it applies the fundamental principle of French public law: equality of individuals before the operation of administrative services and before the costs of government."[153]

It may, however, be objected that the comparison just made between the results reached in the *Fleurette* type of case in the French and American systems is not entirely accurate because it overlooks this fact: that American courts, even in the heyday of their assertion of the authority to set aside statutes, did not declare laws invalid merely because they imposed a special burden on certain individuals. Such laws have, on the contrary, been upheld by our courts unless their violation of the principle of equality was based on arbitrary and unreasonable classification. The mere fact that a statute causes injury to certain individuals is not, in other words, of itself sufficient reason for it to be held invalid. It is only where the statutory classification is not justified by any consideration of public health, safety, or morals that it will be condemned.

Yet an analogous inquiry into the justification for the legislative classification is also made by the Council of State in the *Fleurette* type of case. In a decision rendered the same day as its *Fleurette* decision[154] the French tribunal refused to award compensation to a company professing to be damaged by a law that drastically regulated the export of liquor from Saint-Pierre and Miquelon, two French islands near Newfoundland. The law was enacted to prevent the smuggling of liquor from those islands into the United States, after protests against the smuggling had been made by our government. The plaintiff company, engaged in the smuggling, had built up a large supply of liquor on the islands and was unable to use it because of the law regulating exports, which effectively stopped the smuggling against which it was aimed.

In refusing compensation for the damages alleged to have been suffered the Council of State declared that the law that caused the damage was passed "to suppress fraudulent practices carried on to the detriment of a foreign country." Here we have the difference between this and the *Fleurette* case, where compensation was awarded. In this case, though the plaintiff company was injured by the enactment of the law, the legislative singling out of those in its position was justified by considerations of public morals. "We remind you," the government commissioner stated in his conclusions to the Council of State, "that the goal of the law out of which this case arose was the suppression, on the request of a foreign State, of a fraudulent activity; the fact, asserted

[153] Jèze, *supra* note 72, at 377.
[154] Compagnie générale de la Grande Pêche, January 14, 1938.

by the Company, that its activity was lawful under French law, is not conclusive; it does not change the highly reprehensible quality of that activity." This position, it should be noted, also applied to the law prohibiting the sale of absinthe, already referred to.[155] There, too, the activity prohibited had previously been permitted by law. But even under the *Fleurette* decision those adversely affected need not be awarded compensation, since the legislative classification was clearly justified by the need to protect public health and morals.

Need to Abrogate Sovereign Immunity

Our analysis of the French law of State liability shows clearly that the *droit administratif* has developed a complete system of State responsibility far beyond anything thus far evolved in the common-law world. Not only has the French system been able to free itself from all traces of the doctrine of sovereign immunity: it has gone much farther than to make the State liable for its torts on the same basis as individual citizens. The private citizen in France is still liable primarily for the damages caused by his faults,[156] even though there has been in recent years an extension in the French private law of torts of the rule of absolute liability[157]—an even greater extension than that which has occurred in Anglo-American law. The State in France, on the other hand, is no longer liable only, or even primarily, on the basis of fault. The rule now generally applied by the Council of State is that of absolute liability. The French State is responsible in every case where damage has been caused by its acts.

An American observer who has examined the law of public liability in the *droit administratif* is bound to rebel at every vestige of the doctrine of sovereign immunity that remains in our law. Is there any reason why the American citizen, living in a country that inveterately prides itself on the protection it furnishes to the individual against the State, should be less completely safeguarded from damage by administrative action than the citizen of France? "It requires but a slight appreciation of the facts," an American judge has recently stated, "to realize that in Anglo-American law the individual citizen is left to bear almost all the risks of a defective, negligent, perverse or erroneous administration of

[155] *Supra* note 148.

[156] See H. and L. Mazeaud, *op. cit. supra* note 126, chap. 4.

[157] See Savatier, Du Droit civil au droit public (2d ed., 1950). In large part the extension of absolute liability in the French private law of torts has been influenced by the Council of State's jurisprudence discussed above.

the state's functions—an unjust burden—which is becoming graver and more frequent as the government's activities become more diversified and as we leave to administrative officers in even greater degree the determination of the legal relations of the individual citizen."[158]

The one justification that can be advanced for the doctrine of sovereign immunity is that it is the only practically workable one. To abandon it wholly, it is urged, would be to open the door to the draining of the public treasury by the constant litigation of those who assert injury from State action. The working of the French system shows, however, that the danger referred to is not great enough to justify a doctrine completely indefensible on ethical grounds. The *droit administratif*, as we have seen, has gone far beyond merely discarding sovereign immunity. Yet its system of complete State responsibility has not proved unworkable in practice, and French jurists, far from advocating limitations in the name of expediency, have consistently urged the extension of State liability to its logical limits; *i.e.*, to the point where the State is in effect an insurer against injuries caused by its acts. All Frenchmen from the members of the Council of State down are justifiably proud of the fact that in their system the citizen's protection is more nearly adequate in the field of public torts than it is in any other system. And they feel the same conscious pride from the realization that their law of State liability seems destined to serve as a prototype even to the law of the common-law world, to which enlightened Frenchmen have always been accustomed to look as a model in the field of the protection of individual rights.

An American who looks at the jurisprudential edifice of State liability constructed by the French Council of State can but conclude that our own courts have been derelict in their work in this field. The argument constantly reiterated by American courts that the abrogation of sovereign immunity is entirely a legislative question is merely an easy way of enabling our judiciary to avoid performing their duty. When a doctrine of exclusively judicial origin works manifest injustice the obligation to change it rests primarily on the judge himself, and he must not wait "for the dim distant future in never-never land when the legislature may act."[159] "Certainly we have a duty here," stated a Utah judge, in recording his dissent from a decision applying the doctrine of sovereign immunity. "There are cases where we are powerless

[158] Carter, J., dissenting, in Madison v. San Francisco, 236 P. 2d 141 (Cal. 1951).

[159] Wolfe, J., dissenting, in Bingham v. Board of Education, 223 P. 2d 432, 438 (Utah 1950).

to act because the remedy lies solely with the legislature. But in those cases where we still have control of a rule or doctrine because it was judge made and developed, we may act. Non-action here and 'passing' the problem to the legislature is the easy way out. But I do not think it conscionable for us not to lift our hand when to do so would bring the law up to date and furnish remedies long overdue."[160]

A more difficult question is whether American law should follow the *droit administratif* in placing State responsibility on the basis of absolute liability. Mere abandonment of the doctrine of sovereign immunity, even if it be free of the exceptions contained in a statute like the Federal Tort Claims Act of 1946, would not, it should be noted, do this. It would have only the effect of placing State liability on the same basis as individual liability in our private law of torts—liability that in the vast majority of cases is still only liability for fault.

Many common lawyers have criticized as outmoded the emphasis on fault that still prevails in our law of torts. "The common-law concept of negligence," Mr. Justice Frankfurter has asserted, "is an antiquarian and uncivilized basis for working out rights and duties for disabilities and deaths inevitably due to the conduct of modern industry. In the conscious or unconscious endeavor not to have the human cost of industry fall with cruel injustice upon workers and their families, the law of negligence gives rise to endless casuistry. So long as the gamble of an occasionally heavy verdict is not replaced by the security of a modern system of insurance, courts must continue to apply the notion of negligence in situations for which it was never intended."[161]

Justice Frankfurter's remarks would certainly appear to apply with at least equal force to damage caused by the acts of public officers. Indeed, as we have already observed, the considerations usually seen as making for absolute liability—the inequality of the parties, the creation of a risk for the benefit of those subject to liability, and the possibility of spreading the risk—are all present in the field of State liability to a much greater extent than they can be in any case involving only two private citizens. There is thus every reason to urge the adoption in this country of the present French rule of absolute State liability. It should be recognized, however, that it is most unlikely that our law will go so far in the immediate future. As a practical matter, the most that can be advocated here with any hope of success is the abandonment of the

[160] *Id.* at 442.

[161] Urie v. Thompson, 337 U.S. 163, 196 (1949). See, similarly, Wilkerson v. McCarthy, 336 U.S. 53, 65 (1949).

vestiges remaining in American law of the doctrine of sovereign immunity, by the removal of the many exceptions contained in the Federal Tort Claims Act and by the enactment of statutes providing for State liability in the all too large number of American states that still do not have such laws.

Attainment of this more limited goal remains an ever-growing necessity in a modern democratic State. Certainly, as a judge of one of our state courts recently declared: "The reasoning which supports the doctrine of sovereign immunity in cases of this character is so fallacious and unsound that it should shock the intelligence, as well as the sense of justice, of those who believe in the American way of life. In my opinion, decisions of this kind are not only productive of widespread disrespect for the law and courts but can be used as the basis for propaganda which affects the stability of our government."[162]

[162] *Loc. cit. supra* note 158.

Chapter Ten

DROIT ADMINISTRATIF AND THE RULE OF LAW

"Great critics," reads a famous passage from the writings of Edmund Burke, "have taught us one essential rule. . . . It is this, that if ever we should find ourselves disposed not to admire those writers or artists, Livy and Virgil for instance, Raphael or Michael Angelo, whom all the learned had admired, not to follow our own fancies, but to study them until we know how and what we ought to admire; and if we cannot arrive at this combination of admiration with knowledge, rather to believe that we are dull, than that the rest of the world has been imposed on. It is as good a rule, at least, with regard to this admired constitution (of England). We ought to understand it according to our measure; and to venerate where we are not able presently to comprehend."[1]

Though we may not go so far today as fully to share Burke's religious enthusiasm, there is little doubt but that his words still strike a responsive chord in most Anglo-Americans. Dicey's characterization of the spirit with which our grandfathers and our fathers looked upon the institutions of their country is, even today, not too far wide of the mark as a description of dominant sentiment in the common-law world. "The constitution," he writes, "was to them, in the quaint language of George the Third, 'the most perfect of human formations'; it was to them not a mere polity to be compared with the government of any other state, but so to speak a sacred mystery of statesmanship; . . . it was the fruit not of abstract theory but of that instinct which (it is supposed) has enabled Englishmen, and especially uncivilised Englishmen, to build up sound and lasting institutions, much as bees construct a honeycomb, without undergoing the degradation of understanding

[1] Quoted in Dicey, Law of the Constitution 1 (9th ed., 1939).

the principles on which they raise a fabric more subtly wrought than any work of conscious art."[2]

Rule of Law

The attitude of the Anglo-American toward his constitutional system is particularly manifested with regard to what has been termed the central and most characteristic feature[3] of our common-law polity: the now almost axiomatic concept of the *rule* or *supremacy of law*. Here especially, the Anglo-American has tended to feel that Burke's panegyric is justified. It is the rule of law as a bridle on governmental power that, to the common lawyer, is peculiarly the Anglo-American contribution to political science; and that it is which, in his view, has preserved the common-law world, ever since the abortive attempts at Stuart absolutism, from the extremes of government that have characterized civil-law countries. "Modern Englishmen may at first feel some surprise," states Dicey, "that the 'rule of law' . . . should be considered as in any way a peculiarity of English institutions, since, at the present day, it may seem to be not so much the property of any one nation as a trait common to every civilised and orderly state. Yet, even if we confine our observation to the existing condition of Europe, we shall soon be convinced that the 'rule of law' is peculiar to England, or to those countries which, like the United States of America, have inherited English traditions."[4]

Even so staunch a constitutionalist as Dicey, however, was forced to recognize that the great growth of administrative authority that has occurred during the present century poses a substantial threat to the principle of the rule of law. According to Dicey's now classic attempt at defining that principle, by the rule of law "We mean, in the first place, that no man is punishable or can be lawfully made to suffer in body or goods except for a distinct breach of law established in the ordinary legal manner before the ordinary courts of the land."[5] In the light of the development of the modern administrative process this definition, taken literally, is clearly at variance with fact.

The administration, like the courts, is today vested with the authority to determine private rights and obligations by rendering de-

[2] *Id.* at 2.
[3] Dickinson, Administrative Justice and the Supremacy of Law 32 (1927).
[4] Dicey, *op. cit. supra* note. 1, at 188.
[5] *Ibid.*

cisions in cases involving individual citizens. And it is manifest that the administrative organs that exercise such authority "are not ordinary courts in Dicey's sense. 'Judicial' as their functions clearly seem to be, they are not 'courts' in the common-law meaning of the term. And they differ from common-law courts in precisely the particulars which furnish the reasons for the common law's insistence that every individual shall be entitled to have his rights tried in a law court."[6] That Dicey himself saw this transformation is shown in an article written near the end of his life in which he called attention to the bestowal upon the administration of "functions which in their nature belong to the law courts."[7] "Such transference of authority," he asserted, "saps the foundation of that rule of law which has been for generations a leading feature of the English Constitution."[8]

Must we then answer in the affirmative the question asked by Dicey in this article: Has the development of the administrative process tended to weaken the rule of law as the dominant constitutional principle of the common-law world?

Dicey himself was able to answer it in the negative. The constitutional principle was maintained, in his view, by the existence of judicial control over administrative action. "The fact that the ordinary law courts can deal with any actual and probable breach of the law committed by any servant of the Crown still preserves [the] rule of law."[9]

To one nurtured in Anglo-American constitutional traditions, justice according to law is the outstanding characteristic of the State in which the rule of law prevails. Its dominance does not militate against the possession of wide powers of decision by the administration. The rule of law does not necessarily demand judicial justice in the settling of all disputes. What that concept does require is justice according to law as either the determining or the controlling factor. Whenever disputes are committed to agencies other than courts, judicial control of their determinations is essential. It is only to the extent that judicial justice serves to keep these other agencies in line that the rule of law can be said to be maintained. That is why the question of judicial review of administrative action remains the pivotal one in all discussions of administrative law. "For just in so far as administrative determinations

[6] Dickinson, *op. cit. supra* note 3, at 35.

[7] Dicey, "The Development of Administrative Law in England" 31 L. Q. Rev. 148, 150 (1915).

[8] *Ibid.*

[9] *Id.* at 152.

are subject to court review, a means exists for maintaining the supremacy of law, though at one remove and as a sort of secondary line of defence."[10]

The common lawyer would, then, reply with Dicey in the negative to the question whether the growth of administrative authority has been inconsistent with the rule of law as that principle has been developed in the common-law world. The rule of law is preserved by the assertion by our law courts of the authority to hold administrative action to the standard of legality. Administrative action that does not meet that standard will be set aside on the bringing of the appropriate review action in the competent court. Judicial control, in the Anglo-American view, still ensures the subordination of administration to law, as administered by the ordinary courts of the land.

To the common lawyer the fact that the legality of administrative action is controlled in his system by the ordinary courts of law is of fundamental importance. In a system governed by the rule of law it must, in his opinion, be the law courts that determine questions of administrative law, and the applicable principles are those that have been worked out from the ordinary private law by the method of judicial empiricism. " 'A government of laws and not of men,' " as Mr. Justice Frankfurter has reminded us, "was the rejection in positive terms of rule by fiat, whether by the fiat of governmental or private power. Every act of government may be challenged by an appeal to law, as finally pronounced by this Court."[11]

It is the absence of control of administrative action by the law courts in France that has led Anglo-American observers such as Dicey and Lord Hewart to their well-known denunciations of the *droit administratif*. The French system, Lord Hewart declares, is one "which is fundamentally opposed to the English conception of the 'Rule of Law,' especially as regards exemption from the jurisdiction of the ordinary legal tribunals, in the case of public officials acting in performance or purported performance of their official duties. In countries where this system of administrative law prevails the rights and obligations of all servants of the State, and also of all private individuals in relation to servants of the State acting in their official capacity, as well as the procedure for enforcing those rights and obligations, are governed by special rules which are, in general, administered by special tribunals,

[10] Dickinson, *op. cit. supra* note 3, at 37.
[11] United States v. United Mine Workers, 330 U.S. 258, 308 (1947).

and the principles underlying these rules differ essentially from the principles forming the basis of the law which governs the relations of private individuals towards one another. Under this system, the ordinary Courts of Justice are regarded as having no jurisdiction to deal with any dispute affecting the Government or its servants."[12]

Rule of Law in France

Before undertaking this study of the *droit administratif* the present writer, like most Anglo-Americans, was convinced that control of administrative action by the ordinary courts of justice was the essential element of the rule of law. With Dicey and Lord Hewart, he felt that a system in which the law courts were barred from exercising competence in administrative-law cases was contrary to the first principles of common-law constitutional polity. "The absence of public-law concepts, in the Continental sense," he wrote in 1949, "rather than being a defect of our jurisprudence is, thus, its great strength. It enables control over Executive action to be maintained through the same institutions that administer the normal law of the land, and on the same basic principles of justice."[13]

This view appeared to be particularly valid to an American jurist. "From their own experience and their deep reading of history, the Founders knew that law alone saves a society from being rent by internecine strife or ruled by mere brute power however disguised. . . . The conception of a government of laws dominated the thoughts of those who founded this Nation and designed its Constitution, although they knew as well as the belittlers of the conception that laws have to be made, interpreted and enforced by men. To that end, they set apart a body of men, who were to be the depositories of law, who by their disciplined training and character and by withdrawal from the usual temptations of private interest may reasonably be expected to be 'as free, impartial, and independent as the lot of humanity will admit.' "[14] To an American the rule of law seems to demand that all justiciable controversies be determined by the judges who are our depositories of the law. And the fact that the administration happens to be one of the parties in a particular case does not, in our view, make that case any less a justiciable controversy within the competence of our law courts.

[12] Hewart, The New Despotism 37 (1929).
[13] Schwartz, Law and the Executive in Britain 151 (1949).
[14] *Loc. cit. supra* note 11.

Professor René David, an outstanding French student of comparative law, in discussing the present writer's point of view on this subject as expressed in the 1949 work already referred to, has stated: "Professor Schwartz wrote his book before coming to France for a year to make a study of administrative law. We should be interested in knowing whether, after this experience, he would still write without modification his first chapter entitled 'Executive Power and the Disappearance of Law,' in which he reaffirms the Anglo-American concept of the rule of law and refuses to admit that the needs of justice and those of administration can be reconciled by a system of control and checks established within the administration itself."[15]

To one who has read thus far it is almost needless for the author to state that his views on the compatibility of *droit administratif* with the principle of the rule of law have been modified. Indeed, anyone who impartially analyzes the various aspects of the French system as presented in this book cannot but reject an interpretation of the concept of the rule of law that makes of the *droit administratif* the best example of a system inconsistent with the constitutional concept.

The rule of law demands the subordination of administration to law. In a State governed by it the citizen adversely affected by governmental action can obtain a decision by an independent judge on the legality of such action, just as he can obtain a similar decision when aggrieved by the act of another private individual. The rule of law assumes that the State, to use the French expression already cited,[16] is an "honest man." As such, it will respond in damages for the wrongful acts done by it, just as any ordinary citizen does.

The rule of law rejects the conception of the dual State, in which the administration of justice is characterized by its dualistic quality. In such a State law plays a controlling part only in the ordering of the relations between private citizens. Legal concepts are not applicable to the political sphere, which is regulated by arbitrary measures in which the dominant officials exercise discretionary prerogatives.[17] A system of law and a system of force exist side by side in a State of this type. "There are certain areas into which law penetrates only slightly. For example, a person who is suspected of antagonism to the regime may be picked up by the secret police, held incommunicado for a long

15 David, Book Review, 4 Revue Internationale de Droit Comparé 184, 185 (1952).
16 *Supra* p. 270.
17 See Fraenkel, The Dual State 3 (1941).

period of time, tried secretly by an administrative board, and sentenced to hard labor—without benefit of defense counsel and without any possibility of appeal. On the other hand, there are other areas which are on the whole governed by well-defined legal standards."[18]

The notion that the administration of justice must be dualist in essence—that different rules are to be applied to State action, that differing consequences are to follow where the acts of government officials are involved—is wholly foreign to a State governed by the rule of law. It rejects, in both theory and practice, the consequences flowing from these ideas: that the public officer is to be placed on a higher plane than the individual; that immunity must be given to government officials *qua* officials.

It is, then, a dualized legal order in which acts of the administration are placed in a privileged position of immunity from control by law that is opposed to the constitutional concept of the rule of law. A State in which administration is not vested with any such immunity, in which administrative acts are subject to as strict legal scrutiny as the acts of ordinary citizens, in which the law of public liability is at least as extensive as the private law of torts—such a State is certainly not one whose institutions are inconsistent with the rule of law.

The analysis given in this book of the different facets of the *droit administratif* should have shown sufficiently that the French system, like that which prevails in the common-law world, is governed by the rule of law. In France, as in our own system, administration is subordinated to law. And the principle of administrative legality is enforced by a judge who is today wholly independent of the active administration. The French citizen adversely affected by administrative action possesses a remedy in a court, just as he does when aggrieved by the action of another private individual.

It is true that the remedy afforded him in administrative-law cases is not in the courts that administer justice between ordinary citizens. But that fact, of itself, should not be conclusive. The administrative courts in France, as we have emphasized,[19] are as independent of the active administration as the law courts. Their membership is recruited in much the same way. They decide cases in a genuinely judicial manner, at least according to French notions of judicial procedure. They are infused with the inculcated traditions and techniques that are an indispensable part of any judicial tribunal. In a word, administration

[18] Berman, Justice in Russia vii (1950).
[19] *Supra* pp. 60-62.

in France is as subject to the control of a veritable judge as the acts of ordinary citizens. The Council of State is as much a true court as the Court of Cassation, the supreme law court in the French system.

What, then, is the essence of the rule of law if not that, under it, the acts of the administration, like those of private individuals, must conform to the principle of legality as enforced by a truly independent judge? It matters little that the judge who is authorized to resolve administrative-law disputes is not the same one who is vested with jurisdiction in private-law cases. What does matter is that the administrative-law judge shall be as autonomous of the active administration as his confrere in the law courts, so that he can approach a case without that bias in favor of administration that would inevitably result from a lack of judicial independence. What must be avoided at all costs is a dualistic administration of justice, in which the administration is rendered free from the law that binds everyone else in the community.

Common-law critics of the *droit administratif* who have based their denunciations on the immunity of the French administration from control by the law courts have tended to stress the nonjudicial character of the administrative courts in France. Dicey, as is well known, asserted that the French tribunals were only "so-called courts";[20] that they were fundamentally official or governmental bodies "which may occasionally be swayed by the policy of a ministry, and still more often be influenced by official or governmental ideas."[21]

Dicey's characterization may well have been true a century ago. The Council of State during its early history was more an administrative agency than a court.[22] But since that time there has been a continuous judicialization of the French tribunal—a development that had already progressed far by the time Dicey wrote. It has reached its culmination since his death, and there is little doubt but that the judicial section of the Council is today a wholly independent court whose bias is, if anything, in favor of the citizen rather than the administration. Dicey's description is consequently no longer an accurate one, however weightily it may still influence Anglo-American conceptions.

To say that the administration in France is not subject to the rule of law because its acts are immune from control by the law courts is today to assert only a half-truth. As a prominent councilor of state has recently pointed out, "since the year VIII of the revolutionary era

20 Dicey, *op. cit. supra* note 1, at 340.
21 *Id.* at 366. See also *id.* at 353.
22 *Supra* pp. 10-11.

[1800] and especially since 1872, a remarkable evolution has improved the administrative-court system, elevated the administrative judge to the position of a true judge, fully opened the roads to judicial review, extended the control of legality, and affirmed the liability of the State. . . . Our administration has escaped from one judge only to be subjected to another."[23]

Desirability of Droit Administratif

What has just been said shows what should have been clear by now to any reader of this book: that a system of administrative law such as that of France is not inconsistent with the constitutional principle of the rule of law. What that principle demands is the subordination of administration to law administered by an independent judge. In the *droit administratif* there is clearly such subordination. The principle of administrative legality is effectively enforced by the review power exercised by the Council of State and other administrative courts.

That *droit administratif* is not incompatible with the rule of law does not, however, necessarily mean that its importation would be desirable in the common-law world. Anglo-Americans have, it should be noted, urged the creation of administrative courts in our system, patterned on those of France.[24] The review power exercised today by the ordinary law courts in the common-law world would be transferred, under their proposals, to the suggested tribunals. To an American the most important of the proposals for such administrative courts is that contained in the so-called Administrative Court Bill introduced in our Congress. It provides for an Administrative Court of the United States, to consist of a chief judge and four associate judges. Upon this tribunal would be conferred permissive jurisdiction in cases involving the judicial review of agency action and proceedings for the civil enforcement of administrative rules, orders, or investigative demands. The enactment of such a bill would clearly represent a significant step in the direction of the *droit administratif* in this country.

One of the primary purposes of a comparative study of French administrative law should be to enable an Anglo-American to form a proper judgment of the value of proposals for the creation of administrative courts in the common-law world. An examination of the workings of an actual system of administrative courts such as that in France

[23] Puget, Preface in Schwartz, Le Droit administratif américain: notions générales iii (1952).

[24] *Supra* pp. 20-21.

should be the most effective way to facilitate an equitable assessment of the merits of the proposed tribunals.

As we have emphasized, the first lesson that a study of the *droit administratif* teaches us is that administrative-court proposals ought not to be judged on the basis of their supposed conflict with the principle of the rule of law. "We can establish administrative courts and alter the rules of administrative law as we please without infringing any rule of law. The fact that any proposal is rejected as contrary to the rule of law indicates that the arguments against it are probably weak."[25]

The experience in France should show conclusively that a system of separate administrative courts can exist without infringing upon the constitutional principle. Indeed anyone familiar with the actual functioning of the *droit administratif* must admit, as an acute English observer did: "The 'rule of law' simply has nothing whatever to do with the question. An administrative court would be just as much a part of the ordinary judicial system as the High Court. Administrative law would be neither more nor less a branch of the ordinary law than it is now. There would be just as much and just as little equality before the law as there is now. Dicey's views are not only wrong but irrelevant."[26] The common lawyer, still largely influenced by Dicey's strictures, tends all too often to overlook this truth.

There is, however, another important lesson that a study of the actual working of the *droit administratif* teaches us—one that Anglo-American advocates of separate administrative courts appear wholly to have neglected. The French system, we have seen,[27] suffers from all the defects that inhere in the dichotomization of remedial justice. The citizen in France who seeks a judicial remedy against the administration must first decide whether his case falls within the jurisdiction of the administrative courts or of the law courts. If he brings his suit in the wrong tribunal, the ultimate result will be a dismissal, and he will have to start all over in the correct court. Since the rules of jurisdiction in the French system are hardly defined with anything like mathematical precision, the would-be litigant's need to bring his action in the proper set of courts may cast a great burden on him. In borderline cases the choice of tribunals may well resolve itself into little more than guesswork for the French litigant, with the matter in doubt until his choice

25 Jennings, quoted in Robson, Justice and Administrative Law 460 (3d ed., 1951).
26 *Ibid.*
27 *Supra* pp. 64-75.

has ultimately been confirmed or rejected by a decision of the Court of Conflicts. Justice for the citizen in France is all too often a process of marching the king's men up the hierarchy of one set of courts, only to have to march them down again to the set in which the action should have been brought in the first place.

Those who urge, by the establishment of separate administrative courts, the creation of a two-court system in the common-law world overlook the dangers inherent in the dichotomization of remedial justice. To divide our unified system of justice is to risk a recrudescence of the deficiencies that existed in Anglo-American law before the merger of law and equity. It was to eliminate these defects that our system forsook the division of remedial justice that had formerly distinguished it. Ever since the first efforts toward the merger of law and equity the trend with us has been toward the unification of justice. To set up a separate series of administrative courts in our legal system would be to reverse this tendency. To return to the jurisdictional difficulties that confronted Anglo-American litigants when law and equity were separate and competing systems of justice is surely no answer to the problems raised by the need for adequate judicial control of administrative action.

The difficulties referred to may well be avoided by the establishment of administrative courts with only permissive rather than mandatory jurisdiction. Under the Administrative Court Bill introduced in the American Congress, the proposed tribunal would be given optional competence in administrative-law cases. The jurisdiction of the court would be discretionary with that tribunal. It could be invoked only by a party other than an administrative agency. And except where such jurisdiction is invoked by an outside party and taken by the court, the regular federal courts would still have jurisdiction. Under the proposed law persons adversely affected by administrative action would thus still have a choice of bringing their review actions before the ordinary law courts.

The vesting of only optional jurisdiction in an administrative court would avoid many of the difficulties for the litigant that are inherent in a two-court legal system. One wonders, however, whether the establishment of a court whose competence is not mandatory would itself be desirable. As one study has expressed this doubt, "we believe that such an experiment could not be effectively made on an optional basis, that much of such value as a specialized single court would have would be lost if its jurisdiction were not exclusive and that concurrent jurisdiction might well create an unseemly appearance of competition between the Administrative Court and other Federal courts for the favor of litigants."[28]

Judicial Expertise

The impetus behind the movement for specialized administrative courts in the common-law world has been well described by Mr. Justice Frankfurter. "The same forces which have given rise to the new machinery and a new technique of administrative control have reacted upon the structure and scope of judicial control over these new tribunals. The same need for economy and expertness that led to the development of administrative agencies led to a demand for the same qualities on the part of courts sitting in judgment on these agencies. The American adaptation of the English judicial system, which in turn had its roots in the seventeenth century, was found inadequate for modern industrialized America. The momentum behind specialized administrative tribunals brought forth a demand for specialized courts."[29]

Many Anglo-Americans have felt that the problems posed by specialization in government can best be controlled by specialization in the judiciary. A court set up to deal only with administrative-law cases could hope to become specialists after some experience with work in that field. Such a court would develop precedents and practices of its own, and well-knit, comprehensive legal principles would arise to govern what are in effect the separate legal systems of each agency. On such a tribunal, its advocates urge, we could hope to have in time "expert" judges capable of dealing with the highly technical and complex issues that judicial review of administrative action represents.

It cannot be denied that the call for *expertise* strikes a responsive chord in a society of insecure laymen. "The highly industrialized society in which we live has a great appetite for 'know-how.' Such a society elevates and aggrandizes the position of the expert. His is the voice with the ready answer. His opinions become the facts upon which lesser mortals—laymen—risk life and fortune."[30]

In pointing out that there may be dangers as well as advantages in the specialization of the judiciary, the present writer has no intention

[28] 3 Administrative Law Bulletin, A.B.A. Ad. Law Section 78, 80 (1951).

[29] Frankfurter, "The Business of the Supreme Court of the United States—A Study in the Federal Judicial System" 39 Harv. L. Rev. 587, 588 (1926).

[30] Rifkind, "A Special Court for Patent Litigation? The Danger of a Specialized Judiciary" 37 A.B.A.J. 425 (1951).

of tilting a quixotic lance against the citadel of the expert.[31] At the same time, those who seize upon judicial inexpertness as the reason for ousting the Anglo-American courts of jurisdiction in administrative-law cases are going too far in the other direction. They ignore the affirmative advantage in adjudication by courts of broad jurisdiction, which can bring to the solution of particular legal problems a wide range of experience, knowledge, and understanding as well as a proper detachment from narrower interests.[32]

True, Anglo-American courts are, by their very nature, not technically expert in any one field, for they decide all types of litigation. But that characteristic has usually been considered by the common lawyer as one of the prime virtues of his judicial system: its judges have not the restricted outlook of those accustomed to dealing in only one narrow phase of human experience, but rather exercise a broad over-all judgment on the questions they have to determine. The ideal of the common law has been that disputes be settled by men of general learning in the law rather than by men of great technical knowledge in the cases they decide. For such experts tend too often to become sterile in their outlook and to make their decisions in the pigeonholes of their own restricted experience.

The early common-law judges were clerics, trained not as technical experts in any one field but in the common law, which was based on good faith and equity and the general ideals of Christian conduct. When the earlier flexibility of the common law gave way to a rigidity of form and procedure, the Chancellor's jurisdiction was expanded so that once more cases might be decided on the broad principles of reason and conscience. The emphasis on broad over-all judgment in our legal system has been so great, in fact, that the common lawyer has often tended unduly to distrust experts and adjudication by them. The very concept of the jury system, in which disputes are resolved by laymen of no special competence, shows this distrust. The idea that twelve ordinary men are better than a group of experts is an ancient one. Bracton in one passage asserts that even "if the jurors are altogether ignorant about the fact and know nothing concerning the truth," it is enough if they "speak from belief and conscience at least."[33]

Common-law countries have in the past all too often tended to over-

[31] Compare *ibid.*

[32] *Supra* note 28, at 81.

[33] Pound and Plucknett, Readings on the History and System of the Common Law 153 (3d ed., 1927).

look the fact that the role of the expert in modern government is a vital one. The need to make use of the specialist has been, indeed, one of the prime reasons for resort to the administrative process. "In many cases a principal reason for establishing an agency has been the need to bring to bear upon particular problems technical or professional skills."[34] The utilization of administrative expertness does not, however, militate against control by the courts. "The well-learned lesson of democratic government with 'experts' is that they should be kept on tap but not on top."[35] In ensuring this subordination the nonexpertness of our courts plays an essential part. It is the great virtue of our judicial process that it employs men not specialists in any one field of legal endeavor but capable by disposition and training of dealing with all types of cases. "The judicial process," as an eminent American jurist has put it, "requires a different kind of *expertise*—the unique capacity to see things in their context. Great judges embrace within their vision a remarkably ample context. But even lesser men, presiding in courts of wide jurisdiction, are constantly exposed to pressures that tend to expand the ambit of their ken."[36] The limitations of the expert—inability to see beyond the narrow confines of his own experience, intolerance of the layman, and excessive zeal in carrying out his own policy regardless of the cost to other, broader interests of society—are subjected under our system to the trained scrutiny of the nonexpert judge, who, unhindered by the professional bias of the specialist, is able to take a broader view than that of merely promoting administrative policy in the case at hand without counting the ultimate cost.

Administrative law "does not live in the seclusion and silence of a Trappist monastery. It is part and parcel of the whole body of our law. . . . [It] is separated from the rest of the law not by a steel barrier but by a permeable membrane constantly bathed in the general substantive and procedural law."[37]

It is difficult for one trained in common-law traditions and techniques to see what would be gained by segregating administrative law from other branches of the law. That there are deficiencies in the present system of judicial control in the Anglo-American world cannot be denied. But the answer to one who has studied the *droit administratif*

34 Report of the Attorney General's Committee on Administrative Procedure 19 (1941).

35 H.R. Rep. No. 1383, 73d Cong., 2d Sess. (1934) 16.

36 Rifkind, *loc. cit. supra* note 30.

37 *Ibid.*

is not the creation of separate administrative courts. To set apart administrative law from the rest of the law is to "contract the area of its exposure to the self-correcting forces of the law. In time such a body of law, secluded from the rest, develops a jargon of its own, thought patterns that are unique, internal policies which it subserves and which are different from and sometimes at odds with the policies pursued by the general law."[38]

Conflicts with Administration

Historically, law and administration are rival agencies of social control in the common-law world. The rule of law was considered to require the complete subjection of administration, and attempts to allow it any scope were considered as inroads into the constitutional doctrine. This "bad adjustment between law and administration, traditional in common-law countries for historical reasons, gave rise to conditions of mutual distrust on the part of courts and administrative agencies."[39] Anglo-Americans who have advocated the establishment of separate administrative courts have urged that such tribunals could do much to eliminate the conflicts between law and administration that have characterized common-law jurisprudence. The judges of the administrative courts, they say, being themselves specialists in administrative-law cases, will appreciate the needs of administration. They will be more willing than the judges of our law courts to allow proper scope for the adequate prosecution of administrative activities; for the ordinary judge cannot be expected to possess sufficient knowledge of the necessities of administrative life.

One of the most important advantages, in theory, of specialized courts to review administrative determinations is that they should lead to a more harmonious relation between the administration and the courts. A court that deals exclusively with the work of the administration should become familiar both with the problems involved and with the personalities of those whose work it is reviewing. The building up of a personal relation between two bodies is an important intangible in the efficiency with which they function together, and, though not so important, perhaps, as between two executive agencies, it can mean much in actual practice.

Our study of the *droit administratif* should, however, show that the

[38] *Ibid.*

[39] Pound, Administrative Law 105 (1942).

establishment of a system of specialized reviewing courts can lead to the opposite result. There is at least as much danger of discord between the administration and administrative courts as there is between it and the ordinary law courts. The judges of the administrative courts will not unnaturally tend to consider themselves to be as expert in the field of administrative law as the agencies whose acts they are called upon to review. As tribunals of experts they are bound to consider themselves more competent to review administrative determinations than our present courts consider themselves. There will be much less inclination on the part of the administrative-court judge, himself a specialist, to defer to administrative *expertise*. The result will undoubtedly be a great extension in the scope of review. The natural tendency will be for the administrative court to grant review *de novo*, for, as a group of specialists in the field, it will feel fit to review administrative determinations as to both law and fact. Since it will consider itself as competent as the agencies that it reviews, it will feel justified in substituting its independent judgment instead of merely seeing whether the administrative determination is supported by substantial evidence.

That these are not merely theoretical possibilities is shown by our analysis of the scope of review in France. Anyone familiar with developments in that aspect of the *droit administratif* cannot doubt that the Council of State has been consistently expanding the scope of reviewing power, until the scope of review in France today is far broader than in the common-law world. Indeed, as has been pointed out,[40] the time may not be too distant when the French administrative courts will exercise a full power of inquiry over both the law and the facts in every case in which review of an administrative act is sought.

The reasons for the vast extension by the Council of State of the scope of reviewing power are not difficult to determine. The French tribunal feels few of the pressures that have exacted deference to the administration on the part of Anglo-American courts. It considers itself to be, in the French system, *the* expert in administrative law. The judicial section of the Council has developed from within the active administration itself. The professional careers of its members are devoted almost entirely to the field of administrative law. They need assume none of the leave-it-to-the-expert attitude that has too often dominated the work of Anglo-American courts in this field. "The administrative judge knows administrative law. By reason of the manner of his recruitment he can understand the facts and grasp their reality and complexity.

[40] *Supra* p. 249.

From this understanding his decision acquires the authority needed to make an administration naturally disposed to abuse its prerogatives defer to it."[41]

Nor is it true that the experience of the Council of State is one that would not necessarily be duplicated in a similar tribunal in the common-law world. The tendency to expand the scope of review appears to be an almost inevitable concomitant of a specialized administrative court. In a now nearly forgotten chapter of American administrative law, the Commerce Court of the United States was created in 1910 with jurisdiction to review orders of the Interstate Commerce Commission. The reasons for the establishment of that tribunal were essentially those urged today by the Anglo-American advocates of administrative courts. The expectations of its sponsors were, however, largely defeated by the lack of harmony between the Commerce Court and the Interstate Commerce Commission, whose work it reviewed. The specialized court soon felt that it was as competent as the Commission, and it had no hesitancy in reversing that body whenever it disagreed with its findings. The Commerce Court tended to consider the I.C.C. more or less as a subordinate body whose determinations were merely preliminary to the actual trial before the court.[42]

According to one American judge, "If courts are to weigh the evidence before commissions . . . , the efficiency of administrative action will be greatly impaired. If it must give a trial de novo, the twilight of administrative law is at hand, for the proceedings before the administrative body will be but a perfunctory skirmish, the principal contribution of which will be delay."[43] These words may seem extreme to Americans who feel that the scope of review has been restricted unduly by our courts. Nevertheless, there are few administrative lawyers in this country who do not reject the principle of unlimited judicial review. It is of the utmost importance that those interested in the subject be made aware that establishment of separate administrative courts will lead almost inevitably to a great extension in the scope of review. Even the advocates of such specialized tribunals appear to be unaware that this is an unavoidable aspect of their proposals. Realization that the adoption of *droit administratif* involves full judicial review on both law

[41] Rolland, Précis de droit administratif 277 (10th ed., 1951).

[42] For a discussion of the Commerce Court experiment, see Note, 20 N.Y.U. L.Q. Rev. 220 (1944).

[43] General Accident F. & L. Assur. Corp. v. Industrial Commission, 271 N.W. 385, 389 (Wis. 1937).

and facts is imperative if proposals for the creation of administrative courts in the common-law world are to be intelligently appraised.

Suggestions from Droit Administratif

Our analysis thus far indicates that it is out of key with reality to reject *droit administratif* because it is repugnant to the rule of law. An impartial observer of the French system cannot but conclude that the administration can be controlled by law administered by independent administrative courts as effectively as by law applied by the ordinary courts of justice. At the same time, to a common lawyer it does not seem desirable to establish a system of separate administrative courts in the Anglo-American world, both because it violates the basic principle of unification of remedial justice that has dominated our legal system since the Judicature Acts and their American equivalents and because it invites the dangers inherent in overspecialization by the judiciary. The view of the present writer on this point has been well summed up by an eminent councilor of state. "M. Schwartz is convinced of the merits of the system that prevails in the United States; he was, it seemed to me, even more convinced before carrying his comparative study to its conclusion. Each people possesses institutions and systems which are the product of its history, which have adapted themselves to its way of life, and to which it has become accustomed. There should be no question of recommending rash transpositions from one country to the other."[44]

The fact that a study of the *droit administratif* does not lead to the conclusion that separate administrative courts such as those in France would be desirable in the common-law world does not, however, mean that such a study is not of positive value to the Anglo-American administrative lawyer. One who has read the analysis provided in this book will realize that the problems dealt with in the French system are not unlike those that have confronted students of Anglo-American administrative law. The French answers to these problems should be of great interest to us, particularly where they appear to be superior to those of our own system. "By making inquiries in other countries we can seek inspirations, note advantages or disadvantages, and observe improvements."[45]

To make such an inquiry into the details of the *droit administratif*

[44] Puget, *op. cit. supra* note 23, at vii.
[45] *Ibid.*

has been the prime purpose of this book. Wherever comparison has been feasible the French answer to a particular administrative-law problem has been compared with that given in the Anglo-American world. It may be useful at this point to summarize those aspects of the French system that appear to be in advance of our own law on the subject. Such a summary, together with the suggested changes that they seem to call for in common-law administrative law, follows in the order in which the various points have appeared in different portions of this book.

(1) Proceedings for review.

Anglo-American administrative law has been unduly influenced by the common law's concern with forms of action. The result has been a tendency to lose sight of the need for simplicity of procedure in administrative-law cases. In this respect the *droit administratif*, with its simple petition to annul an illegal administrative act (*recours pour excès de pouvoir*), certainly appears to be in advance of Anglo-American law. And one can without hesitancy urge that our law follow the French system in this respect by the abolition of the extraordinary remedies and the other forms of review action from the field of administrative law and the substitution for them of a uniform nontechnical petition for review in all cases in which a decision by a court is sought on the legality of challenged administrative action.

(2) Cost of litigation.

The French system of administrative law has been able largely to solve a problem still most acute in the common-law world; namely, the expense of litigation. In the common-law world the high cost of justice has meant in most cases the practical preclusion of judicial review for those who do not have the necessary financial resources. "The rule we announce . . . makes a tyrant out of every contracting officer," asserted Mr. Justice Douglas in dissent in a recent case[46] in which the Court held that all review was precluded in a government-contract case. But it is not generally realized that the high cost of litigation makes an equal unreviewable tyrant out of every Anglo-American administrative officer, except where the financial impact of administrative action makes it worth while to incur the expense involved in seeking judicial review.

The *droit administratif* has been able to resolve the problem of the expense of justice by its use of the inquisitorial method.[47] Private parties

[46] United States v. Wunderlich, 342 U.S. 98, 101 (1951).

[47] *Supra* p. 127.

in France can avoid the cost of counsel because of the active role played by the reviewing court itself in developing both sides of the case. It is not, however, suggested that the common-law world adopt the French solution, which works as a practical matter only because the review procedure in the *droit administratif* is inquisitorial rather than adversary. What is needed in the Anglo-American system is an attempt to attain the end already achieved by the French system, inexpensive judicial review of administrative action, while avoiding the inquisitorial procedure on which the French solution is based. This end could be attained by the establishment of an Office of Public Prosecutor in administrative-law cases, as has been suggested.[48] That Office would perform part of the role undertaken in the French system by the reviewing court itself; namely, active development of the plaintiff's case against the administration.

It has already been shown that the desired end cannot be achieved by the mere extension of programs of legal aid, however useful they may be in dealing with many of its aspects. As the most recent survey on legal aid in this country has aptly pointed out, there are advantages to be obtained through the creation of a public agency that cannot be secured by the ordinary legal-aid program. "A distinct advantage of the public bureau appears to be that it carries with it less connotation of charity and takes on more of the character and prestige of a public service. It is generally better-known."[49]

The objection will undoubtedly be raised that politics or graft or inertia would inevitably creep into the Public Prosecutor system and make it useless if not harmful. Experience in this country with the Office of Public Defender, the closest analogy to the type of office here advocated, shows, on the contrary, that the proper devotion to duty can be achieved in a public as well as in a private setting if proper safeguards are observed. "There is no inherent reason why a Public Defender should not be as conscientious and as trustworthy a public official as the judge who sits on the bench."[50]

A more difficult criticism would be addressed to the taking over by the State of a sphere that is today still almost wholly that of the private practitioner. But if the establishment of an Office of Public Prosecutor in administrative-law cases can be said to involve a socialistic element, it does so only in the sense that public prosecution in criminal cases

[48] *Supra* pp. 127-28.
[49] Brownell, Legal Aid in the United States 97 (1951).
[50] *Id.* at 146.

does. There doubtless were complaints of State interference when the blood feud and other primitive methods of proceeding against crime were superseded by direct enforcement in the King's courts by his officers. Such public enforcement was nonetheless seen to be justified by the fact that society's interest in securing enforcement of the criminal law was at least as great as that of the victims of crimes. Does not society have the same direct interest today, in an era of ever-expanding administrative authority, in ensuring enforcement of the principle of administrative legality?

(3) "Trial by battle."

Under the inquisitorial procedure followed by the administrative courts in France much of the adversary nature of the review proceeding is eliminated. In this respect the *droit administratif* differs radically from the system in the common-law world. With us justice in the courts, in both public- and private-law cases, is almost completely dominated by what has been termed the "sporting theory of justice."[51] The common-law theory of litigation, as Dean Pound has expressed it, "is that of a fair fist fight, according to the canons of the manly art, with a court to see fair play and prevent interference. . . . We strive in every way to restrain the trial judge and to insure the individual litigants a fair fight, unhampered by mere considerations of justice."[52]

The procedure in the French administrative courts appears to go to the other extreme of almost entirely excluding the adversary element. There are few Anglo-Americans who would go so far as to urge following the French system in this respect. But more and more we are coming to realize that the fighting method of conducting trials is carried to excess in our system. "It has contributed to lower the system of administration of justice . . . to the level of a mere game of skill or chance. . . . The right to use a rule of procedure or evidence precisely as one plays a trump card, or draws to three aces, or holds back a good horse till the home stretch, is a distinctive result of the common-law attitude toward parties in litigation."[53]

Many Anglo-Americans would like to have our courts play a more active role in cases in order to eliminate the grosser aspects of our fighting theory of justice. "A court striving to do justice," a federal judge has asserted, "should not put on blinders and ignore matters which

[51] See In re Barnett, 124 F. 2d 1005, 1010 (2d Cir. 1942).
[52] Pound, "Do We Need a Philosophy of Law?" 5 Col. L. Rev. 339, 347 (1905).
[53] Wigmore, quoted in In re Barnett, 124 F. 2d 1005, 1011 (2d Cir. 1942).

counsel overlook."[54] It has been urged, too, that the State assume in our system more responsibility for seeing that relevant evidence is presented. Both of these steps are in the direction of the procedure followed by the administrative courts in France. In this respect, of particular significance is what is known in French law as *expertise.* Under it experts are chosen by the court whose sole concern is to arrive at an impartial evaluation of the facts.[55] The abuse of the expert witness, so prevalent in our system, is thus completely avoided. Few if any common lawyers, to be sure, would go so far as to advocate the importation into our courts of the inquisitorial procedure followed by the Council of State. But the fact that "trial by battle" can be almost entirely eliminated from the workings of the French tribunal should furnish strong practical support for those who urge its minimization in our own judicial system.

(4) Standing.

A study of the *droit administratif* cannot but lead one to conclude that American courts have been excessively narrow in their views regarding the availability of review. This observation is especially pertinent to the question whether particular plaintiffs possess the standing prerequisite to the maintaining of a review action. The federal courts in this country, influenced by the "case or controversy" requirement of Article III of our Constitution, have been averse to allowing suits by those alleging only a collective interest, such as that of a taxpayer or a consumer. The Council of State in France has been less hesitant about entertaining such actions, though it has not gone so far as to do away with the requirement of personal interest in would-be challengers of administrative action. Because of constitutional demands it may be that our courts cannot make of the review action an *actio popularis,* maintainable by any citizen. But they should at least be as liberal as the French tribunal in their interpretation of the requirement of standing in particular cases.

(5) Abuse of power.

Anglo-American courts have consistently refused to inquire into the motives that induced a challenged administrative act. In the *droit administratif*, on the other hand, the reviewing court does exercise an authority to examine into the motivation behind an administrative act.[56]

[54] *Ibid.*
[55] *Supra* pp. 137-38.
[56] *Supra* pp. 216-19.

If the French administration has used its authority for a purpose other than that for which the legislature intended it to be employed, its action will be annulled for abuse of power.

Even if one recognizes the limitations on judicial inquiry into cases of this type, it appears that the concept of abuse of power is a valuable adjunct to the authority of the French reviewing court. Under it the judge may go behind the form of a challenged act to determine whether respect for legality did in fact inspire its author. The existence of a similar ground of review would be most useful in our own administrative law, for it would help eliminate American jurists' fears in connection with grants of apparently unrestricted discretionary authority to the administration.

(6) Scope of review.

Many American administrative lawyers have felt that our courts have been unduly restricting the scope of review, particularly where review involves so-called "mixed questions of law and fact" and findings on which jurisdiction depends. True, very few jurists in this country would urge going to the other extreme of full review on both the law and the facts—the direction in which the French Council of State is tending to go[57]—and there are dangers in such overwide review as great as those in the excessively narrow review granted by many American courts. But the French experience does show that as a practical matter courts can exercise broad reviewing power without causing a breakdown in administration. It thus furnishes a pragmatic answer to those who assert that review wider than that now afforded by American courts is not workable. The development in this aspect of the *droit administratif* should provide substantial support for those who feel that review can be broadened in our system without impairing the efficiency of administrative action.

(7) Liability of public officers.

The common lawyer who points to the superiority of his own system over the French with regard to the personal liability of public officers is, in the United States at any rate, closing his eyes to the realities of our law. American courts no longer follow the common-law rule of strict personal responsibility of officers. In its place has been substituted a principle of immunity that is more and more tending to shield officers from having to answer personally for the consequences

[57] *Supra* pp. 247-49.

of their acts. In France, on the other hand, the early rule of personal irresponsibility has given way to one of liability for so-called personal faults; *i.e.*, those that involve willfulness, malice, gross negligence, or action by the officer outside the scope of his official functions.

That the common-law rule of wholesale personal liability has proved unworkable under modern conditions is recognized by most American administrative lawyers. At the same time, from the constitutional point of view a rule of blanket immunity should be avoided if it is at all possible. "It is desirable," as a recent English treatise points out, "that the members of administrative tribunals should be personally liable in the courts of law wherever malice or negligence or corruption or fraud can be proved against them in their official capacity."[58]

The law of officer liability should seek above all to deter officials from committing what the French term personal faults. A rule of liability for such faults, like that which has been developed in the *droit administratif*, is therefore far preferable to the rule of immunity toward which American law is tending. It is, of course, realized that where the State is liable the responsibility of the officer may become a purely academic matter, since the injured citizen will in practice almost always prefer a judgment against the State to one against the officer individually. But in such cases, too, there is the solution of liability of the officer to the State for personal faults that have led to judgments against it. This is the solution finally adopted by the Council of State, though it is still too early to tell how effective it will prove in practice.

(8) Liability of the State.

It is especially on the subject of public liability that the *droit administratif* appears to be in advance of our own system. While our law was still governed by the rigid rule of irresponsibility the Council of State was constructing an edifice of State liability that is a monument to its inveterate concern with giving the citizen justice even against his government. Working first toward the principle that the State is responsible for the consequences of its faults, the French tribunal was able to place the liability of the administration on the same plane as that of the private citizen, at least in its responsibility for fault. But the French law has gone far beyond this stage, and under contemporary jurisprudence the liability of the State is now based even more on risk than on fault.[59] The State in France is more and more coming to be

[58] Robson, *op. cit. supra* note 25, at 629.
[59] *Supra* pp. 291-98.

looked upon as an insurer of the consequences of its acts. The French citizen who is injured by action of the administration is considered to have a right to reparation whether he can prove administrative fault or not.

It would not mean much as a practical matter, in the present state of American law, to advocate that our system go as far as the *droit administratif* has gone in the law of State liability. At the same time, developments in France do show that a comprehensive system of State responsibility is more feasible than most Americans think. It is difficult for an American observer familiar with French law to explain why the American citizen who has a claim against his State should be in a worse legal position than one who has only a claim against a fellow citizen. For our law to be based on a notion like that of sovereign immunity appears manifestly anachronous in a modern democratic society. And the anomaly holds despite a statute like the Federal Tort Claims Act of 1946, for under it, as has been shown,[60] State irresponsibility is far from eliminated. Even if our law cannot at present follow the *droit administratif* in building a system of State liability based on risk, it should take the step, made many years ago in France, of abolishing the vestiges of the doctrine of sovereign immunity. That done, the American State will at least not be in a legal position superior to that of the ordinary citizen on the score of its liability for fault.

Political Questions

The starting point of French administrative law was an absolutist administration wholly uncontrolled by law. After the Revolution of 1789, the law courts in France were completely divested of jurisdiction in administrative-law cases.[61] The result was that the French citizen adversely affected by illegal administrative action was left without any legal redress. He could, it is true, avail himself of whatever remedies he might have within the administration. But this recourse was far short of the remedy that he had in the courts whenever he was injured by the act of another private individual.

Post-Revolutionary France was thus a good example of what has been characterized as a dual State.[62] In it only the relations of private citizens were governed by law administered by courts. The sphere of

[60] *Supra* pp. 273-75.
[61] *Supra* pp. 6-7
[62] *Supra* p. 311.

government was entirely outside the orbit of the law. The legality of administrative acts was controlled only by whatever hierarchical checks the administration itself saw fit to provide. Such a State, in which administration is placed in a privileged position of immunity from control by law, involves the very negation of the constitutional concept of the rule of law.

The history of administrative law in France in the post-Revolutionary era, and especially since the establishment of the Third Republic in 1870, has been one of gradual elimination of this dualization of the legal order by the steady subjection of administration to law. The crucial step in this direction was the development, in the judicial section of the Council of State, of an independent court to determine the legality of administrative acts. This court, once its judicial quality was recognized, was able constantly to expand its jurisdiction until by the end of the last century its competence was conceded in almost all cases involving questions of administrative law.

The enforcement of the principle of administrative legality by the Council of State encountered a serious obstacle, however, in the doctrine of acts of government. Under that doctrine certain administrative acts are placed in a position of complete immunity from judicial control.[63] The acts meant are those touching matters considered to be within the exclusive competence of the political branches of government. It cannot be denied that the doctrine of acts of government has constituted a serious lacuna in the rule of law as it has been developing in France.

Nevertheless an observer of the *droit administratif* cannot avoid the conclusion that this gap is becoming smaller all the time. The doctrine of acts of government as first developed was of very wide application. It operated to bar judicial review in every case in which the author of a challenged administrative act was impelled by political motives. Today the doctrine is much more limited in scope. It is the nature of the challenged act, not the end, that inspired its author, that determines whether review is precluded. And the jurisprudence of the Council of State is more and more restricting the list of acts considered to be acts of government. It may be too early, as has been pointed out,[64] to characterize the doctrine of acts of government as a thing of the past in the French system. But, as the authoritative contemporary treatise on the *droit administratif* puts it, it is clearly a doctrine in a state of retrogres-

[63] *Supra* pp. 160-62.
[64] *Supra* p. 165.

sion, and "we must hope for the complete disappearance of preclusions of review based on that doctrine."[65]

The American observer is bound to be impressed by the consistent progress of the *droit administratif* away from the notion of the dual State. And he is the more impressed because of a tendency visible in this country to expand the list of administrative acts rendered immune from judicial control. The doctrine of "political questions"[66] has not displayed the regressive tendencies that have characterized its French counterpart. On the contrary, while the doctrine of acts of government has constantly been decreasing in importance, the American doctrine is, if anything, being expanded by our courts. For example, in the recent jurisprudence of our Supreme Court there are, as we have seen,[67] clear indications of that tribunal's intention to maintain a hands-off policy in cases at all related to the field of foreign affairs.

It is not contended that there is not a legitimate place in our law for the doctrine of political questions. But such a doctrine, with its effect of exempting administrative action from control by the courts, must not be pushed too far. Carried to its extreme, it would have the effect of rendering the action of the political branches of government immune from legal restraints. There is particular danger in the view that where the issues in a case touch upon foreign affairs they are *ipso facto* not justiciable. Under contemporary conditions this view can have the effect of removing a great many administrative acts from the sphere of judicial control; for a large proportion of such acts can be considered to have at least some effect on our foreign relations.

Review of Presidential Action

Closely connected with the tendency of American courts to refuse review in cases of this type are those in which our courts have articulated the proposition that they are without power to control the legality of acts of the head of the executive branch of the government. "The President," Mr. Justice Jackson has stated for a majority of the Supreme Court, "both as Commander-in-Chief and as the Nation's organ for foreign affairs, has available intelligence services whose reports are not and ought not to be published to the world. It would be intolerable that courts, without the relevant information, should review and perhaps nullify actions of the Executive taken on information prop-

[65] Waline, Traité élémentaire de droit administratif 108 (6th ed., 1951).
[66] *See supra* pp. 162-63.
[67] *Supra* pp. 164-66.

erly held secret."[68] The attitude of our courts is well expressed in the oft-stated principle that a federal court may not issue an injunction against the President. As this principle has been put by Justice Jackson in a more recent case, the presidential office is "relatively immune from judicial review."[69]

The reluctance of our courts to review the legality of acts of the President stems from a perverted construction of the doctrine of the separation of powers. "The Congress," states a leading case, "is the legislative department of the government; the President is the executive department. Neither can be restrained in its action by the judicial department."[70] For the courts to attempt to control the legality of presidential action would, in this view, amount to undue interference by the judiciary with the workings of a co-ordinate independent branch of the government.

The separation of powers, so interpreted, is, in effect, the opening wedge of a system of government like that which prevailed in France after 1789. It places the head of the executive beyond judicial control—a position that, in practice, means that his acts are not subject to law. Such a construction of the separation-of-powers doctrine is neither desirable nor justified. The principle of judicial abstention in administrative-law cases was adopted in France as the leading corollary of the separation of powers for historical reasons totally absent from the common-law world. With our different historical background we need not construe the separation-of-powers doctrine in a way to place the acts of the President beyond judicial review.

It is erroneous to assert that our courts are interfering unduly in the operations of another department when they review the legality of presidential action. The essence of judicial power is the application of the law in cases presented to the courts for decision. The fact that the head of the executive happens to be a party in a given case does not mean that a court, in deciding that case, is exercising other than purely judicial power.

The American administrative lawyer who rejects the notion that the President is immune from judicial control finds strong support in the contemporary French system. Although the starting point of the *droit administratif* was the notion of the dual State, in which acts of

68 Chicago & Southern Airlines v. Waterman S.S. Co., 333 U.S. 103, 111 (1948). See United States v. Bush & Co., 310 U.S. 371 (1940).

69 Youngstown Sheet & Tube Co. v. Sawyer, 343 U.S. 579, 654 (1952).

70 Mississippi v. Johnson, 4 Wall. 475, 500 (U.S. 1866).

administration were not subject to the law governing the acts of private citizens, this has long since ceased to be the basis of the French system. No distinction in French law today places the head of the executive in a privileged position. "An objective act," states Duguit, "whether done by the president of the Republic, or by the humblest official, may be attacked by any citizen on the ground of *ultra vires* and the Council of State will pass on its legality. . . . The citizen is living under the regime of state and law, and where the government violates the law he has the right to demand judicial censure."[71]

Happily, American courts, too, are beginning to see the need for avoiding the dangers inherent in the doctrine that acts of the head of the executive cannot be reviewed. It is true that the federal courts still assert the principle that they cannot enjoin the President, a principle that tends to render him immune from review, since the action for an injunction is the basic remedy in the federal field in the absence of statutory provisions for review.[72] But, even though the courts continue to pay lip service to the principle that illegal acts of the President cannot be restrained, they can nonetheless assert an effective review power over the Chief Executive by a liberal application of the rule laid down in *Williams v. Fanning*.[73] In that case the Court held that the Postmaster General was not an indispensable party in an action to enjoin a local postmaster from carrying out the provisions of a postal fraud order, though all that the postmaster was actually doing was to carry out the orders of his departmental superior. The President, like the Postmaster General, acts in practice through subordinate officials. Under *Williams v. Fanning*, the subordinates through whom the President acts can be enjoined from executing illegal presidential orders. This device enables the courts to review the legality of acts of the President without having formally to order the head of the executive to do, or to refrain from doing, anything.

That this is the approach which our courts are starting to follow is shown by *Youngstown Sheet & Tube Co. v. Sawyer*[74]—the celebrated steel-seizure case—in which the federal courts ruled on the legality of an executive order directing the Secretary of Commerce to seize the steel industry on behalf of the government. The action was brought against the Secretary to enjoin him from carrying out the President's

71 Duguit, Law in the Modern State 172 (tr. Laski 1919).
72 *Supra* p. 117.
73 332 U.S. 490 (1948).
74 343 U.S. 579 (1952).

order. The defendant asserted that the courts were without power to negate action of the President, relying on the principle that the judiciary would not attempt to control the President. "But," said Judge Pine in his now famous opinion in the District Court, "in this case the President has not been sued. Charles Sawyer is the defendant, and the Supreme Court has held on many occasions that officers of the Executive Branch of the Government may be enjoined when their conduct is unauthorized by statute. . . . There is no doubt, therefore, that the defendant is subject to an injunction, and the President not only is not a party but he is not an indispensable party to this action, as held in Williams v. Fanning."[75] In upholding Judge Pine's decision the majority of the Supreme Court clearly appears to have agreed with his opinion on this point. Indeed, even the dissenting opinion of Chief Justice Vinson[76] did not question the propriety of the injunction action against the Secretary.

1984?

"Law has reached its finest moments," Mr. Justice Douglas has stated, "when it has freed man from the unlimited discretion of some ruler, some civil or military official, some bureaucrat. Where discretion is absolute, man has always suffered. At times it has been his property that has been invaded; at times, his privacy; at times, his liberty of movement; at times, his freedom of thought; at times, his life. Absolute discretion is a ruthless master. It is more destructive of freedom than any of man's other inventions."[77]

It cannot be denied that in contemporary conditions there has been a constant increase in administrative discretionary authority. This has been coupled with a tendency in the Anglo-American world constantly to expand the area of executive discretion that is rendered immune from judicial control. "A little inquiry," asserts Lord Hewart, "will serve to show that there is now, and for some years past has been, a persistent influence at work which, whatever the motives or the intentions that support it may be thought to be, undoubtedly has the effect of placing a large and increasing field of departmental activity beyond the reach of the ordinary law."[78]

[75] 103 F. Supp. 569, 576 (D.C. 1952).
[76] 343 U.S. at 667.
[77] Dissenting, in United States v. Wunderlich, 342 U.S. 98, 101 (1951).
[78] Hewart, *op. cit. supra* note 12, at 11.

Courts in the common-law world have consistently imposed self-limitations on their own reviewing power. If this process is carried to its extreme, there is danger that the effectiveness of judicial control of administrative legality will be destroyed. As an English observer points out: "we seem to have fallen between two stools: anxious to maintain a theoretically universal rule of law, we preserve merely the fiction of a formal legalism and in fact abandon the executive to its own unattractive instincts. . . . It is surely essential, if we value our liberties and the very elements of law, that the acts of the administration, however high its standards, should speedily become examinable by some tribunal able to afford to an aggrieved subject public and efficacious redress. The painful contrast between the French and English systems is that such redress is on an increasingly ample scale afforded to the French citizen by the Conseil d'Etat, whereas in England the powers of the High Court have in this respect increasingly become unavailing."[79]

There are, however, those who insist that the great need under modern conditions is to increase the efficiency of administration. Any checks on it, they say, must be largely internal, for to allow an alien branch of government to interfere would unduly hamper administrative efficiency. The great safeguard, in their view, lies in the development of interior checks, similar to those that exist within the judicial process—the formation of professional standards and settled ideals of quasi-judicial conduct, the development of adequate procedural rules, professional criticism, internal review, and the like. Above all, great stress is laid on the acquisition by the administrator of the "judicial mind." "If that can once be grasped," asserted a British administrator before a royal commission, "none of the rest matters."[80]

Such a statement, if more than a pious wish, ignores basic differences between the administration and the courts. The administrative process is by its very nature deficient in characteristics vital to acquisition of the "judicial mind." The administrator necessarily lacks the independence that is the judge's most prized possession. "Administrative tribunals do not have that independence from government which is one of the traditionally prized guaranties of the justice administered by our common-law courts. Their adjudications taking place as very part and parcel of the process of government, are exposed to the influence of all the political forces which act upon government."[81] The administrator

[79] Hamson, Rule of Law in France: I. The Conseil d'État and the Executive, The Times (London), February 20, 1951, p. 5.

[80] Sir Claude Schuster, quoted in Robson, *op. cit. supra* note 25, at 361.

[81] Dickinson, *op. cit. supra* note 3, at 36.

cannot decide disputes with the virgin mind of the judge. The very purpose of administration is to get things done. An administrative agency is created to accomplish certain ends, and it would be derelict in its duty if it were not predisposed in favor of those objectives for which it was created.

These defects are inherent in administration. Attempts to ameliorate them through internal checks alone lose sight of the fact that administration, not justice, is the prime purpose of the administrative process. It is only by recourse to an independent judiciary that the citizen can be adequately protected against administrative illegality. "The principle of checks and balances is a healthy one. An official who is accountable will act more prudently. A citizen who has an appeal to a body independent of the controversy has protection against passion, obstinacy, irrational conduct, and incompetency of an official."[82]

The basic principle of a system of administrative law that seeks to safeguard the rights of the individual even against his government must be that recently articulated by the senior government commissioner in the French Council of State, "the principle according to which every citizen adversely affected in his rights or interests by an administrative act has available to him a judicial remedy to have such act set aside."[83] This principle is one that is bound to grow in importance as the power of the administration increases. George Orwell may have painted an unduly dark picture in his description of the State of the future in his novel *1984*. The State of tomorrow need not be the Orwellian super-State with its omnipotent administration, unrestrained by any checks on its all-pervasive regulatory activities. But there is no reason to doubt that the future will see little diminution in the rate of increase of administrative authority.

In the State of a century ago administration was, after all, but one of many competing power structures. The citizen was affected less by it than by the many private institutions with which he normally dealt. But in the State toward which we are evolving administration tends gradually either to take over or to control the functions heretofore performed by these other institutions. In such a State administration will tend to be all-powerful unless suitable safeguards are imposed. "Unless we make the requirements for administrative action strict and

[82] Douglas, J., dissenting, in United States v. Wunderlich, 342 U.S. 98, 102 (1951).

[83] Letourneur, "Les 'Principes généraux du droit' dans la jurisprudence du Conseil d'État" Conseil d'État, Études et documents 19, 26 (1951).

demanding, *expertise*, the strength of modern government, can become a monster which rules with no practical limits on its discretion."[84]

A sound system of administrative law must recognize that the position of administration is a subordinate one in the hierarchy of lawmakers. The authority to make the law must be vested in the elected representatives of the people. Whatever legislative power the administration possesses must be derived directly from the legislature and exercisable validly only within the limits prescribed. The notion of inherent or autonomous lawmaking powers in the administration is one that must be rejected. Such rejection alone is, however, of little practical value if those who are aggrieved by administrative action do not have recourse to an independent judge who can determine whether the administration has in fact remained within the bounds fixed by the law. The principle of legality is devoid of effective content unless it is enforced by judicial review. "With all its defects, delays and inconveniences," as Mr. Justice Jackson has recently put it, "men have discovered no technique for long preserving free government except that the Executive be under the law, and that the law be made by parliamentary deliberations."[85]

It must be recognized, of course, that even seemingly strong safeguards may prove inadequate. "If not good law, there was worldly wisdom in the maxim attributed to Napoleon that 'The tools belong to the man who can use them.' We may say that power to legislate . . . belongs in the hands of Congress, but only Congress itself can prevent power from slipping through its fingers."[86] This realization should not, however, deter us from constantly asserting the need for an adequate system of control of administration by those impersonal forces that we call law.[87] "The accretion of dangerous power does not come in a day. It does come, however slowly, from the generative force of unchecked disregard of the restrictions that fence in even the most disinterested assertion of authority."[88] It is surely at the present time, when the process of accretion has not yet progressed too far, that we must lay down the foundations of a sound system of administrative law in which even the State can be brought to the bar of justice at the suit of the ordinary citizen. It will be too late to do so in 1984.

[84] Douglas, J., dissenting, in New York v. United States, 342 U.S. 882, 884 (1951).

[85] Youngstown Sheet & Tube Co. v. Sawyer, 343 U.S. 579, 655 (1952).

[86] *Id.* at 654.

[87] The term used in *ibid.*

[88] *Id.* at 594.

APPENDIX A

Bibliographical Note

I. The Founders

The doctrinal founders of modern French administrative law began to publish their works as early as the Second Empire. The first writers sought merely to state the basic principles without any real attempt at combining the various aspects of the subject into a coherent whole. Thus, one of the important early texts, Dufour, *Droit administratif appliqué*, 7 vols. (1854-57), treated the different headings in alphabetical order, much as the legal encyclopedias do with which the Anglo-American lawyer is familiar. As time went on, however, treatises appeared that strove to classify the principles of the *droit administratif* in logical order. The efforts of their authors laid the foundation for the French system described in this book. Of these early works three are of particular interest:

Aucoc, *Conférences de droit administratif*, 3 vols. (1869-76);
Ducrocq, *Traité de droit administratif*, 7 vols. (1897-1905);
Laferrière, *Traité de la juridiction administrative et des recours contentieux*, 2 vols. (2d ed., 1896).

The now classic treatise of Laferrière is especially important. Its author was vice-president of the Council of State during one of the important periods of its development, and his study represented the first successful attempt at synthesis and systematization of the principles worked out by the administrative courts. Laferrière, more than anyone else, can be considered the founder of the modern *droit administratif*.

II. The Classics

The period after 1900 was one of the most important in the history of the *droit administratif*. The Council of State was consolidating its newly won position as a true court and was in process of formulating the basic principles that have dominated its jurisprudence ever since. Leading case followed leading case as the French tribunal progressively carried to completion its task of constructing a sound system of administrative law. And doctrinal writers were not wanting to classify and comment on the Council's work. In this period, indeed, were published the classic treatises of the modern *droit administratif*.

The writing of the period is dominated by the works of Maurice Hauriou, dean of the Law Faculty of the University of Toulouse. His *Précis de droit administratif* (12th ed., 1933) is invaluable to anyone interested in the French system. His writings are noted for a clarity and an ease of expression that make them particularly useful to an outside observer. In addition to his classic treatise Hauriou is important for his Notes on significant cases, which appeared at frequent intervals during his life in the *Recueil Sirey*. These Notes were arranged in logical order by his son and published under the title *La Jurisprudence administrative de 1892 à 1929*, 3 vols. (1929). These volumes, which are still in print, enable a student to have at his command all the important cases in a key period of the *droit administratif*. In addition to Hauriou's comments they contain the text of the decisions commented on and, in many cases, the conclusions of the government commissioners.

Léon Duguit, dean of the Law Faculty of the University of Bordeaux, was, next to Hauriou, the outstanding French public lawyer of this period. Though his main concern was not with administrative law as such, there is much in his writings of interest to a student of the subject, particularly in the field of State liability. His principal work is his *Traité de droit constitutionnel*, 5 vols. (3d ed., 1925-28).

In addition to Hauriou and Duguit the following treatises should be cited:

Berthélémy, *Traité élémentaire de droit administratif* (13th ed., 1933);
Bonnard, *Précis de droit administratif* (4th ed., 1943);
Jèze, *Principes généraux du droit administratif*, 6 vols. (3d ed., 1926-36).

There are also useful texts on specific aspects of administrative law:

Alibert, *Le Contrôle juridictionnel de l'administration* (1926). The leading work on review of administrative action.

Appleton, *Traité élémentaire de contentieux administratif* (1927, supp. 1936).

Duez, *Les Actes de gouvernement* (1935).

Duez, *La Responsabilité de la puissance publique* (2d ed., 1938).

III. Contemporary Works

The outstanding present-day text on French administrative law is the *Traité élémentaire de droit administratif* (6th ed., 1951; supp. 1952) by Marcel Waline, professor on the Law Faculty of the University of Paris. A worthy successor to the work of Hauriou, this treatise has already become a classic.

Other useful contemporary works are:

Duez and Debeyre, *Traité de droit administratif* (1952);

De Laubadère, *Traité élémentaire de droit administratif* (1953); *Manuel de droit administratif* (3d ed., 1951);

Rolland, *Précis de droit administratif* (10th ed., 1951).

On the subject of judicial review the most valuable work is Odent, *Cours de contentieux administratif* (1949-50). Its author, now a councilor of state, was senior government commissioner in the Council of State at the time of its publication.

Since 1947 the Council of State has published annually its *Études et documents.* They contain articles on important aspects of administrative law by its members and distinguished outsiders, as well as statistics, available in convenient form for the first time, on the Council's work. Also worthy of note among Council of State publications is its *Livre jubilaire publié pour commémorer son cent cinquantième anniversaire* (1952), an impressive tome containing contributions from French and foreign administrative lawyers, published on the occasion of the one hundred and fiftieth anniversary of the Council.

Articles and comments of value are also to be found in the *Revue du Droit Public,* the leading law review on French public law.

IV. The Case Law

As a system primarily judge made, the *droit administratif* has its primary source in the case law. The decisions of the Council of State and of the Court of Conflicts are published in the *Recueil des arrêts du Conseil d'État statuant au contentieux,* usually called the *Recueil Lebon.* It is unfortunately about one year late in publishing current decisions. The more important administrative-law cases are printed and commented on in the two great unofficial law reports, the *Recueil Sirey* and the *Recueil Dalloz* and in some other unofficial reports, as well as in the *Revue du Droit Public.* Conclusions of the government commissioners are often contained in these publications. Most of the decisions of the Prefecture Councils have not, until the present, been published. It is to be hoped that, now that those tribunals (under their new title of "Administrative Courts") are to become the courts of general original jurisdiction in the *droit administratif,* their decisions will be published in a report comparable to the *Recueil Lebon.*

To one interested in research in the case law Hauriou, *La Jurisprudence administrative de 1892 à 1929,* discussed above, is invaluable. It contains the leading cases for that period. There being nothing like it for the period since 1929, the researcher must himself seek out the important cases from the reports referred to above.

APPENDIX B

Illustrative Council of State Decision and Conclusions of Government Commissioner

I. Decision of the Council of State in the case of the Widow Trompier-Gravier, rendered May 5, 1944:

"The Council of State;—Under the decrees of the prefect of the Seine of March 13, 1924, December 11, 1924, and January 22, 1934; Under the law of December 18, 1940;—Since it is established that the challenged decision, by which the prefect of the Seine revoked the permit that had been granted to the Widow Trompier-Gravier to sell newspapers from a stand on the Boulevard Saint-Denis, in Paris, was based on a misdeed committed by petitioner;—Since, in consideration of the significance that the revocation of the permit carried in these circumstances, and of the gravity of that penalty, such a measure could not be taken legally without the Widow Trompier-Gravier's having been given an opportunity to be heard; petitioner, not having been afforded the opportunity of presenting evidence in her defense, can validly contend that the challenged decision was rendered by the prefect of the Seine without proper procedures and was, therefore, *ultra vires*:

"Article I.—The decision of the prefect of the Seine of December 26, 1939, is annulled.

"May 5, 1944.—Council of State, judicial section.—M. M. Rouchon-Mazerat, pres.—Barjot, reporter—Chenot, gov't com'r—Alcock, att'y."

II. Conclusions of M. Chenot, government commissioner, in the Trompier-Gravier case:

"Gentlemen.—

"On March 30, 1925, the Widow Trompier-Gravier, *née* Tichy, was named, by a decree of the prefect of the Seine, licensee of Stand No. 65, located on the Boulevard Saint-Denis, in Paris. Being herself employed in the Ministry of Agriculture, she was authorized to entrust the management of her stand to one Mme. Lange. In 1939, upon the complaint of M. Lange, husband of the latter and president of the federation of newspaper dealers, the administration formed the opinion that the Widow Trompier-Gravier had tried to extort from Mme. Lange the sum of 40,000 francs by threatening to withdraw the management of the stand from her. On December 26, 1939, the prefect informed the Widow Trompier-Gravier that the permit that she possessed to sell from the stand would expire on December 31, 1939, and would not be renewed.

"This is the decision that is challenged.

"The petition, contesting the facts on which that decision is based and contending that it is invalid because of abuse of power, sets up almost incidentally the claim that the Widow Trompier-Gravier had not been permitted to state her defenses against the accusations brought against her.

"Examination of the facts does not raise any question. It is for Mme. Trompier-Gravier to establish their inaccuracy. It is established, on the contrary, by the record and especially by the report of the police inspector who investigated the matter (though in a bungling way), that the continuance of Mme. Lange in her management was conditioned on the payment of a substantial sum of money to Mme. Trompier-Gravier. In making this demand petitioner has committed an immoral if not a criminal act, in violation of the regulations governing newspaper stands contained in the prefectoral decree of March 13, 1924: the stand permit is, in principle, a personal one; it is renewable annually; it should not be a subject of trade, still less of extortion.

"In revoking the permit of Mme. Trompier-Gravier, the administration has not, as the petition contends, meddled in a purely private controversy. It has sought, by a proper sanction, to repress a reprehensible scheme.

"The challenged decision thus does not lack a legal base, nor is it invalid because of abuse of power.

"It does nonetheless raise an issue of procedure whose significance goes far beyond the controversy between Mme. Trompier-Gravier and M. and Mme. Lange.

"It is established that the challenged decision was rendered without Mme. Trompier-Gravier's having been *given an opportunity to present her defense.* The procedure that led to the revocation of the permit of which Mme. Trompier-Gravier was the holder thus did not have an *adversary* character.

"Is it irregular because of this fact? This is the question that we must inquire into.

"Your jurisprudence, even in the absence of a legal text, has several times asserted the need for adversary procedure. This rule, based on the principles of our law, is, however, neither general nor absolute, as certain decisions show. What, then, is its scope?

"Your decision *Mlle. Sée* (December 10, 1943) marks out one limit. The permit to open a retail store had been withdrawn from Mlle. Sée on the petition of a trade assocation. 'Having regard to the nature of said petition as well as its object,' reads the decision, 'Mlle. Sée cannot contend that the petition should have been communicated to her so that she could present her views in defense.'

"On the other hand, your jurisprudence assures in the *judicial* sphere the strict application of a rule that is, according to your decision *Mme. Neveu* (December 6, 1933), among those 'which are binding, even in the absence of an express text, on all judicial tribunals.'

"Similarly, in *disciplinary* matters, you have decided that, even where Article 65 of the law of April 22, 1905, is not applicable, a measure such as the withdrawal of an honorary title could not be taken unless the individual affected was given prior notice of the facts for which he was censured. (June 17, 1936, *Gauthier.*)

"Thus, the administration, in its operation of public services, is not required, in the absence of an express legal text so providing, to give those affected by its acts an opportunity to be heard. Such a requirement would needlessly slow down the running of the service and would paralyze the action of the administration. In certain cases, however, this practical rule gives way to a higher principle. Certain decisions, by virtue of their nature and their object, must be preceded by a hearing, or at the very least they must not be rendered before those affected have had some opportunity to present their point of view. So much is true of all judicial decisions and of disciplinary matters involving civil servants. Only a legal text could exempt the administration from following an adversary procedure in these two fields. If these principles are clear and consistently reaffirmed by your jurisprudence, it is nonetheless difficult to mark out the limits of their application in practice. Certain proceedings are not held before a judge and yet derive from their object the need for judicial safeguards. The setting aside of electoral operations by a minister requires, in the public interest, the support of an adversary procedure (July 29, 1943, *Solus, et al.*)

"Your jurisprudence thus extends the rule of adversary procedure to kindred matters outside the judicial field strictly speaking.

"The same extension of the rule can be seen outside the traditional area of the disciplining of public servants. When an administrative decision assumes a penal quality and has a sufficiently serious adverse effect on the situation of an individual, your jurisprudence requires that the individual be given an opportunity to present his point of view on the measure affecting him.

"You have decided this, notably, with regard to the withdrawal of a state scholarship (January 17, 1930, *Ribeyrolles*), the exclusion from a school or a civil-service examination (July 8, 1936, *Widow Hoaran;* April 28, 1937, *Hartwig*).

"Now, if we analyze the measure taken by the prefect with regard to Mme. Trompier-Gravier, we can see clearly that the challenged decision has a penal quality.

"The administration has not proceeded, in the interest of the public domain, to withdraw a permit to use the public way: the newspaper stand still exists. The permit to occupy it has changed hands. It is thus in reality a revocation of Mme. Trompier-Gravier's permit. She has shown herself unworthy of the permit that she held; she has violated the spirit and the letter of the regulations governing newspaper stands. It is upon these reasons and these alone that the challenged decision is based. We are certainly not dealing with a case of public employment. Mme. Trompier-Gravier is in no sense an employee of the administration. She is in the position of the holder of a permit. Such permits are revocable, and the administration could have summarily ordered the closing down of the stand. This is not what it did. It sought to punish a fault. It acted to accomplish a penal end. In these circumstances, it could not, in our opinion, disregard a principle that governs all penal procedure, even outside the field of public employment and in the absence of an express legal text. The victim of a penalty must be given notice and enabled to present his defense.

"We therefore conclude that the challenged decision should be annulled."

TABLE OF CASES

FRENCH

PAGE

Other courts:

ANGLO - AMERICAN

INDEX

Index

Index

Index

www.ingramcontent.com/pod-product-compliance
Ingram Content Group UK Ltd.
Pitfield, Milton Keynes, MK11 3LW, UK
UKHW041131071026
15587UKWH00009B/428

9 781584 777045